# CORPORATE SECRETARIAL PRACTICE

ICSA STUDY TEXT

# CORPORATE SECRETARIAL PRACTICE

2nd Edition

**LUKE THOMAS**

icsa.
Publishing

First published 2010

Published by ICSA Information & Training Ltd
16 Park Crescent
London W1B 1AH

© ICSA Information & Training Ltd, 2012

Designed and typeset by
Florence Production Ltd, Stoodleigh, Devon
Printed by
Hobbs the Printers Ltd, Totten Hampshire

British Cataloguing in Publication Data
A catalogue record for this book is available from the British Library.

ISBN 978 1 86072 516 6

# Contents

# How to use this study text

ICSA study texts developed to support ICSA's Chartered Secretaries Qualifying Scheme (CSQS) follow a standard format and include a range of navigational, self-testing and illustrative features to help you get the most out of the support materials.

Each text is divided into three main sections:

■ introductory material
■ the text itself, divided into Parts and Chapters
■ additional reference information

The sections below show you how to find your way around the text and make the most of its features.

## Introductory material

The introductory section of each text includes a full contents list and the module syllabus which reiterates the module aims, learning outcomes and syllabus content for the module in question.

Where relevant, the introductory section will also include a list of acronyms and abbreviations or a list of legal cases for reference.

## The text itself

Each **part** opens with a list of the chapters to follow, an overview of what will be covered and learning outcomes for the part. Part openings also include a case study, which introduces a real-world scenario related to the topics covered in that part. Questions based on this case and designed to test the application of theory into practice appear in the chapters and at part endings (see below).

Every **chapter** opens with a list of the topics covered and an introduction specific to that chapter. Chapters are structured to allow students to break the content down into manageable sections for study. Each chapter ends with a summary of key content to reinforce understanding.

Part opening

Chapter opening

Part case study

# Features

The text is enhanced by a range of illustrative and self-testing features to assist understanding and to help you prepare for the examination. Each feature is presented in a standard format, so that you will become familiar with how to use them in your study.

The texts also include tables, figures and checklists and, where relevant, sample documents and forms.

## Case Examples

Case examples present short, illustrative case studies which look at how concepts are applied in practice.

## Sample wording

## Checklist

## Case Law

Case law summaries provide overviews of significant legal cases.

## Case Questions

Case questions relate to the part opening case study, encouraging you to apply the theory you're learning to a real-world business scenario.

## Definitions

Key terms are highlighted in bold on first use and defined in the end of book glossary.

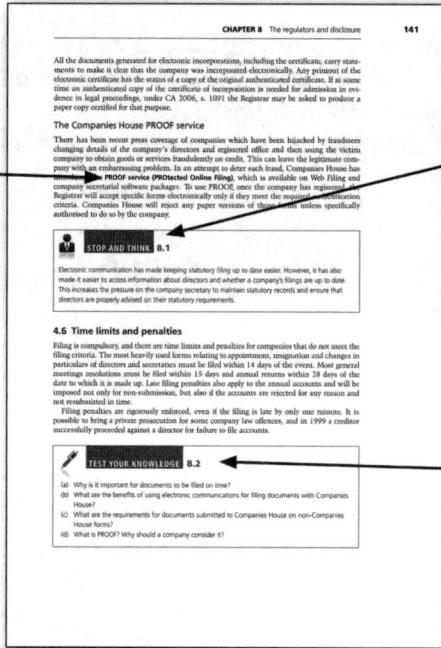

## Stop and Think

Stop and think boxes encourage you to reflect on how your own experiences or common business scenarios relate to the topic under discussion.

## Test your Knowledge

Short, revision-style questions to help you re-cap on key information and core concepts.

## Part case questions

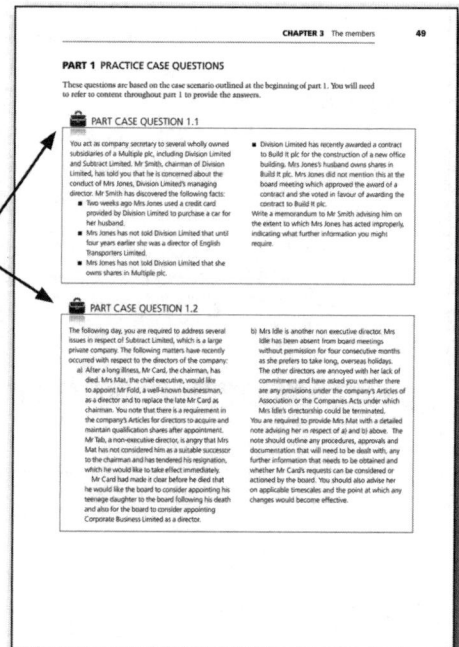

## Glossary

# Reference material

The text ends with a range of additional guidance and reference material. Most texts will include Appendices which comprise additional reference material specific to that module.

Other reference material includes a glossary of key terms, a directory of further reading and web resources and a comprehensive index.

# The Corporate Secretarial Practice syllabus

## Module outline and aims

This module examines the role of the Chartered Secretary in promoting and reinforcing good governance across the organisation by ensuring compliance with statutory obligations and good practice. In particular, this module explains the role of the Chartered Secretary in devising and overseeing appropriate compliance systems and processes to ensure that the company and its directors are compliant with the Companies Act 2006 and with the company's constitution. The module also deals with managing the practical and company law issues in relation to shareholders.

Chartered Secretaries need to understand the application of statutory requirements and other best practice and how this underpins good governance and compliance, irrespective of sector. The module examines corporate secretaryship practices and processes within legal and other frameworks of best practice and the role of the Chartered Secretary in ensuring organisational effectiveness.

## Learning outcomes

On successful completion of this module, you will be able to:

- Identify the scope, role and functions of the company secretary and apply them in the employing or client organisation.
- Critically evaluate and apply the role of company secretary as an advisor to the board.
- Ensure effective communication and dissemination of information to and from the board, both internally and externally, for the optimum benefit of the organisation.
- Understand the law and best practice in key functional matters (for example, meetings and share capital management) and apply them in the secretaryship function and ensure corporate compliance.
- Apply the functions of a company secretary in ensuring corporate compliance through good disclosure and observance of statutory and other regulations
- Take responsibility for the ongoing duties of the secretary as a professional practitioner in the organisation and be responsible for continuing personnel development within the secretariat.
- Identify required actions arising from statutory obligations and best practice in terms of financial, compliance and governance reporting and disclosure; understand why such disclosure is necessary.
- Apply statutory requirements and good practice in relation to shareholder related communications.
- Critically assess the role played by the secretary in supporting compliance, disclosure, and accountability across the organisation to ensure the effective achievement of organisational objectives.

## Syllabus content

The role of the company secretary involves maintaining three key elements of an organisation: the company itself, the board of directors and the shareholders. The aim of the module is to specify and assess the essential knowledge and skills involved in taking overall responsibility for the corporate secretarial function in large-scale organisations. The practice of corporate secretaryship in this module extends to both the strategic and functional contexts, in advising the board, in leading teams in secretarial best practice, in ensuring compliance with law and regulation and in establishing and maintaining appropriate processes in respect of the company's shareholders.

## The secretary, the board and members – weighting 20%

Candidates need to understand the importance of the role of secretary and how the secretary interrelates with others in the board and the company's shareholders. An important aspect of the role of the secretary is the interaction with the board. The role of secretary is quite unusual as it can provide direct access to the board of large organisations at a relatively early career stage. It is therefore all the more important that the secretary is equipped with the professionalism that the board expects. This opening part of the syllabus serves as a useful foundation for the rest of the subject.

### Content
- Role of the secretary, functions, duties, appointment and vacation of office
- The secretary as advisor to the board
- The secretary's role in ensuring compliance
- Directors:
  - Appointment, removal and disqualification
  - Roles and duties
- Members:
  - Types of shareholders
  - Member rights and duties

## Corporate compliance – weighting 40%

This part of the syllabus focuses on the creation of different types of legal entities and ongoing compliance: the importance of the Memorandum and Articles for a company cannot be underestimated, as it is essentially the company's written constitution. The secretary is expected to have a working knowledge of the Articles of Association and to apply that knowledge in a practical way to a variety of situations.

There is a host of statutory returns that need to be submitted to the Registrar of Companies and, in addition, the secretary should have a good understanding of possible offences under the Companies Acts to prevent inadvertent breaches of the law. The directors of a company are held responsible for non-compliance and so depend on the secretary to protect their interests and the reputation of the company in ensuring the company remains compliant.

Candidates may go on to work for listed companies and therefore need to be aware of the framework of regulations for listed companies and the general ongoing requirements. Shareholders, potential investors and other stakeholders need to have a high degree of confidence that a listed company is properly run, not only in accordance with the Companies Act and best practice, but also to the standards demanded by the Listing Regime. It is the secretary's duty to advise the board so that this is maintained.

### Content
- Company formation, company constitutions, different types of companies
- Company insolvency, winding up, striking off and dissolution of companies
- Maintenance of statutory records
- Filing of company returns
- The regulation of listed companies: The UK listing regime, the London Stock Exchange and takeovers and mergers
- Shares:
  - Share capital
  - Share transfer, transmission and registration

- Regulation of the securities industry
- The company registrar function
- Capital events
- Employee share schemes
- Dividends

## Regulation and disclosure – weighting 40%

The company secretary has an important role to play in the dissemination of information about the company, its directors and its members. These are required as most companies have limited liability and hence many third parties will wish to know with whom they are doing business.

Secretaries also need to be mindful of legal implications and best practice with regard to such areas as formal meetings of either the board or shareholders.

The importance of the annual report – both in compliance with the Companies Act and as a shareholder relations tool – cannot be underestimated. The secretary has a pivotal role to play, by ensuring that the annual report is distributed to those who are entitled by law to receive it and also to other important interested parties. The secretary also drafts the directors' report.

### Content

- Regulation of companies and disclosure requirements – Companies House, shareholders, UKLA, Community Interest Companies Regulator.
- The links between disclosure, accountability, transparency and trust.
- Understanding of the importance of the disclosure process for ensuring statutory compliance and for securing support from the organisation's stakeholders. Implications for failing to keep proper records and failing to disclose.
- Company law, statutory rights of shareholders and the public to information about companies.
- Statutory requirements and good practice in relation to member and board meetings:
  - Convening meetings
  - Notice
  - Quorum
  - Voting and other procedures
  - Minutes and resolutions
  - The role of the chairman
  - The role of the company secretary
  - Statutory records
- Meetings of the members:
  - Annual general meetings
  - Other general meetings
  - Class meetings
  - Written member resolutions
  - Meeting procedures (e.g. disorder, dealing with members' questions)
- The annual report and accounts:
  - Role and duties of the company secretary
  - Statutory reporting requirements
  - Narrative reporting
  - EU directives and other developments
- Auditors:
  - Appointment and termination
  - Role, liability, disclosure and other duties

# Acronyms and abbreviations

| | |
|---|---|
| ABI | Association of British Insurers |
| ACT | advance corporation tax |
| AGM | annual general meeting |
| AIM | Alternative Investment Market |
| BACS | Bankers' Automated Clearing System |
| BIS | Department of Business Innovation & Skills |
| CA | Companies Act 2006 |
| CDDA | Company Directors Disqualification Act 1986 |
| CEO | chief executive officer |
| CIC | community interest company |
| CJA | Criminal Justice Act |
| CSOP | company share option plan |
| DCA | dormant company accounts |
| DRIP | dividend reinvestment plan |
| DTRs | Disclosure and Transparency Rules |
| EA | Enterprise Act |
| EEA | European Economic Area |
| EMI | enterprise management incentive |
| EPA | enduring power of attorney |
| EPAA | Enduring Powers of Attorney Act |
| ESOP | executive share option plan |
| EU | European Union |
| FRC | Financial Reporting Council |
| FSA | Financial Services Authority |
| FSMA | Financial Services and Markets Act |
| IA | Insolvency Act |
| IFRS | International Financial Reporting Standards |
| IS | Insolvency Service |
| ISC | Institutional Shareholders' Committee |
| LLP | limited liability partnership |
| LPA | lasting power of attorney |
| LTIP | long-term incentive plan |
| NAPF | National Association of Pension Funds |
| NED | non-executive director |
| NICs | National Insurance contributions |
| PAYE | pay as you earn |
| PDMR | persons discharging managerial responsibility |
| PROOF | protected online filing |
| PIP | primary information provider |
| plc | public limited company |
| RIE | recognised investment exchange |
| RIS | regulatory information service |
| RSB | recognised supervisory body |
| SAIL | Single Alternative Inspection Location |
| SAYE | save as you earn |
| SDRT | stamp duty reserve tax |
| SE | societas euopaea |
| SEAQ | Stock Exchange Automated Quotation |
| SEATSplus | Stock Exchange Alternative Trading Service |
| SETS | Stock Exchange Electronic Trading Service |

| | |
|---|---|
| SETSqx | Stock Exchange Electronic Trading Service – quotes and crosses |
| SIP | share incentive plan |
| SPE | Société Privée Européenne |
| UKLA | UK Listing Authority |
| VAT | value added tax |

# Acknowledgements

The publisher would like to thank the following for permission to reproduce the following material in this study text:

## Sample wordings

Reproduced from *Company Secretarial Practice* by Keith Walmsley and Andrew C Hamer, published by ICSA Information and Training Ltd.

## Company House forms

These are all Companies House-Crown Copyright and are reproduced with the permission of the Controller of HMSO and the Queen's Printer for Scotland.

## Appendices 1 and 2: Model Articles for Private Companies Limited by Shares and Model Articles for Public Companies Limited by Shares

© Crown copyright 2009. Reproduced with permission of the Controller of HMSO and the Queen's Printer for Scotland.

Every effort has been made to locate and acknowledge sources and holders of copyright material in this study text. In the event that any have been inadvertently overlooked, please contact the publisher.

# The secretary, directors and members

**■ LIST OF CHAPTERS**

**1**   The role of the company secretary
**2**   The directors
**3**   The members

**■ OVERVIEW**

Part One looks at the respective roles of the company secretary, the directors and the members (shareholders).

The company secretary is a senior manager in most organisations and may be a main board director in a large public company. He acts as the gateway for information, communications, advice and arbitration between the company, its shareholders and the regulatory authorities, such as Companies House. In order to fulfil these roles effectively, the company secretary must be fully aware of the rights, duties and obligations of these groups so that he can provide independent, impartial advice and support.

In this opening part we look at the administrative structure of a company, and the roles of the three parties who are responsible for it: the company secretary, the directors and the members. Chapter 1 describes the core duties and responsibilities of the company secretary and the skills and knowledge that he requires. We then turn to directors, their responsibilities and liabilities, and how they are appointed and removed from office. Finally, we look at the third side of the administrative triangle, the members, and in particular their responsibilities and rights to information about the company.

This part refers extensively to sections and provisions contained in the Companies Act 2006 (CA 2006). Other legislation and regulation which will be referred to in this text are:

■   the Company Directors Disqualification Act 1986 (CDDA);
■   the Insolvency Acts (IA) 1986 and 2000, and
■   the UK Listing Regime, the regulations for listed companies published by the Financial Services Authority (FSA).
■   While *Corporate Secretarial Practice* is essentially concerned with the practice and application of the law, students will find it useful at times to refer to the *ICSA Study Text in Corporate Law* and the *ICSA Study Text in Corporate Governance*.

## ■ LEARNING OUTCOMES

After reading and understanding the contents of Part One, you should be able to:

- Explain the administrative role and implied powers of the company secretary.
- Understand how the company secretary is appointed and where his express powers come from.
- Understand the statutory duties and responsibilities of the company secretary.
- Distinguish between the different types of director.
- Explain the procedures for the appointment, removal and rotation of directors.
- Understand the duties and powers of directors under CA 2006.
- Understand details of the statutory records concerning directors and be able to advise directors on what they are required to disclose.
- Be able to define and explain the term 'member'.
- Understand when to refuse entry to the register of members for certain persons.
- Be able to describe and appreciate the principal rights of members.
- Understand the duties and liabilities of members.

## PART 1 CASE STUDY

You are the company secretary of Multiple plc, a company listed on the London Stock Exchange. Multiple is a large manufacturing company with operations around the world. Multiple is a very active company and is growing fast. In addition to having the parent company, there are many subsidiary companies which form part of the Multiple group. You are responsible for the Company Secretariat department, which consists of two assistant secretaries, two company secretarial assistants and a share schemes manager. As company secretary, part of your responsibility will be to ensure that:

- your staff are aware of the duties and responsibilities of a company secretary and the best way for the Company Secretariat department to operate;

- all directors of Multiple plc and its subsidiary companies are aware of their duties and responsibilities and that the Company Secretariat department is able to deal with any queries the directors have regarding company law issues;
- all shareholders of the company are properly recorded in the company's books and that the Company Secretariat department understands the rights and duties of members.

As part of the company's growth, new directors will be appointed and new shareholders are expected to be attracted to the company. This will increase the workload of the department and mean that a very high standard of professionalism will be required throughout the department at all times to service the company's growth.

# The role of the company secretary

1

## ■ CONTENTS

## ■ INTRODUCTION

As an officer of the company at the centre of the decision-making process, the company secretary is in a powerful position. He should assist and guide the board in the pursuit of profit and growth, but should also act with integrity and independence to protect the interests of the company, its shareholders and its employees. The company secretary is key to the efficiency and effectiveness of the board and to the smooth running of the company. To fulfil the role, he must not only keep up to date with relevant legal, statutory and regulatory requirements, but also be able to give impartial advice and support to directors.

## 1 Requirement to appoint a company secretary

Under CA 2006, all public companies are required to appoint a company secretary. Private companies are not required to appoint or retain a company secretary, but they may do so, in which case the company secretary has the same duties and responsibilities as he would in a public company. Private companies should check their **Articles of Association** – if there is an express requirement in the Articles to maintain a company secretary and they wish to adopt the provisions of CA 2006, they should amend their Articles accordingly.

It is still too early to determine what the outcome of this change for private companies will be. It may be that many will choose to keep a company secretary. The tasks which used to be the responsibility of the company secretary will still need to be done even if there is no one with that title. As good corporate governance continues to increase in importance, the appointment of a company secretary should be considered best practice for all but the smallest companies. An individual, a partnership or a body corporate can be appointed as secretary.

The law does not state explicitly what the company secretary should do. In practice, however, the company secretary plays a central role in the governance and administration of a company's affairs, with particular responsibilities in three main areas:

1 *The board* – The company secretary provides essential practical support to the chairman and other directors, both as a group and individually, ensuring that statutory and regulatory requirements are met for the conduct and running of board meetings, and that the board has access to the information it requires.
2 *The company* – The company secretary is responsible for ensuring that the statutory and regulatory requirements are met, particularly in relation to the CA and related legislation governing the reporting of the activities of the company (for example, filing statutory returns).

**3** *The shareholders (members)* – The company secretary is the primary point of contact for all shareholders and is principally responsible for the maintenance and management of shareholder records, such as the register of members, and organising shareholder-related events, such as paying dividends, producing and issuing the annual report and accounts, and coordinating general meetings.

Throughout these main areas of activity the company secretary is charged with the responsibility for ensuring that the business is carried on according to the principles of good corporate governance (see the syllabus on Corporate Governance for more details). The company secretary should be aware of the company's **Memorandum of Association** and also needs a detailed working knowledge of the company's Articles of Association (see Chapter 5), which contains requirements and procedures which cover all three of the areas described above.

## 1.1 An officer of the company

The company secretary is an officer of the company. This makes him liable, along with the directors, for breaches of the regulations imposed by the CA. Although responsibility ultimately rests with the directors, in making the company secretary liable, the CA recognises that the directors usually rely on the company secretary and provides a strong indication that they should give him responsibility or involvement in these matters. Some company secretaries are also directors, although in companies where there is only one director, that director cannot also be the secretary. We shall consider the liabilities and penalties for breach of the regulations below.

For companies listed on the London Stock Exchange, the company secretary has a key role in ensuring that board procedures are followed and regularly reviewed. He must also be a source of advice to the chairman and to the board on compliance with **corporate governance** for listed companies (the **UK Corporate Governance Code**). The Code is looked at in more detail in the syllabus on Corporate Governance and text.

## 1.2 The powers of the company secretary

### The secretary's signature

A secretary's signature is sometimes valid as an alternative to a director's signature (e.g. the requirement of one signature on the company's annual return). The secretary's signature may be used with that of one director when a seal (see Chapter 4) is affixed or a deed created as an alternative to the signatures of two directors. Cheques and bank documents can also be signed by the secretary. A company secretary needs to take great care before executing any document. If in doubt, he should make appropriate enquiries before the document is signed. If necessary, professional advice should be taken if the secretary is unsure of the ramifications of executing a document.

### Ostensible authority

The court has been quoted as saying that the company secretary

> 'regularly makes representations on behalf of the company and enters into contracts on its behalf which come within the day-to-day running of the company's business . . . He is certainly entitled to sign contracts connected with the administrative side of a company's affairs . . . All such matters now come within the ostensible authority of a company secretary.'

**Ostensible authority** extends to recruiting staff, ordering office equipment and stationery, and arranging the company's insurance and administrative contracts. Accordingly:

- If the company secretary enters into a contract of an administrative nature on behalf of the company, the company will be bound by his acts.
- If the company secretary enters into a contract of a managerial nature on behalf of the company with express authority from the directors, the company will be bound by his actions.
- If the company secretary enters into a trading contract on behalf of the company without express authority, the company will be bound by his actions, but he may be held personally liable by the company for any resultant loss.

In *Panorama Developments (Guildford) Ltd v Fidelis Furnishing Fabrics Ltd* (1971) the Court of Appeal ruled that the company secretary is 'the chief administrative officer of the company'.

---

### CASE LAW  1.1

*Panorama Developments (Guildford) Ltd v Fidelis Furnishing Fabrics Ltd* **[1971] 2 QB 711**

The company secretary of Fidelis hired a car from Panorama. He signed the hire documents in his own name and added 'Company Secretary'. Panorama believed he was hiring them for meeting Fidelis's clients. In fact, he used the car for his personal use. When Panorama presented the bill to Fidelis they refused to pay, claiming that the secretary was acting contrary to his powers.

In this case the court described the status of the company secretary:

'He is no longer a mere clerk. He regularly makes representations on behalf of the company and enters into contracts on its behalf which come within the day-to-day running of the company's business. So much so that he may be regarded as having authority to do such things on behalf of the company. He is certainly entitled to sign contracts concerned with the administrative side of a company's affairs.'

Fidelis had to pay Panorama and reclaim the money from their company secretary.

---

In summary, the company secretary can be seen as one point in the administrative triangle, the other two points being the directors and the members. Members and directors make the policy and the company secretary administers it. In many ways the company secretary can be described as forming the backbone of the organisation.

---

### TEST YOUR KNOWLEDGE  1.1

a  Outline briefly the role and the powers of the company secretary.
b  In what circumstances will a company secretary become personally liable after signing a company document?
c  What should a company secretary do before executing any document?

---

## 2  Core duties of a company secretary

The duties and responsibilities of the company secretary vary from company to company. The following identifies the core duties, cross-referenced with coverage in the chapters in this text.

1  The secretary should be present at all meetings of the company and of the directors, and is the coordinator of such meetings. He is responsible for drafting the agenda and agreeing it with the chairman and chief executive officer (CEO), as well as collecting, organising and circulating the papers required at the meetings. He is also responsible for organising board committees and acting as a channel of communication for non-executive directors (NEDs).

2  The secretary is responsible for ensuring that the **annual general meeting (AGM)** follows the appropriate procedures and complies with the requirements of CA 2006 and the company's Articles of Association. He will usually coordinate the administration of the meeting (see Chapter 9). Private companies are not required to hold an AGM.

3  The secretary is usually responsible for the minutes of meetings of the company and the directors.

4   The secretary will execute the instructions of the board of directors, for example, regarding notices for meetings. (Chapters 9 and 10 give full coverage of the responsibilities of the secretary at general and board meetings.)

5   The secretary is responsible for ensuring that the company complies with its Articles, drafting and incorporating amendments in accordance with the correct procedures (see Chapter 5).

6   If the company is listed, the secretary is responsible for ensuring compliance with the **Listing Regime**, the **City Code on Takeovers and Mergers** and managing relations with the UK Listing Authority (UKLA) through the company's brokers (see Chapter 6).

7   The secretary must ensure compliance with the Companies Acts and all other relevant legal requirements.

8   The secretary is responsible for the registrar functions within a company, and in particular for the maintenance of statutory registers (see Chapter 8), such as:
   a)  register of members, including monitoring movements to identify any 'stake-building' and the beneficial owners of holdings (s. 793 notices under CA 2006);
   b)  register of company charges;
   c)  register of directors and secretary;
   d)  register of debenture holders (if kept) (see Chapter 8).

9   The secretary must file statutory returns and certain documents with the Registrar of Companies (see Chapter 8) to comply with periodic filing requirements or to notify of changes regarding the company. Examples include:
   a)  annual return;
   b)  report and accounts;
   c)  amended Articles of Association;
   d)  changes to share capital;
   e)  notice of appointments, removals and resignations of directors and secretaries.
   The secretary coordinates the publication and distribution of the company's annual report and accounts and interim statements and the preparation of the directors' report (see Chapter 11).

10   The secretary may implement and administer directors' and employees' share schemes (see Chapter 15).

11   The secretary ensures safe custody and proper use of the common seal (if the company has one) and maintains a register of sealings (see Chapter 4).

12   The secretary is responsible for the administration of any subsidiary companies and for maintaining the record of the group structure.

13   The secretary is the focal point for shareholder communication and is the shareholders' first point of contact with the company. He is responsible for organising the distribution of announcements and circulars, arranging payment of dividends, issuing documentation regarding rights and capitalisation issues, and maintaining good relations with institutional shareholders (see Chapters 6, 12 and 13).

14   The secretary conducts all correspondence with shareholders as regards dividends, calls, transfers, forfeiture, issue and other general enquiries in respect of shares (see Chapter 13).

15   The company secretary is responsible for registering share ownership, dealing with transfers and other matters affecting shareholdings (see Chapter 13).

16   The secretary is responsible for maintaining the statutory requirements for a registered office address, allowing public inspection of documents when required under the law and for ensuring that all business communications, whether in hard copy or electronic form, letters, invoices, websites and signage show the name and any other required details of the company and comply with the current statute and regulation (see Chapter 4).

17   In addition to the core functions, company secretaries can be involved in a wide range of other responsibilities. The careers section of the ICSA website (see Directory) has a sample selection of various job descriptions for secretaries which gives an idea of the diversity of the profession.

# 3 The secretary's role in advising and communicating with the board

## 3.1 The secretary as adviser to the board

In listed companies, the UK Corporate Governance Code emphasises the role of company secretary in ensuring compliance with the proper board procedures and regulation. The Code also requires that the secretary is in attendance at all board and board committee meetings. This places a considerable onus on company secretaries, so the position is not one to be accepted lightly or without an appreciation of its implications. The secretary must not only keep up to date with relevant legal, statutory and regulatory requirements and best practice, but must be able to give impartial advice and support to the directors. This includes advising the board if it appears that (through the officers) it may be acting in breach of legal requirements.

## 3.2 The company secretary as the board's communicator

One of the core duties of the secretary is to be the focal point for all shareholder communication. This is particularly important in a listed company. This will include annual and half-year reports and interim management statements.

Listed companies must maintain a quarterly cycle of announcements: the annual report and accounts as soon as they have been approved by the board, the half-year results from the first six months of the financial year and two interim management statements which must be released between ten weeks after the start of the period and six weeks before its end. This ensures that information is released to the market promptly and fully to minimise the likelihood of inside information being leaked.

Board decisions regarding dividends must also be announced without delay after board approval. The announcement must give details of the exact net amount payable per share, the payment date, the record date (where applicable) and any foreign income dividend election, together with income tax liabilities. This information is required in the case of any interim dividend being declared as well as the final recommended dividend.

### Circulars and other notifications

Apart from the directors' report and the audited accounts, which are required by law, a company must also circulate notices of meetings and any non-routine resolutions to be proposed. There are certain instances where the law requires these circulars to be accompanied by an explanation, often drafted by the company secretary. There are also other instances when information is required following an enquiry made by a member or the public. The inspection of registers by the members and the rights of the public to information under the provisions or the Listing Rules are looked at in later chapters.

## Changes in board composition and other material changes in the business of the company

Listed companies must release information of any changes in board membership without delay, as this is considered to be of material consideration to the company. In addition, information about any material change to the business of the company (e.g. if the directors become aware that its profits will be considerably different from previous expectations) must also be released without delay.

### Investment advertisements

The publication by companies of financial information in newspaper advertisements can be regarded as the issue of an investment advertisement which requires, under the Financial Services and Markets Act (FSMA) 2000, approval by an authorised person. The legislation provides that no advertisement specified by the Listing Rules and Prospectus Rules shall be issued in the UK unless the contents have been approved by the competent authority, UKLA.

The company secretary plays a central role in the circulation of information to the members and to the public, making him, in effect, the communicator for the board. The secretary must always be ready to refuse requests for information to members and outsiders if the law does not specifically entitle them to it or it is not in line with best practice.

## 3.3 Electronic communications

Information to shareholders can be circulated electronically if the company's Articles permit it and shareholders agree and supply the appropriate email addresses. Shareholders may agree to access annual reports including summary financial statements and accounts on a website instead of receiving hard copies through the post. Shareholders may also appoint proxies electronically and give them voting instructions. Companies can canvass shareholders about website notification of documents addressed to shareholders. Provided the correct procedure is followed, if shareholders do not respond and specifically request hard copy documents, they may be deemed to consent to website notification (see Chapter 9).

As with all other forms of communication, steps must be taken to ensure that electronic communication and website notification are available to all shareholders on equal terms. The invitation to members to use electronic means of communication must include an explanation of all the available procedures and details of exactly which documents will be available. Communications that can be sent electronically include:

- the annual report and accounts;
- summary financial statements;
- shareholder circulars;
- notices of meetings;
- proxy appointments.

**STOP AND THINK 1.2**

If shareholders elect to use computer-based electronic communications, they must be warned that any communication found to contain a computer virus will not be accepted. This includes the filing of electronic proxy forms. As the company secretary is responsible for ensuring that the Articles of Association cover matters such as electronic communication, he should review the Articles before decisions can be made about sending documents to shareholders electronically.

**TEST YOUR KNOWLEDGE 1.3**

Apart from the directors' report and the audited accounts, what other information must a company circulate to its shareholders?

## 4 The company secretary's role in ensuring compliance

Company secretaries are deemed to be officers of a company and as such have certain responsibilities and potentially have liabilities (see section 6 below). The company secretary will often be the only expert in many areas of compliance (e.g. the Annual Return requirements – see Chapter 8) and hence the directors will be reliant on him to take responsibility for ensuring full compliance with such areas. Company secretaries operate in a niche area where not many people in an organisation will have knowledge. There is, therefore, a considerable onus on a company secretary to be professional in his duty to ensure compliance.

Company secretaries can employ professional, management and control techniques to ensure that the many different compliance obligations are not overlooked and that their work schedule is properly planned. Typical methods company secretaries use to ensure compliance include:

- establishing and maintaining checklists for all standard procedures (e.g. appointment of a director; filing of annual accounts);
- preparing detailed timetables for scheduled events (e.g. dividend payments);
- for larger companies, using a specialised software package (essentially a database) for holding the statutory registers. These software packages have features which help ensure compliance; for example, they can check the validity of entries made on the database and reminders can be set to ensure compliance events are not overlooked;
- ensuring that company secretaries make use of comprehensive and up-to-date reference materials, such as CA 2006, and for listed companies the various Listing Rules (see Chapter 6). This should be accompanied by sufficient continuing professional development;
- acting promptly after an event has occurred; for example, a company secretary should prepare the minutes of a board meeting as soon as possible after the meeting and should ensure that signed minutes are entered into the minute book without delay;
- if there is more than one person in the company secretary's department, it is helpful to hold regular team meetings to ensure that progress on all compliance matters is being met.

### CASE QUESTION

As company secretary of Multiple plc, you are responsible not only for company law compliance and good corporate governance, but also working with your team to ensure these objectives are met. Some of these responsibilities may include:

- ensuring subsidiary companies have adequate company secretarial support;
- providing high quality support to directors;
- ensuring corporate records are properly maintained;
- ensuring all necessary compliance matters are observed.

How should you as company secretary organise the department to ensure company secretarial matters are dealt with to the best effect? Consider how to address the following:

- reporting lines within the department to ensure good governance is maintained;
- who should act as company secretary to the various subsidiary companies and why;
- how the department can ensure it provides a good and consistent level of service;
- the best way to maintain company records and why.

## 5 Appointment and removal from office

CA 2006, s. 271 states that a public company must have a company secretary, but it does not specify how he should be appointed. However, for listed companies the UK Corporate Governance Code states that 'the appointment and removal of the company secretary should be a matter for the whole board'. Companies incorporated prior to 1 October 2009 are likely to have Articles which provide that the company secretary can be appointed and removed by resolution of the board.

The person named as the secretary on form IN01 (see Chapter 4) – the formal notification to the Registrar of Companies of the first directors and secretary of a company when it is incorporated – is deemed to have been appointed as the first secretary. The name is entered on the register of secretaries. Subsequent appointments are made by the board of directors and notified to Companies House by filing form AP03, which must take place within 14 days of the date of appointment. The register of secretaries must also be updated. In a single-member private company, it is not possible to appoint a secretary who is also the sole director/single member.

Company secretaries appointed do not need to provide a residential address to the Registrar of Companies and may instead provide a service address, which may be stated as the company's registered office (CA 2006, ss. 275–278).

If the company is listed, the appointment or resignation should be notified to one of the regulatory information services (see Chapter 6) and any appropriate press releases issued. The new secretary is likely to be in possession of unpublished, price-sensitive (inside) information from time to time and should therefore be bound by the company's rules regarding securities transactions, but must in any case comply with the **Model Code**.

As the company secretary will be one of the signatories on the company's bank account, the bank will require a specimen signature and it may be appropriate to notify the company's staff, suppliers and customers of the appointment. The company's auditor should also be informed.

## CHECKLIST 1.1 **The secretary's appointment**

✓ A resolution is passed at a meeting of the board to appoint a new company secretary in place of one who is resigning or being removed. The terms of the appointment and any specific delegated authority should be made clear in the resolution.

✓ An employment contract should be executed.

✓ Form APO3 is filed with the Registrar of Companies within 14 days of the date of the appointment.

✓ The necessary entry is made in the register of directors and secretaries.

✓ The company's bank should be notified of the new appointment, the bank mandate should be amended and specimen signatures supplied.

✓ The company secretary should be provided with appropriate induction materials (e.g. the Articles of Association; the most recent annual report, any terms of reference for the board or standing committees, contact details of all directors, etc.) and should be fully briefed (e.g. dates of next board meeting; the company's corporate calendar).

✓ The company secretary should be included in the directors' and officers' indemnity insurance policy.

## 5.1 Qualifications of a company secretary

There is no legal requirement for a company secretary of a private company to have professional qualifications or any previous experience. In the case of a public company, however, the Companies Acts provide that the directors must take all reasonable steps to secure that the company secretary is a person who appears to have the requisite knowledge and experience to discharge the relevant functions. According to CA 2006, s. 273 the company secretary of a public company must be a person who:

1 Is a barrister, advocate or solicitor, called or admitted in any part of the UK.
2 For at least three of the five years immediately preceding his appointment held the office of company secretary of another company other than a private company.
3 Is a member of any of the following professional bodies:
   a) Institute of Chartered Secretaries and Administrators;
   b) the Institutes of Chartered Accountants in England and Wales, Scotland or Ireland;
   c) Chartered Institute of Management Accountants;
   d) Association of Chartered Certified Accountants;
   e) Chartered Institute of Public Finance and Accountancy.
4 Is a person who, by virtue of his holding or having held any other position, or his being a member of any other body, appears to the directors to be capable of discharging those functions.

These provisions also apply when a private company re-registers as a public company. If it has not appointed or retained a company secretary, it will have to do so.

---

**STOP AND THINK** **1.3**

Do you think it appropriate that the ICSA strongly encourages all practising secretaries to reinforce their qualifications through a continuing professional development programme?
Why do professional bodies advocate it?

---

## 5.2 Removal of secretary from office

The secretary is appointed by the directors and may also be removed by them. A secretary may also resign from office at any time. In either case form TM02 must be filed at Companies House within 14 days of the effective date of resignation or removal. In respect of listed companies, the UK Corporate Governance Code recommends that the removal of a secretary should be a matter that the whole board decides. However, although removal is usually a quite simple procedure, like any other employee, the secretary may be able to take action for breach of contract under his service agreement or contract of employment.

As for an appointment, listed companies should also notify the London Stock Exchange and issue a press release as appropriate. The bank will have to be notified and the register of directors and secretaries updated.

---

**STOP AND THINK** **1.4**

Consider the position if a company secretary resigns at short notice. Remember, each public company must have a company secretary and the duties of the company secretary need to be carried out in private companies even if a company secretary is not appointed. CA 2006, s. 274 also provides that if the office of company secretary is vacant, a deputy or assistant secretary or any officer of the company authorised by the directors may act in the secretary's capacity. However, given the responsibilities and potential liability of a company secretary, a decision to provide a short-term replacement needs to be considered.

---

## 5.3 Reporting lines

The company secretary is responsible to the board and should be accountable to it through the chairman on all matters relating to his core duties as an officer of the company. In connection with non-core duties, the company secretary should report to the CEO or to any other director as chosen by the board. The company secretary's remuneration and benefits should be decided by the board or by the remuneration committee of the board. This will prevent the secretary from being exposed to the influence of a single director.

The ICSA Guidance Note *Reporting Lines for the Company Secretary* can be downloaded from the ICSA website (see Directory).

In some larger organisations, the company secretary has a functional reporting line to the company's General Counsel, the most senior in-house lawyer.

# 6 Liabilities

The company secretary can be liable with the directors to default fines for non-compliance with the Companies Acts. Penalties vary depending on the offence, in accordance with the Acts. Even with liability insurance cover the principle of law is that one cannot insure against the effects of an illegal act and the wording of many policies is such that if the legal claim cannot be successfully defended, the policy will not pay out and damages must be paid for out of personal assets. (See Chapter 2 in respect of directors' liabilities and indemnities.)

The current trend seems to be that public opinion and increasingly legislation require that where accidents and/or incidents occur, someone should be held liable. In this climate we may see a situation where employees as well as officers become liable to pay damages to other employees (e.g. in a case of discrimination or harassment of a work colleague). In the issues of safety there have been cases where companies and directors have been found guilty of manslaughter, which carries a substantial fine and/or prison sentence, together with disqualification for several years.

The Corporate Manslaughter and Corporate Homicide Act 2007 does not create any offences for which individual directors will be liable; it does, however, allow unlimited fines to be imposed on companies and other organisations for gross failings in health and safety management which lead to fatal consequences.

Companies may be held liable even when they have prohibited the acts of their employees, as in *National Rivers Authority v Alfred McAlpine Homes East Ltd.*

**CASE LAW** **1.2**

**National Rivers Authority v Alfred McAlpine Homes East Ltd**

Cement was being washed into a stream causing it to be polluted despite Alfred McAlpine's efforts to ensure that its employees complied with the legal and trading guidelines. The Court of Appeal held that the company could not be held liable for employees wilfully breaking rules, but the House of Lords overturned the ruling, imposing heavier fines and threatening jail sentences for future similar cases.

HM Revenue & Customs has stated that if it discovers wrongdoing in the process of an audit which is considered to be the fault of an individual, action will be taken against that individual and not against the directors, the company or the owners. This is also carried through in FSMA, which carries criminal penalties for individuals responsible for giving poor, faulty or biased advice, or laundering money.

Companies should have liability insurance cover, but officers or employees cannot be held harmless for criminal acts and it is a serious offence to fail to report suspicions of criminal acts as it is to carry them out. The largest part of the burden of compliance with the various Acts therefore falls to the company secretary as adviser to the board.

## 6.1 Offences and penalties for non-compliance

The company secretary is held to be liable only where he himself is in default or where he knowingly and wilfully permits the default. There is no excuse if the secretary allows himself to remain ignorant in an attempt to avoid liability.

It is the duty of the company secretary to ensure compliance with the Companies Acts, but as a matter of operating policy, the Registrar of Companies does not generally proceed against the company secretary unless he is also a director. Failure to deliver accounts and annual returns on time to the Registrar is a criminal offence. On average well over 1,000 directors are prosecuted each year for failing to deliver accounts and annual returns on time. On conviction, members of the board could incur a criminal record, their names published in the local press and personal fines of up to £5,000 for each offence.

There are automatic late filing penalties if the accounts miss the statutory filing deadline. These are on a sliding scale and for public companies can reach a maximum of £5,000 if the accounts are filed more than twelve months late.

Persistent failure to deliver statutory documents on time may lead to a director being disqualified from taking part in the management of a company for a period specified by the court. The company secretary should therefore take responsibility for coordinating and monitoring statutory filings on a timely basis.

**CHAPTER** SUMMARY

- Every public company must have a company secretary. Private companies do not have to appoint or retain a company secretary but may do so if they choose (CA 2006, s. 270).
- In a public company the secretary must be suitably qualified for the position. The secretary's role in a listed company is further defined by the UK Corporate Governance Code.
- The company secretary is responsible for his own actions as an officer of the company.
- The secretary's duties and responsibilities should be defined in his contract of employment.
- The appointment or removal of the secretary is a matter for the board and must be notified to the Registrar of Companies. Listed companies must also notify the London Stock Exchange.
- The onus is on the company secretary to advise the board if they are acting in breach of certain legal requirements. In order to do this properly it is essential that he has detailed knowledge not only of statutes such as the CA, but also of the company's Articles of Association. Professional knowledge should be kept up to date by reading materials and continuing professional development programmes.
- The company secretary should act as the board's communicator, particularly in matters of public awareness.
- The company secretary is also a focal point of communication to the company's shareholders.

# 2  The directors

## ■ INTRODUCTION

This chapter looks at the different types of director, their powers, duties, responsibilities and liabilities. It also looks at how directors are appointed and removed. Company secretaries must be in a position to provide directors with concise and accurate advice on these matters and directors will often rely on such advice.

CA 2006 codifies the general duties of directors, replacing previous common law and equitable principles in relation to directors' duties to the company.

Directors' duties were one of the most debated issues leading up to the enactment of CA 2006, with concerns raised that, despite the requirement to have due regard to previous common law and equitable principles, by putting directors' duties on a statutory footing, courts may interpret the statutory wording in a different way from previous case law and equitable principles.

## 1  What is a director?

Companies are incorporated to create a separate legal entity, but they cannot act on their own; they need people to make the decisions and manage them. These people are the directors. CA 2006, s. 154 states that a public company must have a minimum of two directors and a private company at least one.

CA 2006, s. 250 defines a director as any 'person occupying the position of director, by whatever name called'.

A director is an 'officer of the company' and an agent of the company. Directors are the company's most senior level of management and have the right to take part in the board of management. They are also the people appointed by the shareholders to manage the company. The definition is wide in order to include those who are effectively dealing with the affairs of the company but do not bear the title 'director'. It also includes corporate bodies – a company can be a director of another company. The Act does not specify any qualifications that must be held in order to qualify as a company director. However, a company's Articles may require that a director holds a specified qualification, for example, directors of a residents' management company may be required to be property owners or tenants of the particular development.

## 1.1 Executive directors

Directors are often employees too. If this is the case, they are known as executive directors and the company as employer is represented on the board by a director who is also an employee. Directors with specific responsibilities are usually denoted by a special title, such as finance director, but their legal position remains the same as any other director of the company. They are members of the board of directors, but also full-time employees with a clear executive role.

Some companies appoint a managing director. Managing directors have a special position and are usually granted wide apparent powers, although as with all directors, they must exercise their powers in accordance with the company's constitution and for the purposes for which they are conferred (CA, 2006, s. 171). Their duties may also be delegated to a committee that comprises one or more directors (Model Article 5; public company Model Article 5). Any appointment of a director to an executive office will terminate if he ceases to be a director.

## 1.2 Non-executive directors (NEDs)

A **non-executive director (NED)** is a member of the board of directors without executive responsibilities in the company. A NED is not an employee of the company of which he is a NED. However, because he is a director, he is legally liable in the same way as an executive director.

The criteria for selecting a NED are varied, and consideration needs to be given by the board (or by any appointed nomination committee of the board) as to the qualities and experience required for the role. NEDs are usually expected to contribute judgement and objectivity to the deliberations of the board by bringing relevant experience from outside the company. A NED has to understand the company's business, but the experience and qualities required of a NED can be obtained from working in a different industry or in other aspects of commercial and public life. NEDs might therefore include individuals who:

- are an executive director in another company;
- hold NED positions and/or chairmanship positions in other companies;
- have professional qualifications (e.g. as a partner in a firm of solicitors);
- have experience in government (e.g. politicians or former senior civil servants).

A NED should bring an independent and objective view to board decision-making; this is particularly important in respect of listed companies (see below). However, it is possible for a NED's independence to be compromised under certain circumstances. Checklist 2.1 shows the potential relationships and circumstances which the UK Corporate Governance Code states may affect the independence of a NED in a listed company.

### CHECKLIST 2.1 **NED independence**

The independence of a NED may be affected if the NED:

- ✓ has been an employee of the company in the last five years;
- ✓ has, or has had within the last three years, a material business relationship with the company;
- ✓ has received or receives additional remuneration from the company apart from a director's fees; participates in the company's share option or a performance-related pay schemes; or is a member of the company's pension scheme;
- ✓ has close family ties with any of the company's advisers, directors or senior employees;
- ✓ holds cross-directorships or has significant links with other directors through involvement in other companies or bodies;
- ✓ represents a significant shareholder; or
- ✓ has served on the board for more than nine years.

The selection and appointment of NEDs is a cornerstone of corporate governance. The guiding principle is that there should be a sufficient number of independent NEDs on the board to create an appropriate balance of power and to prevent the dominance of the board by one individual or a small number of individuals. For listed companies, this includes one of the NEDs acting as senior independent NED. The senior independent NED should be available to shareholders if they have concerns that contact through the normal channels of chairman, CEO or finance director has failed to resolve or for which such contact is inappropriate.

---

**STOP AND THINK** **2.1**

While NEDs are generally supposed to bring independence of judgement to the board, it is important to note that this may not always be the case. Common sense should be used to assess whether there is a conflict of interest.

For example, imagine a very small, family-run business where the father and mother are the only shareholders. They have retired, but both remain NEDs as they have useful experience. They have handed the running of the business to their daughter, who is the sole employee and an executive director. Although the composition of the board is clearly non-independent, how likely is it that there will be a conflict of interest?

---

**CASE LAW** **2.1**

***Re Continental Assurance Co. of London plc* [1997] 1 BCLC 48**

This was the first indication of the court's approach to the status of NEDs. The case involved a holding company, its subsidiary and a senior bank officer who was a NED of both boards. Both companies collapsed and it emerged that the subsidiary had made a series of cash transfers to the holding company in breach of CA provisions on financial assistance. There was a note on the transfer in the holding company's accounts. The NED stated that he did not know of the transfers and that if he had, he would have stopped it.

The court held that any competent director, especially a banker, would understand the accounts and his conduct made him unfit to be concerned in the management of a company. He was disqualified for three years.

---

## 1.3 Corporate directors

CA 2006, s. 155 requires that each company shall have at least one natural person as a director so that every company has at least one individual who can be held to account for the company's actions. Company secretaries should therefore review the board's composition upon the formation of a company and each time there is a change in directorship to ensure the constitution of the board is in line with section 155.

## 1.4 Other types of director

It is possible for a company's Articles to allow employees to have the word 'director' as part of their title (e.g. divisional director or associate director) when they are not a director within the meaning of CA 2006, s. 250. The title is sometimes given to add status to senior executives. Even if the position is absolutely clear from the Articles, it is nevertheless misleading to have the word 'director' in a job title if that person is not subject to the legal duties of a director.

A *de facto* **director** is a person who has not been formally appointed but who is 'occupying the position of a director'. Such a person is treated as a director and therefore bears all the responsibilities of being a director without enjoying any of the authority.

Where there is a group of companies, the solution is often to appoint the executive to the board of the particular subsidiary with which he is most concerned. In that case there is no doubt about his status as a full director of the subsidiary, but not of the parent company. Another practical alternative is to use a different job title, for example, head of sales instead of sales director.

Shadow and alternate directors are described in sections 9 and 10.

## 1.5 Who can become a director?

There are no formal requirements or qualifications to become a director, but certain categories of individual are excluded. Persons cannot become a director if:

1 They are bankrupt and not discharged. If a director becomes bankrupt after appointment, he must immediately resign unless the courts give permission for him to continue (CDDA 1986, s. 11).
2 They are disqualified by the court because they have committed criminal offences whilst director of another company (CDDA 1986, ss. 2 and 5).
3 They are disqualified by the court because, during the directorship of a previous company now insolvent, they were declared unfit to manage.
4 They have accepted a voluntary disqualification undertaking (see section 8).
5 They are the auditor of the company.
6 The Articles may contain special restrictions or provide further instances where appointment cannot be made or must cease, for example:
   a) if the person is suffering from a mental disorder (Model Article 18, public company Model Article 22);
   b) if a composition is made with the director's creditors in satisfaction of the director's debts (Model Article 18, public company Model Article 22).

A private company can, as a minimum, have one director. A public company must have at least two. Most companies will have at least two directors, even if one of them also acts as the company secretary. When documents are to be signed by a director and the secretary, the signatories must be two different people.

## 1.6 Chairman

The appointment and role of the chairman is examined in Chapter 10.

---

**TEST YOUR KNOWLEDGE 2.1**

a What is the difference between an executive and a NED?
b What factors might prevent a person from being eligible for appointment as a NED in a listed company?
c Who is excluded from being a director?

---

## 2 Appointing directors

The first directors of a company are those named on form IN01, which is submitted to the Registrar of Companies on **incorporation** (see Chapter 4). Subsequent appointments are governed by the company's Articles of Association, which usually state that the board may fill casual vacancies or appoint additional directors up to any maximum number permitted. A casual vacancy can arise from the death or resignation of a director, if an elected director fails to take up office or for any reason other than retirement by rotation (see section 4). For public companies, elections or re-elections of directors following retirement by rotation or removal must be approved by the company in general meeting.

Public company Model Article 21 provides that at the public company's first AGM, all the directors retire from office and must be re-elected by the shareholders at the meeting. Public company Model Article 21 further provides that at every subsequent AGM any directors who have been appointed by directors since the last AGM or who were not appointed or reappointed at one of the preceding two AGMs must retire and seek re-election. These provisions do not apply to private companies operating under the private company Model Articles. A director is appointed, therefore, by being:

■ named in form IN01 when the company is formed;
■ individually appointed by ordinary resolution of the company in general meeting; or
■ appointed by the existing board to fill a casual vacancy until the next AGM.

## 2.1 Appointment procedure

### CHECKLIST 2.2 Appointing a director

✓ If appropriate, the board (or if applicable, a nomination committee of the board) should draw up a profile of a suitable candidate for the position. It may be necessary to use recruitment consultants to find an appropriate person.
✓ Select a candidate for consideration by the board.
✓ Before the board meeting, the secretary should send to the other directors:
   a) all relevant information about the director;
   b) a summary of the director's proposed remuneration arrangements;
   c) a draft of the service contract; and
   d) copies of any press releases which will be issued upon the director's appointment.
✓ The board resolves to appoint the new director.
✓ The secretary writes to the newly appointed director confirming his appointment by the board as follows:
   a) requesting personal details which are required to complete form AP01, specifically name, residential address, date of birth, nationality, business occupation and other directorships held within the past five years. Under CA 2006, directors can provide a service address (the registered office address) instead of their residential address for the public register held with the Registrar of Companies. The director's residential address continues to be supplied to the Registrar, but the residential address will not appear on the public records of the company. This abolishes the prior requirement for directors to seek a Confidentiality Order before being able to suppress their residential address from the public register;
   b) requesting signature of the consent section of form AP01;
   c) obtaining a specimen signature to be lodged at the company's bank if the director is to sign cheques on the company's behalf;
   d) informing the director of any share qualifications which he must acquire under the Articles and the time allowed in which to do this. This provision is in respect of companies that have amended their Articles, as the Model Articles do not contain any requirement for directors to have a qualification shareholding;
   e) if the company's shares are traded on a regulated market (see Chapter 6), the director should be informed of the obligation to disclose any interests in the shares or debentures of the company. This is necessary as the director's interests in shares or debentures (or any changes thereto) must be announced to the market through a regulatory information service (RIS) as required under the Disclosure and Transparency Rules (DTRs);
   f) inviting the director to give the appropriate notice of interests in any of the company's contracts;
   g) obtaining details of how the director wishes to be paid, including pay as you earn (PAYE) coding and National Insurance contributions (NICs). Most companies pay salaries direct to bank accounts, so it is usually advisable to request bank account details at this stage.
✓ If the company is listed, UKLA should be notified of the appointment by the end of the business day following the decision to appoint. Details of the director's other business activities must be disclosed to UKLA within 14 days.
✓ The secretary should update the necessary entries in the register of directors and secretaries.
✓ The completed form AP01 should be sent to the Registrar of Companies within 14 days of appointment.
✓ If the company stationery/letterhead shows the names of all directors, it should be amended.

In accordance with
Section 167 of the
Companies Act 2006.

# AP01
## Appointment of director

Companies House
*for the record*

**You can use the WebFiling service to file this form online.**
Please go to www.companieshouse.gov.uk

✓ **What this form is for**
You may use this form to appoint
an individual as a director.

✗ **What this form is NOT for**
You cannot use the form to appoint
a corporate director. To do this,
please use form AP02 'Appointment
of corporate director'.

For further information, please
refer to our guidance at
www.companieshouse.gov.uk

---

## 1   Company details

| | |
|---|---|
| Company number | |
| Company name in full | |

→ **Filling in this form**
Please complete in typescript or in
bold black capitals.

All fields are mandatory unless
specified or indicated by *

---

## 2   Date of director's appointment

| | |
|---|---|
| Date of appointment | d d  m m  y y y y |

---

## 3   New director's details

| | |
|---|---|
| Title* | |
| Full forename(s) | |
| Surname | |
| Former name(s) ❶ | |
| Country/State of residence ❷ | |
| Nationality | |
| Date of birth | d d  m m  y y y y |
| Business occupation (if any) ❸ | |

❶ **Former name(s)**
Please provide any previous names
which have been used for business
purposes in the past 20 years.

Married women do not need to give
former names unless previously used
for business purposes.

Continue in section 6 if required.

❷ **Country/State of residence**
This is in respect of your usual
residential address as stated in
Section 4a.

❸ **Business occupation**
If you have a business occupation,
please enter here. If you do not,
please leave blank.

---

## 4   New director's service address ❹

Please complete your service address below. You must also complete your usual
residential address in **Section 4a**.

| | |
|---|---|
| Building name/number | |
| Street | |
| Post town | |
| County/Region | |
| Postcode | |
| Country | |

❹ **Service address**
This is the address that will appear
on the public record. This does not
have to be your usual residential
address.

Please state 'The Company's
Registered Office' if your service
address is recorded in the company's
register of directors as the
company's registered office.

If you provide your residential
address here it will appear on the
public record.

---

BIS | **Department for Business Innovation & Skills**

CHFP000
05/10 Version 4.0

Other practical work includes providing the director with general information, a copy of the Memorandum and Articles, and copies of annual report and accounts and relevant circulars if he is new to the company. A schedule of the dates of forthcoming board meetings for the year would be helpful and, if appropriate, a press announcement regarding the appointment should be sent to newspapers or through the company's press agents.

## Induction and briefing

Induction arrangements and briefing materials should be prepared as appropriate (e.g. visits to any main operational sites for the business). If the company is listed, the UK Corporate Governance Code and related guidance provides additional assistance regarding induction. In particular it prescribes that:

- all directors should receive induction on joining the board and should regularly update and refresh their skills and knowledge;
- it is the responsibility of the chairman to take the lead in providing a properly constructed induction programme for new directors that is comprehensive, formal and tailored, facilitated by the company secretary;
- the company should offer major shareholders the opportunity to meet a new NED;
- specific induction and training may be required for NEDs who serve on the key committees of the board, particularly the audit committee.

As all directors of listed companies are required to comply with the Listing Regime, it is good practice to provide them with a copy of the Listing Rules, Prospectus Rules, DTRs and the UK Corporate Governance Code.

Before a director accepts an appointment, the secretary should ensure that he is fully aware of his responsibilities, duties and potential liabilities. There are several books available which can be provided. Alternatively, the company may prefer to produce in-house guidance and it is usually the company secretary's responsibility to prepare the guidance or organise its preparation. Additional guidance material is available from other sources, for example, the Companies House Directors and Secretaries Guide, which is available free of charge from the Registrar of Companies or can be downloaded from the Companies House website (see Directory). There are also institutions (e.g. the ICSA or the Institute of Directors) that provide training courses for new directors to help them understand their legal position.

---

**STOP AND THINK 2.2**

It is often the duty of the company secretary to arrange induction materials, site visits, and so on for a new director. This means that the company secretary needs to have a good understanding of how the business operates and who will be the most appropriate employees to meet the new director.

---

A good company secretary will ensure that the training materials are suited to the director's existing knowledge about his legal responsibilities. Additional help is available from the ICSA Guidance Note *Induction of Directors*, available on the ICSA website (see Directory).

## Shareholder proposal to appoint a director

Although it is usually the board that recommends the appointment of directors, shareholders may also propose the appointment of directors by requisitioning a proposal at a general meeting.

> **STOP AND THINK 2.3**
>
> When shareholders use their powers to appoint a new director whom the directors have not proposed, this is normally an indication that there is a considerable difference of opinion between major shareholders and the board about who should be serving as a director. A good company secretary should be alert and prepared to handle the potential consequences; for example, are the current directors likely to resign if a new director is appointed to the board against their wishes?

## Age of a director

The CA 2006 does not require a director to vacate office once they have reached a particular age. However, CA 2006 does contain restrictions on the appointment of underage directors, and the appointment of directors under the age of 16 years is prohibited.

## 2.2 Directors' service contracts

It is useful to the director and the company if the terms of employment for executive directors are set down in a formal service contract. As NEDs are not employees, they do not have service contracts; instead they usually have a simple letter of appointment. However, the provisions of CA 2006, ss. 227–230 apply whether it is in respect of an executive or NED.

Apart from setting out the director's remuneration, pension rights and entitlements to holiday and sick pay, the agreement may define his duties or even impose a time-limit against the director joining a competitor company. Any service contract must be kept at the registered office or at the Single Alternative Inspection Location (SAIL). (See Chapter 8 for further details on the location of statutory registers and provisions of CA 2006 in respect of the inspection of service contracts.) Furthermore, service contracts must be retained for at least one year following cessation of the director's appointment and must be available for inspection during that time.

It may be the case that a member would like to inspect a service contract but is too far away from its location to make this practical. CA 2006, s. 229 provides that any member may, upon payment of the prescribed fee, request a copy of the service contract and the company must provide such a copy within seven days of the request.

The information contained in a director's service contract should include the following:

- the name of the employing company;
- the date of the contract and details of any notice period;
- full details of the director's remuneration, including salary and other benefits. There should also be information as to when remuneration will be reviewed (e.g. annually or as the remuneration committee considers appropriate);
- any commission or profit-sharing arrangements;
- any compensation due for early termination;
- any other information regarding possible liability on early termination of the contract.

A service contract gives the executive director the usual statutory employment rights under employment law. It is best practice for the board as whole to approve the terms of the service contract.

A director's contract which cannot be terminated within a period of two years, other than for breach of contract, must be approved by shareholders in general meeting (CA 2006, s. 188). This serves as an important safeguard for shareholders to ensure that directors do not become too entrenched on boards and that, in the event of termination, any termination payments made are not excessive.

The UK Corporate Governance Code encourages listed companies to have service contracts that carry a notice period of not more than one year. Many institutional shareholders will vote against the election or re-election of any director with a notice period longer than this.

## 2.3 Directors' remuneration

Model Article 19 (public company Model Article 23) states that directors are entitled to such remuneration as the directors determine for their services to the company as directors and for any other service which they undertake for the company. Model Article 19 further provides, subject to the Articles, that a director's remuneration may take any form, and include any arrangements for pensions or other benefits.

Model Article 20 (public company Model Article 24) permits a company to pay any reasonable expenses for a director. The expenses must be properly incurred as a result of attending board or shareholder meetings or otherwise in connection with the exercise of the director's powers and the discharge of their responsibilities in relation to the company. This typically includes items such as travel and hotel costs. If the company is listed, the directors are recommended to delegate remuneration to a remuneration committee comprising only of NEDs.

## 2.4 Change of particulars

If a director or company secretary changes address or name, form CH01–02 must be completed and filed, and the relevant statutory registers (register of directors and secretary) updated. The company secretary should also consider who else may need to be informed of the change, for example, the Personnel Department.

## 2.5 When an appointment is defective

CA 2006, s. 161 provides that the acts of a person acting as a director are valid notwithstanding any defect in their appointment, or if the director had previously been disqualified or had otherwise ceased to hold office. On discovering that the director's appointment is invalid, the company secretary should take steps to rectify the situation. This will depend on the reason for the invalidation; for example, if there is a minimum share qualification required of a director and the director has not yet taken his shares, this should be corrected.

Once the appointment is discovered to be defective even though it may be some years since the appointment was made, it is appropriate to consider passing a resolution in general meeting to ratify the acts of the director (see Sample Wording 2.1). This will ensure that the members will be informed of the position and will, so far as possible, ratify all earlier appointments and acts of the directors and avoid any question of remuneration received having to be repaid to the company.

Any resolution rectifying a defective appointment should ratify the acts of all directors. This may be necessary where the acts of other directors would have otherwise become invalidated (e.g. for lack of a quorum), if the director with the defective appointment would have been excluded.

Remedying a defective appointment can be problematic and embarrassing for both the directors and the company secretary. Careful planning and awareness by the company secretary together with the use of checklists to ensure that the appointment has been correctly dealt with should mean that no appointment is ever defective.

In accordance with
Section 167 of the
Companies Act 2006.

# CH01
## Change of director's details

**Companies House**
*for the record*

**You can use the WebFiling service to file this form online.**
Please go to www.companieshouse.gov.uk

✓ **What this form is for**
You may use this form to change the details of an individual who is a director.

✗ **What this form is NOT for**
You cannot use this form to change the details of a corporate director. To do this, please use form CH02 'Change of corporate director's details'.

For further information, please refer to our guidance at www.companieshouse.gov.uk

---

**1** **Company details**

| Company number | |
|---|---|
| Company name in full | |

→ **Filling in this form**
Please complete in typescript or in bold black capitals.

All fields are mandatory unless specified or indicated by *

---

**2** **Director's current details on the Register ❶**

| Date of birth* ❷ | d d  m m  y y y y |
|---|---|
| Title* | |
| Full forename(s) | |
| Surname | |

❶ **Current details**
This information is used to identify your details on the public record.

❷ This is voluntary information and if completed it will be placed on the public record.

---

**3** **Date of change of details**

| Date of change of details | d d  m m  y y y y |
|---|---|

Please complete the appropriate sections to indicate which of your details have changed.

---

**4** **Change of name details**

| Title* | |
|---|---|
| Full forename(s) ❸ | |
| Surname ❸ | |

❸ **New name**
Please enter your new name.

---

**5** **Change of service address ❹**

| Building name/number | |
|---|---|
| Street | |
| | |
| Post town | |
| County/Region | |
| Postcode | |
| Country | |

❹ **Service address**
This is the address that will appear on the public record. This does not have to be your usual residential address.

Please state 'The Company's Registered Office' if your service address is recorded in the company's register of directors as the company's registered office.

If you provide your residential address here it will appear on the public record.

Please complete Section 5a if your usual residential address has changed.

☐ I confirm that there has been no change in the company's register of directors' residential addresses.

---

**BIS** | **Department for Business Innovation & Skills**

CHFP000
05/10 Version 4.0

**Resolution validating acts of directors**

That all appointments and reappointments of directors of the company made and all acts of the directors done prior to the date of this resolution be confirmed and ratified, notwithstanding any defects in any such appointments or reappointments that might otherwise cause their validity to be in doubt.

**TEST YOUR KNOWLEDGE 2.2**

**a**   Which statutory registers should be updated upon appointment of a director?
**b**   What documentation would you need to prepare an appointment of a new director?

# 3   Vacation of office and removal

## 3.1 Vacation of office

By Model Article 18 (public company Model Article 22), a person ceases to be a director as soon as notification is received by the company from the director that the director is resigning from office. For companies operating under Articles which provide for retirement by rotation, this can also be effected by the director not offering himself for re-election when his term of office comes to an end under the rules of rotation (see below). Private companies operating under the private company Model Articles do not have provisions for retirement by rotation. The date of resignation is the date the letter is received unless it states a subsequent date, and does not have to be approved by the board to be effective.

The office of director is obviously vacated on death. Where companies have only one director and that director resigns or dies, any shareholder can request the company secretary to convene a shareholders' meeting to appoint a new director. This would also be the case if a company with more than one director found itself with no directors as a result of mass resignations or some collective fatality.

Vacation of office can also arise if the company's Articles provide that a director must obtain and hold a share qualification and the director has not complied with this provision. Neither CA 2006 nor the Model Articles require such a share qualification from directors.

## 3.2 Removal of a director

According to CA 2006, s. 168, a company may remove a director at any time by ordinary resolution with special notice, regardless of anything to the contrary in the Articles or any agreement with the director. Removal does not deprive the director of any right he may have to compensation or damages payable in respect of the termination. CA 2006, s. 169 provides that the director who has been proposed for removal is entitled to protest against their removal, which includes circulating their representations on the matter to the members of the company and having the right to be heard at the general meeting at which the removal is to be considered. The provisions of the Act must be strictly complied with and it may be advisable to obtain legal advice as to the precise procedure. Chapter 9 gives full details of the procedure required for special notice.

If the Articles allow, a director can be removed from the board by fellow directors by a notice given to him by them all or by a board resolution. If the Articles empower the board to call on a director to resign and cease to hold office and he does not, the other directors must act in the interests of the company.

The Model Articles do not contain provisions to remove a director solely by board resolution. Instead, Model Article 18 (public company Model Article 22) sets out that the office of the director shall be vacated if he:

- is disqualified by any provision of CA 2006 or otherwise by law;
- becomes bankrupt;
- is mentally or physically incapable of acting as a director;
- makes a composition with his creditors in satisfaction of his debts; or
- resigns his office by notice to the company.

The statutory power for removal may also be limited, for example, if the director holds weighted voting rights as in the case of *Bushell v Faith* (1970). Such weighted voting rights are not permitted for listed companies. Whatever the reason for vacating office the following actions should be taken.

### CHECKLIST 2.3 **Vacation of office by director**

✓ If possible, obtain a letter of resignation from the director. If being removed, follow special notice procedure set out in Chapter 9.
✓ The board should formally minute the vacation of office, including the reason for vacation. The minutes should include an instruction to the secretary to update the statutory registers, make all necessary returns and to take any other actions required.
✓ Record the date of ceasing to be a director in the register of directors and secretaries.
✓ Complete form TM01 and send it to the Registrar of Companies within 14 days of the date of vacation of office.
✓ Any fees and expenses for the period to the date of cessation of office should be paid to the director, or if he is deceased, to his personal representatives. Inform HM Revenue & Customs of the cessation of fees.
✓ Check whether any share options or other incentives held by the director have been triggered by the vacation of office (e.g. the ability to exercise share options).
✓ Remove the name of the director from any company stationery.
✓ If the director was authorised to sign cheques or authorise other forms of payments, inform the bank.
✓ If the company is listed, notify the UKLA without delay and, if appropriate, issue a press release.
✓ Ask the director to return all documents and company property and make arrangements for the return of a company car if relevant.

## 3.3 Rotation of directors

CA 2006 does not impose general requirements for directors to retire by rotation, but provisions do appear in Model Article 21 for public limited companies. These provisions do not apply for private companies operating under the private company Model Articles. The provisions for companies operating the Model Articles are as follows:

1 At the first AGM, all the directors must retire and be elected by the company in general meeting.
2 At every subsequent AGM any directors:
   a) who have been appointed by the directors since the last AGM, or
   b) who were not appointed or reappointed at one of the preceding two AGMs,
   c) must retire from office and may offer themselves for reappointment by the members.

Under the public company Model Article provisions, no director is exempt from the requirement to retire by rotation. In order to keep track of the position, company secretaries should draw up a schedule which shows when directors were last subject to retirement by rotation and when the director will be next subject to such retirement.

The rotation clauses enable the company not to re-elect a director at the expiry of his period of office if it does not wish to do so, although it could be useful to have alternative powers of removal in the company's Articles.

In accordance with
Section 167 of the
Companies Act 2006.

# TM01
## Termination of appointment of director

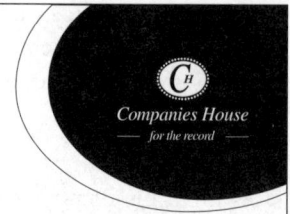

Companies House
— for the record —

**You can use the WebFiling service to file this form online.**
Please go to www.companieshouse.gov.uk

✓ **What this form is for**
You may use this form
to terminate the appointment of a
director (individual or corporate).

✗ **What this form is NOT for**
You cannot use this form to
terminate the appointment of a
secretary. To do this, please use form
TM02 'Termination of appointment
of secretary'.

For further information, please
refer to our guidance at
www.companieshouse.gov.uk

## 1 Company details

Company number

Company name in full

→ **Filling in this form**
Please complete in typescript or in
bold black capitals.

All fields are mandatory unless
specified or indicated by *

## 2 Director's current details on the Register

Please give us the current appointment details of this director held on the
public Register.

Date of birth* ❶   d d m m y y y y

Title*

Full forename(s)

Surname/Corporate
name

❶ **Date of birth**
Providing a date of birth will help
us identify the correct person on
the public record. This is voluntary
information and if completed it will
be placed on the public record.

## 3 Termination date ❷

Date of termination of
appointment   d d m m y y y y

❷ Only one director appointment can
be terminated per form.

## 4 Signature

I am signing this form on behalf of the company.

Signature

Signature   X                                            X

This form may be signed by:
Director ❸, Secretary, Person authorised ❹, Liquidator, Administrator,
Administrative receiver, Receiver, Receiver manager, Charity Commission receiver
and manager, CIC manager, Judicial factor.

❸ **Societas Europaea**
If the form is being filed on behalf
of a Societas Europaea (SE) please
delete 'director' and insert details
of which organ of the SE the person
signing has membership.

❹ **Person authorised**
Under either section 270 or 274 of
the Companies Act 2006.

## Listed companies and public companies

The Articles of most listed companies provide for the election and re-election of directors at the AGM. The UK Corporate Governance Code recommends that all directors of listed companies should be subject to election by shareholders at the first opportunity after their appointment, and to re-election thereafter at intervals of not more than three years (however, directors of FTSE 350 companies should be subject to annual re-election).

In respect of public companies, CA 2006, s. 160 provides that the resolutions at a general meeting for the appointment or reappointment of directors must be voted on individually unless the meeting has first agreed that the appointment or reappointment may be made by a single resolution.

---

**TEST YOUR KNOWLEDGE 2.3**

**a** According to the Model Articles, how can a director vacate office?

**b** Which document must be filed with the Registrar of Companies when a director vacates office? When must it be filed?

**c** What proportion of the board must offer themselves for re-election at the first AGM of a company?

**d** What are the provisions in the Model Articles for a public company for the election and re-election of directors of a listed company?

---

# 4 Directors' duties

## 4.1 Statutory duties

The statutory statements in CA 2006 codify the general duties of directors, replacing previous common law and equitable principles in relation to directors' duties to the company. However, the Act makes it clear that regard must be made to such previous common law and equitable principles when interpreting the statutory statements.

Each general duty is considered further below. In addition to the general duties, CA 2006, s. 182 requires a director to declare a direct or indirect interest in an existing transaction or arrangement. It is a criminal offence for a director not to comply with s. 182.

## 4.2 Duty to act within powers

A director must act in accordance with the company's constitution. Constitution is defined by CA 2006 as including not only the Articles, but also any other relevant resolutions, decisions or agreements. Company secretaries must therefore take care that all such constitutional documents have been collated, are up to date and have been communicated to directors.

## 4.3 Duty to promote the success of the company

A director is required to act in a way he considers in good faith and shall promote the success of the company for the benefit of its members as a whole. CA 2006 provides a non-exhaustive list of factors which directors should take into account when considering this duty:

- the likely consequences of any decision in the long term;
- the interests of the company's employees;
- the need to foster the company's business relationships with suppliers, customers and others;
- the impact of the company's operations on the community and the environment;
- the desirability of the company maintaining a reputation for high standards of business conduct;
- the need to act fairly as between members of the company.

This replaces the previous duty to act in the best interests of the company and, according to the government, merely codifies the previous legal position. The duties reflect the government's desire for the principle of enlightened shareholder value (i.e. good governance and corporate social responsibility, taking into account the interests of employees, suppliers, customers and the environment over the longer term) to be embedded in CA 2006.

There has been much debate on the practical implication for directors to ensure any decisions they make have been made after taking due regard to the above factors. Much of the debate has commented that good companies would already be making decisions after taking such factors into account and that such processes need to be embedded into the decision-making processes for each organisation. It may be the case that in certain decisions directors take, they will need to weigh up the competing interests of the above factors and may conclude that one factor is more important than another. It should be noted, however, that the overriding factors that need to be considered are that directors must promote the success of the company.

## 4.4 Duty to exercise independent judgement

Directors are required to exercise independent judgement. However, the ability of a director to exercise his judgement may at times be restricted because of other agreements which bind the company. CA 2006, s. 173 takes note of these potential restrictions. It provides that the duty is not infringed if the director is acting in accordance with an agreement duly entered into by the company that restricts the future exercise of discretion by directors or is otherwise authorised by the company's constitution.

## 4.5 Duty to exercise reasonable care, skill and diligence

A director must exercise reasonable care, skill and diligence. This provision closely tracks the previous common law position. CA 2006, s. 174 states that this means the care, skill and diligence that would be exercised by a reasonably diligent person with:

■ the general knowledge, skill and experience that may reasonably be expected of a person carrying out the functions carried out by a director (i.e. an objective test); and
■ the general knowledge, skills and experience that the director has (i.e. a subjective test).

## 4.6 Duty to avoid conflicts of interest

CA 2006, s. 175 requires that directors must avoid situations where they may have a direct or indirect interest which is, or could potentially be, in conflict with the interests of the company. This statutory duty replaces the previous common law position in relation to conflicts of interest, but the statutory position would appear to be wider in application. It is possible for the duty to avoid conflicts not to be infringed if the matter has been authorised by the directors:

■ for private companies, if there is nothing in the company's constitution that would invalidate such an authorisation, the matter may be proposed and authorised by the directors;
■ for public companies, where the constitution includes provisions enabling the directors to authorise the matter, by the matter being proposed and authorised by the directors in accordance with the company's constitution.

In order for boards to authorise conflicts, it may be necessary for companies to propose changes to their Articles of Association to insert the relevant provisions to allow such an authorisation. Where the directors make such an authorisation, the director who is the subject of the conflict of interest may not be counted in the quorum of the meeting and must not vote on the matter. The previous power of members to authorise conflicts is also maintained in CA 2006.

Company secretaries must ensure that there is an appropriate system in place for directors to make full disclosure of conflicts or potential conflicts and for the board to consider them in a timely manner. Company secretaries should also ensure that a procedure to record such conflicts is put in place.

**STOP AND THINK** 2.5

Although it is the responsibility of the director to ensure that the company is informed of any interests he may have, particularly one which may cause a conflict, it is a good idea for the company secretary to be proactive and to perform an annual check of directors' declared interests. This could coincide with the company's financial year-end. In this way, directors will be encouraged to make any declarations promptly and will be reminded of the importance of keeping their declarations up to date.

## 4.7 Duty not to accept benefits from third parties

CA 2006, s. 176 requires that directors must not accept benefits from third parties in respect of their position as a director of a company. This is designed to prevent putting directors into a position where they may have a conflict of interest. Section 176 further provides that the duty is not infringed if the acceptance of the benefit cannot be reasonably be regarded as likely to give arise to a conflict of interest. However, care needs to be exercised as s. 176 (unlike s. 175) has no provision which allows the other directors to authorise the benefit. The only possibility for such authorisation under s. 176 is, therefore, to seek the authorisation of shareholders.

## 4.8 Duty to declare an interest in a proposed transaction or arrangement

CA 2006, s. 177 provides that a director must declare a direct or indirect interest in a proposed transaction of arrangement. This is in relation to an interest of which he is aware or ought to be reasonably aware. The director must make the declaration either at a board meeting or by notice to the directors, and the declaration must be made before the directors consider the transaction or arrangement. No declaration is necessary if the interest cannot be reasonably regarded as likely to give rise to a conflict of interest. The company secretary should take care to ensure that any declaration is properly recorded in the minutes if the declaration is made at the board meeting, or at the next possible board meeting following a notification by the director.

## 4.9 Breach of duty: remedies

CA 2006, s. 178 provides that the consequences of breach in respect of the general duties of directors are the same as would apply if the corresponding common law rule or equitable principle applied. Prior to the enactment of CA 2006 the following remedies were available:

- If failure to disclose an interest results in the company having the ability to avoid the contract and make the director account for any profits; there is also a criminal penalty of a fine to the statutory maximum.
- Directors are also liable for damages through negligence when it is appropriate.
- If the company considers it appropriate, the director can be dismissed.

## 4.10 Directors' duty of disclosure

Disclosure for directors extends to statutory information about them and any interests they may have in contracts or the company's shares or debentures. Every company must keep a register of directors and secretaries at the company's registered office. It must be open for inspection by any member free of charge and by the public on payment of the appropriate charge. The register of directors must contain the following information pursuant to CA 2006, ss. 163–164:

- full name, including any previous name(s);
- nationality;
- a service address (companies are required to keep a separate register of directors' residential address for individuals);

- the country or state or part of the UK in which the director is usually resident;
- date of birth;
- business occupation;
- particulars of other directorships held during the preceding five years, but not for companies that are dormant;
- if the director is a corporation, its corporate name, registered office, registered number, legal form and the law by which it is governed.

## 4.11 Other legislation

Directors also need to observe much other legislation, for example, there are statutes in respect of:

- health and safety
- anti-bribery processes
- ensuring fair competition
- environmental regulations.

Issues such as these should be covered, as necessary, during the induction process. Company secretaries should take responsibility for ascertaining the actual level of knowledge of the director and for ensuring the induction process is appropriately tailored so that the director is aware of his key statutory obligations.

---

**TEST YOUR KNOWLEDGE 2.4**

a  To whom do directors owe their duties?
b  What are the general duties of a director?
c  What are the key factors directors need to consider in respect of the duty to promote the success of the company?
d  Summarise the directors' duty to exercise reasonable care, skill and diligence.
e  What should a director do to avoid potential claims of conflict of interest?
f  What particulars must be recorded in the register of directors?

---

# 5   Power and liabilities

The directors are generally responsible for the management of the business of the company, but the extent of their authority depends on the provisions of the Articles and any overriding provisions in the Companies Acts. Model Article 3 (public company Model Article 3) provides that 'subject to articles, the directors are responsible for management of the company's business, for which purpose they may exercise all the powers of the company'.

Directors act as agents of the company and are therefore bound by all the provisions of agency law (i.e. actual and ostensible authority). In order to safeguard their position, directors should ensure that the company secretary makes full board minutes showing the directors' reasons, the factors they took into account and the arguments against or for any proposed course of action.

## 5.1 Directors' liabilities and powers

As directors are responsible for the general management of the company it follows that they are liable to some extent for their actions. CA 2006 confirms that directors and officers may be indemnified against civil proceedings (both defence costs and damages) brought by third parties and criminal proceedings. It also permits companies to reimburse directors in respect of costs incurred prior to the outcome of those proceedings.

There are some exceptions. The basic statutory position under CA 2006, s. 232(1) remains, insofar as companies cannot exempt a director from liability in respect of his negligence, default, breach of duty or trust. In addition, for public policy purposes, indemnification will not be permitted if the director is found guilty in criminal proceedings or is liable to a fine imposed by a government body.

If the company itself is seeking damages against one of its own directors, the company may pay the director's defence costs as they are incurred. However, defence costs must be repaid by the director if he unsuccessfully defends the company's claim (unless the company still decides to provide indemnification against defence costs anyway). The director will still be liable to pay any damages awarded to the company (i.e. indemnification would not be available in respect of actual damages payable).

CA 2006, s. 236 provides that any qualifying indemnity provisions must be disclosed in the company's annual directors' report. In addition to the disclosure obligation, s. 238 stipulates that members may inspect the qualifying indemnity provision. Section 237 requires the qualifying indemnity provision to be retained and made available for inspection for at least one year after it has expired or terminated. Section 238 also provides that members may, upon payment of the prescribed fee, request a copy of the qualifying indemnity provision and that the company will be obliged to provide the copy within seven days of the request.

Companies wishing to take advantage of the provisions of the Act in respect of the indemnification of their directors should check their Articles. Model Article 52 (public company Model Article 85) provides that the company may indemnify every director or officer against any civil or criminal proceedings.

The directors are responsible for ensuring that the company fulfils its statutory duties and may be liable to penalties should the company fail to carry them out. The secretary will usually be responsible for the performance of most of the duties imposed by the CA, for example, the duty to maintain proper books and records (see Chapter 8) and the preparation of the company's statutory accounts and directors' report (see Chapter 11).

If a company is involved in a takeover, the responsibility of the full board for the conduct of the offer arrangements has been stressed by the Panel on Takeovers and Mergers (see Chapter 6).

## 5.2 Delegation

Models Articles 5 and 6 (public company Model Articles 5 and 6) provide that directors may delegate any of their powers to any person or committee as they think fit. For listed companies, the UK Corporate Governance Code recommends that key matters are reserved for whole board consideration only.

CA 2006 does not provide any statutory guidance on the delegation of powers. In the past, the courts have laid down the following principles governing liability where directors delegate a matter:

■ Directors have, collectively and individually, a duty to acquire and maintain sufficient knowledge and understanding of the company's business to enable them to discharge their duties properly.

■ While directors are entitled (subject to the company's Articles) to delegate particular functions to those below them in the management chain, and to trust their competence and integrity to a reasonable extent, directors are not absolved from the duty to supervise the delegated functions. In this situation it is possible to delegate authority, but not responsibility.

Questions may arise as to whether the delegation has been made to an appropriate person or whether the individual with overall responsibility should have checked how his subordinates were discharging their delegated functions.

Where there is an issue as to the extent of a director's duties and responsibilities in any particular case, the level of reward that he is entitled to receive or which he may reasonably have expected to receive from the company may be a relevant factor in resolving the issue. It is not that the fitness or otherwise of a respondent depends on how much he is paid. The point is that the higher the reward, the greater the responsibilities that may reasonably be expected (*prima facie* at least) to go with it.

The company secretary has an important practical role to play in ensuring authority is delegated responsibly by directors. For example:

- If authority needs to be delegated for a specific transaction, full details of the delegated authority should be stated in the board minute. This provides all parties with an understanding of who is responsible for specific actions.
- If authority needs to be delegated for re-occurring transactions, formal terms of reference for a committee should be drawn up specifying who should be authorised to handle the transactions, the constitution and the remit of the committee.
- Model Article 6 (public company Model Article 6) provides that the proceedings of committees to which directors have delegated authority shall, unless the directors provide otherwise, follow the provisions in the company's Articles which govern the taking of decisions by directors. The company secretary should therefore take care that all decisions by committees have been made in accordance with the Articles or other directions of the directors.

## 5.3 Directors' and officers' insurance

Because of the heavy potential liabilities to which directors and other officers are subject, it is becoming increasingly common for companies to take out indemnity insurance. Model Articles 52 and 53 (public company Model Articles 85 and 86) provide that the company may indemnify every director or officer against the costs of any civil or criminal proceedings and that directors may purchase and maintain insurance at the expense of the company. (See section 5.1 in respect of the indemnification of directors under CA 2006.)

## 5.4 Derivative claims

Under the **derivative claims** procedure in CA 2006, ss. 260–269 any member may, on behalf of the company, bring a claim against a director for an actual or proposed act or omission involving negligence, breach of duty or breach of trust. The member making the claim must apply to the court for permission before the claim can continue by establishing a *prima facie* case. This step is designed to filter out frivolous claims. Permission to proceed will not be given where the court finds that:

- a person acting in accordance with the duty to promote the success of the company (see section 4.2) would not seek to continue such a claim; and
- the act or omission which is the cause of the claim has been authorised or ratified by the company.
- In addition, before giving permission to proceed, the court shall take into account:
  - the views of other 'independent' shareholders;
  - whether the claimant is acting in good faith and would be likely to bring the claim in their own name;
  - whether the subject of the claim is likely to be authorised or ratified by the company;
  - the importance of the claim to a person responsible for promoting the success of the company; and
  - if the company itself had not decided to bring a claim against the director.

---

**STOP AND THINK 2.6**

During the passage of CA 2006, concern was expressed that the combination of the codification of directors' duties and the introduction of the derivative claims process would increase the risk of directors being sued. This has been emphasised by certain features in the statutory provisions, for example, any single shareholder, no matter how small their shareholding, may commence an action. In addition, the shareholder commencing the action does not have to show that any actual loss has been suffered by the company before commencing the action. Some companies are therefore reviewing the adequacy of their arrangements for directors' and officers' insurance and their indemnity provisions – a task which is often the responsibility of the company secretary.

---

**a**  Who can bring a derivative claim? Summarise the procedure.
**b**  In whose name is the action brought?
**c**  What safeguards are in place to prevent frivolous claims being made?

# 6   Loans to directors

Under CA 2006, ss. 197–214 companies may make loans, **quasi-loans** (under which the company reimburses the director's creditor) or other related transactions to directors. This is provided there has been prior approval by ordinary resolution of the members. If the company's Articles require a higher standard of resolution in general meeting (e.g. a special resolution), this will override the statutory position. In order for approval to be given in general meeting there needs to be full disclosure in advance by including the following information in a memorandum:

- the purpose of the loan or transaction;
- the amount of the loan or value of the transaction;
- the liability to which the company may be exposed under the loan or transaction.

Where the resolution is to be passed in writing, the memorandum must be circulated to members. Where the resolution is to be passed in a general meeting, the memorandum must be available for inspection at the registered office for at least 15 days ending with the date of the meeting and must also be available for inspection at the place of the general meeting.

Shareholder approval is not required under the following exceptions, which apply where loans or transactions are in respect of small amounts, or if the company is in the business of lending money, or if funds have been made available to the director to meet expenditure for the purposes of the company:

- loans or quasi-loans up to £10,000;
- up to £15,000 for credit transactions under which the director acquires goods from the company on deferred payment terms;
- to enable a director to meet expenditure incurred for the purpose of the company's business to enable him to perform his duties. The aggregate amounts outstanding must not exceed £50,000;
- if a loan is made by a money-lending company in the ordinary course of its business and on normal terms, there is no limit to the loan amount.

One category of transaction should be distinguished from loans. Articles of Association commonly empower directors to use their company's funds to meet the expense of carrying out their functions as directors. When a director spends the company's money for that purpose, he does so as an agent of the company and not as a borrower.

A further exemption arises as a result of CA 2006, which relaxes some of the restrictions on companies indemnifying their directors in advance of the outcome of civil or criminal proceedings. As stated in section 5.1, it is possible for companies to make loans to directors in respect of their civil and criminal defence costs as and when those costs occur. If the director is unsuccessful in defending the civil or criminal proceedings, he will be required to reimburse the company. If the director is successful, the loan can be repaid in accordance with its repayment terms or the company can write off the loan.

## 7 Substantial property transactions

CA 2006, ss. 190–196 set out the provisions in respect of substantial property transactions between a company and a director. The term director for the purposes of substantial property transactions includes **connected persons** to the director. Generally, a company may not transfer to a director, or a director to a company, a non-cash asset (e.g. property) if its value exceeds 10% of the company's net assets and is more than £5,000, or if the value exceeds £100,000, unless approved by the company in general meeting. A transaction may be entered into which is conditional on shareholder approval being granted; this may be useful where time is of the essence in an urgent transaction.

No shareholder approval is required if the value is less than £5,000, or if the transaction is between two companies within the same group, or between a member acting in his capacity as member and the company. No approval is required if the transaction is already specified in the director's service contract (e.g. the purchase of a house or car).

A substantial property transaction which has not received the appropriate shareholder approval is generally voidable. This could have serious implications for the director concerned should the company subsequently become insolvent. It is possible under CA 2006, s. 196 for subsequent shareholder approval to be obtained to approve the transaction, in which case it will no longer be voidable.

---

**TEST YOUR KNOWLEDGE 2.6**

a When must shareholder approval be sought in respect of a loan to a director?
b When must shareholder approval be sought in respect of a director's proposed property transaction?

---

## 8 Disqualification of directors

As explained in section 4, directors should exercise their powers in good faith and in the interests of the company. Before the IA 1986, directors were liable to creditors only for 'fraudulent trading'. Honest directors who were ignorant, or who believed the assurances of their fellow directors, had nothing to fear. IA 1986 introduced a new offence of 'wrongful trading'. If a company goes into insolvent liquidation and the director either knew or ought to have concluded there was no reasonable prospect of avoiding insolvency, the court may order the director to make a personal contribution to the company's assets.

The standard of care required and expected of directors is now mainly objective not subjective; ignorance and/or incompetence are not accepted as a defence.

Since the introduction of IA 1986, further offences have been created. For example, a director may be disqualified from acting as a director or taking part in the management of a company for a specified period laid down by the court.

The leading case authority on the duty of care is *Re City Equitable Fire Insurance Co. Ltd.*

---

**CASE LAW 2.2**

**Re City Equitable Fire Insurance Co. Ltd [1925] Ch 407**

The directors of an insurance company delegated virtually all aspects of management to its managing director. The managing director stole large amounts of cash from the company, largely because of inadequate supervision by the other directors. It was held that the directors had been in breach of their duty of skill and care. In his judgment, Romer J laid down the directors' duties of skill and care:

- The director must exhibit the skill that would be reasonably expected of a person of his knowledge and experience.
- The director is not bound to give continuous attention to the company affairs.
- A director may delegate his duties to some other official in the company and trust him to perform them properly.

But the situation is changing and there is now a general trend towards holding directors accountable.

**CASE LAW 2.3**

**Re D'Jan of London Ltd [1994] BCLC 561**

A liquidator brought proceedings in negligence against a director. Hoffmann LJ stated that the standard expected of a director today was as stated in the IA 1986, s. 214 (where the provisions regarding wrongful trading are to be found), namely, a director must show the higher of either the skill actually possessed by him or that which would objectively be expected of such a director of such a company.

## 8.1 The Insolvency Act (IA) 1986

IA 1986, s. 214 deals with wrongful trading in circumstances where:

- the company is in the process of being wound up;
- the company is insolvent;
- the liquidator applies to the court for a declaration that a director contribute an appropriate sum to the company's assets.

Before the court will order a director to contribute, it requires proof that he knew, or ought to have known, that there was no reasonable prospect of the company avoiding insolvency. In order to establish this criterion IA 1986, s. 214(4) provides the following test:

'the facts which a director of a company ought to know or ascertain, the conclusions which he ought to reach and the steps which he ought to take are those which would be known or ascertained, or reached, or taken, by a diligent person having both:
(a) the general knowledge, skill and experience that may reasonably be expected of a person carrying out the same functions as are carried out by that director in connection with the company; and
(b) the general knowledge, skill and experience that that director has.'

The important question is: What would a reasonably diligent director have done in the circumstances? The keys to minimising problems are:

- be reasonable;
- plan ahead;
- prepare and use financial information;
- document (e.g. in board minutes) the reasons for continuing to trade;
- take professional advice.

---

CASE LAW **2.4**

*Re Produce Marketing Consortium Ltd* (No. 2) (1989)

Produce Marketing Consortium Ltd imported and stored fruit on a commission basis. Although initially successful, it lost customers and, by 1981, was trading at a loss. By 1985 the directors knew that they had to find new business and contracted with R Ltd, an importer of citrus fruit and an unsecured creditor. The company persuaded the bank to extend overdraft facilities, which were granted. In January 1987 the accounts for 1984/85 and 1985/86 were submitted late and the auditors referred to the company's present trading position as insolvent and warned of fraudulent trading. The directors believed that their company was the best placed to service R's contract as it held R's goods in store. They continued to trade, paying off the overdraft and increasing the credit line with R. R realised what was happening and put the company into creditor's winding up. The liquidator asked for the directors to contribute £100,000.

The judge dismissed any defence that the directors were unaware because of late submission of accounts. From their position the directors had access to the relevant financial information, which they would be reasonably expected to know. But they would also be expected to know more; their optimism that R Ltd would wait forever for payment was unjustified. The judge ordered payment of £75,000.

---

## 8.2 The Company Directors Disqualification Act (CDDA) 1986

Under the Act, directors can be disqualified automatically following a defined event, or by application to the court declaring that a person is unfit to be a director. A person who has been disqualified under the Act cannot, during the period of disqualification, act as a director, liquidator, administrator, receiver or manager of a company without the consent of the court. Contravention of an order is a criminal offence and can carry a two-year prison sentence or unlimited fine.

The court has power to disqualify a director for between two and 15 years where:

1 The director was in charge of a company that is or has become insolvent and where his conduct has made him unfit to be a director. Unfitness can be as a result of his actions or inaction.
2 The director has been convicted of an indictable offence in connection with the management or formation of a company.
3 The director has persistently failed to file accounts, annual returns or other documents required by Companies House, or has failed to keep statutory records.
4 The director is guilty of fraudulent trading during the course of a winding up, or some other offence where the director is required to make a contribution to the company's assets for insolvent trading.
5 The director is disqualified by the court following an application by the Secretary of State on the grounds of public interest. This usually follows an investigation by the Department for Business, Innovation and Skills (BIS).
6 The director has been issued a competition disqualification order under the Enterprise Act (EA) 2002 for acting in a manner which breaches competition law.

The following cases illustrate some of these provisions:

1 *Phoenix companies* – In *Re Ipcon Fashions* (1989), the director had run a clothing business for 15 years using different companies, three of which collapsed. His method was to go into insolvent liquidation and start up a new company on the same premises. He was disqualified for five years.
2 *Arrears of Crown debts* (i.e. PAYE and value added tax (VAT)) – In *Re Stanford Services Ltd* (1987), the courts considered there was a practical difference between Crown debts and ordinary trade debts. Most traders extended credit and realised they were taking risks, but the Crown was an involuntary creditor: employers had to deduct PAYE and NI contributions;

non-payment affects both the Crown and employees. By allowing Crown debts to build up the directors were culpable and disqualified for two years. It is interesting to note, however, that in *Re Bath Glass* (1988) substantial Crown debts were held insufficient in themselves to disqualify the directors of an insolvent company. Two factors will be significant in deciding which side of the line a case falls; failure to pay Crown debts and failure to file documents with Companies House.

3 *Directors' remuneration* – In *Re D. F. Ltd* (1987), a director continued to award himself high remuneration and to arrange for rent to be paid to a company owned by him while allowing Crown debts and trade creditors to remain unsatisfied. He was disqualified for four years.

4 *Accounts and accounting records* – In *Re Rolus Properties* (1988), a director of two companies not only failed to maintain any books, but failed to file returns and prepare audited accounts. He was disqualified for two years. (It would have been longer, but a fellow director was a Chartered Secretary on whom he had relied.)

---

**STOP AND THINK 2.7**

In the last few years the FSA has sought views on proposals as to whether it should have the authority to disqualify directors of listed companies (see Chapter 6). Do you think the FSA should have these powers?

---

## 8.3 Disqualification (voluntary) undertaking

IA 2000 provides an alternative to disqualification through the court by a process of **disqualification (voluntary) undertaking**. This is an out-of-court procedure which allows the Secretary of State to accept a binding undertaking from a director (most likely a prospective defendant) not to act as a director for a defined period without the consent of the court. A disqualification undertaking has the same legal effect as a disqualification order from a court; for example, a breach of the undertaking could result in a prison sentence of up to two years.

Similarly, a director may provide a competition disqualification undertaking. Again, this is binding on the director but does not require a court order.

## 8.4 Personal liability

Directors are agents of the company and if they are properly exercising their duties, they will not incur personal liability in the event of a breach of contract. However, if they have not made it clear that they are acting as agent and have given personal guarantees, they may be liable. Personal liability comes from a breach of duty or statutory offence including the following:

■ acting as a director whilst disqualified;
■ evading the payment of VAT;
■ failing to show the company name on correspondence, cheques, etc.;
■ fraudulent trading;
■ wrongful trading;
■ employing workers without valid work permits.

---

**TEST YOUR KNOWLEDGE 2.7**

a What are the main provisions for which a director may be disqualified under CDDA 1986?
b What is a disqualification undertaking?

# 9   Shadow directors

A **shadow director** is defined in CA 2006, s. 251 as

> 'a person in accordance with whose directions or instructions the directors of the company are accustomed to act'.

A shadow director is, in other words, a person who either controls the management of a company or on whose instruction the directors act. Professional advisers are not a shadow directors as their advice is usually limited to a particular part of the business, such as accounts or commercial property transactions. In *Re Unisoft* (1994) the definition was explained as requiring that the outsider control the whole of the board or at least a governing majority to qualify as a shadow director.

A shadow director may be an outside person or corporate body who, for commercial reasons, is influencing the directors' actions. Even a controlling shareholder or a creditor may be regarded as a shadow director, but s. 251 provides that a corporate body is not to be regarded as a shadow director of any of its subsidiary companies for the purposes of the general duties of directors, transactions requiring members approval or a contract with a sole member who is also a director.

Practical steps which can be taken to avoid potential shadow directorships arising are:

- professional advisers should have a letter of engagement setting out their terms of reference and expressly stating that they are not to be treated as directors of the company;
- it is good practice to ensure that third parties are made aware that professional advisers are not acting as directors of the company;
- advisers (and senior employees) should avoid frequent attendance at board meetings if this is not necessary.

---

**STOP AND THINK** **2.8**

People who are subsequently judged to be shadow directors are unlikely to have made the required returns to the Registrar of Companies and will therefore automatically be in breach of legislation.

Consider the impact of whether other breaches of legislation may have occurred. For example, what if a large loan had been made to a person who is subsequently judged to be a director? The loan would be voidable by the company (see section 6 above). If the company had become insolvent, what would the liquidator be likely to do in respect of any such loan?

---

Shadow directors are just as liable as every other director and must comply with the provisions of CA 2006 as follows:

- Form AP01–02 must be filed with Companies House on appointment. Personal details must be entered in the register of directors.
- Any interests in contracts of the company must be disclosed by written notice to the directors.
- Service contracts must be available for inspection by the members (and a copy must be sent to members on request).

Shadow directors are often discovered only after something has gone wrong with the company, for example, insolvent liquidation and the liquidator (who is responsible for recovering as much money as possible for the creditors of the company) has claimed that an individual was *de facto* a director of the company. This may be particularly onerous if there is a claim against the directors for wrongful trading (i.e. failing to take reasonable steps to minimise loss to creditors when the directors ought to have reasonably known that there was little or no prospect of avoiding insolvency).

**CASE LAW 2.5**

*Secretary of State v Deverel* [2000] 2 All ER 365

A company went into liquidation with £4.6 million of deficit. Disqualification of the directors was applied for and also against two people involved in the management of the company and described as 'consultants'. At first instance the judge held that the consultants were not shadow or *de facto* directors, but this was reversed in the Court of Appeal. The Court of Appeal was unhappy with the use of phrases describing boards as the cat's paw, puppet or dancing to the tune of the shadow director. They implied more than what the statutory definition required. The question was simply one of whether the alleged shadow director had real influence in the corporate affairs of the company.

## CASE QUESTION

As company secretary of Multiple plc, you are responsible for making sure all arrangements for the appointment of new directors are in place. As this is a complex area, how would you ensure that you have considered all relevant processes and have the right documentation to hand? Which other departments within your organisation do you think you will need to work with?

Mrs Baxter is being proposed as a new director and the chairman has asked you to prepare several matters for consideration:

■ A schedule of all the documents which need to be prepared in respect of the appointment.
■ Any approvals that need to be given in respect of the appointment.
■ The key messages to tell Mrs Baxter about the duties of directors. How would you suggest this is done?
■ The necessary checks on Mrs Baxter's background to ensure she is fit to be a director.

## 10 Alternate directors

An **alternate director** is a person appointed by a member of the board to act and speak during periods of absence or incapacity of the director. An alternate may only be appointed if the Articles of Association provide for it, and the private company Model Articles do not contain provisions for alternate directors. Similarly, there are no such provisions within CA 2006. Private companies incorporated after 1 October 2009 or otherwise operating under the private company Model Articles and wishing to be able to appoint alternate directors must therefore establish appropriate provisions in their Articles. Provisions for alternate directors are included in the Model Articles for a public company (Articles 15, 25, 26 and 27).

During his appointment the alternate director is certainly a *de facto* director and the Articles should provide that he is an officer of the company for all purposes. Public company Model Article 25 states that a director can appoint another director to be his alternate or may appoint any other person as his alternate, subject to that person being approved by the board of directors. Any appointment of an alternate must be effected by a notice in writing signed by the director making the appointment and must contain a statement signed by the proposed alternate that he is willing to act as an alternate (public company Model Article 25).

The particulars of an alternate director should be entered in the register of directors and a form AP01 filed with Companies House. Alternate directors are subject to the same rules as directors with regard to loans and other transactions with the company. They may act only in the absence of the appointing director, who may also revoke the alternate's appointment at any time by notice in writing to the company. If an appointing director ceases to hold office for whatever reason, the alternate director will automatically cease to hold office unless the alternate director is already a director.

Public company Model Article 26 sets out the rights and responsibilities of alternate directors and provides that they are entitled to the same rights as the person making the appointment in relation to any directors' meeting or written resolution. They are entitled to:

■ receive notice of all meetings of directors and all meetings of committees of which his appointer is a member;

■ attend and vote at any such meeting at which the director appointing him is not personally present;

■ perform all the functions of his appointer as a director in his absence.

The alternate director will not, however, be entitled to receive any remuneration from the company for his services, although this does not preclude the negotiation of a separate fee. The alternate will be deemed for all purposes to be responsible for his own acts and omissions, i.e. he will not be deemed to be the agent of the director appointing him.

Company secretaries also need to consider how other provisions in the Model Articles affect board procedures in relation to alternate directors, in particular:

■ Board resolutions are decided on a simple majority of votes. A director who is also an alternate director is entitled in the absence of his appointer to a separate vote in addition to his own vote (public company Model Article 15).

■ The quorum for a board meeting is two directors. A person who holds office only as an alternate director shall, if his appointer is not present, be counted in the quorum. This removes any possibility of double-counting representation of the same director in determining the quorum.

■ Public company Model Article 18 (and private company Model Article 8) requires unanimous consent to written resolutions of the board (i.e. all directors must sign them). The public company Model Articles state that a written resolution signed by an appointing director need not also be signed by his alternate, and vice versa. Although the alternate's signature may not be required, it would still appropriate to send the alternate the same documentation as public company Model Article 26 stipulates that an alternate director has the same rights in relation to directors' written resolutions as the appointing director.

Company secretaries should take great care when advising alternate directors regarding interests they may have in the company. Public company Model Article 13 provides that, subject to some exceptions in the Articles, if a director has an interest in an actual or proposed transaction, the director and his alternate may not vote on any proposal relating to it. This does not, however, preclude the alternate from voting in relation to the transaction on behalf of another appointor who does not have such an interest. The practical application of this is to stop an unscrupulous director who has a material interest appointing an alternate who (i) would be part of a quorum to decide on the transaction in which the appointer is interested; and (ii) would have a vote on the particular transaction.

## CHAPTER SUMMARY

■ Directors must act as a board and not as individuals.

■ The final decision as to whether a person is a director or not rests on interpretation of his functions (e.g. by the court) and not the individual.

■ Directors cannot deny their true position or evade their statutory obligations by removing the word 'director' from their title.

■ There is no statutory distinction between an executive director and a NED.

■ There are no statutory qualifications required to become a director.

■ The company's first directors are the persons named on form IN01. Subsequently, the appointment of a director is usually made by the board. The decision as to whether to re-elect a director is a matter for the general meeting.

■ The directors can exercise all the powers of the company except those functions removed by statute or the Articles; if both are silent, the directors' actions are the company's actions.

■ The directors are at the apex of the company administration and are accountable to the shareholders.

■ The CA 2006 prescribes the general statutory duties of directors.

■ Companies are allowed to make loans to directors or to enter into other property transactions provided prior approval of the shareholders is obtained or if the amount is small and qualifies for an exemption.
■ Directors can be disqualified if they fail to perform their duties.
■ Having someone who might be deemed to be shadow director is undesirable.
■ Directors may appoint alternates to represent them in their absence.
■ Company secretaries need to be aware of the law and regulation relating to directors appointed to act as alternate directors in the absence of the appointed director.

# 3 The members

■ **INTRODUCTION**

This chapter looks at who is a member and the conditions which need to be met for someone to become a member, including the different types of shareholder and restrictions on membership. The section on members' rights explores their duties and liabilities. This chapter also deals briefly with the register of members, although this is covered in detail in Chapter 8. You may also find Chapters 12 and 13, on share capital and share registration, useful reading in relation to this chapter.

## 1 What is a member?

Generally, the **members** of a company are the shareholders. They are:

■ the subscribers to the company's Memorandum who become members when the company is incorporated; and
■ every other person who agrees to become a member and whose name is entered on the **register of members** (CA 2006, s. 112).

Two conditions have to be met for a person to become a member:

1 A person cannot become a member unless he agrees to do so.
2 The shareholder's name must appear on the register of members. If his name has not yet been entered, he may be the beneficial owner of the shares concerned, but he is not entitled to the full rights of membership.

For example, a person may become entitled to the **shares** of another on the death, bankruptcy or insanity of a member. However, a person entitled to shares in these circumstances does not become a member simply because he is entitled to them. He is not a member until the change of ownership is formally registered and his name appears in the register of members. The procedures associated with the **transmission** of shares are described in Chapter 13.

### 1.1 Number of members

CA 2006, s. 123 permits either private or public limited companies to have just one shareholder (a single member company). The sole shareholder could be the subscriber at the incorporation of the company or the number of members could subsequently be reduced to one. If a company reduces its membership to one, the register of members must be annotated to state that the company has only one member and the date when the change occurred (CA 2006, s. 123). Similarly, if the membership increases, a note must be added to the register of members stating this fact and the date when the change took place (see Sample Wording 3.1). If the company was incorporated with one member, then the register merely has to state that the company has one member.

---

> **SAMPLE WORDING 3.1**
>
> **Wording of entries to be placed on the register of members in respect of a single member**
>
> With effect from [date], the company has only one member.

---

Where there is a single member, the quorum for general meetings is one, and this overrides any contrary provisions in the Articles of Association (CA 2006, s. 318). Members of private companies are also permitted to approve matters by written resolution instead of in general meetings (CA 2006, s. 288). This flexibility is not available to members of public companies.

## 1.2 Members of companies limited by guarantee

In **companies limited by guarantee** (usually not-for-profit organisations) the members do not generally hold shares. The subscribers to the Memorandum become members before being registered. Subsequently, each person wishing to become a member becomes liable under the guarantee in the Memorandum that in the event of the company being wound up, he will contribute an agreed amount to the company's assets. As with members holding shares, he does not acquire the status of member until he is entered on the register of members.

## 1.3 Restrictions on membership

As a general rule, any person or legal entity can become a member of a company and their ability to do so is determined by the ordinary rules of the law of contract. The members and the company are bound by the provisions of the Memorandum and Articles as if they had been signed by each member (CA 2006, s. 33) (see Chapter 5).

### Partnerships, clubs and associations

An unincorporated body, such as a partnership, club or association, not registered under the Companies Acts should not be accepted as a member of a company because it does not possess a legal personality. If such a body wishes to hold shares, the shares should be registered in the name of a trusted individual or individuals of the unincorporated body (e.g. a club secretary or club treasurer). Alternatively, the shares could be registered with a person having a legal personality, such as a bank nominee or a trustee company. A partnership which is registered as a **limited liability partnership (LLP)** can become a member, because it is a legal entity.

### Restrictions under the Companies Act (CA)

1 CA 2006, s. 136 states that a company cannot be a member of its own holding company. An exception to this rule applies where the subsidiary is holding the shares as a nominee, personal representative or trustee of a third party (e.g. for a group employee share scheme or pension scheme) and that neither the subsidiary nor the holding company has the beneficial interest in the shares held.
2 CA 2006, s. 658 expressly prohibits a company from being a member of itself. There are a number of exceptions to this rule, including purchases of own shares, treasury shares (see Chapter 13), the redemption of redeemable shares or where shares are forfeited or surrendered for non-payment of any part of the amount payable in respect of them or where the acquisition is of fully paid shares and is gratuitous.

### Minors

Although minors are not prevented by the CA from becoming members, it is not good practice to accept minors as members of a company in their own names, as the responsibilities relating to those liabilities will be void while they remain minors. If the Articles provide that a minor can be a member, under common law the minor will be able to avoid any allotment or **transfer** of shares while he is a minor or within a reasonable time after attaining the age of majority. If the minor does avoid the allotment or transfer, he ceases to be a member.

If a company is listed, the Listing Rules require that the Articles contain no restriction on the transfer of fully paid shares. In practice, minors may well become members of a company without the company's knowledge. Any member transferring shares to a minor, even in ignorance, is liable for any future calls on those shares until the minor comes of age and remains the registered holder.

## 1.4 Exceptions to membership

Members are generally the shareholders of the company. However, there are some exceptions. These are:

1 holders of share warrants to bearer;
2 letters of allotment; or
3 unregistered transfers.

### Share warrants to bearer

A **share warrant to bearer** is a **negotiable instrument** issued by the company, entitling the bearer (holder) to the number of shares in the company stated in the warrant (CA 2006, s. 779). The key terms of the issue (e.g. how communication between the company and the holder are to be transacted) are usually set out on the warrant. The name of the holder of the warrant does not appear on the warrant. Share warrants can be issued by any limited company provided the Articles allow. Public company Model Article 51 sets out provisions in respect of warrants. However, there are no such provisions in the private company Model Articles and any company operating under the private company Model Articles will need to amend the Articles accordingly.

The company usually communicates notice of general meetings and declarations of any dividends to warrant holders by advertising in a particular newspaper and holders may claim any dividends outstanding by detaching a coupon which accompanies the warrant and sending it to the company. As share warrants to bearer are negotiable instruments, ownership of the warrant is transferred by passing the warrant to someone else.

Share warrants to bearer are not popular in the UK for two main reasons:

■ Directors of companies usually prefer to know who holds shares in the company; and as share warrants to bearers do not appear on the register of members, this lack of visibility is unattractive to them.
■ The ability to transfer by delivery does not provide good security against theft of a warrant.

### Letters of allotment

A **letter of allotment** is confirmation that shares have been allotted to an individual and that share certificates will be issued by a certain date. The name of the transferee on an **unregistered transfer**, the holder of a letter of allotment and the owner of a share warrant do not appear in the register of members, so they are not members of the company. The Articles may confer any of the rights of a member on the owners of share warrants and may impose any of the obligations of a member on them. Although there seems no reason why the holders of letters of allotment should not be treated in the same way as members, in practice this is not done. If the holder of a share warrant or letter of allotment is not expressly put in the position of a member by the Articles, he is not a party to the statutory contract under CA 2006, s. 33 between the company and its members, by which they undertake to conform to the provisions of its Articles of Association.

## 1.5 Cessation of membership

A person ceases to be a member of the company when he ceases to be registered in the register of members. This happens in one of the following ways:

■ voluntary transfer of shares (i.e. the holder sells or gives his shares);
■ transmission of shares on death, bankruptcy or mental disorder;

■ compulsory transfer of shares, i.e. enforcement of a **lien** as provided in public company Model Article 60 (the private company Model Articles provide that all shares are to be fully paid up, hence there is no concept of a lien for private companies operating under the private company Model Articles).

---

### TEST YOUR KNOWLEDGE 3.1

**a** At what point does a person become a member of a company?
**b** What groups or categories of individual may not or should not become members?
**c** In what circumstances are shareholders not members?
**d** When would a membership be forfeited according to the Model Articles?

---

## 2 Types of shareholder

### 2.1 Institutional shareholders

Shareholders (or members) are the owners of the company and **institutional shareholders** own a large part of the share capital of public quoted companies. This puts a burden on institutional shareholders to act in the best interests of their clients. This includes maintaining effective channels of communication with the board in order to understand the company's aims and objectives and to support the board by positive voting, unless they have a good reason to do otherwise. Listed companies should ensure they understand the policies of their major institutional shareholders. This gives the company valuable insight into to how institutional shareholders are likely to vote at a general meeting.

The Institutional Shareholders' Committee (ISC) report, *The Responsibilities of Institutional Shareholders in the United Kingdom*, and the 2010 **Stewardship Code** suggests that in the interests of good corporate governance institutional shareholders should work to the following principles:

1 They have a responsibility to make considered use of their votes.
2 Reasons for voting against a resolution or withholding a vote should be made known to the board in advance of the vote taking place.
3 They should take steps to ensure their voting intentions are being translated into practice.
4 They should endeavour to eliminate unnecessary variations in the ways they apply their criteria to the performance of the companies in which they invest. However, institutions should give due weight to all relevant factors drawn to their attention by a company which may explain a departure from a particular criteria.
5 They should be ready to enter into dialogue with companies based on the mutual understanding of objectives.
6 They should take an interest in the board of directors, particularly in relation to the composition of the board, the concentration of decision-making power and the appointment of NEDs.
7 Institutional shareholders should, on request, make information on votes lodged with respective companies available to their clients.
8 Major institutional shareholders should be prepared to attend AGMs where appropriate.

### 2.2 Nominee shareholders

If the beneficial owner of shares does not wish to have the shares registered in his own name, it is possible to have them registered in the name of a person, group of people or a company as a **nominee shareholder**. The beneficial owner of the shares usually has no contact with the company, since the company has to address all communications to the registered shareholder, in this case the nominee. The beneficial holder is permitted to remain anonymous, but, under CA 2006, s. 793, the identity of the beneficial holder must be disclosed at the request of the company (see Chapter 8).

In practice, one or more of the shares in the subsidiary will be registered in the name of a nominee on behalf of the company.

### Exercise of member rights

CA 2006, Part 9, ss. 145–153 give certain rights to those holding shares through nominees. There are two aspects to this. First, if a company's Articles give certain rights to underlying beneficiaries, the references to members in the relevant parts of CA 2006 are deemed to cover the beneficiaries also. The Articles may specify which rights are given, although this may not include the right to transfer shares. Second, nominees may request a company to provide 'information rights' to those on whose behalf it holds shares and who have indicated that they wish to have such rights. These requirements apply only to companies quoted on the main Stock Market and not to private companies or those with shares traded on the Alternative Investment Market (AIM).

A company planning a takeover might also build a stake in the target company through nominees.

## 2.3  Joint holders of shares

Subject to the Articles, a company may register a transfer of shares into the joint names of any number of persons, although the number of holders is commonly limited to four. Private company Model Article 26 contains an unqualified right for directors to refuse to register any transfer (regardless of the number of proposed transferees). Public company Model Articles 63 and 64 provide that in respect of both certificated and uncertificated transfers (see Chapter 13) the directors have the discretion of refusing to register a transfer if it is in favour of more than four transferees. The UKLA states that the limit must not be less than four.

Company secretaries need to bear the following in mind when dealing with joint holders:

- Model Article 24 (public company Model Article 46) provides that for joint holders, only one certificate may be issued in respect of the holding. Thus delivery of a certificate to one joint holder is deemed to be delivery to all.
- All joint holders are jointly and severally liable to pay all calls if the shares are partly paid (public company Model Article 55).
- If one of the joint holders dies, the shares pass automatically to the surviving joint holder(s). CA 2006, s. 286 provides that the proxy vote of the 'senior' joint holder is accepted to the exclusion of the votes of any other joint holder(s). Seniority is determined by the order in which the names of the holders appear in the register of members, with the first named being the most senior. Section 286 permits this to be subject to any provision of the company's articles.
- Dividend warrants, notices and other communications are sent to the 'senior' joint holder, unless otherwise directed (Model Article 31; public company Model Article 72). This is deemed as delivery to all joint holders.
- The signature of all joint holders is required on a transfer of shares.

---

🖋 **TEST YOUR KNOWLEDGE 3.2**

a  What is an institutional shareholder? What principles should they adhere to?

b  What is a nominee shareholder? What rights are available to those who invest through a nominee?

c  What are the key provisions of the Model Articles in respect of joint shareholders?

# 3 Members' rights, duties and liabilities

Essentially the rights and liabilities of the members are expressed in terms of the rights and liabilities attaching to the types of shares they hold. These are usually defined by a combination of CA 2006 and the company's Articles.

## 3.1 Members' rights to information

The principal rights of members to information about the company are:

- to inspect and request copies of various statutory books and records (see Chapter 8);
- to inspect directors' service contracts or request a copy of a service contract;
- to inspect written memoranda of the terms and conditions of a director's contract of service for the company and any of its subsidiaries;
- to be provided with a copy of the company's Memorandum and Articles of Association;
- to receive a copy of the annual accounts at least 21 days before the general meeting at which they are to be laid (public companies only);
- to be provided with a copy of the latest accounts of the company;
- to receive notice of all general meetings;
- to inspect minutes of general meetings and to request copies;
- to attend general meetings and to ask questions of the directors.

In practice, a member holding **preference shares** may have the same right to inspect the register of members of the company as a member holding **ordinary shares**, but the Articles may give the two classes different rights. In companies limited by guarantee, the rights of members attach solely to the member as no shares exist, but it is still common for such companies to create classes of membership, some having lesser rights and thus referred to as associate members for example.

## 3.2 Other members' rights

These include the following:

1 *Unfair prejudice* – If a member considers that any act of the company could result in an unfair prejudice to his interests, he can petition the court to obtain relief (CA 2006, s. 994).
2 *Member's application for winding up* – A member can apply to the court for the winding up of a company if it is unable to pay its debts, or on just and equitable grounds (see Chapter 7).
3 *Derivative claims* – A member may bring an action on behalf of the company against a director or a third party for an act or omission if the company has suffered loss (CA 2006, ss. 260–269) (see Chapter 2).
4 *General meetings* – A member is entitled to attend general meetings and to vote on any resolution. In addition, a member can requisition a general meeting or require that a resolution be added to the business of the AGM (see Chapter 9). A member can also appoint a proxy to attend and vote at a general meeting on his behalf (CA 2006, s. 324).
5 *Members' audit report* – Where a company is exempted from the requirement to have its annual accounts audited (see Chapter 11), CA 2006, s. 476 provides that any member(s) holding at least 10% of the **nominal value** may require the company to obtain an audit of its accounts. This will result in an auditor's report being produced for the members.
6 *Compulsory acquisition* – Where a major shareholder has acquired 90% or more of the share capital of a company, the holder is entitled to give notice to the other shareholders that he desires to acquire their shares (CA 2006, ss. 979–989) (see Chapter 6).
7 *Share certificates* – Members are entitled to receive a share certificate in respect of their shareholding.

Read literally, CA 2006, s. 33 appears to create a contract between the company and its members to observe all the provisions of the Articles whatever they relate to. However, the section has been construed to create a contract only in respect of the rights and duties of members as such, so that if the Articles provide for other matters, those provisions do not form part of the contract. Members cannot be compelled to take more shares or to increase their liability in any way.

## 3.3 Limitations of members' rights

Members do not have a specific right to:

- be paid a dividend, unless the board recommends one;
- increase a dividend above the amount recommended by the board;
- access to the minutes of board meetings, the accounting records or other sensitive internal documents;
- be consulted on every business issue affecting the company.

## 3.4 Duties and liabilities of members

Where a person or group of people have rights by virtue of their association with a particular body, it follows that they will also have duties and responsibilities and, in most cases, some liabilities. A member of a public company, if so requested by the company, must:

- disclose their interest in the shares (CA 2006, s. 793);
- notify the company if they acquire 3% or more of the company's total voting rights and if their holding subsequently falls below 3%. Once a holding reaches 3% or more there is an obligation to advise of any changes which take the holding above or below the next percentage point (DTRs).

Other duties and liabilities include:

- To contribute to the assets of the company in respect of any amounts outstanding on the shares which they hold on a winding up. Members of companies limited by guarantee will be liable to pay the amount agreed in the Memorandum – often £1.
- To pay any amounts that are unpaid on the shares if called on to do so by the company.

If a member has fully paid for his shares, there is generally no further liability on that member. This is the essence of the concept of limited liability.

---

**TEST YOUR KNOWLEDGE** **3.3**

**a** What rights to information does a member have?
**b** How can a member require a company to produce an audit report?
**c** What are the main liabilities of a member?

---

## 4 The register of members

By CA 2006, s. 113, every company must keep a register of members. The register should be kept at the registered office or at the **single alternative inspection location** (see Chapter 8). The Registrar of Companies must be informed of the address when the register is not kept at the registered office. The register must be maintained in the same country as the registered office, i.e. for companies registered in England and Wales the register of members must be kept in England or Wales but not Scotland.

The management and maintenance of the register of members is dealt with in much more detail in Chapter 8, but it is useful here to give a very brief summary.

The register must contain the following information:

- names and addresses of members;
- the date that person became a member and, if applicable, the date on which that person ceased to be a member;
- the number, class and amount paid up on shares and, if appropriate, the split between the different classes;

- further details where shares have been converted to stock. The register must be open for inspection by any member without charge and by any other person on payment of the prescribed fee.

When requesting copies of the register of members, certain information will have to be given and the request must be made 'for a proper purpose' (see Chapter 8).

It is customary for additional information (e.g. dividend mandate instructions) to be found with the register of members. However, such information does not form part of the register and should not be made available for inspection or be included in the annual return.

For single-member private companies, a note should be added to that person's entry in the register stating that the company only has one member and the date on which the transaction took place (see Sample Wording 3.1).

Names of partnerships, other than LLPs, trusts or settlements must not be registered as the holders of shares as they have no legal capacity.

If the company has issued share warrants to bearer (see section 1.4), it should also establish and maintain two additional registers:

- a register recording details of warrants issued and cancelled;
- a register showing dividend coupons issued with warrants and subsequently returned to claim a dividend payment.

## CHAPTER SUMMARY

- The members are the shareholders of the company who have agreed to become members and whose names are entered in the register of members.
- Any person or legal entity can become a member of a company; however, it is best practice not to allow minors or unincorporated bodies, such as unlimited partnerships, clubs and associations to become members.
- The minimum number of shareholders is normally one (a single member company).
- Institutional shareholders have a responsibility to act in the best interests of their clients. In respect of listed companies, the 2010 Stewardship Code encourages institutional shareholders to participate in a dialogue with the companies they are investing in.
- Nominee shareholders arise when the beneficial owner of the shares has the shares registered in another person's or company's name.
- Those who hold shares through a nominee have rights to receive information direct from the company.
- Members are entitled to receive information about the way the company is constituted and managed, inspect the directors' service contracts and attend all the general meetings of the company.
- A member can apply to the court for the company to be wound up.
- Members can requisition general meetings.
- It is a statutory requirement that details regarding the members must be recorded in the register of members. The company secretary is usually responsible for maintaining the register and for its safekeeping, although for companies with large numbers of shareholders this is usually outsourced to a firm of professional share registrars.

# PART 1 PRACTICE CASE QUESTIONS

These questions are based on the case scenario outlined at the beginning of Part One. You will need to refer to content throughout Part One to provide the answers.

## PART CASE QUESTION 1.1

You act as company secretary to several wholly owned subsidiaries of a Multiple plc, including Division Limited and Subtract Limited. Mr Smith, chairman of Division Limited, has told you that he is concerned about the conduct of Mrs Jones, Division Limited's managing director. Mr Smith has discovered the following facts:

■ Two weeks ago Mrs Jones used a credit card provided by Division Limited to purchase a car for her husband.

■ Mrs Jones has not told Division Limited that until four years earlier she was a director of English Transporters Limited.

■ Mrs Jones has not told Division Limited that she owns shares in Multiple plc.

■ Division Limited has recently awarded a contract to Build It plc for the construction of a new office building. Mrs Jones's husband owns shares in Build It plc. Mrs Jones did not mention this at the board meeting which approved the award of a contract and she voted in favour of awarding the contract to Build It plc.

Write a memorandum to Mr Smith advising him on the extent to which Mrs Jones has acted improperly, indicating what further information you might require.

## PART CASE QUESTION 1.2

The following day, you are required to address several issues in respect of Subtract Limited, which is a large private company. The following matters have recently occurred with respect to the directors of the company:

a) After a long illness, Mr Card, the chairman, has died. Mrs Mat, the chief executive, would like to appoint Mr Fold, a well-known businessman, as a director and to replace the late Mr Card as chairman. You note that there is a requirement in the company's Articles for directors to acquire and maintain qualification shares after appointment. Mr Tab, a non-executive director, is angry that Mrs Mat has not considered him as a suitable successor to the chairman and has tendered his resignation, which he would like to take effect immediately.

 Mr Card had made it clear before he died that he would like the board to consider appointing his teenage daughter to the board following his death and also for the board to consider appointing Corporate Business Limited as a director.

b) Mrs Idle is another non executive director. Mrs Idle has been absent from board meetings without permission for four consecutive months as she prefers to take long, overseas holidays. The other directors are annoyed with her lack of commitment and have asked you whether there are any provisions under the company's Articles of Association or the Companies Acts under which Mrs Idle's directorship could be terminated.

You are required to provide Mrs Mat with a detailed note advising her in respect of a) and b) above. The note should outline any procedures, approvals and documentation that will need to be dealt with, any further information that needs to be obtained and whether Mr Card's requests can be considered or actioned by the board. You should also advise her on applicable timescales and the point at which any changes would become effective.

# Compliance

## ■ LIST OF CHAPTERS

## ■ OVERVIEW

Part two is concerned with the formation and ending of a company and compliance for companies listed on a stock exchange.

Chapter 4 deals in detail with the statutory requirements for incorporating the separate legal personality that is the company and we look at the statutory documents and necessary processes before a new company will be recognised.

Chapter 5 deals with the key components of a company's constitution. It also analyses the process for amending the constitution and related issues for the company secretary.

Chapter 6 deals with the requirements of the UKLA (part of the FSA) for companies listed on the London Stock Exchange. It also briefly examines provisions in respect of the takeover of listed companies.

Chapter 7 deals with the various ways in which a company's existence is brought to an end, through insolvency, winding up, dissolution or striking off.

Unless modified, default Model Articles for public and private companies apply to all companies incorporated after 1 October 2009, replacing Table A (which, where applicable, contained default Articles for companies formed under the CA 1985). Unless the Articles have been amended, companies formed prior to 1 October 2009 under the Companies Act 1985 will have Table A Articles and company secretaries will need to consider whether such companies should have their Articles amended to operate under the new Model Articles. Company secretaries, therefore, have an important part to play in ensuring that the best decision for each company is reached.

For reference, the Model Articles for private and public companies are included in this text as Appendices 1 and 2 respectively.

## ■ LEARNING OUTCOMES

After reading and understanding the contents of Part Two, you should be able to:

- Recognise the different types of company that can be formed and their characteristics, including oversea companies.
- Understand the filing requirements for the incorporation of a new company, and the procedures for re-registering companies.
- Define the requirements of CA 2006 with regard to a company's constitution.
- Explain the significance and legal importance of the Articles of Association, and their role in the relationships between company directors and members.
- Apply the procedures and requirements for changing the Articles.
- Understand the regulatory framework controlling financial services of securities in the UK, including the respective roles of the FSA, UKLA and the London Stock Exchange.
- Outline the process and procedures involved in applying for listing and bringing a new issue to the market.
- Explain the regulations governing takeovers and mergers, especially in listed companies.
- Be aware of offences under the Criminal Justice Act (CJA) 1993 and FSMA 2000, and the purpose of The Model Code.
- Identify the different ways in which a company can be wound up, and why.
- Understand the role of the liquidator, receiver and administrator, and when they are appointed.
- Apply the procedures for the striking off and dissolution of a company, and identify the powers of the Registrar of Companies in striking off and dissolving companies.

## PART 2 CASE STUDY

As company secretary of Multiple plc, you recognise that the structure of the business will change as the business changes. New companies will need to be incorporated as the company enters new markets and companies will need to be wound up when they are no longer needed. This is part of normal corporate life for a large organisation and you will need to decide what type of company should be formed to best suit the business's needs and what route should be followed if a company is no longer required.

In addition, as Multiple plc is a company with a listing on the London Stock Exchange, the regulation of the company has a dimension apart from observing company law. Listed company regulation is a niche area of expertise, particularly in respect of ongoing disclosure and compliance obligations, and it is your company secretariat department that will take most of the responsibility for ensuring full compliance with these obligations. However, in the main, you recognise that it is the directors who will be liable if these obligations are not met, so your focus will be (i) to help the directors understand what they need to know and do; and (ii) to provide the directors with some assurance that the company secretariat department has good control over listed company obligations.

# Company formation

**4**

■ **CONTENTS**

■ **INTRODUCTION**

The registration or incorporation of companies is an important area of the company secretary's work, so a clear understanding of the different types of entity is essential. This chapter describes the general characteristics of a company and explains the process of incorporation. It covers the documents that must be filed with the Registrar of Companies in order for a company to begin trading as a limited company.

## 1 The company as a legal entity

Companies are incorporated primarily to create a separate legal entity as distinct from the members, directors, employees and creditors. This was established in *Salomon v Salomon & Co. Ltd.* A company cannot act on its own, however, and needs directors and shareholders to make the decisions and manage the company.

---

### CASE LAW 4.1

#### *Salomon v Salomon & Co. Ltd* (1897) AC 22

Salomon ran a small leather business as a sole trader. He then formed a limited company in which he himself took up shares and sold his business to the company. Payment was not in cash but by shares and a debenture, which was secured on a **floating charge**.

Salomon became managing director. The company continued in business and raised further loans. But the company failed and went into liquidation owing over £7,000 and with insufficient funds to pay all the creditors. One of those creditors was Salomon himself because of his debenture. The special feature of a debenture with a charge is that it must be paid before unsecured creditors are paid. At the same time that the company went into liquidation Salomon's personal affairs were not much better – he had gone bankrupt. So there were two sets of creditors: those of the company and those of Salomon personally.

The liquidator, representing the company's unsecured trade creditors, claimed that the company's business was in reality still Salomon's, the company being merely a sham designed to limit Salomon's liability for debts incurred in carrying it on, and therefore he should be ordered to indemnify the company against its debts, and payment of the debenture should await payment of the other creditors.

The House of Lords held that a limited company is a separate legal personality distinct from those who own, work in and manage it. This applied even though the company was in reality one man. The debenture was to be paid first. *Salomon v Salomon & Co. Ltd* established something else, the second important feature of the limited company: the reason limited liability can operate is that the company is an independent legal person.

Businesses do not have to be incorporated; a person may choose to set up as a sole trader, which is a business run by one person. In this case, the life of the business extends only to the life of the owner; there is no separate identity and no limit to the liability of the individual.

# 2  Classification of companies and partnerships

In this section we look at each type of company and detail the particular characteristics that govern each form of incorporation.

Before incorporating a company it is sensible to clarify the aims and objectives of the company to decide the most appropriate trading entity (see Table 4.1).

## 2.1  Private limited companies

**Table 4.1**  Types of trading entity

| Factors to consider | PLC | Ltd | Unlimited | Guarantee | LLP | Unincorporated |
|---|---|---|---|---|---|---|
| Profit | ✓ | ✓ | ✓ | | ✓ | ✓ |
| Not for profit | | | | ✓ | | |
| Liability of the members limited | ✓ | ✓ | | ✓ | ✓ | |
| Liability of the members unlimited | | | ✓ | | | ✓ |
| Profits of the business assessed for tax on owners | | | | | ✓ | ✓ |
| Profits of the business assessed for tax on the trading entity | ✓ | ✓ | ✓ | ✓ | | |
| Shares offered for subscriptions to the public (> 50 persons) | ✓ | | | | | |
| Ownership offered to a defined restricted membership | | ✓ | ✓ | ✓ | ✓ | ✓ |

The great majority of companies registered at Companies House are private companies limited by shares. CA 2006, s. 4 states that, by definition, a private company is a company 'that is not a public company'. Private companies must have a name ending with the word 'Limited' or 'Ltd' because this is the only visible sign that it has limited liability but is not a public limited company or 'plc'. (Welsh language equivalents may be used by companies with their registered offices situated in Wales.) A fixed amount must be paid to the company for each share held by a member. Model Article 21 provides that, with the exception of the subscriber share(s), no share is to be issued for less than the aggregate of its nominal value and any premium. Shareholders of companies operating under the private company Model Articles should therefore have no further liability for the debts of the company.

### Single member companies

Under CA 2006, s. 7 any company (including public companies) may be formed with one subscriber.

## 2.2  Public limited companies

Public limited companies (plc) are limited by shares and must have been registered (or re-registered) on or after 22 December 1980.

Just because a company has been registered as a public limited company, this does not mean that it becomes listed on the Stock Exchange or AIM. There is a separate process for public companies to be admitted to public stock markets, and companies must meet additional criteria before admission is granted (see Chapter 6).

A plc has access to capital markets and may be able to offer its shares for sale through a **recognised investment exchange (RIE)** or another public stock market. It can also issue advertisements offering any of its securities for sale to the public; however, this process is regulated. In contrast, a private company may not offer its shares to the public. The following list sets out the key requirements on public companies. These do not apply to private companies.

## Key requirements: public limited companies

- The name of the company must end with 'public limited company', 'plc' or 'PLC' (or the Welsh equivalent).
- The Memorandum must be in the appropriate form and must be in accordance with the provisions of CA 2006, s. 8 (see Chapter 5).
- Before the company can commence business it must have issued shares with a nominal value of the authorised minimum £50,000 or the equivalent value in Euros (CA 2006, s. 763). Unlike private companies operating under the private company Model Articles, the Model Articles for a public company permit shares to be partly paid. The issued shares must be paid up to at least 25% of their nominal value, with the whole of any premium (see Chapter 12).
- A public company may offer its shares to the public (CA 2006, ss. 755 and 756).
- It must file its accounts with the Registrar of Companies within six months of the end of its financial year (CA 2006, s. 442).
- CA 2006, s. 154 requires that there must be a minimum of two directors (one of whom may also be the company secretary). At least one director of every company must be a natural person (i.e. not a corporation) (CA 2006, s. 155).
- Under CA 2006, s. 7, any company (including a public company) may be formed with one subscriber.
- The company secretary must be suitably qualified as:
  - a barrister, advocate or solicitor called or admitted in any part of the United Kingdom; a member of any of the following bodies:
    - the Institute of Chartered Secretaries and Administrators
    - the Institute of Chartered Accountants in England and Wales
    - the Institute of Chartered Accountants of Scotland
    - the Association of Chartered Certified Accountants
    - the Institute of Chartered Accountants in Ireland
    - the Chartered Institute of Management Accountants
    - the Chartered Institute of Public Finance and Accountancy
  - a person who was a secretary on 22 December 1980 or, by virtue of holding or having held any other position or being a member of any other body, appears to the directors to be capable of discharging the functions of secretary.
- They do not qualify for the provisions enabling small or medium-sized private companies to file abbreviated accounts.
- There are strict regulations regarding the purchase of their own shares (see Chapter 12).
- They may not allot shares for a non-cash consideration without a supporting independent valuer's report (see Chapter 12).
- They may not pass written resolutions in place of general meetings (see Chapter 9).
- The election of directors in a general meeting must be dealt with by separate rather than composite resolutions.

As a company secretary you may be asked to give advice on whether it is more appropriate to establish a private limited company or a public limited company. It is useful therefore to compare some of the key differences between them. These are summarised in Table 4.2.

**Table 4.2** Key differences between private companies limited by shares and public limited companies

| LTD | PLC |
|---|---|
| **Share Capital and Shareholders** (see Chapter 12) | |
| May not issue shares to the public. | May issues shares to the public |
| May allot shares for a non-cash consideration without consideration the need for a supporting independent valuer's report. | May not allot shares for a non-cash without a supporting independent valuer's report. |
| No minimum share capital requirement. | Must maintain a share capital of at least £50,000 (or equivalent in Euros) with at least 25% of the minimum paid up |
| Able to take advantage of more flexible arrangements. | Able to purchase its own shares but there are more concerning financial assistance in the purchase of its stringent requirements own shares. |
| May have pre-emptive rights on the allotment of shares permanently excluded via incorporation into period the Memorandum and Articles of Association. | Must pass a special resolution to exclude pre-emptive rights for a specified period, usually limited to the between successive annual general meetings. |
| Can purchase or redeem shares out of its own capital. | Cannot purchase or redeem shares out of its own capital. |
| **Directors and Officers** (see Chapters 1 and 2) | |
| Can operate with only one director. | Must have at least two directors. |
| Does not need to have a company secretary. | Must have a company secretary qualified in accordance with the CA. |
| May appoint one or more directors at a general meeting by passing a single resolution. | May make multiple appointments, but will need to first pass a resolution permitting this. |
| Subject to specific exemptions there is a general prohibition against a company making loans to a director. A private company may take advantage of certain additional exemptions in respect of quasi-loans and loans. | Unable to take advantage of additional exemptions in respect of quasi-loans and loans to a director. |
| **General Meetings** (see Chapter 9) | |
| Not required to hold an AGM. | Required to hold an AGM. |
| May pass written resolutions of the members in lieu of members passing resolutions in general meetings. | May not pass written resolutions of the members. |
| Not required to convene a general meeting following serious loss of capital. | Required to convene a general meeting following a serious loss of capital. |
| **Statutory Registers and Compliance** (see Chapters 8 and 10) | |
| Does not need to maintain certain statutory registers, for example a register of substantial interests. | No such exemptions in respect of statutory registers. |
| **Accounts** (see Chapter 11) | |
| Can operate as a dormant company. Dormant companies are entitled to be exempted from the requirement to have their accounts audited. | Cannot operate as a dormant company. |
| Must file its annual accounts within nine months of the year end. | Must file its accounts within six months after the year end. |
| According to size, may be able to produce abbreviated accounts. | Cannot produce abbreviated accounts. |

## 2.3 Companies limited by guarantee

In a company limited by guarantee the liability of the members is limited to the amount that they undertake to contribute to the assets of the company if it is wound up.

Companies limited by guarantee are usually charitable or not-for-profit organisations. This type of incorporation can also be used for professional bodies, trade associations and for management purposes – for example, a block of flats where the individual owners of the flats become members to achieve continuity of ownership of the common parts and the provision of services on a non-profit-making basis. Companies limited by guarantee typically have a low commercial risk.

In a company limited by guarantee, members are not required to provide funds on becoming a member. However, companies being formed limited by guarantee under CA 2006 are required to submit a statement of guarantee that it is to be limited by guarantee. The statement must contain such information as required so that the subscribers to the Memorandum of Association can be identified (CA 2006, s. 11). It must also state that each member undertakes that, if the company is wound up while he is a member, or within one year after he ceases to be a member, he will contribute the specified amount towards the debts and liabilities of the company. The liability of the members in the event of insolvent liquidation is limited to the guarantee, usually fixed at some low nominal value, such as £1 per member. The rest of the company's Memorandum is similar to that of a company limited by shares.

Since 22 December 1980, companies limited by guarantee may only be formed without share capital. Before that date, a company limited by guarantee could be formed with or without a share capital, as well as a guarantee. If the company was formed before 1 October 2009 and has a share capital, the Articles state the amount of its nominal capital and the nominal value of the shares into which it was divided. Such companies may continue to exist as companies limited by guarantee with a share capital, but no new company may be incorporated in that form and no existing company (whether limited or unlimited) may now be re-registered as such a company.

A company limited by guarantee must have its own Articles of Association, and all such companies incorporated after 1 October 2009 operate under the Model Articles, unless the Model Articles are modified or excluded. A company limited by guarantee formed prior to 1 October 2009 will need to assess to what extent it wishes to amend its constitution to reflect the Model Articles.

A company limited by guarantee may apply to the Registrar of Companies under CA 2006, s. 60 to omit the word 'Limited' from its name, provided that the following conditions are met:

■ the objects of the company are the promotion of commerce, art, science, education, religion, charity or any profession, and anything incidental or conducive to any of those objects; and
■ the company's Articles must:
  – require any profits or other income to be applied in promoting its objects,
  – prohibit the payment of dividends; and
  – require all the assets which would otherwise be available to its members on its winding up to be transferred to another body with either similar or charitable objects.

An application to omit 'Limited' from the name may be made at the time of incorporation or subsequently by special resolution. A company is obliged to inform the Registrar of Companies if any action is taken that would contravene the conditions for omitting 'Limited' from its name (e.g. if the objects of the business were amended in such a way that they no longer met the required criteria) and the company would be required to reinstate the word 'Limited' accordingly.

Despite this dispensation, the company must disclose on its stationery that it is limited by guarantee. As with any other limited company, other regular requirements, such as filing accounts and annual returns with Companies House, must be observed.

---

> **STOP AND THINK 4.1**
>
> The responsibility of directors and the secretary is no less in a company limited by guarantee than for other types of company. Indeed, if the company has applied to omit the word 'Limited' from its name, additional care needs to be taken that the company does nothing to contravene its status. The secretary should therefore be familiar with the requirements of companies limited by guarantee and be prepared to advise the directors accordingly.

## 2.4 Community Interest Companies

The Companies (Audit, Investigations and Community Enterprise) Act 2004 introduced the **Community Interest Company (CIC)**. The purpose of a CIC is to encourage the provision of products and services that benefit the social and environmental regeneration of wide sections of local communities. Any profits generated from CICs must therefore be used for the public good. This helps to provide a more straightforward way of locking business assets to a public benefit purpose other than applying for charitable status.

Companies wishing to qualify for CIC status are required to satisfy the community interest test that 'a reasonable person might consider that its activities are being carried on for the benefit of the community'. The expectation is that the CIC will help to meet the need for a transparent, flexible model, clearly defined and easily recognised.

The Act outlines that much the same company law applies to CICs – for example, directors have the usual responsibilities associated with running a company and CICs are required to file annual accounts.

A CIC may be incorporated as a company limited by shares or limited by guarantee. In addition to the usual incorporation documents, directors are required to sign a statement which confirms that the CIC will only be used for public good purposes. In much the same way as companies limited by guarantee (see above), the surplus assets of a CIC on transfer or winding up shall be applied only to similar organisations or for charitable purposes.

A regulator for CICs oversees that the appropriate purposes of each CIC are maintained. The regulator has powers on the appointment and removal of directors, investigations, auditing, winding up and striking off. In addition, the regulator must confirm that any change to the purpose of the CIC is consistent with the community interest test of a CIC before it can be accepted by the Registrar of Companies. The CIC website contains useful information and guidance, including a model Memorandum and Articles, and forms which can be downloaded (see Directory).

In order to encourage flexibility in financing, CICs have access to financial markets, and investors are entitled to dividends or interest on debentures limited to a fixed or capped rate of return set by reference to the prevailing published interest rates. The CIC regulator is responsible for amending from time to time the maximum cap on rates of return for investors.

---

> **STOP AND THINK 4.2**
>
> If you were requested to incorporate a company for charitable purposes, consider if it would be more appropriate to incorporate a company limited by guarantee or a CIC. It would be necessary to compare and contrast the requirements and regulations governing each type of entity and then match it to the needs of the business.

## 2.5 Societas europaea

A **societas europaea (SE)** is a public limited company operating across two or more countries in the European Union (EU) and governed predominantly by laws applicable in the EU country in which the company has its registered office. For companies which have operations across several EU countries introduction of SEs can simplify their corporate structures; for example, it may not be necessary to establish a separate subsidiary company in each EU country of operation.

SEs can be formed by:

- merging two or more public companies in different EU countries;
- transforming a plc which has had a subsidiary company in another EU country for two or more years; or
- creating a subsidiary from companies in two or more EU countries. Conversely, a holding company from companies in two or more EU countries may also be created.

SEs are required to have a minimum issued share capital of €120,000. The company name must either begin or end with 'SE' to denote the type of company, in place of any other description (e.g. 'plc'). Constitutional documents (i.e. Memorandum and Articles of Association) are required. The registered office of an SE may be in any EU country in which it has an administrative head. Unlike UK companies, an SE can change its registered office to another EU country.

Like UK companies, directors will be required to run the business and this may take the form of the traditional UK unitary board known as an 'administrative organ' (i.e. executive and non-executive directors serving on one board) or a two-tier board (i.e. a management organ consisting of executives which reports to a supervisory organ consisting of NEDs). Two-tier boards are the norm in many EU countries and the Regulations require a minimum number of two members for each of the management and supervisory organs. Generally, where a two-tier system operates, no person may be a member of both organs. The Regulations also require the company to have some employee participation through consultation.

Companies House has produced guidance notes for companies on the formation of SEs, the use of the 'SE' description, general administration and the various Companies House filing requirements.

If, after an SE is formed, the company no longer feels it is appropriate, the Regulations permit an SE to revert to being a plc.

Proposals in respect of a private company which can operate throughout the EU are also being considered. The Société Privée Européenne (SPE) has yet to be approved by the European Council and European Parliament.

## 2.6 Partnerships and Limited Liability Partnerships

A partnership can be formed by simple agreement and need not attract substantial formation expenses. Other characteristics are as follows:

- There is no separate legal entity (partners are jointly and severally liable for any debts).
- Partnership accounts are private.
- The constitution of the partnership can be changed by agreement.
- Profits are subject to income tax (payable by the partners).
- Partners usually take an active part in the business.
- The partnership ends on death, resignation or removal of a partner.
- There is no upper limit on the number of partners.

### Limited Partnerships

In addition to general partnerships, it is possible to form Limited Partnerships, which are governed by the Limited Partnership Act 1907. Limited Partnerships are formed with one or more persons (called general partners), who are liable for all debts and obligations of the firm, and one or more persons called limited partners, who contribute money or property. Limited partners are only liable for the debts and obligations of the firm to the extent of the amount contributed. Limited partners are not permitted to take part in the management of the Limited

Partnership and may not receive back their contribution while they remain a limited partner. A person cannot be a general and a limited partner at the same time.

Limited Partnerships do not have a separate entity (except for Limited Partnerships formed in Scotland). Limited Partnerships must be registered at Companies House and any subsequent change in details of a partner must be notified. As with general partnerships, a Limited Partnership's accounts are private. Limited Partnerships can be brought to an end through dissolution.

### Limited Liability Partnerships (LLPs)

Under the Limited Liability Partnerships Act 2000 and in the Limited Liability Partnerships Regulations 2001, which apply parts of the Companies Acts to limited liability partnerships, it is possible to form partnerships with limited liability. Unlike members of ordinary partnerships, the LLP itself, and not the individual partners, is responsible for any debts it runs up. An LLP has the organisational flexibility of a partnership and is taxed as a partnership, but in other respects it is very similar to the concept of a limited company. For example:

- Incorporation procedures for an LLP follow the same model as for a limited company (but using form LL IN01). An LLP is issued with a certificate showing its place of registration and registration number.
- An LLP is required to maintain at least two designated members (the nearest equivalent to being a director) at all times. Details of the appointment, resignation and change of particulars of a member are provided to the Registrar of Companies using forms LL AP01–02, LL TM01–02 and LL CH01–02.
- Annual accounts and annual returns must be filed with the Registrar of Companies.
- All LLP names must end with the words 'Limited Liability Partnership', 'LLP' or their Welsh language equivalents. This name and partnership registration number must be used on headed notepaper and other official documents.

Limited liability partnerships are not available for some activities such as non-profit-making activities.

## 2.7 Unlimited companies

An unlimited company, like a limited company, is a corporation and is therefore subject to the same rules concerning its capacity to enter into transactions and incur liabilities. Unlike a limited company, however, its members are liable to contribute their personal assets in order to satisfy its debts and liabilities in the event of winding up. Unlimited companies are usually professional practices or special types of trading organisations that require corporate status and perpetual succession. This means that the company can carry on regardless of the changes in membership that may occur from time to time.

An unlimited company must be a private company. Its name must not end with the word 'Limited', but need not include the word 'Unlimited'. If it does, this must be used as the last word of its name.

An unlimited company has its own Articles of Association, which must state the amount of its share capital, if it has one. CA provisions regulating the alteration of a company's share capital do not apply to unlimited companies. Capital may be returned to members by resolution.

It is possible to re-register an unlimited company as a limited company, and vice versa. This change of status may take place only once in the life of a company. An unlimited company is not required to file statutory accounts at Companies House unless it is a holding company or a subsidiary of a limited company.

## 2.8 Holding and subsidiary companies

This relationship is defined by CA 2006, ss. 1159 and 1160, which set out the following regulations. A company is a holding company of another company if it:

- holds a majority of the voting rights;
- is a member of it and has the right to appoint or remove a majority of the board of directors;

- is a member of it and controls on its own the majority of voting rights by virtue of agreements with other shareholders;
- is a subsidiary of a company which is itself a subsidiary of another company.

A company becomes a wholly owned subsidiary if the holding or parent company owns all the shares by itself or through the holding company's nominees. A holding company and its subsidiaries are collectively called a group. The importance of this classification relates to:

- the requirement to publish group accounts (i.e. consolidated accounts which reflect the performance of both the holding company and all the subsidiary companies);
- financial assistance in the purchase of shares: a holding company may help in the purchase of shares in its subsidiary but not vice versa;
- the avoidance of provisions on fair dealing by directors, for example, provisions on loans to directors do not apply when the loan is to a director of a subsidiary company (see Chapter 2);
- the increase in limited liability: a major company law consideration favouring the use of subsidiaries is the increased level of limited liability afforded to the group as a whole. Valuable assets such as group freehold properties might, for example, be transferred to a non-trading group company, or a high-risk trading activity carried on within a subsidiary which has no other activities.

---

**TEST YOUR KNOWLEDGE 4.1**

a  Can a plc be formed with a single subscriber?
b  Why is a plc not necessarily a listed company?
c  What are the key differences between a private limited company and a public limited company?
d  How can you become a member of a company limited by guarantee?
e  Will the death of a shareholder in a single member company terminate the company?
f  How is a Limited Liability Partnership formed? What are the benefits of a Limited Liability Partnership?
g  What is the purpose of a Community Interest Company?
h  How is an SE formed? What are the benefits of operating an SE?
i  When is a company a subsidiary of another company?

---

## 3  The registration process

Registration is the process of forming a legal entity which is separate from its owners (the shareholders). This can also be referred to as incorporation or formation. Registration is effected by delivering the relevant documentation to the Registrar of Companies. Companies House provides a starter pack for the incorporation of new companies, which includes relevant guidance and the necessary statutory forms. This is available by post or from the Companies House website (see Directory). The website is a very useful source of information generally on company formation and statutory returns. Students are strongly encouraged to take the time to visit it to familiarise themselves with the information available.

A number of documents are required to complete registration, all of which take time to prepare. If time is limited, it may be a better option to buy an **'off the shelf' company** and adapt it to the company's needs. These companies have already been registered and have Certificates of Incorporation, Memorandum, Articles and name, all of which can be changed by the new owners.

> **STOP AND THINK** **4.3**
>
> Companies may be purchased off the shelf from a variety of sources, most commonly from solicitors, accountants or formation agents. It is a good idea to keep a contact list of such sources in case you need to acquire or incorporate a company urgently.

The CA 1985 (Electronic Communications) Order 2000 allows registration documents to be submitted electronically using approved software or a provider approved by Companies House. To take advantage of this service you must register as an electronic filer first (see below).

## 3.1 Business name

The rules relating to the name a company can use are provided in the CA 2006, which has the following guidelines:

1 Before submitting any documents, every new business name must be checked against the index of company names held by the Registrar of Companies to ensure that the intended name of the company is not the same as or 'too like' the name of any existing company or otherwise objectionable (see below). It is the responsibility of the person registering the company to check the index, which can be done via the Companies House website, or through a registration agent. It is not possible to 'reserve' prospective names ahead of formation.

2 A company can be registered with any name provided the following two sets of provisions are satisfied:

*Set one*

a) the name is not already on the company index;

b) the words 'Limited', 'Public Limited Company' or 'Unlimited' (or the abbreviated forms and Welsh language equivalents) are only at the end;

c) the name is not offensive;

d) the use of the name is not a criminal offence.

As a result of the introduction of the SE (see section 2.5), the Registrar will not permit any other company other than an SE to use the initials 'SE' either at the beginning or the end of the company name. 'SE' can still be used if it forms part of a company name, for example 'ABC Builders of London SE25', but it cannot be used on its own at the beginning or end of the name. The same principles will apply to companies seeking a change of name.

*Set two (sensitive words)*

The Secretary of State for Business Innovation & Skills (BIS) (previously known as Business Enterprise and Regulatory Reform (BERR)) can designate certain words as sensitive enough to require permission for their use. A complete list is given in the Companies House Guidance Booklets GBF 2, *Company Names*, and GBF 3, *Business Names*, available on the Companies House website. Prior consent must be obtained from the Secretary of State for BIS for the following words or expressions:

a) words that imply national or international pre-eminence, e.g. English, National, European;

b) words that imply business pre-eminence or representative or authoritative status, e.g. Association, Institute, Society;

c) words that imply specific objects or functions, such as Assurance, Fund, Stock Exchange, Trade Union.

### Business names and company names

There is a difference between a 'business name' and a 'company name'. The Business Names Act applies to all business activities, sole traders, partnerships and companies not trading under their name as it appears on the index of company names. In this case they must disclose the registered name on correspondence. There is no facility for registering a business name. There is a further requirement that if the business name implies association with the government or is in the 'specified regulations', prior permission must be obtained from the Secretary of State. It is possible for the company to use a business name as well as its incorporated name, e.g. Tesco plc trading as Tesco.

## The Registrar's power to order a change of name after incorporation

The Registrar has the power to order a change of name as follows:

1 Within twelve months of registration if the name is the same as or similar to ('too like') a name in the existing index of company names (CA 2006, s. 67(1)).
2 Within five years of registration if misleading information was given on registration (CA 2006, s. 75).
3 At any time if use of the name is misleading and is likely to cause harm to the public (CA 2006, s. 80).

## Objections to company names

Under CA 2006, ss. 69–74 complaints can be made where a company name has been registered with the intention of extracting money from a complainant or preventing the registration of a company name in which a person or business has some goodwill (sometimes referred to as an 'opportunistic registration'). Under these provisions, a Company Names Tribunal has been established as part of the UK Intellectual Property Office to review objections. Any person or company may object to a company name. The Company Names Tribunal has the power to order a change of name and, if the company fails to comply, it may select a new name for the company. These provisions are separate and in addition to the Registrar's powers to order a change of name as set out above.

## Use of the words 'limited' or 'public limited company' as part of company name

CA 2006, ss. 58–59 require companies to have 'limited' or 'public limited companies' (or the Welsh equivalents or accepted abbreviations) at the end of the company name. Section 60 does, however, provide some exemptions from using these words where the company is either a charity or a company limited by guarantee (see 2.3 above).

---

**STOP AND THINK** **4.4**

What's in a name? As you begin your career and start to form companies you will see how the importance of brand and name is growing. Be careful: companies try to trademark numbers and words which are variations of their existing names. There may be no name on the company register, but an action for passing off may drop through the letterbox once the company begins to trade.

---

## 3.2 Memorandum of Association

The Memorandum of Association sets out the subscribers' intention to form a company and to become a member of that company on formation. There has to be at least one subscriber to the Memorandum of Association who agrees to take at least one share in the company (prior to October 2009 a public company was required to have at least two members). The Memorandum of Association shows the name of each subscriber and the authentication (e.g. signature) of each subscriber. A subscriber can be a corporate body or an individual. Information on capital and shareholdings is not required as this is given in form IN01 (see below). Once the company has been incorporated, it will not be necessary usually to amend the Memorandum of Association as it does not reflect the future operation of the company. Once a company is formed, the Memorandum of Association essentially becomes an historical document.

## 3.3 Articles of Association

The purpose of the Articles is to govern the internal affairs of the company. It is usual to adopt the Model Articles and make any specified modifications. The effect of the Articles is looked at in Chapter 5, together with a detailed summary of the Model Articles. The Model Articles are included as Appendices 1 and 2. The Articles of Association are therefore usually the key document in determining the constitution of the company, and, unlike the Memorandum, can be amended going forward (see Chapter 5).

## 3.4 Documents required

### Form IN01

Form IN01 contains all the details required to enable the incorporation of a company; the presenter (in many cases the company secretary) will be required to prepare it. Key areas to note on the form include the following:

- The address of the registered office and respective jurisdiction (e.g. England and Wales) must be stated. The registered office address must be within the respective jurisdiction. A physical registered office address should be supplied. PO Box or DX addresses will be rejected.
- Names and particulars of the first director(s) and secretary(ies) must be provided and signed by the individual to signify their consent.
- Details of any alteration to the respective Model Articles must be provided.
- Information on the capital of the company and its shareholders must be provided. This will include details of the initial shareholders (subscribers) or a statement of guarantee by the guarantors of any company limited by guarantee. Any particular rights attaching any of the shares must also be disclosed.
- Every subscriber to the Memorandum of Association must sign a statement of compliance (this is contained within the form). The statement confirms that the subscriber has complied with the requirements of CA 2006 in respect of registration.

A summarised version of Form IN01 is provided on page 65. A pro-forma **Memorandum of Association** for a company with share capital is provided on page 78.

### Memorandum and Articles of Association

The Memorandum of Association (see 3.2 above) must be provided. The respective Model Articles of Association (see 3.3 above) will apply to the company in default if no other Articles are provided on registration. Companies are free to modify and/or exclude some or all of the Model Articles by attaching different Articles with their registration (see Chapter 5).

### Form SH50 (public companies only)

This is the application by a public company for a certificate to commence business and to exercise borrowing powers under CA 2006, s. 761. Although the public company will exist from the date of incorporation, unlike a private company it cannot commence business until the Registrar issues a 'trading certificate'. This is not issued until the company has allotted at least £50,000 (€65,600) worth of shares, of which at least 25% of the nominal value of each share is paid up, together with the whole of any premium.

If the company commences its business before the issue of the trading certificate, the company and any of its officers may be liable to criminal proceedings.

### Form formats

The Registrar of Companies is specific about hard copy forms submitted and the ink used to complete them. The documents and forms delivered to Companies House are scanned to produce an electronic image. The original documents are then stored and the electronic image used as the working document. (Form formats are dealt with in Chapter 8.)

In accordance with
Section 9 of the
Companies Act 2006.

# IN01
## Application to register a company

**Companies House**

**A fee is payable with this form.**
Please see 'How to pay' on the last page.

✓ **What this form is for**
You may use this form to register a
private or public company.

✗ **What this form is NOT for**
You cannot use this form to register
a limited liability partnership. To do
this, please use form LL IN01.

For further information, please
refer to our guidance at
www.companieshouse.gov.uk

## Part 1    Company details

### A1   Company name

To check if a company name is available use our WebCHeck service and select
the 'Company Name Availability Search' option:

**www.companieshouse.gov.uk/info**

Please show the proposed company name below.

Proposed company
name in full ❶

For official use

**→ Filling in this form**
Please complete in typescript or in
bold black capitals.

All fields are mandatory unless
specified or indicated by *

**❶ Duplicate names**
Duplicate names are not permitted.
A list of registered names can
be found on our website. There
are various rules that may affect
your choice of name. More
information on this is available in
our guidance booklet GP1 at:
www.companieshouse.gov.uk

### A2   Company name restrictions ❷

Please tick the box only if the proposed company name contains sensitive
or restricted words or expressions that require you to seek comments of a
government department or other specified body.

☐ I confirm that the proposed company name contains sensitive or restricted
words or expressions and that approval, where appropriate, has been
sought of a government department or other specified body and I attach a
copy of their response.

**❷ Company name restrictions**
A list of sensitive or restricted
words or expressions that require
consent can be found in our
guidance booklet GP1 at:
www.companieshouse.gov.uk

### A3   Exemption from name ending with 'Limited' or 'Cyfyngedig' ❸

Please tick the box if you wish to apply for exemption from the requirement to
have the name ending with 'Limited', Cyfyngedig' or permitted alternative.

☐ I confirm that the above proposed company meets the conditions for
exemption from the requirement to have a name ending with 'Limited',
'Cyfyngedig' or permitted alternative.

**❸ Name ending exemption**
Only private companies that are
limited by guarantee and meet other
specific requirements are eligible
to apply for this. For more details,
please go to our website:
www.companieshouse.gov.uk

### A4   Company type❹

Please tick the box that describes the proposed company type and members'
liability (only one box must be ticked):

☐ Public limited by shares
☐ Private limited by shares
☐ Private limited by guarantee
☐ Private unlimited with share capital
☐ Private unlimited without share capital

**❹ Company type**
If you are unsure of your company's
type, please go to our website:
www.companieshouse.gov.uk

**BIS** | Department for Business
Innovation & Skills

CHFP000
05/12 Version 5.0

In accordance with
Sections 761 & 762 of
the Companies Act 2006.

# SH50

## Application for trading certificate
## for a public company

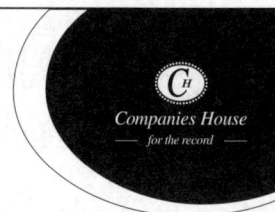

*Companies House*
*— for the record —*

✓ **What this form is for**
You may use this form to make an
application by a public company for
a trading certificate.

✗ **What this form is NOT for**
You cannot use this form to
make an application for a trading
certificate following a
re-registration from a private
company to public company.

For further information, please
refer to our guidance at
www.companieshouse.gov.uk

---

**1** **Company details**

Company number

Company name in full

→ **Filling in this form**
Please complete in typescript or in
bold black capitals.

All fields are mandatory unless
specified or indicated by *

---

**2** **The application**

The above company applies for a certificate entitling them to do business and
exercise borrowing powers and confirms that:

1. the aggregate nominal value of the company's allotted share capital is not
   less than the authorised minimum.

2. the company is designating its authorised minimum capital in ❶

   ☐ Sterling

   ☐ Euros

3. the ❷

   ☐ amount of preliminary expenses

   ☐ estimated amount of the preliminary expenses of the company is

❶ One of the boxes needs to be ticked
only where the company satisfies
the authorised minimum in both
Sterling and Euros.

❷ Please tick one box only.

---

**3** **Amount paid or benefit given**

Has any amount or benefit been paid or given or is intended to be paid or given
to any promoter of the company?

→ **Yes** Complete **Section 4**.
→ **No** Go to **Section 5** Statement of compliance.

---

**4** **Promoters**

**Promoter number 1**

Amount paid or intend
to be paid

Any benefit given or
intended to be given

Consideration for such
payment or benefit

---

## Other documents

Other registration documentation may be required as follows:

- *Form AA01* – unless otherwise altered, the company's accounting period will end on the last day of the month in which it was incorporated. A company may, however, alter this date by choosing a new date on form AA01 and returning the form to the Registrar. The change of date can be made at incorporation or subsequently (see Chapter 11).
- *Form SH01* – return of allotments of further shares issued for cash, shares issued wholly or in part for a consideration other than cash or as bonus share issues.

## 3.5 Registration fee

The registration documents must be accompanied by the applicable registration fee. Companies House offers a same-day incorporation service, this though is more expensive.

Chapter 8 looks at same-day registration, and quicker still, electronic incorporation. Schedules of Companies House fees can be found on their website (see Directory).

---

**STOP AND THINK** **4.5**

CA provisions regulating the alteration of a company's share capital do not apply to unlimited companies.

Limited liability is a privilege and the price paid for it is publicity and the regulation that ensures a basic minimum standard of behaviour:

'It is easy to lose confidence in a company that doesn't meet its legal obligations, if you don't tell us about your company's financial state in time and you don't send in details of changes, anyone wanting to do business with you will not have access to the most up to date information about your company. It could cause trading problems or affect your company's credit rating. It could even stop a potential investor from putting money into your company, or prevent you from getting a loan when you need it.' (Companies House information booklet GBF1/V5, *Company Formation*)

---

## 3.6 Certificate of incorporation

If all is in order, the Registrar of Companies will issue a certificate of incorporation (see specimen certificate overleaf). This is effectively the 'birth certificate' of a company and is issued under the authority of CA 2006, s. 15. It contains:

- the company's allocated registered number;
- if the company is a public company, this will be stated on the certificate;
- the actual date of incorporation, not the date when the certificate was issued.

CA 2006, s. 15 states that the certificate when issued is conclusive evidence that the company has been duly registered. The effect is that should an irregularity in the registration procedure be discovered after the issue of the certificate of incorporation, it would not be possible to attack the validity of the company's incorporation. The evidence to prove the irregularity would not be admissible in court. The certificate of incorporation is an important document. The company secretary should therefore ensure that it is kept safe and secure.

A private company may commence business on incorporation without further formality. A company cannot subsequently alter the place of registration from that which has been stated on the certificate of incorporation (e.g. a company incorporated in England and Wales cannot later be registered in Scotland).

Companies are often asked by third parties (e.g. banks, creditors or suppliers) to produce evidence that they are validly incorporated. This is usually evidenced by the company secretary supplying a certified copy of the certificate of incorporation.

### CHECKLIST 4.1 Company registration

✓ Check the index of company names to ensure that the proposed name is not the same or too similar to an existing company.

✓ Consider whether the proposed name may be construed as misleading.

✓ Check whether the name contains sensitive words and, if it does, whether permission has been obtained.

✓ Check whether there may be a conflict with a registered trade or service mark of another business.

✓ Consider whether the business will use a business name which is different from the company name.

✓ Submit the following documents to the Registrar:
   – Articles of Association;
   – Memorandum of Association
   – Form IN01, containing details of first directors and secretary share capital, initial shareholders and statutory declaration of compliance;
   – if a plc and you wish to trade immediately, a completed form SH50.

✓ Consider whether the accounting reference date will be changed and complete form AA01 if necessary.

✓ Complete and return form SH01 in respect of any additional share allotted.

✓ Include the fee.

## 3.7 Procedure following incorporation

Once the certificate of incorporation has been issued, a private company may commence trading. As we have seen, a public company must wait for the issue of a trading certificate. A private company which has re-registered as a public company does not need to wait for the trading certificate to continue trading.

Checklist 4.2 sets out the key matters to be attended to after incorporation.

### CHECKLIST 4.2 Matters arising following incorporation

✓ The first directors, secretary and registered office will be stated in the form IN01 filed on incorporation. If any changes are required (e.g. if the company has been purchased from company registration agents), these should be formalised at the first board meeting (see below) and forms AD01 or AP01–04 or CH01–04, as necessary, filed with the Registrar.

✓ Obtain a seal (if required) and arrange for the directors at the first board meeting (see below) to adopt as the common seal and to lay down any necessary regulations for the use of the seal and attestation of sealed documents.

✓ At the first board meeting, the directors should:
   a) appoint a chairman and, if relevant, a managing director;
   b) appoint the company's bankers and adopt the resolutions set out in the opening of account mandate;
   c) appoint auditors;
   d) determine the company's **accounting reference date** (see Chapter 11);
   e) approve the registration of any necessary transfers of subscribers' shares;
   f) make any necessary allotments of share capital;
   g) approve the issue of share certificates;
   h) dispense with the distinguishing numbers of all issued fully paid shares in the company, if appropriate (CA 2006, s. 543);
   i) appoint persons to represent the company at meetings of members or creditors of other companies (CA 2006, s. 323);
   j) approve directors' service contracts if applicable and notify the Registrar of the place where they are kept if not at the registered office. (See the SAIL provisions of CA 2006, s. 1136 in Chapter 8);
   k) note and receive any declaration of directors' interests;
   l) notify the Registrar of the place where the register of members is kept, if not at the registered office (as j) above: see the SAIL provisions in Chapter 8).

✓ Further details about the agenda and minutes of the first board meeting are given in Chapter 10.
✓ File return of allotments with the Registrar (form SH01) for allotments for cash and for allotments for consideration other than cash.
✓ The accounting reference date will automatically be the last day of the month in which the anniversary of incorporation falls (CA 2006, s. 391). If a different date is required by the company, the date must be changed by submitting form AA01.
✓ Obtain statutory registers for the company (e.g. a combined register, preferably in loose-leaf form, available from law stationers) and make all necessary entries.
✓ Organise headed stationery for the company and arrange for the full name of the company to be shown outside every place of its business.
✓ Inform HM Revenue & Customs as necessary regarding the company. Consider arrangements regarding corporation tax, income tax (PAYE), National Insurance and VAT (if relevant).
✓ Arrange insurance cover as appropriate, for example property, employer liability, directors and officers liability.
✓ If the company was purchased from company registration agents, it may be necessary for the secretary to review the Articles of Association to ensure they are appropriate for the company. If any amendments are required, it will be necessary for the directors to convene a general meeting as shareholder approval will be required.

## Note

On incorporation the subscribers should be entered in the register of members as the holders of the shares subscribed (CA 2006, s. 112); no formal allotment is needed of these shares and they should not be included on a return of allotments.

## 3.8 Display of the company name

The name, registered number and country of incorporation provide evidence of a company as a separate legal entity. These characteristics need to be used to ensure that those dealing with them are aware of the identity of that legal person.

Once the company has been incorporated, its full name, registered office address and registered number, as shown on the certificate of incorporation, must be stated on:

- all business letters;
- all notices and other official publications;
- all bills of exchange and cheques;
- all invoices, receipts and letters of credit;
- all company emails, faxes and websites (CA 2006, s. 82).

Where a company uses a trading name that is different from its registered name, this can be shown on the headed paper. However, the company's full name, as registered, must be shown in legible characters – usually in small print at the foot of the page.

Unless the company is and has been dormant since it was formed, the company name must also be displayed in a conspicuous position in legible letters at all premises where business is carried on.

When premises are shared (e.g. in a large office) it is sufficient to place the name at the entrance to that part of the premises used by the company. If six or more companies share the same premises, CA 2006 permits the name of the company to be displayed for 15 seconds every three minutes. This will be particularly suited to electronic display screens which are common in the reception areas of many large offices.

If the premises are primarily used for living accommodation, it is not necessary to display the company name at the premises.

---

**STOP AND THINK 4.6**

Consider these regulations within a large organisation with a number of business sites. The company secretary should work closely with the company's property managers to ensure that each of the business premises displays the correct business name and should share the responsibility of ensuring that statutory requirements are met.

## 3.9 Common seal

CA 2006, s. 45 provides that a company may have a seal, but need not have one. Most substantial companies continue to have a company seal, particularly for use overseas where local law requires that documents are executed under seal. The seal should have the company name engraved in legible characters and should be kept by the company secretary, who should keep a record of all documents to which the seal is affixed (the sealing register). The seal should be kept securely (usually in a safe or locked cabinet) to avoid potential misuse.

If a company has decided to dispense with using a seal, any document signed by two directors or a director and the secretary which is expressed to be executed by the company has the same effect as if it were executed under the company's seal. The same principle applies if a document needs to be executed as a deed; provided the company has made it clear that the document is being executed as a deed, there is no need for a seal to be used.

Under CA 2006, s. 768 a share certificate issued under the common seal of the company is *prima facie* evidence of a member's title to the shares, which the certificate represents. Although companies are no longer obliged to have a company seal, many public companies have adopted and continue to use 'securities seals', which can be used to seal certificates relating to the securities of the company. Such seals are useful where the register of members is maintained by external registrars, so that the company can retain the use of its common seal under its own control.

The actual use of the seal is determined in the Articles (Model Article 49; public company Model Article 81). The directors may specify via board resolution who may execute documents under seal, but in the absence of instructions a document may be sealed in the presence of a director and the secretary, or two directors. It is common for large companies to delegate authority for the use of the seal to various officers of the company.

Again subject to the Articles, a company with a common seal may keep one or more official seals for use overseas. The person who affixes the seal to documents in the country concerned must first be appointed by the company in writing under common seal, often by power of attorney. It is usually the responsibility of the secretary to ensure that the sealing register is kept up to date, to inform the directors at board meetings of documents which have been executed under seal and to maintain any schedule of authorised signatories of those permitted to execute documents under seal.

---

**TEST YOUR KNOWLEDGE 4.2**

a  Which documents must be submitted to the Registrar of Companies on incorporation of a private company?

b  What are the restrictions on the selection of a company name?

c  What information appears on a certificate of incorporation?

d  What is a trading certificate? Why is it required?

e  What matters should a board consider following incorporation?

f  What information about a company must be included on a company's letterhead?

g  How is the use of a company's seal determined?

---

# 4    Re-registration of companies

## 4.1 Private company to a public company

Both a private company limited by shares and an unlimited company with a share capital may re-register as a public company, but a company without share capital cannot do so. To qualify for re-registration a private company must meet the necessary minimum criteria to become a public company.

Namely, it must have:

- at least one shareholder (CA 2006, s. 123);
- at least two directors (CA 2006, s. 154(2));
- a suitably qualified company secretary (CA 2006, s. 273);
- issued at least £50,000 (€65,600) of share capital, in nominal value of which all of a premium and at least 25% of the nominal value must be paid (CA 2006, ss. 763 and 764).

## Procedure

The board should resolve to convene a general meeting. Any deficiencies (such as an issued share capital which is below the required amount) must be addressed. A special resolution (see Chapter 9) is required to re-register as a public company and a copy of the resolution, together with an application form, must be delivered to the Registrar. The resolution must make any required alterations to the Articles of Association of the company.

---

**SAMPLE WORDING 4.1**

**Special resolution for re-registration of private company as public company**

THAT pursuant to the provisions of sections 90–94, CA 2006, the company be re-registered as a public company [with effect from ................... 20xx or from such other date as may be approved by the Registrar of Companies] and that the Articles of Association of the company be thereupon altered as follows:

a   by deleting the existing article 1 and substituting therefor the following articles to be numbered 1 and 2:

   1. The company's name is '................... Public Limited Company'.

   2. The company is to be a public company;

b   by renumbering the existing articles [...] as articles [...] respectively.

---

The application to re-register must made be on form RR01 and filed within 15 days of the resolution being passed. It should be accompanied by the following documents:

1 a copy of the revised Articles;
2 a copy of the signed special resolution;
3 a copy of a balance sheet prepared not more than seven months before the application date and containing an unqualified report by the company's auditors;
4 a written statement by the company's auditor that in his opinion at the balance sheet date the amount of the company's net assets was not less than the aggregate of its called-up share capital and undistributable reserves;
5 a valuation report on any shares issued as fully or partly paid up except in cash after the balance sheet date;
6 a statement on form RR01 confirming that the resolution has been passed, that there has been no change in the company's financial position causing its net assets to be reduced to less than its called-up share capital and undistributable reserves, that the nominal value meets the minimum required and disclosing whether any shares have been allotted since the balance sheet date.

On approval, the Registrar will issue a certificate of incorporation stating that the company is a public company. Alterations to the Articles take effect when the certificate is issued. The change of company status is not effective until the certificate has been issued.

In accordance with Sections 94 & 765(4) of the Companies Act 2006.

# RR01

Application by a private company for re-registration as a public company

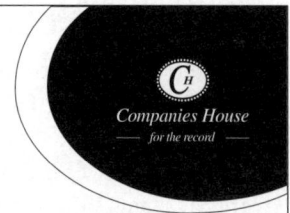

Companies House
*for the record*

**A fee is payable with this form.**
Please see 'How to pay' on the last page.

✓ **What this form is for**
You may use this form to make an application by a private company for re-registration as a public company.

✗ **What this form is NOT for**
You cannot use this form to make an application by a private limited company for re-registration as a private unlimited company.

For further information, please refer to our guidance at www.companieshouse.gov.uk

# Part 1

## A1    Company details

Company number

Company name in full

→ **Filling in this form**
Please complete in typescript or in bold black capitals.

All fields are mandatory unless specified or indicated by *

## A2    Re-registration

The above company applies to be re-registered as a public company by the name of:

Full name of re-registered company ❶

and for that purpose delivers the following documents for re-registration:
1.    A copy of the special resolution that the company should re-register as a public limited company (unless previously delivered).
2.    A printed copy of the articles as proposed to be amended.
3.    A copy of the auditors written statement in relation to section 92(1)(c) of the Companies Act 2006.
4.    A copy of the relevant balance sheet. ❷
5.    A copy of the auditors unqualified report.
6.    If applicable, a copy of the valuation report in accordance with section 93(2)(a) of the Companies Act 2006.
7.    If there is no company secretary appointed, a statement of the company's proposed secretary in accordance with section 95 of the Companies Act 2006 needs to be completed. Please complete the secretary details in Part 2.

❶ **Name**
Please insert the full name of the company including the appropriate name ending for a public company.

❷ The balance sheet must be made up to a date not more than 7 months before the date of this application.

## A3    Authorised minimum share capital

The above company confirms that:
1.    the aggregate nominal value of the company's share capital is not less than the authorised minimum.
2.    the company is designating its authorised minimum capital in ❸

☐    Sterling.

☐    Euros.

❸ One of the boxes only need to be ticked where the company satisfies the authorised minimum in both Sterling and Euros.

An unlimited company must in addition:

- include a statement in the resolution that the liability of the members is limited and what the company's share capital is to be; and
- make such alterations to the Articles as are necessary for them to conform to those of a company limited by shares.

The company must also satisfy the statutory minimum share capital requirements.

## 4.2 Public company to a private company

A public company limited by shares may re-register as a private company by passing a special resolution. However, if members representing not less than 5% in nominal value or not less than 50 members object, under CA 2006, s. 98 they may apply to the court to cancel the resolution within 28 days of it being passed. The registrar must be informed of the application and once the court has ruled, it will notify the company that must send a copy of the court order to the registrar, usually within 15 days.

A court may also order a public company to re-register as private on approving a 'minute of reduction' of share capital which results in the **issued share capital** falling below the statutory minimum. In such a case the court will also specify alterations to the company's Articles. A special resolution to re-register is not required (see Chapter 12).

Similarly, a public company may be required to re-register as private if its issued capital falls below the statutory minimum by other means. These include **redemption**, forfeiture or repurchase of shares. In these cases a special resolution to re-register is required.

Except where a court has specified in an order the alterations to be made, a resolution must also be passed to alter the Articles to those required for a private company.

---

**SAMPLE WORDING 4.2**

**Special resolution for re-registration of public company as private company**

THAT pursuant to the provisions of section 97, Companies Act 2006, the company be re-registered as a private company [with effect from ........... 20xx or from such other date as may be approved by the Registrar of Companies] and that the Articles of Association of the company be thereupon altered as follows:

**a** by deleting the existing articles [1 and 2] and substituting therefor the following article to be numbered 1:

The company's name is '..................... Limited';

**b** by renumbering the existing articles [...] as articles [...] respectively.

---

## Procedure

The board should resolve to convene a general meeting to pass a special resolution to re-register as a private company, altering the Articles so that they no longer state that the company is a public company and making any other necessary alterations. This will include changing the name of the company to delete public limited company (or any abbreviation) and substituting the word 'Limited' or 'Ltd'.

Once passed, the resolution must be sent to the Registrar within 15 days. The application for re-registration (using form RR02) must be accompanied by a signed copy of the resolution and a copy of the Articles as modified to meet the company's new circumstances. Form RR02 contains the necessary statement of compliance that the requirements of CA 2006 have been met (s. 100).

If the Registrar of Companies approves the application, a certificate of incorporation will be issued stating that the company is a private limited company. Alterations to the Articles take effect when the certificate is issued.

In accordance with
Section 100 of the
Companies Act 2006.

# RR02

## Application by a public company for re-registration as a private limited company

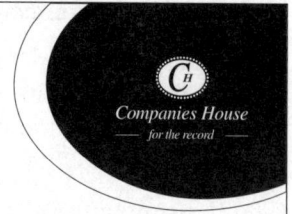

*Companies House
— for the record —*

**A fee is payable with this form.**
Please see 'How to pay' on the last page.

✓ **What this form is for**
You may use this form to
re-register a public company as a
private limited company.

✗ **What this form is NOT for**
You cannot use this form to
re-register a public company as a
private limited company following
a court order reducing capital, a
cancellation of shares or a reduction
of capital due to re-denomination.

For further information, please
refer to our guidance at
www.companieshouse.gov.uk

## 1 Company details

Company number

Company name in full

→ **Filling in this form**
Please complete in typescript or in
bold black capitals.

All fields are mandatory unless
specified or indicated by *

## 2 Re-registration

The above company applies to be re-registered as a private limited company by
the name of:

Full name of
re-registered company ❶

and for that purpose delivers the following documents for registration:
1. A copy of the special resolution that the company should re-register as a
   private limited company (unless previously delivered).
2. A printed copy of the articles as proposed to be amended.

❶ **Name**
Please insert the full name of the
company including the appropriate
name ending for a private limited
company.

## 3 Statement of compliance

I am signing this form on behalf of the company and confirm that the
requirements of Part 7 of the Companies Act 2006 as to re-registration as a
private limited company have been complied with.

Signature

Signature
X                                                                    X

This form may be signed by:
Director ❷, Secretary, Person authorised ❸, CIC manager.

❷ **Societas Europaea**
If the form is being filed on behalf
of a Societas Europaea (SE) please
delete 'director' and insert details
of which organ of the SE the person
signing has membership.

❸ **Person authorised**
Under either section 270 or 274 of
the Companies Act 2006.

## 4.3 Other re-registrations

An unlimited company may be re-registered as a private company by shares or by guarantee unless it has been previously converted from a limited to an unlimited company (CA 2006, s. 105). A private company cannot re-register as a public company if it has previously been re-registered as unlimited.

A public company can re-register as an unlimited company with a share capital, providing all of its members agree and it has not previously re-registered as a limited or unlimited private company (CA 2006, s. 109). A general meeting will be required to pass the resolution. A special resolution should be passed to amend or delete any Articles which are not consistent with becoming an unlimited private company. The company must also ensure that its name is consistent with it being an unlimited private company.

A private company limited by shares or by guarantee, and which has not previously been an unlimited company, may re-register as an unlimited company with or without a share capital provided all its members consent and its Articles are altered so as to conform to those of an unlimited company (CA 2006, s. 102).

All applications for re-registrations must be lodged with the Registrar of Companies. There are separate forms, depending on the type of re-registration, but each of the forms is similar (see the Companies House website for each of the various forms). Amended Articles should be provided, along with any required statements of compliance. If all is in order, the Registrar will issue a statement of incorporation on re-registration.

## 4.4 The cost of re-registration

Fees apply for re-registration by Companies House's standard service; higher fees apply if the company wishes to take advantage of a premium same-day service. If the company is re-registering and changing its name at the same time, an additional change of name fee is payable. Deleting the words 'company' or 'and company' (or their abbreviations or Welsh equivalents) from a company name would normally be a change of name, but this is not so on re-registration. See Chapter 5 for the procedure for changing a company name.

---

**TEST YOUR KNOWLEDGE 4.3**

a  What is the procedure for re-registering a private company as a public company?
b  Why might a public company be required to re-register as a private company?
c  A public company cannot re-register as an unlimited company. True or false?
d  What documents must be filed with the Registrar following re-registration? When must they be filed?
e  What majority is required when re-registering limited to unlimited? Why is this level of majority required?

---

**CASE QUESTION**

As company secretary of Multiple plc, you have formed part of a project team which is looking at the structure of the company as it grows. The project team asks you to prepare: (i) a report setting out the most appropriate types of new subsidiary companies which may be required to support the business; and (ii) a 'starter pack' for your department for the formation of new subsidiary companies.

■ What considerations do you need to take into account when determining the appropriate type of subsidiary company?
■ Who should act as director(s) and secretary for these companies and why? What other considerations need to be thought about, such as accounting reference date?
■ What will be in the contents of the starter pack? How can you ensure that your department uses it?

# 5   Oversea companies operating a UK establishment

The term **oversea company** applies to all companies incorporated outside the UK, which establish a place of business within the UK. It is usually more convenient for a foreign company to conduct business operations within the UK via a registered subsidiary company. However, there are a number of circumstances where it may be preferable to open an establishment in the UK.

The CA 2006 simplified the rules for oversea companies, replacing two regimes (branch and place of business) for which the filing requirements, etc. were different, with one unified regime. The following documents must be filed with the Registrar of Companies within one month of establishing an oversea company:

- a statutory form OS IN01 and registration fee;
- a copy of the company's constitutional documents. This is usually the company's certificate of incorporation, Memorandum and Articles of Association (or equivalent). If the constitutional documents are not in English, duly certified translations must be provided;
- a copy of the latest audited accounts (again translated into English if necessary).

The oversea company will be required at all times to have a person authorised to accept the serving of formal documents. Changes in particulars must be notified and also details of any charges created over assets in the UK.

An overseas company can be registered in its corporate name under the laws of the country in which it is incorporated or under an alternative name in the UK. The controls and restrictions which apply to the selection of company name also generally apply to overseas companies.

Once an overseas company is established it must notify Companies House of any changes to the original information delivered at formation, usually within 21 days of any such change. Appropriate forms for overseas companies are available from the Companies House website. Overseas companies are also subject to broadly equivalent regulations to UK companies in respect of the display of the company name at business premises and also providing company details on formal correspondence, letterheads, invoices etc.

In respect of the delivery of annual accounts, if an overseas company is required to prepare and disclose accounting documents under its parent law (i.e. the law of the country in which the company is incorporated), it must also send accounts to Companies House. Such accounts must be delivered to Companies House within three months of the date on which the document is required to be disclosed under the company's parent law. This requirement is often overlooked when foreign companies are considering business operations in this country and hence it will be vital for company secretaries to diarise such events.

Even if the overseas company is not required to disclose accounts under its parent law, it must still file accounts with the Registrar of Companies. In this case an oversea company is required to deliver accounts within 13 months of the end of the relevant accounting reference period.

## CHAPTER SUMMARY

- Registration or incorporation is the process of creating a separate legal entity. A certificate of incorporation provides conclusive evidence that a company has been incorporated.
- Businesses may be set up as a sole trader or partnership.
- Companies can be unlimited, private limited by guarantee, private limited by shares, or public limited companies. A public limited company is not necessarily listed.
- A company can be formed with a single member.
- Other business entities include the Community Interest Company and the SE.
- Companies cannot be incorporated with a name that already exists or that is too similar to an existing name. The company name must not be misleading and there are certain words which cannot be used or where permission must first be sought.
- Company names must be displayed on documents and at places of business.
- Apart from the statutory forms, companies may file the Articles of Association on registration.
- It is possible to re-register companies from private to public and from public to private; unlimited to limited and limited to unlimited. In order to re-register as a public company, minimum requirements concerning the number of directors, share capital and a qualified company secretary must be met.
- Businesses which have been incorporated outside UK may create a business presence within the UK by forming an oversea company.

# Company constitution

## 5

## ■ CONTENTS

1 The Memorandum of Association
2 Articles of Association
3 Alteration of the Articles
4 Other elements of a company's constitution, registered office address and company name

## ■ INTRODUCTION

The CA 2006 made major changes to a company's constitution. From October 2009 a company's key constitutional document is essentially its Articles, with the Memorandum of Association becoming simply an historical statement of the subscribers to it.

The internal rules that govern the company are found in the Articles of Association. For companies incorporated after 1 October 2009, CA 2006 introduced new default Model Articles for both public and private companies which replaced previous default Articles for companies incorporated prior to 1 October 2009 under CA 1985. The Articles should be appropriate for the company and its circumstances and so company secretaries need to decide whether to amend the company's Articles to bring them into line with the Model Articles or to suit the particular needs of the company.

Later chapters deal with the specific Articles as they occur – for example, Model Articles provisions on voting are covered in Chapters 9 and 10.

## 1   The Memorandum of Association

Under CA 2006, the Memorandum is a short document showing the intent to form a company and the identity of the initial subscriber(s). Companies incorporated prior to 1 October 2009 had an old-style Memorandum which included other information in relation to the company's capital, its activities and its country of registration. CA 2006, s. 28 operates to move these provisions into the Articles of Association. The Memorandum for all companies is, therefore, an historical document as there is no need to change it if constitutional changes are required to the company as it goes forward.

Companies incorporated before 1 October 2009 had within their Memorandum of Association objects clauses, which set out the permissible activities of the company, or that the company acted as a 'general commercial company', enabling it to carry on any trade or business whatsoever and have the power to do all such things as are incidental or conducive to the carrying on of any trade or business. As noted above, all such provisions would have moved to the Articles of Association and CA 2006, s. 31 provides that, unless a company's Articles expressly restrict objects, a company's objects are unrestricted. If a company incorporated before 1 October 2009 wishes to have unrestricted objects, the Articles (inclusive of objects as of 1 October 2009) should be reviewed and any restrictive objects clause removed. Many companies decided after 1 October 2009 to amend their Articles to take s. 28 into account, so that its Articles reflect the statutory position.

# COMPANY HAVING A SHARE CAPITAL

## Memorandum of association of

Each subscriber to this memorandum of association wishes to form a company under the Companies Act 2006 and agrees to become a member of the company and to take at least one share.

| *Name of each subscriber* | *Authentication by each subscriber* |
| --- | --- |
| | |

Dated

---

**TEST YOUR KNOWLEDGE 5.1**

**a**  What is the purpose of the Memorandum of Association?
**b**  How likely is it following the formation of a company that the Memorandum of Association will be amended?

---

## 2 Articles of Association

A company's Articles are the regulations governing its internal management. They usually cover such matters as:

■ rights of shareholders;
■ transfer or transmission of shares;
■ rights attaching to shares;
■ appointment, removal and powers and conduct of directors;
■ conduct of board meetings and general meetings;
■ dividends.

### 2.1 Model Articles

Model Articles have been created under the powers of the CA 2006, which apply to companies incorporated on or after 1 October 2009. Different Model Articles have been created for private companies and public companies. The Model Articles for private and public companies are included in this text as Appendices 1 and 2. Model Articles have also been created for private companies limited by guarantee. Companies limited by guarantee usually adopt byelaws in addition to the Articles. This is essential where companies limited by guarantee operate a membership separate from their shareholders or guarantors.

The Model Articles do not apply to companies incorporated prior to 1 October 2009 unless those companies choose to adopt some or all of the new Model Articles' provisions. Hence companies incorporated prior to 1 October 2009 are able to retain their existing Articles or adopt some or all of the Model Articles.

If a company is incorporated without Articles (see Chapter 4), the Model Articles will apply by default. If the company is incorporated and the Articles registered do not modify or exclude the Model Articles, relevant parts of the Model Articles shall apply to the extent applicable. Companies being incorporated which do not want the new Model Articles to apply should therefore register a full set of Articles and expressly state in the Articles that the Model Articles shall be excluded in their entirety.

---

**STOP AND THINK 5.1**

Consider the Model Articles as the foundation for all company Articles going forward. As a good company secretary you will have a detailed working knowledge of the Model Articles and will find that, even when a company has modified its Articles, many original features of the Model Articles remain. The Model Articles must therefore be read in their entirety.

## 2.2 The legal effect of the Articles

A company's Articles of Association form a key part of the company's constitution (see section 4 below). CA 2006, s. 33 states that the company's constitution binds the company and its members as though they had individually covenanted to obey their provisions. Evidence of this can be found on share certificates, which state that the shareholder is a member subject either to the Memorandum and Articles of the company or to the constitution of the company. This has achieved the following results:

1 The company is bound to its members according to the terms in the Articles.

---

**CASE LAW** **5.1**

**Salmon v Quin & Axtens Limited (1909) 1 Ch 311**

The Articles provided that although the general management of the company was under the control of the directors, no resolution could be passed by them for acquiring or letting premises without the express consent of Salmon, the managing director. A resolution was passed by the directors for acquiring or letting premises in circumstances where Salmon expressly dissented. It was held that Salmon could obtain an injunction to restrain the company from acting in breach of this Article.

---

2 The members are bound to the company according to the terms in the Articles.

---

**CASE LAW** **5.2**

**Hickman v Kent or Romney Marsh Sheepbreeders Association (1915) 1 Ch 881**

The Articles contained a clause stating that in the event of a dispute between a member and the Association, the dispute was to be settled by reference to arbitration. Hickman was expelled by the Association and went to court. Hickman failed. It was held that the Articles were to be treated as a contract between company and member. Hickman should have gone to arbitration and accepted the decision of the arbitrator.

---

3 The members are bound to each other according to the terms in the Articles.

---

**CASE LAW** **5.3**

**Rayfield v Hands (1960) Ch 1**

An article of the company provided that every member who intended to transfer shares should inform the directors, who would take the said shares equally between them at fair value. A member informed the directors that he wished to transfer his shares, but they refused to buy them. It was held that the Article created an obligation on the directors as members to take the shares and the member wishing to leave the company could force the directors to acquire them.

---

4  But, the company is not bound to any person except in that person's capacity as a member.

---

**CASE LAW** **5.4**

***Eley v Positive Life Assurance Co. Limited* (1876) 1 Ex D 20**

An Article of the company stated that Eley should be the solicitor to the company for life. He bought shares in the company. Subsequently, the company disposed of his services. Eley sued for breach of contract. It was held that his action must fail since the Article gave rights to him in a capacity other than as a member of the company. In other words, they gave him the right as legal adviser. The court said that the Articles only gave rights to members in their capacity as members.

---

## 2.3 Format

CA 2006, s. 18 specifies the format the Articles of Association should take. It must be printed, contained in a single document, divided into paragraphs, numbered consecutively and dated.

## 3  Alteration of the Articles

A company may at any time alter all or any of the provisions contained in its Articles by special resolution (CA 2006, s. 21). No reason needs to be given and any alterations are deemed to be as valid as if they had been contained in the original Articles. When altered, a copy of the amended Articles, together with a printed copy of the special resolution, must be delivered to the Registrar of Companies (see below).

The following rules apply:

- The alteration must be for the benefit of the company as a whole (*Shuttleworth v Cox*, 1927; *Sidebottom v Kershaw Leese & Co. Ltd*, 1920).
- The alteration may be retrospective (*Allen v Gold Reefs of West Africa Ltd*, 1900).
- There must be no infringement of minority rights under CA 2006, s. 994.
- If there are different classes of shares, CA 2006 s. 630 must be followed. Essentially, the consent of the majority is required either by 75% in value in writing or a special resolution passed at a general meeting of holders of the minority class.

---

**CASE LAW** **5.5**

***Sidebottom v Kershaw Leese & Co. Ltd*, 1920**

A proposed alteration of the Articles would have allowed the directors to expropriate the shares of any member who carried on a competing business. It was held that such an alteration was valid as being genuinely for the protection of the company.

---

## 3.1 Entrenched Articles

It is possible, with unanimous shareholder approval, for any company to incorporate conditions within Articles which must be met before particular Article changes can be made. These is referred to in CA 2006, s. 22 as 'entrenched' Articles. Such conditions could include, for example, that a higher level of shareholder approval (more than the 75% needed for a special resolution) is required prior to the approval of a certain Article changes. Articles which have been entrenched in this way may be subsequently amended by unanimous shareholder approval or by Court Order (CA 2006, s. 22).

It is also possible to protect class rights from being varied by utilising these entrenchment provisions (see Chapter 12, Classes of share and share rights).

In respect of companies incorporated under CA 1985, any provision which was previously entrenched in the Memorandum and which subsequently moves to the Articles will remain entrenched. Such entrenched Articles can only be amended by a court order.

## CHECKLIST 5.1 **Alteration of articles**

✓ The board resolves to amend the Articles.

✓ They must convene a general meeting (or wait until the next AGM or circulate a written resolution if it is a private company) to consider the necessary special resolution, approve a circular to members explaining the proposed alteration and include it with the notice of the meeting. If it is proposed to adopt new Articles, the circular should summarise the main provisions of the new Articles and state that a copy of the proposed Articles is available for inspection at the company's registered office or at the company's solicitors[1] and at the general meeting.

✓ A proxy form should be sent with the notice of meeting.

✓ As Articles are changed by special resolution, all amendments in wording should be included in the resolution (see Sample Wording 5.1), although where a number of amendments dealing with separate matters are proposed it may be more practical to prepare individual resolutions to cover each alteration so that shareholders can consider each matter separately and vote accordingly.

✓ If a significant proportion of the shares are held by institutional holders, it would be prudent to obtain confirmation that the proposed new Articles are acceptable. This can be relevant where the changes proposed require greater involvement of the shareholders, for example as part of the company's corporate governance strategy.

✓ A certified copy of the resolution, with a verified copy of the Articles as amended or a certified copy of the new Articles, must be sent to the Registrar within 15 days of the resolution being passed (CA 2006, s. 30).

✓ If the company is listed, two copies of the resolution should be sent to UKLA.

✓ If the company is listed and an altered copy of the Articles is sent to the Registrar, two copies should also be sent to UKLA.

### Note

1   Provided that the circular, proposed Articles, notice of meeting and proxy comply with the UK Listing Rules, there is no need to submit them in draft for approval to UKLA. However, if the proposals contain any unusual features, the documents will have to be submitted in draft for approval.

---

**SAMPLE WORDING 5.1**

**Special resolution to alter Articles of Association**

THAT the Articles of Association of the company be altered as follows: by deleting in article ..............the words '....................';

by substituting for the existing article .................... the following article: '...........................'; and

by deleting in article ............. the words '............' and substituting therefore the words '.................'.

---

**SAMPLE WORDING 5.2**

**Special resolution to adopt new Articles**

THAT the regulations contained in the [printed] document [marked 'B'] submitted to this meeting and, for the purpose of identification, signed by the chairman hereof be approved and adopted as the Articles of Association of the company in substitution for and to the exclusion of all the existing Articles thereof.

---

**TEST YOUR KNOWLEDGE 5.2**

**a**  If a company is registered without Articles of Association these must be drafted after receiving the certificate of incorporation. True or false? Why?

**b**  What is the legal effect of the Articles?

**c**  In *Sidebottom v Kershaw Leese & Co.* the alteration of the Articles did not benefit one shareholder, but was approved by the court. Briefly why?

**d**  Who should receive copies of revised Articles after they have been altered?

---

# 4  Other elements of a company's constitution, registered office address and company name

## 4.1 Constitution

CA 2006, s. 17 defines a company's constitution to include the company's Articles, and any resolutions and agreements to which CA 2006, s. 29 applies. Section 29 outlines the resolutions and agreements affecting a company's resolution, which are generally:

■ any special resolution;

■ any resolution or agreement agreed to by all the members of a company that, if not so agreed to, would not have been effective for its purpose unless passed as a special resolution; and

■ any resolution or agreement that effectively binds all the members of a class of shareholders if it has not been agreed to by all those members.

CA 2006, s. 30 requires each such resolution or agreement to be filed with the Registrar of Companies within 15 days after it is passed or made.

## 4.2 Change of registered office

Any change to the registered office is made by resolution of the directors (see Sample Wording 5.1). By CA 2006, ss. 86–87 it is not necessary to obtain shareholder approval in respect of a change of registered office. The registered office must be situated in the country within which the company was incorporated. Thus a company registered in England and Wales may not change its registered office to an address in Scotland.

---

**SAMPLE WORDING 5.3**

**Board resolution for change of registered office of a company**

THAT the situation of the registered office of the company be changed from

. . . . . . . . . . . . . . . . . . . . . . . . to . . . . . . . . . . . . . . . . . . . . . . .

---

If a company is unavoidably forced to change its registered office and it was impracticable to give the required 14 days' notice, provided it continues operating at other premises as soon as is practicable and gives notice to the Registrar within 14 days of resuming business, it will not be penalised for failure to comply.

## CHECKLIST 5.2  Change of registered office

✓ The board resolves to change registered office address (see Sample Wording 5.1) within the same country of jurisdiction.
✓ Notify the change of registered office address to the Registrar on form AD01. The change will not be effective until registered. During the 14 days beginning with the date on which the change is registered a person may validly serve any document on the company at either registered office. The company secretary will therefore need to ensure that he is able to collect post from both addresses during that period.
✓ Amend company headed stationery and ensure the new details are included on all electronic forms of communication (faxes, emails and the company's website(s)). Signage should be placed outside the new registered office (and removed from the old) within 14 days of the change. The company secretary should ensure that old stationery is destroyed.
✓ Notify the company's tax office, bank, auditors, solicitors, customers and suppliers. If the company is listed, it should also inform UKLA. It may be appropriate to inform the company's shareholders.
✓ Make arrangements with the postal authorities and, if possible, with the occupiers of the old property to ensure that any mail sent to the old address is forwarded to the new address.

## 4.3  Change of company name

A special resolution (see Chapter 9) is required to change a company's name (CA 2006, ss. 77–78). The change takes effect from the date of issue by the Registrar of a certificate of incorporation on change of name. The special resolution to change the company's name should be filed at Companies House within 15 days after the date it was passed. CA 2006, s. 79 also provides for a company's Articles to allow a change of name without a special resolution. Under CA 2006, ss. 77–79, companies may also prescribe in their Articles the manner in which the company name may be changed. The change may be accomplished, for example, by resolution of the directors. Notification must be given to the Registrar of the change of name, together with a statement that the change has been effected pursuant to powers in the company's Articles.

After the change of name takes effect, a listed company is required by the Listing Rules to make a regulatory announcement to the London Stock Exchange without delay notifying the change and stating the date on which it has taken effect. It must also inform UKLA in writing on receipt of the change of name certificate issued by Companies House, enclosing a copy of that document.

During company reorganisations it often happens that companies swap their names simultaneously. This can be achieved by writing an explanatory letter to the Registrar enclosing the respective special resolutions.

It is often desirable to plan that the change of name takes effect from a future date to give the company time to prepare and make the necessary arrangements. In this case, the best solution is to use the same-day name change facility.

## CHECKLIST 5.3  Change of company name

✓ Check that the new name is available for use or whether permission must be sought before use (see Chapter 4).
✓ The directors resolve to convene a general meeting (or circulate a written resolution if it is a private limited company) to consider the necessary special resolution to change the name unless the resolution is to be taken as special business at an AGM.

In accordance with Section 87 of the Companies Act 2006.

# AD01
## Change of registered office address

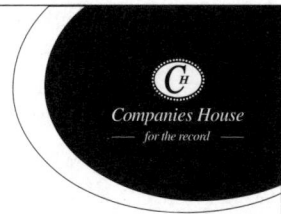

Companies House
*for the record*

**You can use the WebFiling service to file this form online.**
Please go to www.companieshouse.gov.uk

✓ **What this form is for**
You may use this form to change a company's registered office address.

✗ **What this form is NOT for**
You cannot use this form to change the registered office address of a Limited Liability Partnership (LLP). To do this, please use form LL AD01's Change of registered office address of a limited liability partnership (LLP).

For further information, please refer to our guidance at www.companieshouse.gov.uk

---

**1** **Company details**

Company number [ ][ ][ ][ ][ ][ ][ ][ ]

Company name in full

→ **Filling in this form**
Please complete in typescript or in bold black capitals.

All fields are mandatory unless specified or indicated by *

---

**2** **New registered office address ❶**

The change in registered office address does not take effect until the Registrar has registered this notice.

A person may validly serve any document on the company at its previous registered office for 14 days from the date that a change of registered office is registered.

Building name/number

Street

Post town

County/Region

Postcode [ ][ ][ ][ ][ ][ ]

❶ **Change of registered office**
For England and Wales companies, the address provided can either be in England or Wales.

For Welsh companies, the address provided must be in Wales.

For companies registered in Scotland or Northern Ireland, the address provided must be in Scotland or Northern Ireland respectively.

---

**3** **Signature**

I am signing this form on behalf of the company.

Signature

Signature
X

X

This form may be signed by:
Director ❷, Secretary, Person Authorised ❸, Liquidator, Administrator, Administrative receiver, Receiver, Receiver manager, Charity commission receiver and manager, CIC manager, Judicial factor.

❷ **Societas Europaea**
If the form is being filed on behalf of a Societas Europaea (SE), please delete 'director' and insert details of which organ of the SE the person signing has membership.

❸ **Person authorised**
Under either section 270 or 274 of the Companies Act 2006.

---

**BIS** | Department for Business Innovation & Skills

CHFP000
05/10 Version 4.0

✓ The directors approve a circular to members, which explains the reasons for the proposed change of name and includes notice of the general meeting. If the resolution is to be considered at an AGM, the explanation may be included in the directors' report or as a note in the notice of the AGM.

✓ A proxy form should be sent with the notice of meeting.

✓ If the company is listed, when the final documents are posted, two copies each of the notice, any related circular and the proxy card should be sent to UKLA.

✓ If passed, file a copy of the special resolution certified by the chairman or company secretary with the Registrar of Companies within 15 days (CA 2006, s. 30) with the appropriate fee (see below). If the company is listed, two copies of the special resolution should also be sent to UKLA.

✓ A new certificate of incorporation on change of name will be issued showing the effective date of the change (a sample is given below).

✓ Change the name displayed outside the registered office and other places of business, and elsewhere, such as on email addresses or packaging.

✓ Reprint company stationery, including company cheques. Destroy obsolete stationery.

✓ Ensure the change is made to all forms of electronic communication such as faxes, emails and the company's website(s).

✓ Attach a copy of the special resolution to all copies of the Articles.

✓ It is not necessary to file a new copy of the Articles with the Registrar, but people known to hold copies of the Articles, such as directors or the company's professional advisers, should be sent a copy of the special resolution.

✓ If required, a new common seal (and if necessary a new securities seal) should be obtained and submitted for adoption by the directors at a board meeting. The previous seal(s) should be destroyed.

✓ Any stock of the previous version of the Articles should be destroyed.

## Same-day service (name swap)

At the opening of business on the day that the name change is to take effect, which, under CA, 2006 s. 30, is within 15 days of the special resolution being passed (see above), the following should be delivered to Companies House or to one of its satellite offices:

■ a certified copy of the special resolution of the change of name to enable a 'name swap' to be processed;

■ a certified copy of a change of name special resolution by the company that has provided the new name, changing its name to another name;

■ if approval of the name has already been obtained, a copy of the Companies House approval;

■ a remittance for two sets of fees payable to Companies House for the fees for two same-day changes of name. Companies House will expect the change of name certificate to be collected on issue, unless it is made clear in a covering letter from the company that the certificate is to be sent by post.

Provided that the documents listed above are lodged by 3 pm, the Registrar will issue a certificate of incorporation on change of name on the same day, and the change of name will have legal effect from the date of the certificate.

The envelope should be marked for the attention of 'SAME-DAY SERVICE', making it clear in the covering letter that same-day name changes are required. Fees for a same-day service are higher than the standard service (see the Companies House website).

> **STOP AND THINK 5.2**
>
> In large organisations, planning a change of name is a considerable undertaking, requiring months of planning. The company secretary will need to work closely with the company's corporate communications department to ensure the design of any new stationery and signage meets the statutory requirements.

**COMPANIES ACT 2006**
**SPECIAL RESOLUTION ON CHANGE OF NAME**

**Company number:** _____

**Existing company name:** _____

**At an Annual General Meeting\* / General meeting\*** (\*delete as appropriate)
**of the members of the above named company, duly convened and held at:**

_____

_____

**On the** _____ **day of** _____ **20**_____

**That the name of the company be changed to:**

**New name:** _____

**Signed:** _____
\*Director / secretary / CIC Manager (if appropriate) / administrator / administrative receiver / receiver manager / receiver, on behalf of the company.
(\*delete as appropriate)

Notes:

- This form is for use by PLC's or private companies who choose to hold Annual General Meetings or general meetings for the purpose of a special resolution.

- A copy of the resolution must be delivered to Companies House within 15 days of it being passed.

- A fee of £10 is required to change the name (cheques made payable to "Companies House").

- Have you checked whether the name is available at www.companieshouse.gov.uk ?

- Please provide the name and address to which the certificate is to be sent.

# CERTIFICATE OF INCORPORATION

# ON CHANGE OF NAME

## Company No. 1234567

The Registrar of Companies for England and Wales hereby certifies that

having by special resolution changed its name, is now incorporated

under the name of

SPECIMEN

Given at Companies House, Cardiff, the [date]

THE OFFICIAL SEAL OF THE
REGISTRAR OF COMPANIES

*Companies House*
— *for the record* —

---

🖊 **TEST YOUR KNOWLEDGE** **5.3**

**a** Does the change in registered office require shareholder approval?

**b** Which document must be filed with the Registrar of Companies in respect of a change of registered office? What is the significance of the 14-day period following such a filing?

**c** What is the procedure in respect of a same-day change of company name?

---

## CASE QUESTION

As company secretary of Multiple plc, you and your team act as secretary to many different subsidiary companies. Some of the companies may have joined the Multiple group following an acquisition and some of them were incorporated prior to 1 October 2009 and some after. What considerations are there for or against:

■ amending the Articles of all the subsidiary companies to make them consistent?

■ amending the registered offices of all the subsidiary companies to the same address?

Are there any restrictions to this and if so how would such restrictions be overcome?

The Business Development Director of Multiple plc is considering the formation of a new company in order to support a new business venture. One of the considerations is whether the new company should be a private company limited by shares or a public company. Explain the main differences between the Model Articles for a private company limited by shares and a public company.

## CHAPTER SUMMARY

■ The Memorandum sets out the details of the subscribers and their intent to form a company.

■ With the exception of an SE, a company cannot change its domicile once registered.

■ A change of registered office does not require shareholder approval; a resolution of the board will suffice.

■ The Articles are the regulations governing a company's internal management, covering matters such as the rights of shareholders, the appointment of directors and the conduct of board meetings. Resolutions and other agreements may also form part of the company's constitution.

■ Model Articles are default Articles for companies incorporated after 1 October 2009. Companies incorporated before that time may be operating with default Articles under prior legislation. Many companies have updated their Articles to reflect the Model Articles or to suit their particular business need. You should take time to familiarise yourself with the new Model Articles.

■ The Articles are treated as a covenant between the company and its members.

■ The Articles bind the members to each other according to the terms in the Articles. But the Articles do not bind a person in any other capacity, except as a member.

■ Alteration of the Articles is by special resolution.

■ It is the secretary's responsibility to ensure that all practical matters concerning alterations to the Articles are managed in a timely, professional and effective manner. The secretary is responsible for providing amended Articles to the Registrar, other required recipients (including any copy on the website) and for maintaining the company's stock supply of Articles.

# 6 Regulation of listed companies

## ■ CONTENTS

## ■ INTRODUCTION

This chapter introduces the FSA, the competent authority which has the power and responsibility to regulate the financial services industry in the UK. We look at the rules governing admission of securities – all types of stocks and shares – to the Official List, the UK market for the largest quoted companies and the regulations (the continuing obligations) governing securities once they have been admitted for trading. The chapter also covers trading on the AIM. Other sections cover the controls and regulations concerning takeovers and mergers, including the City Code on Takeovers and Mergers and the Competition Commission. The role of the Registrar in takeovers and mergers is also covered.

The FSA website (see Directory) contains extensive information about its role and activities, including the Listing Rules, the Prospectus Rules and the DTRs and practical guidance notes.

## 1 Regulating listed companies

The FSMA 2000 provides the framework for the regulation of the financial services industry in the UK. It establishes the FSA as the UK's financial services regulator, with power to issue rules and guidance across the financial services industry. The FSA acting as the competent authority for listing is referred to as the UKLA, which regulates, through the Listing Rules, DTRs and Prospectus Rules (see below) the admission of securities to the UK **Official List** and the **continuing obligations** on companies once they are listed.

The FSA has power to impose unlimited civil penalties on companies and directors of listed companies for breaches of the applicable rules. The FSA is not a government department, but its powers extend to the right to take investment businesses to court and carry out criminal prosecutions. It also has the ultimate sanction of withdrawal of authorisation.

As the statutory body for authorising investment business in the UK, the FSA is also responsible for approving the various financial markets. Recognition as a RIE or clearing house enables the body concerned to operate in the UK. In order to become and remain recognised, certain requirements must be met covering the maintenance of appropriate financial resources, proper monitoring and enforcement, and the promotion and maintenance of standards and safeguards for investors.

In addition to the Listing Rules, DTRs and Prospectus Rules, a company whose securities are traded on the Stock Exchange must comply with the Stock Exchange's Admission and Disclosure Standards.

As well as the compliance aspects for companies whose securities are traded on the Stock Exchange, the importance of disclosure cannot be underestimated. Confidence in the stock market is focused on the prompt release of accurate and comprehensive information about each company. Any information released must be prepared to a high standard and must first be released through certain channels. The company secretary often plays a pivotal role in ensuring such information is accurate and is released promptly through the right channel. Hence, the company secretary plays an important part in ensuring good disclosure and helping to maintain market confidence.

## 2 The role of the stock exchange

The role of a stock exchange is to provide a regulated **primary market** and **secondary market** for **securities**. The largest stock exchange in the UK for securities is the London Stock Exchange and the main markets are as follows:

■ *UK and foreign company shares* – The Stock Exchange operates three markets for securities:
   a) the Official List for large established companies;
   b) AIM for new companies, smaller companies and companies not eligible for the Official List;
   c) **techMARK** for innovative technology companies. techMARK has its own performance index. Companies may be on both the Official List and techMARK.
■ *Government stocks (gilts)* – Gilt-edged securities form a separate market and are interest-bearing bonds issued by the Bank of England in return for a loan of money from investors.
■ *Options* – These are options (i.e. the right to acquire or sell shares in the future at a particular price or by reference to a particular price formula) for shares and are traded in much the same way as shares are bought and sold.

The London Stock Exchange does not have an exclusive right as a market for securities. Other organisations (e.g. PLUS Markets) (see Directory) may provide competing stock exchanges, provided they meet the requirements set out by the FSA.

### 2.1 The stock exchange as a primary market

The new issue (primary) market is used by companies and public bodies for raising capital (cash) by issuing securities (shares). This method of bringing securities to the market is sometimes referred to an initial public offering. Capital raised may be used to fund the issuer's own ongoing business or as consideration for the purchase of another business.

As a primary market, stock exchanges are subject to a number of safeguards, and companies seeking admission have to demonstrate the soundness of their business and its future to convince **sponsors** to act on their behalf.

There are several methods by which securities can be brought to the market:

■ **Offers for sale or subscription** – The company issues a prospectus inviting investors to apply for shares. An offer for sale relates to new or existing securities first acquired by an issuing house and then offered to the public. An offer for subscription is in the form of new securities issued directly to the applicants by the company.
■ **Placings** – Securities purchased by the issuing house are placed with investment clients with possibly a small proportion being sold through the market.
■ *Intermediaries offers* – Shares passed mainly to private client investors, who then allocate the securities to their own clients.
■ **Vendor consideration issue or vendor placing** – A company acquiring a business can issue securities to the vendor instead of, or in addition to, cash. This is sometimes referred to as a vendor placing. It is not uncommon for the vendor to sell all the shares immediately or to sell the shares in tranches in accordance with the terms of an agreement to sell the business.
■ *Rights issues* – A company offers new shares to its existing shareholders in proportion to the number of shares they already hold.
■ **Open offers** – The same as a rights issue, but the benefit of the rights cannot be traded.

- *Capitalisation (bonus) issues* – Fully paid shares are allotted for no payment to existing shareholders in proportion to their holdings. As the shares are allotted for no payment this method of issuing securities will not raise any capital.
- *Exchanges and conversions* – New securities are listed as a result of existing securities being exchanged or converted into new ones.
- *Exercise of options or warrants* – Rights for the holder to subscribe cash for further securities which are issued when the rights are exercised.
- *Other issues* – Anything apart from the above so long as the relevant conditions are fulfilled, for example, shares issued under employee share schemes.

## 2.2 The London Stock Exchange as a secondary market

The London Stock Exchange operates the following services to facilitate trading:

### SETS (Stock Exchange Electronic Trading Service)

SETS provides member firms with electronic trading for securities via an electronic order book. This allows buyers and sellers to be matched and for the trade to be executed automatically, thus improving the liquidity of the company's shares. Access to SETS is generally restricted to member firms, all of whom must abide by the rules of the Stock Exchange. Unmatched orders are retained on the order book for future execution or returned to the originating member firm. The largest companies or companies with the most liquid stocks (i.e. companies with the highest volume of shares traded), including FTSE 100 and FTSE 250 securities, are traded on SETS, along with some UK listed Irish securities.

### SETSqx (Stock Exchange Electronic Trading Service – quotes and crosses)

SETSqx is a trading platform for securities less liquid than those traded on SETS. SETSqx combines a periodic electronic auction book with stand-alone quote driven market making.

### SEAQ (Stock Exchange Automated Quotation)/SEATSplus (Stock Exchange Alternative Trading Service)

This provides support for trading in the remainder of the UK market (see section 5).

---

**TEST YOUR KNOWLEDGE 6.1**

a  What is the role of the FSA?
b  What is the role of the London Stock Exchange?
c  In what way is an offer for sale different from an offer for subscription?
d  What is the difference between a placing and a vendor consideration issue?
e  On which London Stock Exchange services are FTSE250 shares usually traded?

---

# 3  The UK Listing Regime

## 3.1 Introduction

**Listed companies** and companies applying for listing must comply with the Listing Regime established by the UKLA. The various sets of rules contain the requirements and procedures for listing the securities on the market, the continuing obligations while the securities are listed and the circumstances giving rise to suspension of the listing.

In applying the rules, the authority has regard to the following objectives and principles:

- to seek a balance between ready access to the market and protection for investors;
- to promote standards of disclosure that will give confidence to investors and the market as a whole;

- to facilitate an open and efficient market for trading in a number of securities;
- to ensure full and timely disclosure about its listed securities;
- to give holders of securities enough time to consider any changes in the company's business operations or matters concerning the company's management and constitution.

UKLA provides additional guidance materials and support which help company secretaries, directors and financial institutions to ensure they comply with the plethora of regulations. These include:

- a comprehensive website (see Directory), which includes the Listing Rules, DTRs and Prospectus Rules, as well as recent press releases from UKLA; it is also possible to register to receive regular news updates via email;
- a Model Code on which companies can base their internal procedures to prevent directors and certain other employees from abusing their position in the purchase and sale of securities (see section 7.3);
- dedicated telephone helplines;
- templates for announcements which must be made to the market; this helps to ensure that all required information is included in announcements;
- a free newsletter, *Primary Market Bulletin*, available via email.

The listing regime is centred on three rules:

1 *The Listing Rules* – These include guidance on continuing obligations, Listing Principles, the Model Code and the listing application process (see sections 4.1 and 7.3).
2 *The Disclosure and Transparency Rules* – The DTRs implement the provisions of EU legislation contained in the Market Abuse Directive and govern the disclosure of price-sensitive information and information regarding dealings by persons exercising managerial responsibilities for companies trading on a regulated market. They also implement the Transparency Obligations Directive, which covers financial reporting, notifications of major interests in voting rights and some continuing obligations, several of which were previously in the Listing Rules.
3 *The Prospectus Rules* – These implement the provisions of EU legislation contained in the Prospectus Directive. The Prospectus Rules provide guidance on:
   - when a company is required to produce a prospectus;
   - the format and contents of a prospectus;
   - the process for submitting a prospectus (and related documents) to the FSA for approval;
   - a requirement for companies to produce an 'annual information update' (see section 3.4).

## 3.2 Conditions for listing

Companies will first need to consider the advantages and disadvantages of seeking a listing. These can be summarised as:

### Advantages
- access to a refined and regulated world-class stock market;
- the prestige of having a full listing;
- considerable ability to raise finance through debt and equity.

### Disadvantages
- the costs of maintaining a listing, such as listing fees;
- additional employment resource to meet continuing obligations;
- many additional disclosure requirements, e.g. directors' remuneration report, more detail in the business review, and so on;
- management time and effort in satisfying best practice for corporate governance, for example, the UK Corporate Governance Code.

The requirements for the admission of securities to listing come from FSMA, which also provides for UKLA to modify the requirements. The main criteria are:

- The company must be duly incorporated and acting in accordance with its Articles of Association.
- Companies wanting a full listing must, in most circumstances, have filed audited accounts for the last three years.
- At least 75% of the business must be supported by an historic revenue-earning record that covers the period for which accounts are required (i.e. usually the last three years).
- The current key executives must have played a significant role in the company's activities.
- The company must be capable of making decisions independently of any controlling shareholder.
- The shares must be freely transferable. This is necessary to encourage the liquidity of the shares.
- The first shares to be listed must have an aggregated market value of at least £700,000 capital (or £200,000 for debt securities).
- At least 25% of the company's share capital must be in public hands. This will assist in the creation of an open market for the shares.
- The shares must be eligible for electronic settlement (i.e. CREST; see Chapter 13).
- The company must be a public limited company.

## 3.3 The listing process

The decision to seek a listing may follow years of gradual preparation or can be undertaken very rapidly (e.g. within a few weeks of the company beginning to trade). Before a company can be listed, it must produce a **prospectus**, which must be approved by the FSA. This will be developed with the professional advisers appointed to assist with the issue. A certain amount of 'housekeeping' may also be required, such as the appointment of NEDs or the adoption of new Articles.

### Professional advisers

Every company wishing to have its securities listed must appoint a sponsor to submit its application, lodge the supporting documents and act as a channel for discussion between the company or its advisers and UKLA. Their role includes sponsoring capital issues and the sale of securities to the public generally. They will advise on the form that the issue should take, timing, any capital reorganisation that may be required and the issue price. Together with the directors, they will also be responsible for the accuracy of the information provided in the prospectus. The sponsors will therefore need access to company records and will need to have extensive discussions with the company's directors, company secretary and senior managers.

The prospectus must contain specific financial information, so a firm of accountants must be appointed to report jointly to the sponsor and the company. Solicitors specialising in new issues should also be involved. They will cooperate with the company's usual solicitor in preparing issue documents.

A company coming to market for the first time may also want to appoint a number of other advisers, including public relations consultants, registrars and a receiving agent, often the new issues arm of the company's registrar. Their role is to process applications and payments, report the results to the company and then act accordingly regarding the issue of allotment letters and share certificates (see Chapter 12).

Once the company has resolved to go ahead with a listing or a new issue, all the principal financial and legal advisers – usually the chairman, chief executive, finance director and company secretary – will meet with the company's representatives. They will decide:

- the amount and nature of the capital to be issued;
- the approximate price (subject to final pricing immediately before trading begins);
- the issue structure;
- fees and commissions to be paid;
- timing.

### The prospectus

The prospectus contains information about the company and its shares, which will enable prospective investors to judge the issue. The solicitors or sponsors will prepare the first draft of the prospectus for agreement by the company. All parties involved in the issue should be satisfied that the information is complete and gives an accurate report of the company, its history and future plans. A prospectus should follow a set format, which is prescribed in great detail in the Prospectus Rules. The content of a prospectus includes:

- details of the persons responsible for the prospectus, the auditors and other advisers;
- the types of share;
- the issuer and its capital;
- a description of the group's activities;
- the issuer's assets and liabilities, financial position, including its working capital and profits and losses;
- the management;
- the recent development of, and prospects for, the group, including any risks.

Certain information may also be included by way of incorporation by reference. This applies only to information already approved by the FSA or notified to it in accordance with the Prospectus Rules. The company may therefore simply refer to the information which has been filed with the FSA instead of setting it out again in the prospectus.

Under the Prospectus Rules, a prospectus may be prepared in one of two ways:

1 as a single document; or
2 as a three-part document consisting of a registration document, securities note and a summary.

The registration document contains information about the company and, once lodged with the FSA, is valid for twelve months. The securities note contains information about the shares of the company to be offered and admitted to the Official List. The summary provides key information about the company, the shares to be offered and any associated risks. If the company wishes to issue new securities (which would normally require the publication of a full prospectus) during the life of the registration document, it needs only to update and publish its securities note and summary. This saves time and cost.

It is essential that confidentiality is maintained in the preparation of the prospectus. Key details, such as profit forecasts and proposed issue price, should be omitted from drafts for as long as is practicable to avoid the risk of sensitive information leaking. If the application is for a new issue, an application form for investors should be included in each copy of the prospectus, with a closing date for receipt of applications. Once the receiving agent has processed the applications, the allotment committee, comprising representatives of the company, the sponsor and the broker, must decide the basis of allotment (see issue price below).

## The application

In order to become a listed company, several documents, as prescribed in the Listing Rules, must be submitted. Applications must be made in respect of:

- UKLA – to have the securities admitted to the Official List; and
- the London Stock Exchange – to have the securities admitted to trading.

Before submitting any of the required documents, an applicant should contact the FSA to agree the date on which the FSA will consider the application.

On the penultimate day before listing, a board meeting is held to approve all the documentation (the '48-hour documents') and to give the go-ahead for the applications to be made. The following are the key documents, which must be submitted to the FSA by midday two business days before the FSA is to consider the application:

- a completed application for admission of securities to the Official List;
- a standard application to the London Stock Exchange for the securities to be admitted for trading. This should be sent to the London Stock Exchange on a provisional basis at least ten business days prior to consideration of the application for admission to trading;
- a prospectus;
- any circular that has been published in connection with the application;
- a copy of the resolution of the board allotting the securities. If necessary, the company should have already obtained shareholder approval for any allotment.

Once the documents have been submitted, the FSA will review them and may raise queries or ask for additional documents. A completed shareholder statement signed by a sponsor, using the prescribed FSA form, must also be submitted to the FSA by 9.00 am on the day the FSA is to consider the application. The admission to the Official List becomes effective when the FSA's decision to admit the securities to listing has been announced through a RIS.

The following documents must be submitted to the FSA as soon as practicable after the FSA has considered the application:

■ a statement of the number of securities that were issued; and
■ a completed issuer's declaration, using the prescribed FSA form.

The applicant company must also pay listing fees.

After a prospectus is approved for release by the FSA, it must be filed with the FSA and made available to the public in accordance with the Prospectus Rules, which provide that it is published:

■ in one or more widely circulated newspapers (e.g. a national newspaper); or
■ in a printed form available from the company or their agent; or
■ on the company's website or the London Stock Exchange's website.

## The issue price

One of the major considerations is the issue price of new securities and the manner in which the price is to be fixed and paid. While companies and their advisers will have a reasonable idea of what issue price they can expect, it cannot be fixed until just before the issue because it has to reflect prevailing market conditions.

If the price set is too low, the issue will be oversubscribed and the company will obtain less than the full value of its shares; if the price is too high, there will be insufficient applications and a number of shares will be subject to **underwriting**. To err on the side of too low a price is preferable, provided it is only a modest margin, as a low take-up could cause problems for the underwriter and also adversely affect the public's appetite for the company's securities in the future.

In an offer for subscription or offer for sale, the issue price is fixed. All successful applicants pay the same. If the issue or offer is oversubscribed, some or all allotments may be reduced so that some or all applicants will be allotted fewer shares than they applied and paid for, and some applications may be rejected altogether. Application monies in excess of the amount required to satisfy allotments are returned.

As an alternative to an issue at a fixed price, applicants may be required to tender at a price at or above a stated minimum. The securities applied for will then be allotted at a 'striking price' agreed by the issuer and its advisers – usually a price that ensures full subscription on the basis that no applicant pays more than the price at which he tendered, and all pay the same price.

The main underwriter (usually the company's merchant bank) must agree in writing to purchase any securities that are not subscribed for and to pay the fixed issue price for those shares. There will be an underwriting fee of around 2.25% of the issue value and the underwriter may also offset his risk by sub-underwriting with a number of banks and pension funds. Underwriting provides assurance for the issuer that the issue of shares will be fully subscribed; this is especially important where the issuer has to raise a specific amount of capital for a particular purpose.

## 3.4 Annual information updates

Under the Prospectus Rules, each year a listed company must prepare an **annual information update**. Essentially, this refers to or contains all information that has been released by the listed company to a RIS or otherwise made public pursuant to the Companies Acts over the previous twelve months. It is, therefore, necessary to include filings with the Registrar of Companies. If the annual information update refers to the information (rather than containing it), it must give a short description of the nature of that information and must also state where the information can be obtained. A company must file the annual information update with the FSA by releasing it to a RIS within 20 working days after the publication of its annual report and accounts.

---

**STOP AND THINK 6.1**

Many listed companies will make the company secretary responsible for preparing the annual information update. It is essential, therefore, that the company secretary maintains an adequate system for the full and accurate record of all information released and made public by the company.

---

## 3.5 Premium and standard listings

Following a review of the listing regime in 2010, the FSA amended the listing regime, introducing the concept of companies having securities (e.g. shares) with a 'premium' listing or a 'standard' listing on the London Stock Exchange. The main purpose of the review was to ensure the listing regime's structure and responsibilities of listed companies was clear. In summary, a premium listing is only open to equity shares that are issued by commercial companies. A listed company holding a premium listing is subject to 'super-equivalent' provisions, which are higher standards than the EU regulatory requirements in respect of governance and disclosure. If the securities of a company do not meet the criteria for a premium listing, it must be designated as a standard listing. The securities of each company must be described as either premium or standard so that any third party will know to which standard the securities meets.

---

**TEST YOUR KNOWLEDGE 6.2**

a  What conditions does a company have to meet to be admitted on the Official List?
b  Who are the main advisers on an issue?
c  What is a sponsor?
d  What is a prospectus and what should it contain?
e  Identify the '48-hour' documents.
f  What is the annual information update?

---

# 4  Continuing obligations and key disclosure requirements

Continuing obligations is the term used for the regulations and obligations with which a listed company must comply following admission of its securities to the Official List. The continuing obligations are set out in the Listing Rules and in the DTRs. Continuing obligations are designed to ensure a fair market, with equal access to information by all parties and easy entry to and exit from the market. The continuing obligations also reinforce the importance of a properly regulated market and thus help to increase investor confidence.

## 4.1 The Listing Principles

The purpose of the Listing Principles is to ensure that listed companies pay due regard to the fundamental role they play in maintaining market confidence and ensuring fair and orderly markets. The Listing Principles are designed to assist listed companies in identifying their obligations and responsibilities under the Listing Rules and the DTRs. In essence, the Listing Principles ensure both the spirit and the letter of the Listing Regime are observed.

There are six Listing Principles. They require that a listed company must:

1 Take reasonable steps to enable its directors to understand their responsibilities and obligations as directors.
2 Take reasonable steps to establish and maintain adequate procedures, systems and controls to enable it to comply with its obligations.
3 Act with integrity towards holders and potential holders of its listed equity securities.
4 Communicate information to holders and potential holders of its listed equity securities in such a way as to avoid the creation or continuation of a false market in such listed equity securities.
5 Ensure that it treats all holders of the same class of its listed equity securities that are in the same position equally in respect of the rights attaching to such listed equity securities.
6 Deal with the FSA in an open and cooperative manner.

---

**STOP AND THINK** 6.2

The Listing Principles provide a useful summary of how listed companies are expected to behave. Company secretaries of listed companies are often responsible for ensuring their directors, particularly newly appointed directors, understand their responsibilities. The Listing Principles form an important part of the education process for listed company directors and company secretaries should ensure their directors are familiar with them.

---

## 4.2 Disclosure of information

The DTRs provide guidance on the release of information to the public. Companies must submit announcements to a **RIS**, which is a primary information provider (PIP) service approved by the FSA to disseminate regulatory information to the market. Information which needs to be notified to a regulatory information service must be given to them before being released elsewhere to ensure that no one person or section of the population receives the information ahead of any other.

If an RIS is closed and a company has information to disclose, the company must distribute it to at least two national newspapers and to two newswire services to ensure that there is adequate coverage. An RIS should also be informed so that it can release the news as soon as the market reopens.

The underlying principle in the DTRs is that important information must be released to the market as promptly as possible and, in any event, usually by the end of the following business day. Continuing obligations require a company to notify UKLA of the following:

- any information on new developments which could lead to a substantial movement in the price of its listed securities (e.g. if the company had been awarded a major or lucrative contract);
- any change in the company's expected performance which is materially different from the expectation of the market. This could include a profit warning that the company does not expect to achieve the level of profit it had previously in a given financial period;
- alterations to capital;
- changes in class rights;
- any major acquisitions or disposals;
- the announcement of a company's full and half-year results (see Transparency Rules below);
- purchase of own shares or redemption of securities;
- information relating to major shareholders where they control major voting rights;
- the outcome of any decisions made by shareholders in general meeting;
- any substantial change in the way the company is managed, for example, a change in the accounting reference date;
- the board's decisions on dividends;

- any change in directors (including to their areas of responsibility);
- in respect of a person discharging managerial responsibility, any change in their interests in the shares or debentures of the company, including any options granted to or exercised by them under an employee share scheme (see Chapter 15);
- the issue of the company's statutory accounts and the half-year report.

There are some limited circumstances where a delay may be warranted under the DTRs prior to releasing an announcement. If the company experiences an unexpected and significant event, a short delay may be justified if it is needed to clarify any material uncertainties prior to announcement. In this case, the directors should consider whether a provisional 'holding' announcement is warranted, particularly if there is the possibility that the announcement may be prematurely leaked. A delay may also be acceptable if it is required to avoid prejudice to the listed company's legitimate interest. However, the delay in announcing must not mislead the public, and the company must ensure that confidentiality is maintained so as to avoid leaks ahead of the formal announcement. Legitimate interests may include, for example, where negotiations are ongoing with a third party and the outcome of the negotiations could be affected by the disclosure. Such a delay cannot be used, however, merely because the listed company is in financial difficulty.

The DTRs require that inside information (see section 7) that has been released to an RIS must also be posted on the company's internet site by the close of the business day following the day of announcement. A company must ensure that such information does not appear on their website before it has been released through a RIS. A company is then required by the DTRs to keep all such announcements on their website for at least one year following publication.

---

**STOP AND THINK 6.3**

The effect of the DTRs is to require listed companies to have effective systems in place to identify inside information and to release such information promptly. The establishment and maintenance of these effective systems is usually the responsibility of the company secretary. Furthermore, statute and the listing regime make it clear that the directors are responsible for the content of all announcements. Regulations were issued in 2010 which amend s. 90A of the Financial Service and Markets Act 2000. The effect is that the statutory liability regime (for fraud and recklessness) covers all information published via an RIS and creates a liability for dishonest delay in disclosing information. The company secretary should therefore ensure that appropriate procedures are in place to verify the content of announcements before they are released and to ensure information is released promptly.

The company secretary should also ensure that appropriate procedures are in place for the company to deal with market rumours and press speculation. Generally, a company is not required to make a formal announcement through an RIS to deny inaccurate rumours, however, if speculation and rumours are substantially accurate, the directors will need to consider whether an announcement needs to be made.

---

All notices and circulars (except those of a very routine nature, such as proxy forms, if they comply with the provisions of Chapter 13 of the Listing Rules and do not have any unusual features) should be submitted to UKLA for prior approval. However, two copies of all circulars and proposed resolutions must be lodged with the FSA at the time they are issued. In addition, two copies of the following documents must be lodged if they are issued or amended, although if they have no unusual features they will not need prior approval:

- Articles of Association;
- trust deeds;
- employees' share schemes;
- temporary documents of title including renounceable documents;
- definitive documents of title;
- proxy forms.

Listed companies are also required to produce accounts conforming to International Financial Reporting Standards (IFRS).

The DTRs introduced important changes to financial reporting for listed companies:

- The annual report must be published within four months of the year-end.
- Preliminary results statements are now optional, but if made they must comply with the relevant requirements of the Listing Rules.
- Half-year reports must be published within two months of the period-end; there is no longer any requirement to send them to shareholders or publish them in a newspaper.
- There is a new requirement to publish interim management statements during a period which is no more than ten weeks from the start of the financial period and six weeks from its end.

Two copies of the accounts should be sent to the UKLA's Document Viewing Facility (see below).

In order to maintain good communication between a listed company and the FSA each listed company must, pursuant to the Listing Rules and DTRs, appoint a named primary point of contact. The purpose of the contact is to provide the FSA with a named individual whom the FSA can contact if they have a query. The contact should be a senior employee of the company or a responsible person acting on behalf of the company (e.g. a representative from the company's brokers).The employee or other person must have a good understanding of the business of the company and of the Listing Regime.

As part of the continuing obligations regime, certain documents made public by listed companies (such as annual accounts, shareholder circulars and shareholder resolutions other than ordinary business at AGMs) are available for public inspection on the **National Storage Mechanism (NSM)**. All copies of documents that listed companies are required to place on the Document Viewing Facility can be viewed on the NSM. Previously, it was required for listed companies to send hard copies of documents to the Document Viewing Facility but this is no longer required as the listed company now uploads the document on the NSM via a website.

## 4.3 Protection of shareholder interests

All the requirements listed above are intended to protect the interests of the members of a listed company, but there are other shareholder protection safeguards required by UKLA:

- There is to be no restriction on the registration of transfers of fully paid shares.
- An open offer (see section 2.1) of securities to shareholders cannot be purchased by the directors, unless there are exceptional circumstances.
- Publication of regular financial information (see above).
- Any notice of general meeting of shareholders at which non-routine business is to be transacted must be accompanied by an explanatory circular.
- If matters are to be raised at a general meeting at which members have a right to vote, the directors must include a recommendation as to whether the proposal is in the best interests of the members as a whole and whether the directors intend to support the proposal with any shares they hold.
- Three-way proxy cards must be issued with the notice of general meeting (see Chapter 9).
- Changes to the board (appointment and/or resignation of directors, plus any changes to a director's area of responsibility) must be notified.
- Any changes to the company's name or accounting reference date must be notified.

## 4.4 Oversea companies

Oversea companies that apply to have a primary listing must comply with the Listing Regime, provided compliance is not contrary to the rules in the country of incorporation. The only exception us that the oversea company does not have to comply with the disclosure requirements introduced by corporate governance codes, other than those concerning directors' service contracts.

Oversea companies seeking a secondary listing are subject to various modifications of the rules, for example:

- Its sponsor does not have to report on the company's working capital position.
- It is usual to submit three years' annual accounts, but the most recent can be up to twelve months old.

- If securities are listed on an overseas stock exchange, the company must confirm compliance with that authority.

Continuing obligations for oversea companies are similar, except for those with a secondary listing. The latter only have to make available information that is not misleading, false or deceptive and must not omit anything significant.

## 4.5 Delisting from the Official List

It may be necessary or desirable for a company to delist from the Official List (i.e. cancel its listing), for example, if it is stepping down to the AIM (see section 5) or becoming a private company.

    If a company wishes to delist, it must inform the FSA and obtain the approval of its shareholders by way of special resolution. The company must send a circular to its shareholders convening a general meeting and the circular must include the anticipated date of cancellation (which must be not less than 20 business days following the passing of the resolution). The circular must include an explanation of the reason for seeking delisting. At the same time as issuing the circular, an announcement must be made through an RIS explaining the intended cancellation and the convening of the general meeting. If the special resolution is passed, a further announcement must be made through an RIS and various documentation as prescribed in the Listing Rules must be sent to the FSA.

## 4.6 The role of the company secretary

It is a requirement that all directors of a listed company agree to abide by the Listing Rules, DTRs and Prospectus Rules. A good company secretary of a listed company will, therefore:

- have detailed knowledge of the Listing Regime and advise the board appropriately;
- provide the board with updates in respect of any changes to any of the rules as appropriate;
- clarify any queries raised by the board;
- advise the board of the practical implications of any changes in the Listing Regime.

It is worth noting that the FSA has power to levy unlimited fines on individual directors as well as issuers for breaches of the rules. These may not be reimbursed under directors' and officers' liability insurance cover, so it is essential for the company secretary to be fully briefed to ensure compliance.

---

**TEST YOUR KNOWLEDGE 6.3**

a What is the purpose of a RIS?
b Give four examples of the type of information a listed company is required to release. When should this information be released?
c Which listed company documents do not require UKLA approval before they are issued?

---

## 5 The Alternative Investment Market (AIM)

AIM is the London Stock Exchange's market for smaller public limited companies. AIM companies are regulated separately from the listing regime described above. Instead, they are controlled by the AIM rules for companies, published by the London Stock Exchange. They are still subject to a Model Code (see section 7.3), the CJA 1993 (see section 7.1) and FSMA 2000. The requirements of Chapter 5 of the DTRs (vote holder notifications) also apply to AIM companies.

    The requirements for admission to AIM are less demanding than those for the Official List. The company does not have to be a particular size or have a lengthy trading history; nor is it required to have a certain percentage of its shares in public hands. However, where the company's main activity is a business which has not been independent and revenue-earning for at least two years, it must agree that any director or employee owning more that 0.5% of the shares must not dispose of them for at least one year from the date of admission.

AIM is managed by a separate team within the London Stock Exchange. To join, a company should appoint a nominated broker and a nominated adviser to:

- help the company with the application process and ensure the directors are aware of their responsibilities and obligations;
- confirm to the London Stock Exchange that the company has complied with the relevant rules and that the prospectus is complete and correct;
- bring buyers and sellers of the company's shares together and do their best to match transactions;
- act as the point of contact for information between the company and the investment community.

The adviser must be drawn from a register of approved firms kept by the London Stock Exchange. A single firm may fill the role of both broker and nominated adviser. The nominated adviser is often referred to as a **nomad**.

## 5.1 Admission to AIM

A company seeking admission to AIM must supply certain information to the London Stock Exchange at least ten business days before the expected date of admission. This will enable the London Stock Exchange to publish an announcement to the market in respect of the proposed admission. The information includes:

- the company's name, registered office address, country of incorporation and directors;
- a brief description of the business;
- details about the company's securities and whether it intends to raise further capital as part of its admission;
- details of any major shareholders;
- name and address of the nominated adviser and broker.

At least three days before the expected date of admission, the company will be required to pay the AIM admission fee and submit an admission document (see below) and an application form executed by the directors of the company, together with a confirmation declaration executed by the nominated adviser. A letter from the company's broker confirming the ongoing appointment will also be required. The admission will become effective when the London Stock Exchange issues a dealing notice to the market.

The company will also be required to produce an admission document (in essence, a prospectus), which must be placed on the company's website and remain there after admission. The admission document typically includes the following:

- prospectus information required by applicable statute or AIM rules. AIM companies will only find themselves affected by the Prospectus Directive where they are doing a public offer, rights issue or takeover which triggers the Prospectus Directive and exceeds applicable exemption limits in relation to the size of the offer. Where the information required does not have to be made subject to the Prospectus Directive, the London Stock Exchange has established a shorter disclosure requirement called AIM-PD. The information required under either the Prospectus Directive or AIM-PD is in relation to a full description of the company and its principal activities, its trading history, market trends, performance and details of its management structure;
- audited financial information regarding the company, including working capital;
- names, functions and other details about the directors (or any proposed director), in particular any bankruptcies, criminal convictions, etc.;
- statements by the directors that they have taken due care in the preparation of financial forecasts, etc.;
- details of any major shareholders;
- an anticipated timetable in respect of the admission.

The company's admission to AIM becomes effective when the London Stock Exchange issues a dealing notice confirming the admission. Once a company's shares have been traded on AIM for two years, it can apply to join the Official List without producing a full prospectus.

## 5.2 AIM companies: continuing obligations

AIM companies have an obligation to appoint and retain a nominated adviser and broker who must assist the directors to comply with the rules. As AIM is not a regulated market under EU regulations, the DTRs do not generally apply. However, there are other continuing obligations. They must:

■ have published accounts that conform to applicable IFRS;
■ have appropriate arrangements in place for the settlement of securities;
■ adopt the Model Code for AIM companies by board resolution;
■ publish annual audited accounts within six months of the year-end;
■ prepare half-year reports (which may be unaudited) within three months of the half-year-end;
■ make copies of any documents sent to shareholders available to the public for at least a month from the date of announcement to an RIS;
■ ensure that their shares remain freely transferable;
■ forward six copies of all announcements, circulars, reports and other documents to an RIS as and when they are issued to shareholders.

The announcements that must be notified are:

■ changes in the financial conditions that are not public knowledge and may be price-sensitive, in other words, likely to cause a substantial movement in the company's share price;
■ directors' disclosures regarding their interests in the company;
■ changes of directors' details;
■ publication of audited accounts and any change in accounting reference date (i.e. the financial year-end);
■ the resignation, dismissal or change of the nominated adviser and broker;
■ any issue of new securities or cancellation of existing securities;
■ decisions made to pay a dividend or other distribution;
■ details of substantial transactions;
■ transactions with related parties where the size of the transaction is in excess of 5% of any one of a prescribed set of ratios;
■ material differences between forecast and actual performance.

The rules for AIM have separate rule books for AIM companies and for nomads. One key requirement for AIM companies is to publish certain details on a website. Key points are:

■ The company must notify the market of the relevant website address.
■ The website should be their own website (but may be hosted by another party).
■ The information must be kept up-to-date and the date of the last update must be given.
■ The information must be easily accessible; it should not be necessary to use a search facility to find it.
■ There must be a statement that the information is being disclosed for the purposes of the AIM rules.

The information about the company which must be disclosed is as follows:

■ a description of its business;
■ if it is an investing company, its investing strategy;
■ the names and brief biographical details of directors;
■ a description of the responsibilities of the board of directors and of any board committees;
■ its country of incorporation and main country of operation;
■ if it is not a UK company, a statement that members' rights may differ from those of a UK company;

- its current constitutional documents (e.g. Memorandum and Articles of Association);
- details of any other exchanges or trading platforms on which its securities are listed or traded;
- in relation to its AIM securities:
  - the number in issue (with a note of any held in treasury),
  - the percentage not in public hands,
  - the identity and percentage holdings of its significant shareholders.

  This information should be updated at least every six months;

- any restrictions on the transfer of its AIM securities;
- its most recent annual report and all half-yearly, quarterly or similar reports published subsequently;
- all notifications it has made in the past year;
- its most recent admission document and any circulars or similar documents sent to shareholders in the previous year;
- details of its nomad and other key advisers.

## 5.3 Delisting from AIM

A company may wish to cease trading on AIM for a number of reasons, for example, where the company is going into private ownership. The AIM Rules require that a company must notify the market at least 20 business days ahead of the proposed delisting, stating the reasons for delisting.

Shareholder approval is required. A shareholder circular convening a general meeting must be issued which contains the reasons for, and consequences of, delisting and a special resolution must be passed to effect the delisting. Limited exemptions from the requirement to pass a resolution are available from the London Stock Exchange.

---

**STOP AND THINK 6.4**

Compare the admission and continuing obligation requirements between fully listed companies and AIM companies and consider what type of companies may be best suited for each. In addition to companies having progressed from AIM to the Official List, some have delisted and moved to AIM. Why might a company decide to change markets?

---

**TEST YOUR KNOWLEDGE 6.4**

**a** What is AIM?
**b** What are the conditions for admission to AIM?
**c** How does the delisting process differ between AIM companies and listed companies?
**d** Can a private company be admitted to AIM?

---

## 6 Takeovers and mergers

The purpose of a takeover is the acquisition by one company of the whole or majority of the share capital of another in exchange for an issue of shares, cash payment or a combination of the two. The main types of takeover are:

- *Purchase by* **public offer** – This is the most common form of takeover, where an offer is made to the shareholders of a company to acquire all, or a proportion of, their holdings. The City Code on Takeovers and Mergers should be carefully observed if the company is listed.
- *Purchase by acquisition of individual blocks of shares, i.e.* **stake-building** – This is used to build a base from which to launch a takeover for all the shares. If any of the companies

involved are listed, the bidding company must take care to follow the City Code. Even if the company is not listed, any financial advisers acting on behalf of the bidding company will need to consider the City Code.

■ *Purchase by formal agreement with individual shareholders* – This is only practicable where there are only a few shareholders in the company to be acquired.
■ *Arrangements and reconstructions* – covered by CA 2006, Part 26.

## 6.1 The City Code on Takeovers and Mergers

The City Code on Takeovers and Mergers (the Code) sets out regulations for the acquisition of shares in listed companies. First published in 1968 as the product of a working party organised by the Bank of England, it is now published by the Panel on Takeovers and Mergers (the Panel), which is responsible for the administration of the Code and is available for advice and consultation before or during takeover and merger transactions. Copies of the Code are available from the Panel (see Directory) and it can be viewed on the Panel's website.

The following bodies nominate members of the Panel:

■ The Association of British Insurers (ABI).
■ The Association of Investment Companies.
■ The Association of Private Client Investment Managers and Stockbrokers.
■ The British Bankers' Association.
■ The Confederation of British Industry.
■ The Institute of Chartered Accountants in England and Wales.
■ The Investment Management Association.
■ The London Investment Banking Association (with separate representation for its Corporate Finance Committee and Securities Trading Committee).
■ The National Association of Pension Funds (NAPF).

Whether a listed company is defending or making a bid, professional financial advisers will need to be retained to advise on the merits of the bid. Although these advisers will take the Code into consideration, it is necessary for the company secretary to be familiar with it as he will form part of the team preparing documentation which will be issued to the shareholders of the target company.

The Code is intended to ensure fair and equal treatment of all shareholders during a takeover. It does not set out to deal with the financial implications. Its provisions apply when a bidder increases their shareholding to 30% or more.

The general principles of the Code are:

1 All shareholders of the **offeree** must be given equivalent treatment. Moreover, if a person acquires control of a company, the other holders of securities must be protected.
2 The shareholders of the offeree must have enough information to make an informed decision on the bid and enough time to consider it. The board of the offeree company must give its views on the effects of implementation of the bid on employment, conditions of employment and the locations of the company's places of business.
3 The board of the offeree must act in the interests of the company as a whole and must not deny shareholders the chance to decide on the merits of the bid.
4 False markets must not be created in the shares of the offeree, the **offeror** or any other company concerned by the bid.
5 An offeror must ensure that they can meet any cash consideration in full before announcing a bid.
6 An offeree company must not be hindered in the conduct of its affairs for longer than is reasonable by a bid for its securities.

These six principles are supported by extensive rules and provisions.

### Summary of the principal rules

1 Any offer must first be made to the board of the offeree company or to its advisers disclosing the identity of the offeror.
2 When any firm intention to make an offer is notified to a board from a serious source, the board must publicise it by a press notice without delay, regardless of whether the board

approves the offer. A copy of the press notice or a circular setting out the content of the notice should be sent promptly by the offeree company to its shareholders. If approaches are received which may or may not lead to an offer, or if there are any significant movements in the market price of the company's shares, it may be appropriate to request the Stock Exchange temporarily to suspend dealings in the company's shares to avoid creating a false market. Clearly it is advisable to keep in close contact with professional advisers and with the relevant regulatory bodies during this time.

3  In the period prior to the announcement of an offer, it is essential that absolute confidentiality is maintained; company secretaries should be responsible for the arrangements.

4  The boards of both companies must obtain competent independent advice and the substance of such advice should be made known to shareholders.

5  Any information, including particulars of shareholders, given to an offeror company should on request be given promptly to a less welcome but bona fide potential offeror.

6  Any document or advertisement addressed to shareholders in connection with an offer must be prepared with the same standards of care regarding statements made as if it were a prospectus.

7  The rules also contain detailed provisions covering the content of announcements and offer documents. There are also requirements regarding the timetable of an offer to ensure that all shareholders are given a fair opportunity to consider it.

Following several high profile takeovers in the UK, the Code was revised and re-issued in September 2011 following an extensive public consultation process. Amendments to the Code included the following provisions:

- the identity of the offeror must be made clear at the first formal announcement;
- potential offerors must clarify their position within a short period of time. This is often referred to as the 'put up or shut up' regime and a potential bidder is now required to clarify its position within 28 days following announcement, unless an extension is granted from the Takeover Panel. This provision increases the protection for target companies against protracted bids;
- clarification that the board of the offeree company is not limited in what they can take into account in giving its opinion on an offer. In particular, it is entitled to comment on more than just the financial merits of the offer;
- improved quality of information about the offeror's intentions regarding the offeree company and its employees. Also, a better ability for employees to make their views known on the potential impact of the takeover.

## Announcements and documentation

If a takeover or merger is proposed, the company secretary of each company will need to obtain and collate a considerable amount of information regarding the affairs of the company, including details of dealings by directors in the securities of the company, to prepare announcements and offer documents. He should liaise closely with the company's brokers in doing so.

Copies of all public announcements made and all documents bearing on a takeover transaction must be lodged with the Panel at the same time as they are made or despatched.

The board of the offeree company should ensure that share transfers are registered promptly (see Chapter 12) during a takeover so that shareholders may freely exercise their voting and other rights.

The Code contains important provisions regarding dealings prior to the announcement of any offer that could give rise to the acquiring company being obliged to make an offer. Once an offer has been announced, the offeror should take considerable care regarding any further acquisitions of the securities in the offeree company.

If any such dealings take place for a price in excess of the offer price, which could result in an obligation to increase the price specified in the general offer, this must be disclosed.

The Code also requires the offeror and offeree and their associates to disclose holdings of traded options and other derivatives in the offeree company.

The Panel is endorsed by the FSA and has been designated as the supervisory authority to carry out certain regulatory functions in relation to takeovers under the EU Directive on Takeover Bids. Its statutory functions are set out in CA 2006. Compliance with the provisions of the Code is now a statutory obligation and failure to comply may result in various sanctions or disciplinary actions. It is acknowledged by both government and other regulatory authorities as an appropriate way to conduct high business standards when a takeover is in process. This means that the FSA can, at the request of the Panel, take enforcement action against a person authorised under the FSMA who contravenes the Code or a Panel ruling. Compliance with the Code's provisions would, in addition, be taken into account by a court in assessing the reasonableness of conduct in a contentious situation.

## Substantial acquisitions

A company planning a takeover bid may launch a **dawn raid**, where it acquires a substantial shareholding in the target company before the price rises.

The DTRs include the procedures to be followed by listed companies and substantial shareholders in notifying UKLA and an RIS of a substantial shareholding. The key notification requirement is triggered when a shareholder holds 3% or more in a listed company. Further notification requirements are triggered when the substantial shareholder increases or decreases their holding by a whole % integer (e.g. from 4.7% to 5.1%).

# 6.2 Public offers

A public offer is a takeover offer made to all shareholders of a target company to acquire all, or a proportion, of their holdings in return for cash or shares or other securities in the offeror company. In this instance, the company secretaries and directors of both companies would be closely involved in the preparation of draft documentation for approval by their respective boards.

Strict compliance with the Code, FSA requirements, the Listing Rules and the Prospectus Rules (where shares of the offeror company are being offered to shareholders of the target company) is required. Under FSA requirements, the offer documents are usually sent to the shareholders of the target company by a merchant bank or issuing house.

It may be necessary to call a general meeting if, in respect of the bidding company, the offer is a 'shares for shares' offer, to approve the allotment of shares as the consideration for the shares of the target company. The appropriate documents should be sent to UKLA for approval if the company is listed.

If the shares to be issued in connection with the offer are to be listed on the Official List and admitted to trading on the Stock Exchange, the offer documentation should also include the prospectus, in compliance with the Listing Rules and Prospectus Rules.

## The Competition Commission

If the offer could lead to two major companies in the same field joining forces, the proposed takeover may be referred by the Office of Fair Trading to the Competition Commission for investigation. Under the EA 2002 a company may notify the Competition Commission voluntarily in advance of an intended merger. If the merger is not referred to the Commission within the period allowed for consideration following the pre-notification, it cannot subsequently be referred if the merger is effected within the following six months. However, advance clearance may attract publicity and cause the share price to rise, increasing the cost of the acquisition.

In many instances, the offeror will make the offer conditional on the matter not being referred to the Commission. Instead of referring the merger to the Commission, the Secretary of State may accept undertakings from the parties involved – for example, the disposal of one part of the new merged business to remedy or prevent any effects of the merger being adverse to public interest. These undertakings are legally binding and must be published, with the advice of the Director General of Fair Trading.

If a merger is referred to the Commission, the bidder(s) may not acquire shares in the target company without consent from the Secretary of State while the investigation is carried out, until the referral is either withdrawn or the Commission has made its report.

## Preparing the documentation

The company secretary will be closely involved in preparing the documentation and making other arrangements. Detailed logistical timetables should be prepared to ensure every aspect of document production has been considered.

## CHECKLIST 6.1 Preparing the offer documents

✓ Appoint printers to produce the documents. If the documents contain price-sensitive material it is not uncommon to use specialist financial printers. Such printers have established security procedures to ensure that the information remains confidential until publication.

✓ Although the issuing house and the companies' respective solicitors will carry out most of the work in preparing the offer documents, the directors of the two companies concerned in the takeover are legally responsible for the accuracy of the documents.

✓ If either or both of the companies concerned are listed, the documentation must comply with the Listing Regime. Three copies of the offer document and related documentation will need to be submitted in draft to the listing applications department for approval prior to release.

✓ The document issued to shareholders of the offeree company must constitute a transfer (see Chapter 13) of the securities to the offeror company.

✓ Any existing dividend mandate (see Chapter 14) applicable to the shares in the offeree company will be applied to the shares in the offeror company unless otherwise instructed.

✓ Companies whose shares are settled within CREST (see Chapter 13) will need to liaise with their registrars to ensure that the appropriate procedures are established to enable shareholders to accept the offer within CREST.

Since takeovers can move fairly quickly it is sensible to prepare in advance:

■ envelopes addressed and ready for the offer documents to be sent to shareholders in the offeree company, with reply-paid envelopes for the return of forms of acceptance and transfer with the relevant share certificates;

■ envelopes addressed and ready for any circular letters to be sent to the offeror's shareholders, either explaining the takeover or convening a general meeting to approve any increase in capital that may be necessary;

■ further sets of address labels for both companies' shareholders in case further circulars are issued, for example, if the terms of the offer are changed.

## The closing date

Most shareholders will not accept the offer until just before the closing date, so the offeror company or its receiving agent must be prepared for a last-minute rush of acceptances. The Panel on Takeovers and Mergers requires that stringent procedures are followed to avoid the possibility of double counting. The basic procedure is:

■ Cross-check with the register of members of the target company that the form of acceptance and transfer has been completed correctly and the correct share certificate has been returned.

■ Although acceptance forms without share certificates are usually treated as valid, care should be taken to keep these separate so that they may be completed when the share certificate is received.

■ Acceptances may also be allowed if, following a recent purchase, the share certificates have not yet been prepared.

If a shareholder has lost his certificate(s), the usual procedure will apply (see Chapter 13). Similarly, if forms of acceptance have been signed by a representative or under a power of attorney, the appropriate documents must have been registered first (see Chapter 13).

During the period of the offer, the offeree should notify the offeror of any transfers received for registration so that offer documents can be sent to the new shareholders. The copy of the register of members of the offeree company should be updated.

It is usual to advertise a reminder of the final acceptance date in the press. If there is a cash alternative to the share offer, which is subject to underwriting arrangements, this will restrict the amount of time cash alternatives may remain open for acceptance. If no underwriting is involved, the offer may be extended indefinitely with the proviso that the offer must be declared **unconditional** by the 60th day after it was first posted.

## After the closing date

■ Calculate the totals of the complete and incomplete acceptances so that the board of the offeror company can decide whether the level of acceptances is sufficient for the bid to be declared unconditional, or, if the number of acceptances is small, whether it should be extended for a further period, possibly improving the terms of the offer.

■ Once the bid has been made unconditional, prepare share certificates for shares or other securities in the offeror company to be issued to shareholders in the offeree company.

■ Draw cheques for those who have accepted a cash alternative.

■ The offeror company should establish a committee to make allotments of securities.

■ Send out the certificates or cash consideration 21 days after the date the valid acceptances are received.

■ Arrange to obtain a listing of the securities issued if the company has increased its share capital in order to implement the offer.

■ If employees of the offeree company had share options under any employee share schemes (see Chapter 15), the terms of the acquisition would have stated how the options would be treated on a change of control of the offeree (e.g. some or all of the options may become exercisable). It is therefore necessary to ensure that option holders of the offeree company are provided with the appropriate documentation in accordance with the terms of the acquisition.

## Omnibus transfer

The transfer executed by or on behalf of the offeror company to put the shares of the offeree company into their own name is known as an **omnibus transfer**. This is a slightly simplified arrangement where a schedule detailing the forms of acceptance is sent to HM Revenue & Customs and the stamp duty calculated on this basis, instead of having each of the forms of acceptance stamped individually. It may be possible to obtain exemption from stamp duty in respect of the transfers. The completed forms of acceptance and transfer, together with the covering share certificates and the stamped bulk transfer, are lodged with the offeree company.

## 6.4 Agreement with individual shareholders

This is a simple way of transferring ownership, but is suitable only where small numbers of shareholders are involved. A formal agreement is entered into between the parties setting out the full details of the shares to be acquired, the price, the date for completion and arrangements for paying for expenses such as legal costs.

### CHECKLIST 6.2 **Agreement with individual shareholders**

✓ The purchase and sale agreement is drawn up, with legal advice, ensuring that the interests of both parties are adequately protected.

✓ The final agreement is executed and formally exchanged between the parties and a date set for completion.

✓ On completion the share transfers (see Chapter 13) with share certificates are exchanged for payment.

✓ The Registrar should be notified of any changes (e.g. to directors or secretary, or to the registered office). A return of allotments should also be submitted on form SH01 (see Chapter 12).

✓ The various statutory registers should be updated reflecting the registration of the transfers (see Chapter 8).

If the company is listed, announcements should be made to UKLA, the press (if appropriate) and the company's customers and employees.

**STOP AND THINK** 6.5

A good company secretary will need to think laterally about what other actions need to be taken following a major allocation of shares. For example, if there were any existing major shareholders prior to the acquisition, it is likely that their reportable percentage holding in the company will have decreased as a result of the issue of additional shares. The company secretary should investigate this in case the major shareholder needs to issue the company with a new notification of its revised percentage shareholding.

 The corporate calendar should be scrutinised for any potential complications. For example, is the record date for a dividend payment near to the closing date of the offer?

## 6.5 Compulsory acquisition

Compulsory acquisition is dealt with in CA 2006, ss. 974–989. These provisions are designed to protect the rights of the minority to resist compulsory acquisition if they have reasonable grounds to do so, and to ensure that they are treated no less fairly than shareholders who have accepted the offer.

Under CA 2006, s. 979 the offeror has the right, within three months from the last day on which the offer may be accepted, to give notice (on form 980(1)) to any shareholder who has not accepted the offer that it plans to acquire minority holders' shares on the terms of the offer. Shares which were already held in the offeror's name, or contracted to be acquired but not registered in the offeror's name, at the time the offer was made are excluded from the 90% minimum. Treasury shares (see Chapter 12) must also be excluded from the calculation of the 90% level.

A copy of the notice, together with a statutory declaration (on form 980(dec)), signed by a director, if the offeror is a company, must be sent to the company within two months of the date on which the 90% acceptance is reached.

Unless the shareholder applies to the court to cancel or vary the order within six weeks of the date of the form 980(1) notice and the court agrees, the bidding company must acquire the shares on the original terms of the offer. This may include the terms of a related cash alternative even if this has closed, under the terms for its underwriting, some time earlier.

The offeror company sends a copy of the notice to the offeree company, together with an instrument of transfer executed on behalf of the shareholder concerned by a person appointed by the offeror company for that purpose. This is accompanied by a cheque or certificate, drawn in favour of the offeree company, for the purchase consideration.

The offeree company must register the transfer and hold the consideration on trust for the former shareholder, with any cash being held in a separate bank account. The special provisions that apply to compulsory acquisition of shares held through CREST are outlined in the Uncertificated Securities Regulations 2001.

The former shareholder can obtain the consideration by applying to the offeree company, surrendering any share certificates or giving an indemnity if the certificate is lost. If the consideration is in the form of shares, these will have to be transferred to the former shareholder in the usual way.

The target company has a duty to take reasonable steps to trace the former shareholder so that the cash or shares may be passed on. If the person cannot be found, when the consideration has been held for twelve years (or if the offeree company is liquidated before this) the consideration, together with related interest, dividends or other benefits, must be paid into court (ss. 982(4) and (5)). The expenses of the required enquiries can be met out of the consideration and other property held for the dissenting holders (s. 982(9)).

Minority shareholders who have not accepted an offer are also given the right for their shares to be bought out by an offeror where the offeror has reached the 90% level (CA 2006, ss. 983–985). The offeror must send notice (on form 984) to any shareholders who have not assented to the takeover offer. The notice on form 984 must be sent by the offeror within one month of reaching

**Companies House**
— for the record —

*Please complete in typescript,*
*or in bold black capitals.*
CHFP000

# 980(1)

## NOTICE TO NON-ASSENTING SHAREHOLDERS
Pursuant to section 980(1) of the Companies Act 2006

*Name(s) and address(es) of non-assenting shareholder(s)

To*

** Insert date of offer

A takeover offer was made on

| Day | Month | Year |
|-----|-------|------|
|     |       |      |

**by

"the offeror(s)"

§ Insert description of class or classes of shares or convertible securities to which offer relates

for §

shares / securities in

"the company"

The offeror(s) has/have, within the relevant time period specified in section 980(2) of the Companies Act 2006, satisfied the conditions contained in subsection (2) or (4) of section 979 of that Act. The offeror(s) give(s) notice that he/they now intend(s) to exercise his/their right under section 979 of the Companies Act 2006 to acquire shares held by you in the company. The terms of the offer are †

† Insert terms of offer

†† State address to which acceptance should be sent

If these terms include a choice of consideration, you should within 6 weeks of the date of this notice inform the offeror(s) in writing at ††

which of the choices you wish to accept. If you fail to make a choice and do not make application to the court (see below) the offeror(s) will acquire your shares/securities on the following terms:

**NOTE:** You are entitled under section 986 of the Companies Act 2006 to make application to the court within 6 weeks of the date of this notice for an order either that the offeror(s) shall not be entitled and bound to acquire your shares or that different terms to those of the offer shall apply to the acquisition. If you are contemplating such an action you may wish to seek legal advice.

§§ If this notice is given by a company, it should be signed by a director or the secretary.

Signed§§

Date

the 90% level and will explain the rights which are exercisable by the minority shareholder and the period within which the rights can be exercised. S. 984 provides that the rights of a minority shareholder to require the offeror to acquire their shares are not exercisable after the end of the period of three months from when the offer can be accepted, or, if later, the date of the notice given on form 984. Any non-assenting shareholder may require the offeror company to acquire his shares on the original terms of the offer or such other terms as may be agreed.

## 6.6 Schemes of arrangement

The forms of takeover described above cover the relatively simple situation where one company wishes to acquire a substantial part or the whole of the share capital of another. However, more complicated arrangements may arise, for example, where a new holding company is established to take over the two companies concerned with a view to merging their operations. This could be achieved by agreement between the boards of the companies concerned, usually with the approval in general meeting of both companies. Alternatively, the takeover could be achieved by liquidation under the provisions of IA 1986, s. 110, or under a **scheme of arrangement** under CA 2006, s. 897, which provides for a 'compromise or arrangement' with members (or a class of members) and creditors. Schemes of arrangement can make possible mergers and other restructurings which would not otherwise be possible, for example where a bidder wants to acquire 100% ownership of a business, but where it is not possible to obtain the required 90% level of acceptances necessary for compulsory acquisition (see section 6.5).

A scheme of arrangement requires approval of the court and resolutions of the members and/or creditors of the company passed by a 75% majority rather than the 90% required for compulsory acquisition. Because the shares acquired are not transferred but cancelled by the court order, there is no stamp duty liability (see Chapter 13). Because of the involvement of the court, the documentation for such a scheme must be settled by counsel, and the legal advisers of the companies concerned will be closely involved in the various procedural steps.

The company secretary may well be asked to help facilitate the process as part of the support provided to the board of a listed company.

---

### TEST YOUR KNOWLEDGE 6.5

a Name the key principles of the City Code on Takeovers and Mergers.
b Are listed companies and financial advisers obliged to follow the City Code on Takeovers and Mergers?
c What is the role of the Competition Commission?
d What documentation needs to be prepared in respect of a public offer?
e Outline the procedure for compulsory acquisition of shares.
f Under what circumstances might a scheme of arrangement be appropriate?

---

# 7 Insider dealing, market abuse and the Model Code

## 7.1 Insider dealing

**Insider dealing** occurs where an individual with inside knowledge of developments within a company uses this knowledge to his advantage (e.g. by dealing in shares). This is a criminal offence under the CJA 1993, Part V. The offence of insider dealing may take the following form:

- knowingly dealing in securities on the basis of inside information;
- encouraging another to engage in such dealing;
- disclosing inside information otherwise than in the proper performance of one's employment, office or profession.

**Inside information** in relation to securities is described in FSMA, s. 118C and CJA, Part V as information of a precise nature which:

- is not generally available;
- relates directly or indirectly to a company;
- would, if generally available, be likely to have a significant effect on the price of the company's securities. The test to be applied here is whether or not a reasonable investor would be likely to use the inside information as part of the basis of their investment decisions.

It should be noted that the mere fact that information about a company is unpublished does not itself make that information 'inside information'; the above criteria must also be met. To be guilty of the offence, the information must have been obtained by the defendant as a director, employee or shareholder of the company concerned, or directly or indirectly from such a person and he must have known that the information was inside information.

General information that relates to securities or issuers generally is not inside information, nor is information that has already been made public. The provisions contain detailed guidance on the meaning of 'made public' (CJA, s. 58). For example:

- it is sufficient for the information to be published in accordance with the rules of a recognised market or to be readily available (e.g. on enquiry) to any person likely to deal;
- information may be treated by the court as having been made public even if it is available on a restricted basis, for example, if it can be acquired only by 'persons exercising diligence or expertise or by observation' or if it is communicated only to a section of the public or is communicated only on payment of a fee or is published only outside the UK (CJA, s. 58(3)).

It is a defence to the 'disclosing' offence to show that the defendant did not, at the time of the disclosure, expect any person to deal because of the disclosure or alternatively that he did not expect any such dealing to result in a profit attributable to the price sensitivity of the information.

It is a defence to the dealing offence to show that the defendant would have dealt in the same way even if he had not had the information. Thus, a director who is under financial pressure to sell securities may possibly not commit an offence even though he is in possession of inside information. This defence could also be of assistance to trustees acting on advice.

In addition to dealings in company shares, debentures and loan stock, the insider dealing provisions cover dealings in:

- futures and options;
- futures linked to indexes and related options;
- gilt-edged securities.

Dealings are covered only if they occur on a regulated market or if the person concerned relies on or is himself a professional intermediary. The Treasury is given power to limit, by order, the types of instrument or market to restrict the insider dealing rules to situations in which there is a ready market (see the Insider Dealing (Securities and Regulated Markets) Order 1994, SI 1994/187).

## 7.2 Market abuse

FSMA, Part VIII enables the FSA to impose unlimited civil fines on, or to censure, any person found guilty of **market abuse**. Market abuse can be summarised as behaviour in relation to securities or investments traded on a UK market which amounts to:

- *Misuse of information* – Behaviour based on information that is not generally available to the market, but which a regular user would regard as relevant when deciding the terms on which transactions of the kind in question should be effected.
- *Misleading/false impression* – Behaviour likely to give a regular user of the market a misleading or false impression as to the supply of, demand for or the price or value of investments.
- *Market distortion* – Behaviour that would be regarded by a regular user of the market as likely to give rise to market distortion.

Under FSMA, s. 123(1) the FSA may impose a penalty on, or censure, any person who has engaged in market abuse or on any person who, by taking or refraining from taking any action, has required or encouraged another person to engage in such behaviour.

The FSA is required under FSMA to publish a Code of Market Conduct giving guidance on the application of the market abuse regime.

Though wider-ranging than insider dealing, the misuse of information category of the market abuse regime enables the FSA to impose civil penalties for behaviour that has the characteristics of insider dealing but for which it might be difficult to secure a criminal prosecution. As market abuse is a civil offence, it will only be necessary for the FSA to prove that the behaviour was illegal on the balance of probabilities.

Rigorous compliance with a code of dealing similar to the Model Code (see below) should help to avoid breaches of the misuse of information provisions by directors and other persons discharging managerial responsibility (PDMR) (i.e. senior executives). However, individuals who are required under a company's code to approve dealings by others will need to exercise caution in cases of doubt, not least to avoid falling foul of the market abuse regime themselves (e.g. by encouraging others to deal and thereby creating a misleading impression).

## 7.3 The Model Code

The freedom of directors and certain senior employees of listed companies to deal in their company's securities is restricted in a number of ways:

- by statute (as seen above);
- by common law;
- by the requirement of the Listing Rules that listed companies require their directors and certain senior managers (together referred to as PDMR) to comply with a code of dealing in terms no less exacting than the Model Code.

This requirement imposes restrictions beyond those that are imposed by law.

Under the Listing Rules, a listed company must require its directors and other senior managers to comply with a code and take all proper and reasonable steps to secure such compliance.

Compliance with the Model Code should also help to avoid conduct that could amount to market abuse under FSMA, particularly under the category of misuse of information. It should be noted, however, that market abuse includes behaviour not regulated by the Model Code and could be relevant to a wider range of employees.

### The principal terms of the Model Code

1 PDMR must not deal in the securities of a listed company during a **prohibited period**.
2 A PDMR within a company should not buy or sell any securities in the company without first giving a written notification of the intention to deal. Clearance to deal must be given as follows:
   a) a director (other than the chairman or CEO) or company secretary must notify and receive clearance to deal from the chairman or a designated director;
   b) the chairman must notify and receive clearance from the CEO (or in his absence, the senior independent director or other duly authorised committee of the board or officer of the company);
   c) the CEO must notify and receive clearance from the chairman (or in his absence the senior independent director or other duly authorised committee of the board or officer of the company). If the role of chairman and CEO is combined, that person must notify and receive clearance from the board;
   d) persons who are not directors discharging managerial responsibilities must notify and receive clearance from the company secretary or a designated director.
3 PDMRs may not be given clearance to buy or sell securities in the company during a **close period**, that is, the 60-day period immediately preceding:
   a) the preliminary announcement of the company's annual results;
   b) the announcement of the half-yearly results; or
   c) if shorter, the periods from the relevant financial period end to the time of the announcement; or
   d) if the company publishes quarterly accounts, the close period is the 30-day period immediately preceding the announcement of the first, second or third quarter results or,

if shorter, the period from the relevant financial period-end to the time of the announcement. For the fourth quarter results (i.e. the preliminary announcement of the annual results) the applicable close period is again the 60-day period immediately preceding announcement, or, if shorter, the period from the relevant financial period end to the time of the announcement. At present, a close period does not automatically apply in the run-up to the release of an interim management statement required under DTR 4. If a company considered, however, that such a statement might be price-sensitive, it should impose its own prohibition on dealing. UKLA has indicated that it will keep this under review.

4 Sales of securities may be permitted in exceptional circumstances, even though otherwise prohibited. Where such a sale is permitted and is required to be notified to the Stock Exchange, such notification must include a statement of the circumstances in which the dealing was permitted. Any dealing by a person discharging managerial responsibility in the company's securities, whether in a close period or not, requires a prompt notification by the company to the Stock Exchange under the DTRs.

5 Under the Code definitions, securities include securities listed in any member state or traded on any regulated market. It also includes any other securities that are convertible into such securities as well as the granting or exercise of certain types of employee share options. A member state is defined in the definitions section of the Listing Rules as being any member of the European Economic Area (EEA) (a wider grouping than the EU).

6 PDMRs may not deal in the company's securities on considerations of a short-term nature. This is considered as the buying and selling of securities within a period of one year.

7 PDMRs should take reasonable steps to ensure that connected persons do not deal in a prohibited period and also to observe the code. Connected persons should inform the company when they deal in its securities.

PDMRs may take advantage of a provision in the Model Code to enter into a **trading plan**. This is a provision made in accordance with the Model Code under which a PDMR may enter into an agreement to deal in shares in an open dealing period which may be subsequently executed in an open or a prohibited dealing period. Trading plans must be in writing and made with an independent third party. The trading plan must set out such details as the quantity, price and timescales of envisaged dealings, and such an agreement can only be entered into in an open dealing period and subject to the usual process of seeking permission to deal.

**STOP AND THINK 6.6**

The company secretary will need to be proactive in considering any matters which may fall in a closed dealing period. For example, if a director is appointed with a requirement to hold qualification shares (see Chapter 2), the secretary should make every effort to ensure the director concerned is advised appropriately to avoid the compulsory purchase of the qualification shares in a close period.

If there is any doubt as to whether a PDMR's proposed dealing would be caught under the Model Code (or a company's equivalent code), UKLA or the company's corporate broker advisor should be contacted for guidance prior to the transaction.

It is usually the company secretary's role to ensure PDMRs are aware of close periods. This should be done by sending a written notification informing them well in advance of the close period starting, and if necessary, attaching a copy of the Model Code. It may be appropriate to send the notification in duplicate so that the recipient can countersign one copy and return it to the secretary to acknowledge receipt.

## 7.4 Insider lists

Listed companies are required to maintain a register of persons who have access to inside information of the company. In addition to employees of the company, this extends to persons of the company's advisers who have access to inside information. A listed company must make suitable arrangements to ensure that their advisers either maintain a list or the listed company must maintain such a list.

The DTRs require **insider lists** to be kept for at least five years from when they were created or last updated. The FSA may also demand the insider list from a company, which is then obliged to provide it to the FSA as soon as possible.

---

**TEST YOUR KNOWLEDGE 6.6**

**a** What is insider dealing?
**b** What is market abuse?
**c** What are the main aims of the Model Code?
**d** When are (i) close periods; (ii) prohibited periods?
**e** Explain the purpose of insider lists. Who is entitled to inspect them?

---

## CASE QUESTION

As company secretary of Multiple plc, you realise that the company has certain obligations as a result of being listed. In particular you need to help the directors understand what they need to know and do about the listing regime; and also to provide them with some reassurance that the Company Secretariat department has good control over listed company obligations. In order to address this, you have decided the following:

**1** You will prepare a section of an induction pack for a new NED which addresses the main obligations in the listing regime. What needs to go in the induction pack? Following induction, how would you suggest keeping the director up to date on the listing regime?

**2** You will design a calendar for the department in respect of actions under the listed company regime for the forthcoming year. The calendar will show what needs to be disclosed, why and when.

The following events will require an action in the timetable:

**a** The company's annual accounting reference date is 31 December. Final dividends are due to be proposed in respect of the year end;

**b** The company's half-year accounting reference date 30 June. Interim dividends are due to be approved by the board for the half-year;

**c** The company also publishes quarterly results for the periods 31 March and 31 October;

**d** The AGM is due to be held on 10 May. One of the resolutions includes a proposal to amend the Articles of Association;

**e** The Annual Report and Accounts are due to be published on 24 March. The notice of AGM and proxy cards will also be issued on that day;

**f** The new NED is due to be appointed on 30 October.

## CHAPTER SUMMARY

■ The London Stock Exchange operates several markets for securities, including the Official List for larger established companies, and AIM for newer, smaller companies not eligible for the Official List.

■ The FSMA 2000 establishes the framework for regulating financial services in the UK (through the FSA). The UKLA regulates the admission of securities to the UK Official List and the continuing obligations on companies once they are listed.

■ The detailed regulations are covered in three rule books: the Listing Rules, the Prospectus Rules and the DTRs. It is vital for the company secretary of a listed company to become familiar with the Listing Regime and to be in a position to provide assistance to the directors.

■ Companies wishing to join the Official List should appoint professional advisers, and must meet the criteria laid down in the Listing Rules and Prospectus Rules, including publication of a formal prospectus which sets out the business, assets and liabilities and financial position of the company, together with details of the management and recent development and prospects. Application must be made both to UKLA and to the London Stock Exchange.

■ Once a company has been admitted to the Official List, it becomes subject to the continuing obligations which regulate the disclosure of information to the market and the public.

■ Listed companies are required to produce an annual information update which summarises all information which has been released to the market and made public under the CA over the previous twelve months.

■ AIM is not regulated by its own rules, which are published by the London Stock Exchange.

■ The City Code on Takeovers and Mergers regulates takeovers in the UK. It is intended to ensure fair and equal treatment of all shareholders during a takeover bid.

■ The most common form of takeover is a public issue where an offer is made to all the shareholders of a company to acquire all, or a proportion of, their holdings. Other forms of takeover are by stake-building, or by agreement with individual members.

■ Where a takeover or merger might result in two leading companies in the same field joining forces, the Office of Fair Trading may refer the proposal to the Competition Commission for investigation.

■ When shareholdings in a company by a single holder or group working together reach 3%, the provisions of the DTRs apply. When holdings by a single holder or group reach 30%, the provisions of the City Code apply. If a bidding company acquires 90% of the value of the shares in a target company, under CA 2006, s. 979 it may compulsorily purchase the outstanding shares.

■ Directors and senior employees of listed companies and those who are members of AIM should be aware of offences under the CJA (insider dealing) and under the FSMA (market abuse).

■ Directors and senior employees of listed companies and members of AIM must also act under the provisions of the Model Code, which prohibits dealing in securities when the director or employee is (or is deemed to be) in possession of inside information.

■ Listed companies are required to maintain insider lists of those persons who have access to inside information. The FSA may inspect this list at any time.

# 7

# Insolvency, winding up and dissolution

■ **INTRODUCTION**

In the same way that a company is formed through the process of incorporation, there are formal procedures for winding up or dissolution. This chapter looks at what happens when a company is wound up, and the processes involved in striking off, dissolution and restoration. The life of a company comes to an end when it is dissolved. Dissolution may be voluntary, at the request of the directors, or compulsory, because the company cannot meet its ongoing liabilities. Not all companies being brought to an end are in financial trouble, however, and there are other ways of ending a company apart from winding up.

## 1   Voluntary liquidation

Voluntary liquidation occurs when the company decides that it should be wound up. This could be because the purpose of the business no longer exists or the directors consider that the company will not be able to meet its future liabilities.

There are two types of voluntary liquidation, which reflect the financial position of the company:

1 *Members' voluntary liquidation* – This is where the directors of a company, after making full enquiries as to the financial position of the company, including all of its assets and liabilities, are able to make a **statutory declaration of solvency**. A majority of the company's directors must make a statutory declaration of solvency in the five weeks before a resolution to wind up the company is passed.

2 *Creditors' voluntary liquidation* – If the directors are not able to make a statutory declaration of solvency in a voluntary liquidation, it is by default a creditors' voluntary liquidation. The directors either know or suspect that there may be a risk that the company will not be able to meet all of its liabilities. If the company cannot make the statutory declaration, it is important that reasonable effort is made to identify and contact every creditor so that they are aware of the situation. As the company must cease trading to avoid increasing its existing liabilities, which it may not be able to meet, employees will have to be dismissed.

### 1.1 Members' voluntary liquidation

Both types of voluntary liquidation begin with a shareholder resolution. A members' voluntary liquidation usually requires a special resolution. A copy of the resolution must be delivered to

*The Gazette* within 14 days and to the Registrar within 15 days, together with the statutory declaration. A **liquidator** will need to be appointed and the appointment must be notified to *The Gazette* and to the Registrar within 14 days and advertised in a newspaper local to the business.

If at any time during a members' voluntary liquidation the liquidator forms the view that the company's financial position is not sufficient to pay all its liabilities in accordance with the statutory declaration of solvency, the liquidation process must be altered. A meeting of the creditors must be convened and held within 28 days, and the liquidation becomes a creditors' voluntary liquidation. It is important, therefore, that directors make extensive enquiries of the company's financial position before authorising a declaration of solvency.

## 1.2 Creditors' voluntary liquidation

A creditors' voluntary liquidation usually requires a special resolution. The board should resolve to convene a creditors' meeting and the board resolution should appoint a chairman for the creditors' meeting. (Model Article 39 (public company Model Article 31) does not apply as it states that the chairman of the board is the chairman of a shareholders' general meeting.) The directors and secretary will need to act promptly as a creditors' meeting must be convened within 14 days of the shareholder resolution being passed and at least seven days' notice must be sent to creditors. In addition, in an attempt to contact other potential creditors, the creditors' meeting must be notified to *The Gazette* and advertised in two local newspapers.

In order to assess the extent of the company's ability to meet its debts, the directors must prepare a **statement of affairs** for review at the creditors' meeting.

A liquidator should be appointed and the appointment must be notified to *The Gazette* and to the Registrar within 14 days and advertised in a local newspaper.

The liquidator should be provided with the statement of affairs and is required to send it to the Registrar with the relevant forms within five business days of the creditors' meeting. If the voluntary liquidation commenced on or before 5 April 2010, the liquidator must also send a statement of receipts and payments for the first 12 months of liquidation. After that, statements must be sent every 6 months until the winding up is complete. If the voluntary liquidation commenced on or after 6 April 2010, the liquidator must send a liquidator's report for the first 12 months of liquidation. After that, a liquidator's report must be sent every 12 months until the winding up is complete.

Directors and officers of the company, including the company secretary, should cooperate fully with the liquidator and should ensure that company's records are complete and up to date. Following the creditors' meeting, the liquidator is required to prepare accounts for delivery to the Registrar of receipts and payments over the first twelve months in liquidation. After that a liquidator's report must be sent every twelve months until the winding up is complete.

---

**STOP AND THINK 7.1**

Read the official notices section of your local newspaper. You should find advertisements published by liquidators there.

---

Depending on the size and complexity of the assets and liabilities, it may take some time to wind up a company. Once the assets have been realised and distributed, the company is wound up. The liquidator must then prepare a final account for presentation to meetings of the members and creditors. At least one month's notice must be given, which includes publication in *The Gazette*. Within one week of the meeting, the liquidator must send the final progress report to the Registrar attached to a return of final meeting form. Unless the court makes an order deferring the dissolution, the company is dissolved three months after the return and account are registered at Companies House.

# 2  Compulsory liquidation

Compulsory liquidation occurs when a court order is issued to wind up a company. The liquidation is compulsory as it relates to the court order under which the company is compelled to wind up its affairs. The process is usually initiated by creditors who consider that the company is unable to pay its debts, but it may also be started by the company itself, its members or by the Secretary of State on grounds of public interest.

The most common reason is the company's inability to pay its debts where:

- a sum of £750 or more is owing and remains unpaid;
- the company has failed to settle a debt in full or to the acceptance of one or more creditors;
- a formal statutory demand (see specimen overleaf) has been served in respect of a debt which has not been settled.

---

**STOP AND THINK 7.2**

As a statutory demand will be served on the registered office address of the company, the company secretary may be the first person in the organisation to receive the document. It is essential that company secretaries recognise the document when it is received and realise its importance. The directors must be alerted promptly as urgent action must be taken.

---

The petition to wind up the company must be publicised before the court hearing so it should appear in *The Gazette*. If the petition has been approved at the court hearing, a court order will be granted that the company be wound up. This must be made public immediately by the company delivering a copy of the court order to the Registrar. An **official receiver** will usually be appointed as the liquidator. His first duty will be to review the assets and liabilities of the company and to investigate the circumstances which have led to the court order. The directors will be required to produce a statement of affairs to assist the official receiver in his preliminary duties. This review is important as it may reveal that the directors have breached their duties in such a way that a disqualification order against them needs to be considered (see section 8).

## 2.1  Duties and powers of the official receiver

Following the appointment of the official receiver, most of the directors' powers are transferred to him. As a court order has been issued to wind up the company, employees must be dismissed. The rules of liquidation regarding the priority in which creditors may be entitled to the assets of the company come into force and any frustrating action by creditors, such as seizure of company property, is void. Company secretaries should bear in mind that no further transfers may be registered in the register of members without the court's permission.

After conducting an initial investigation, the official receiver will need to consider whether meetings of the creditors and **contributories** are necessary. If the meetings are held, a liquidator is usually appointed to take over from the official receiver to progress the realisation and distribution of assets. The appointment of the liquidator must be notified to the Registrar without delay. If the official receiver concludes that it is not appropriate to convene such meetings, the creditors, contributories and the court must be informed.

The official receiver or other appointed liquidator must wind up the company according to the relevant legislation (e.g. the Insolvency Rules 1986). Once the winding up is completed, a final report is prepared and sent to the Registrar, who will usually dissolve the company not less than three months following receipt of notification.

If the company's financial position is so bad that it will be unable to meet the costs of the official receiver, liquidator or other winding up costs according to the Rules, the official receiver may use a fast-track procedure to apply to the Registrar for the company to be dissolved, again three months following receipt of notification.

---

**TEST YOUR KNOWLEDGE 7.1**

**a** What is the key difference between a members' voluntary liquidation and a creditors' voluntary liquidation?
**b** What steps are taken by the official receiver following his appointment in a compulsory liquidation?
**c** What is the function of *The Gazette*?

# 3 Administration orders

An **administration order** is a court order giving power to manage the business to an **administrator**. The court order can be sought by the company itself, the directors or creditors, and can be sought if the company is unable to pay its debts or is likely to become unable to do so. A company in such a situation is usually described as being 'in administration'. The law and process of administration orders are covered by the EA 2002.

The purpose of the administration order varies with the circumstances but it is usually:

■ primarily to keep the business operational as a going concern; or if this is not possible, to restructure or operate the business so that it may be sold (in whole or in part) to raise a greater sum or obtain a better result for the creditors than would have otherwise been the case had the company been wound up; or if the above two purposes cannot be achieved, to realise property in order to make distributions to secured or preferential creditors, where this would not unnecessarily harm the interests of other creditors; or
■ as part of a voluntary arrangement (see below); or
■ as part of a compromise arrangement.

An administration order does not necessarily mean that the business will be sold or shut down; business closure will be avoided if possible. Rather, it provides a protective breathing space because, in most cases, during the period of administration, the company cannot have an administrative receiver appointed (see below) and it cannot be wound up.

An administrator can also be appointed out of court by the company's directors or by a **qualifying floating charge holder**. Documentation for an out of court appointment must be filed with the court so that they are aware of the administration and can provide the administrator with directions as required.

## 3.1 Duties and powers of the administrator

Following the court order, the administrator is required to prepare proposals for managing the affairs of the business for presentation to the company's creditors for approval. As soon as practicable and before the end of eight weeks after the company enters administration the administrator must make a statement setting out proposals for achieving the purpose of the administration or explaining why they cannot be achieved. The proposals may include a voluntary arrangement, a compromise or arrangement with creditors or members. The administrator is required to lodge a copy of the court order and the details of the proposals as presented to the creditors' meeting with the Registrar. An advertisement regarding the court order should also be made in *The Gazette* and in a local newspaper. The administrator will then be required to lodge accounts showing receipts and payments of the business at least every six months.

In addition to his general powers, the administrator has a statutory duty to act with speed and efficiency and in the interests of the company as a whole. The directors are not automatically removed and continue to hold office, but cannot exercise their powers without the administrator's consent. The administrator also has general statutory powers, if needed, to remove or appoint directors and to convene meetings of creditors or members. This may involve the assistance of the company secretary, for example, to maintain statutory registers or to provide an up-to-date list of members. During the period of administration, officers of the company are under a duty to co-operate with the administrator.

An administration usually ends one year following commencement, unless the purpose of the order has been achieved earlier. The administration period can be extended by a further six months by approval of creditors or by a further court extension order.

Whilst the company is in administration, there is no exemption for the requirement to continue filing returns with the Registrar of Companies, but it is unlikely that breaches will be enforced during the period of administration.

# 4   Corporate voluntary arrangements

## 4.1 Unanimous creditor arrangement

If a company is in financial trouble, it may be able to reach an agreement with all its creditors for a settlement arrangement, for example, agreement that each creditor will receive 80% of their respective debt. This is known as a unanimous creditor arrangement and is relatively informal, as each creditor has agreed to the arrangement and each is being treated equally.

## 4.2 Formal voluntary arrangement

If a unanimous decision cannot be reached among the creditors, a formal **voluntary arrangement** is required (CA 2006, s. 899). This is an agreement approved by the court for a company to reach a composition in satisfaction of debt (i.e. an agreement to settle the terms of the debt) with its creditors. Voluntary arrangements may be proposed by administrators, liquidators, members or the directors themselves. As it is voluntary in nature, it cannot be proposed by creditors.

### Procedure
A nominee is appointed to oversee the proposal to reach a composition in satisfaction of the debt. Two meetings are convened to consider the proposals – one of the creditors, the other of the members. It is essential that the company secretary ensures the register of members is fully up to date when notice of the meeting is sent to the members.

At the meetings of the creditors and members, only certain amendments to the proposed plan of voluntary arrangement are permitted. If the voluntary arrangement is approved by creditors, it is binding on every creditor who was entitled to receive notice of the meeting. If there is a difference of opinion about the proposals between the creditors and the shareholders, the views of the creditors will prevail. The proposal from the meetings must then be submitted to the court for approval.

Following approval of the voluntary arrangement, the nominee becomes the supervisor of the voluntary arrangement. The supervisor must prepare a report of the meetings for submission to the Registrar. While the voluntary arrangement is in force, the supervisor must submit accounts showing receipts and payments to the Registrar and all other interested parties at least annually.

The appointment of the supervisor comes to an end when the arrangement is satisfied or revoked. The Registrar must be informed within 28 days once this occurs.

### Moratorium under the Insolvency Act (IA) 2000
In limited circumstances, it is possible for the nominee to enforce a statutory moratorium under the IA 2000 so that no creditor can proceed with an action against the company's assets over a stipulated period (initially 28 days but this may be extended by a further two months). The moratorium is available for small companies as defined under CA 2006 (see Chapter 11) and provides an opportunity to review further whether a voluntary arrangement can be achieved.

# 5 Receivers

A **receiver** is appointed to manage the whole or part of a company's property. The terms of appointment and powers of the receiver are contained in a debenture or other instrument creating a secured charge over the company's property. The appointment is triggered by default – for example, the company fails to pay a debt due.

Generally, there are two types of receiver:

1 An administrative receiver is a person appointed under a debenture which is secured by a floating charge over all, or substantially all, of the company's assets. By their nature, floating charges are usually at least in respect of substantially all of the company's assets.
2 A receiver (other than an administrative receiver) is any other person appointed under an instrument which is secured by a charge on the company's assets.

## 5.1 Power and duties of receivers

The person who appointed the administrative receiver or receiver (i.e. the debenture holder or other charge-holder) must inform the Registrar within seven days of the receiver's appointment. An administrative receiver must also advertise his appointment in *The Gazette* and in a national or local newspaper to the business.

Within three months of his appointment, the receiver must prepare a report to the company's creditors and floating charge-holders which explains why he has been appointed and details the steps he will take in respect of the debt. The receiver must decide whether a statement of affairs of the company is required (i.e. a list of the company's assets, liabilities and creditors) and if so, he will request the company's directors and officers to prepare it. If a statement of affairs has been prepared, a summary of the statement must be included in a report sent to creditors and charge-holders. Both the report and the statement of affairs must also be sent to the Registrar.

The receiver will then dispose of the asset(s) necessary to satisfy the secured debt. During the period of receivership, the receiver will send accounts to the Registrar showing payments and receipts for the first year and then at subsequent annual intervals for administrative receivers, or six-monthly intervals for receivers other than administrative receivers, whilst the company is in receivership.

The receivership is brought to an end when the secured debt is satisfied or waived by the creditor, or another arrangement is agreed such as an administration order. The Registrar must be notified of the end of the receivership by the receiver.

## 5.2 Receivers under the Enterprise Act (EA) 2002

The Enterprise Act (EA) 2002 was intended to reform corporate insolvency so that emphasis is placed on rescuing businesses, where possible, rather than winding them up. Under EA, enforcement of any floating charges created after 15 September 2003 (with some limited exceptions) requires court approval by way of an administrative order (see section 3). Floating charges created before 15 September 2003 can be enforced via administrative receivership.

---

**TEST YOUR KNOWLEDGE 7.2**

a  What are the purposes of an administration order?
b  What are the powers of a holder of a floating charge under the EA 2002?
c  What meetings must be held to approve a formal voluntary arrangement?
d  What are the differences between a voluntary arrangement and voluntary liquidation?

# 6   Striking off

## 6.1 Application by the directors to strike off a company

Provisions for striking off a company are contained in CA 2006, Part 31, ss. 1000–1034.

If a company has ceased trading and is no longer required, the directors may apply to the Registrar to have the company struck off and dissolved. This is not an alternative to insolvency proceedings and directors must be certain that the company will meet the qualifying requirements for striking off. The secretary may well be asked to coordinate the process and it will be essential that a methodical approach is adopted, keeping detailed records, checklists and a timetable of actions and events.

The company must meet certain conditions before it is eligible for striking off:

■ it must not have changed company name in the last three months;
■ it should not have undertaken any trading activities or disposed of any assets in the ordinary course of business over the last three months;
■ the only permitted activities in the last three months must be to help prepare for the striking off application (e.g. the disposal of business assets as part of a business closure);
■ it must not be the subject of insolvency proceedings or have applied for a scheme of arrangement under CA 2006.

The decision to apply for a striking off is made by board resolution. Unanimous board consent is advisable in case of subsequent objections (see section 6.3). Once board approval is received, a checklist of actions should be prepared to ensure the following:

■ the qualifying conditions have all been met;
■ a plan of action has been prepared to dispose of all assets, as any remaining assets at the point of dissolution will go *bona vacantia* to the Crown;
■ third parties are informed in a timely manner.

Once the board is satisfied that the company qualifies for the striking off application, form DS01 should be completed and submitted to the Registrar, along with the applicable filing fee, signed as follows:

■ if the company has a sole director, he must sign the form;
■ if there are two directors, both must sign;
■ if there are more than two directors, a majority of the directors must sign.

## 6.2 Informing interested parties of an application to strike off

All interested parties must be informed of the company's intention to be struck off and dissolved. This is in order to give them an opportunity to object prior to the company's assets being disposed of or becoming *bona vacantia*. All parties must be informed by providing them with a copy of form DS01 within seven days of its being filed. The company secretary should work with the directors to provide a comprehensive list of persons who must be informed. They include:

■ creditors;
■ directors who did not sign form DS01;
■ managers or trustees of any company pension scheme;
■ the applicable VAT office if the company is registered for VAT;
■ shareholders;
■ employees;
■ any persons who becomes a creditor, director, etc. following the original notification.

Notification should be by hand or via recorded delivery, as it is good practice to have proof of delivery in the event of future query. A thorough check of records should be made prior to notification to ensure that the notification is sent to the most current address; additional copies should be sent to both the business address and the registered office address (if different) of any incorporated entities. The Registrar will also place a notice of the intention to apply for a striking off on the public records of the company.

## 6.3 Objections to an application to strike off

Any interested party may object to the application on the grounds that:

- the company does not meet the criteria listed in section 6.1 above;
- a fraud is being attempted;
- the interested party has not been informed of the application to apply for a striking off;
- legal proceedings are being taken against the company.

Directors must withdraw the application if they become aware that any of the qualifying criteria no longer apply. Alternatively, any one director may withdraw an application by signing form DS02 and submitting it to the Registrar of Companies. It will be necessary to inform all previously notified parties who received form DS01 that the application has been withdrawn.

## 6.4 Striking off and dissolution

Once the Registrar has received an application on form DS01 and is satisfied with it, he will publish a notice in *The Gazette* informing of the proposed application and inviting any objections. If no objections or withdrawals have been received after no less than three months following publication, and the Registrar remains satisfied with the application, the Registrar may dissolve the company by publishing a further notice to this effect in *The Gazette*.

---

**STOP AND THINK** **7.3**

The process of applying to have a company struck off and dissolved requires a considerable amount of planning. The company should consider any potential problems or objections prior to taking any action. Applying for striking off when the company is ineligible or failure to notify interested third parties are offences under the Companies Acts, which in the worst case can lead to fines being levied against directors and the possibility of disqualification.

The secretary is often central in the planning process and should be prepared to give advice and support to the board so as to avoid any embarrassing or costly mistakes.

---

## 6.5 Registrar of Companies and striking off (defunct companies)

Even if a company is dormant or is being retained only to protect its name (e.g. where a company has been incorporated to prevent a competitor using a particular company name), it is vital that:

- all statutory returns are filed with the Registrar of Companies on time; and
- a postal address is maintained for receipt of documentation at the registered office address.

Failure to do so may lead the Registrar to conclude that a business is defunct unless there is evidence to the contrary. If the Registrar does not receive statutory returns and mail sent to the company's registered office address is returned undelivered, he may consider that the business is not being operated and that it is appropriate for it to be struck off and dissolved.

Before striking a company off the register, the Registrar is required to write two formal letters and send notice to the company's registered office to inquire whether it is still carrying on business or is in operation. If the company is being operated, it is important that it responds quickly to the inquiry letter and files any overdue returns. If there is no response to the inquiry letters, a notice will appear in *The Gazette* inviting objections to a proposed striking off and dissolution. Any interested party, which may include the company itself, may lodge such an objection.

The Registrar will also place a notice of the intention to apply for a striking off on the public records of the company. After no less than three months, if no objections have been upheld and the Registrar remains satisfied that the company is defunct and should be struck off, he

In accordance with
Section 1003 of the
Companies Act 2006.

# DS01
## Striking off application by a company

**Companies House**

**A fee is payable with this form**
Please see 'How to pay' on the last page.

✓ **What this form is for**
You may use this form to strike off a company from the Register.

✗ **What this form is NOT for**
You cannot use this form to strike off a Limited Liability Partnership (LLP). To strike off an LLP please use form LL DS01 'Striking off application by a Limited Liability Partnership (LLP)'.

For further information, please refer to our guidance at www.companieshouse.gov.uk

### Warning to all interested parties

This is an important notice and should not be ignored. The company named has applied to the Registrar to be struck off the Register and dissolved. Please note that on dissolution any remaining assets will be passed to the Crown. The Registrar will strike the company off the register unless there is reasonable cause not to do so. Guidance is available on grounds for objection. If in doubt, seek professional advice.

**1** **Company details**

Company number

Company name in full

→ **Filling in this form**
Please complete in typescript or in bold black capitals.

All fields are mandatory unless specified or indicated by *

**2** **The application**

**Warning to all applicants**
It is an offence to knowingly or recklessly provide false or misleading information on this application.

You are advised to read Section 4 and to consult the guidance available from Companies House before completing this form. If in doubt, seek professional advice.

**I/We as director(s) / the majority of directors apply for this company to be struck off the Register and declare that none of the circumstances described in section 1004 or 1005 of the Companies Act 2006 (being circumstances in which the directors would otherwise be prohibited under those sections from making an application) exists in relation to the company.** ❶

This form must be signed by the sole director if only 1, by both if there are 2, or by the majority if there are more than 2.

→ **Go to Section 3** 'Name(s) and Signature(s) of the directors'

❶ Please read the guidance on our website at www.companieshouse.gov.uk or section 1004 or 1005 of the Companies Act 2006 for circumstances under which an application may not be made.

Please note that on dissolution all property and rights etc will be passed to the Crown.

CHWP000
05/12 Version 6.0

In accordance with
Section 1010 of the
Companies Act 2006.

# DS02

## Withdrawal of striking off application by company

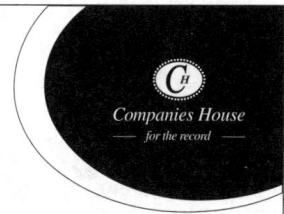

**Companies House**
— *for the record* —

✓ **What this form is for**
You may use this form to withdraw
a company's striking off application.

✗ **What this form is NOT for**
You cannot use this form to:
- withdraw a striking off
  application by a Limited Liability
  Partnership (LLP).
- to stop the Registrar striking off a
  company for default filing.

For further information, please
refer to our guidance at
www.companieshouse.gov.uk

| **1** | **Company details** | |
|---|---|---|

Company number

Company name in full

→ **Filling in this form**
Please complete in typescript or in
bold black capitals.

All fields are mandatory unless
specified or indicated by *

| **2** | **Notice of withdrawal of application** |
|---|---|

The directors hereby withdraw the application in which it was requested that
this company be struck off the Register.

| **3** | **Signature** ❶ |
|---|---|

I am signing this from on behalf of the company.

Signature

Signature

✗                                                                    ✗

❶ This form can be signed by any
director.

Please see our guidance at
www.companieshouse.gov.uk or
section 1009 of the Companies
Act 2006 for the circumstances
under which the application may be
withdrawn.

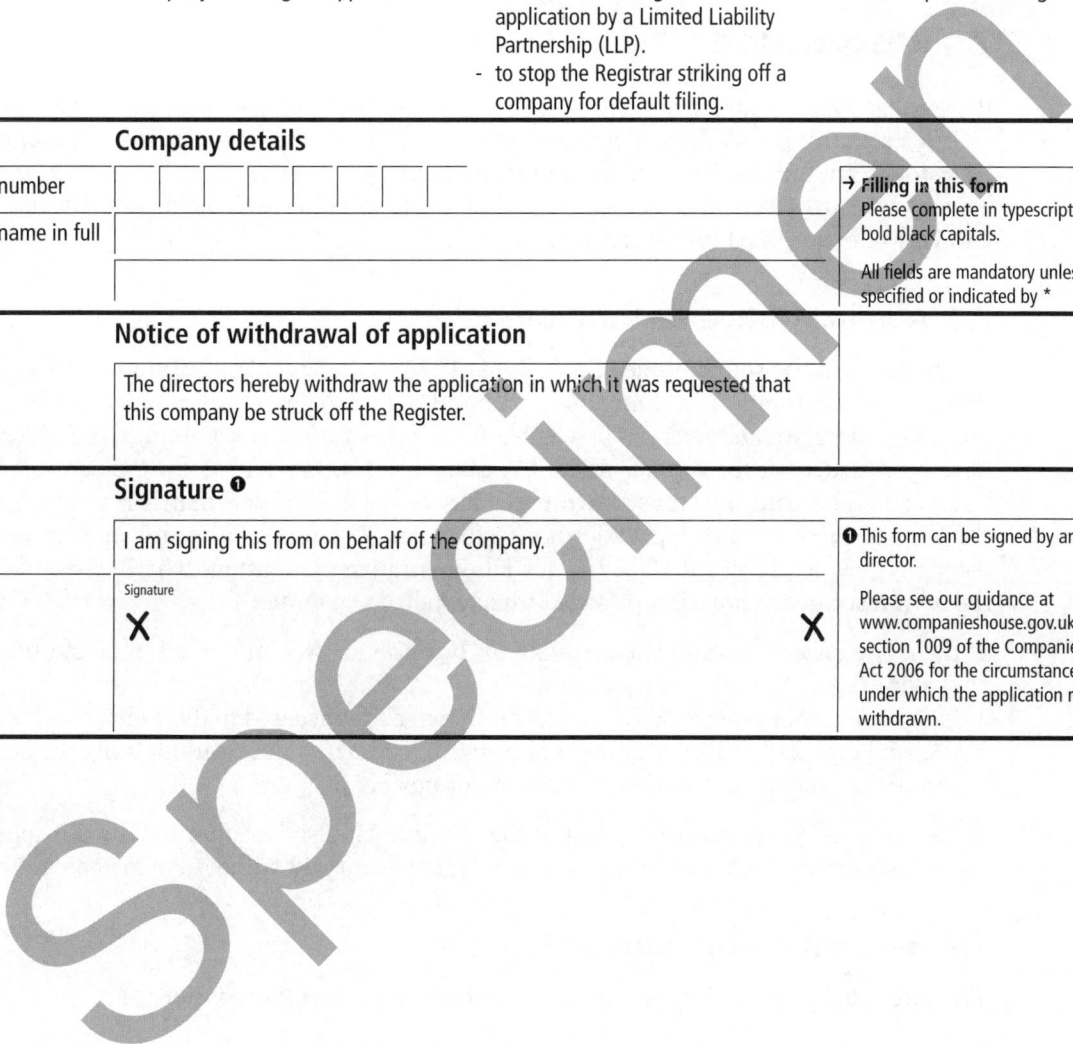

will strike off the company. The company will then be dissolved when the Registrar publishes a further notice in *The Gazette* to that effect. Any assets held by the company at the point of dissolution will become *bona vacantia* and will be held by the Crown.

---

**STOP AND THINK** **7.4**

An important part of the secretary's job is to ensure that a registered office address is maintained to enable the serving of formal documents and also to respond to correspondence, for example, from the Registrar of Companies. This applies even to dormant companies.

---

# 7   Restoration

If a company should not have been struck off and dissolved, or if, subsequent to the dissolution, an interested third party discovers that they have unfinished business, the former company can be restored, but only under limited circumstances and with a court order. The effect of restoring a company is to reverse the decision to strike it off. Any property held *bona vacantia* by the Crown will be returned to the company.

## 7.1  Administrative restoration

Restoration may be sought under CA 2006, s. 1025 by way of **administrative restoration**. This provides the restoration of companies without the need for a court order, so making the procedure more streamlined. To be eligible for administrative restoration, the company must have been struck off the register under CA 2006, ss. 1000 and 1001 (or the equivalent under CA 1985). The company must have been dissolved for no more than six years at the date the Registrar receives the application for restoration. The former directors or members of the company may apply to the Registrar for administrative restoration. The Registrar will grant the administrative restoration provided three conditions are met:

1  the company in question was carrying on business or was in operation at the time of the striking off;
2  if any property became *bona vacantia*, the Crown has consented to the company's restoration;
3  the applicant has delivered to the Registrar all documents necessary to bring the company's records up to date (e.g. annual returns, accounts, etc.).

A statement of compliance in respect of the above must also be submitted by the applicant. If the Registrar does not allow the application, the applicant will still be able to apply to the court.

## 7.2  Restoration by court order

The interested parties who may apply to the court for a restoration order are:

■ the former company itself, its former members or creditors where the company has been declared defunct and struck off by the Registrar;
■ any interested party who should have received a form DS01 where the directors have applied to strike off the company. The reasons for the restoration order are essentially the same as the reasons for objecting to an application to strike off (see section 6.3);
■ any interested party following the winding up of a company under insolvency proceedings;
■ the Secretary of State if it is considered there are just grounds in the public interest.

Generally, the restoration order must be sought within 20 years of the striking off. CA 2006, however, has repealed previous legislation which barred the restoration of companies which were dissolved prior to 1969 where parties wish to bring a claim for damages in respect of personal injuries or fatal accidents. Where the company was wound up following insolvency proceedings, the restoration order must be sought within two years. If the restoration order is successful, notification will appear in *The Gazette*.

> **STOP AND THINK 7.5**
>
> As the effect of restoration is to reverse a striking off and dissolution, a company will need to bring its corporate records up to date. For example, if the company has not filed annual accounts since dissolution, these must be prepared. There will also be statutory penalties for any accounts which have been filed late.

> **TEST YOUR KNOWLEDGE 7.3**
>
> a What conditions must be met in order for the directors of a company to apply for a voluntary striking off?
>
> b Which parties must be informed if directors of a company are seeking a voluntary striking off? What document must the company send?
>
> c Why might the Registrar instigate the striking off of a company? What notification does the Registrar give prior to such a striking off?
>
> d Who is authorised to order the restoration of a company? What are the applicable timescales for such a restoration?
>
> e Explain the procedure of administrative restoration.

## 8 Directors of insolvent companies

Directors' duties are covered in Chapter 2. They extend to situations where the company has become or may become insolvent. For example, directors must:

- act in the best interests of the company;
- avoid entering into transactions that will place them in a personal conflict of interest with the company;
- demonstrate reasonable care, skill and knowledge in respect of the day-to-day running of the business and also any major transactions which have the potential to affect the solvency of the business.

### 8.1 Disqualification

Chapter 2 deals with the grounds for disqualifying directors, including wrongful trading or fraudulent trading under IA 1986. A director is not automatically disqualified if the company of which he is a director becomes insolvent. However, the liquidator, administrative receiver or official receiver is obliged to send the Secretary of State (in this case at the BIS) a report on the conduct of any director who held office up to three years prior to insolvency. It is then the Secretary of State's decision to seek a disqualification order against any of the directors concerned. CDDA 1986, Sch. 1 provides a non-exhaustive list of the grounds for seeking a disqualification order:

- persistent breaches of company legislation;
- failure to pay taxes in due time;
- fraud;
- fraudulent or wrongful trading, as defined under IA 1986;
- failure of the directors to comply with the any other provision of IA 1986; for example, failure to convene a creditors' meeting in a creditors' voluntary liquidation, or failure to prepare a statement of affairs in a liquidation;
- inappropriate conduct in entering into transactions at an undervalue or giving undue preferential treatment to one or more creditors prior to the company becoming insolvent;
- the extent of the director's responsibility for the causes of the company becoming insolvent.

A prosecution for a disqualification will be heard in court. If the director is disqualified, the court will inform the Registrar so that the register of disqualified directors (which is a public register) can be updated.

STOP AND THINK 7.6

The statutory power to disqualify a director is reflected in the provisions of the Model Articles in respect of the termination of a director. Model Article 18 (public company Model Article 22) provides that a person ceases to be a director by virtue of any provision of the CA 2006 or is prohibited from being a director by law.

The liquidator will review company documentation, including board minutes. Although the conduct of the business is ultimately the responsibility of the directors, company secretaries can provide assistance to directors in their day-to-day function by:

■ recommending to the directors that board meetings are held at sufficiently frequent intervals in order to consider the status of the business;
■ recommending to the directors that board meetings regularly consider the trading and financial position of the company;
■ preparing a schedule of statutory returns (particularly the accounts) and reminding directors, if necessary, that action needs to be taken so as to comply with statutory deadlines;
■ ensuring that the going concern principle is reviewed when preparing annual accounts (see Chapter 11).

## 8.2 The effects of disqualification

CDDA 1986 provides that a disqualified person or an undischarged bankrupt cannot act as a director or be concerned in the promotion, formation or management of a company unless permission has been granted by the court.

CDDA, s. 15 provides that if a person acts in the capacity of a director whilst disqualified, he is both personally and jointly and severally liable with the company for all the relevant debts of a company during the time he acted as a director. This applies if the company becomes insolvent and could therefore have a considerable personal financial impact on the disqualified director.

IA 1986, s. 216 prohibits a director of an insolvent company from being a director or being involved in the promotion, formation or management of another company with the same or a substantially similar name within five years of the insolvency. If a director acts in contravention of this, he will be personally liable, along with the company, for its debts. This provision is to prevent directors from being involved in **phoenix companies** whereby a new company is set up which appears to have taken on the character of the previous business. Company secretaries involved in company incorporation should check both the company name and the register of disqualified directors.

## 8.3 The Insolvency Service

The Insolvency Service (IS) is an executive agency within BIS. Through its official receivers, IS administers and investigates the affairs of individual bankrupts and companies in liquidation and the suspected misconduct of directors of insolvent companies. The service is authorised to deal with the disqualification of directors in all corporate failures. It also provides practical help for directors by providing plain English guidance booklets on liquidation and related matters (see Directory). IS also provides a hotline for anyone to report defiant directors and undischarged bankrupts who disregard disqualification orders made against them. IS is empowered to conduct the authorisation and regulation of insolvency practitioners.

# 9 Issues for the company secretary

Although the company secretary does not play an active role in insolvency proceedings, it is vital that he is aware of the circumstances under which liquidation may arise and the procedures which are subsequently followed. There are also practical and procedural matters which the company secretary should bear in mind.

## 9.1 Incorporating a new company or appointing a new director

Company secretaries should use checklists which cover appropriate questions, including insolvency of companies and personal bankruptcy of directors, when involved in the incorporation of new companies or when appointing new directors. This is for their own protection and also for the protection of other directors and the company itself.

The Companies House website contains an index of disqualified directors. The index can be searched by name and shows the general reason for the director's disqualification and the disqualification period. IS also has an online database on its website (see Directory) where anyone can check if an individual (such as a director) is an undischarged bankrupt or has other similar restrictions, orders or arrangements.

The Listing Rules require a listed company to notify certain information to a RIS when a new director is appointed. The information must state whether the director has served in an executive function within twelve months of any company going into receivership, compulsory liquidation, creditors' voluntary liquidation, administration, a company voluntary arrangement or any other composition or arrangement with its creditors. It is also necessary to declare whether the appointee has ever been disqualified by a court from acting as a director or from acting in the management or conduct of the affairs of any company, even if the disqualification no longer applies. Although these matters are not necessarily a bar to the person becoming a director of a listed company, they must still be reported to UKLA.

## 9.2 General advice to directors and drafting board minutes

If it has become clear that the company is in financial difficulties and no action has been taken, the company secretary should inform the directors that potential insolvency is a serious matter and requires urgent attention. Directors must consult an appropriately qualified insolvency practitioner and the speed in which they seek professional advice, in addition to their general conduct, may well have a bearing on whether disqualification proceedings should be enforced. Directors should also be advised about the IS, which strongly recommends that urgent action is taken to confront financial difficulty.

If a company is subject to compulsory liquidation, the official receiver or liquidator will investigate the conduct of the business in the period prior to the court order. Any major transactions are likely to be reviewed in case the liquidator can disclaim any onerous property or reclaim the fair value of property which the company had previously disposed of at an undervalue. Such major transactions should be fully and accurately recorded in the board minutes as and when they occur so that they can stand the test of scrutiny in the future – the company secretary should bear this in mind when drafting board minutes. The company secretary should also ensure that any supporting papers that are used for board meetings are retained.

**STOP AND THINK 7.7**

Unless otherwise proved, board minutes provide conclusive evidence of matters the directors have considered. A great deal of thought should therefore be given by company secretaries when writing minutes on important matters, as they may be subject to review by third parties later.

## 9.3 Statutory documentation and statutory registers

All company documentation (letter heading, receipts, invoices, etc.) must be amended to indicate whether a company is in administration, liquidation or administrative receivership. The name of the administrator or liquidator must appear on the documentation. As the company secretary is often responsible for ensuring that letter heading and other stationery complies with the Act and will also have practical knowledge of where stocks of stationery are printed and maintained, he may be asked to assist the administrator or liquidator.

The company secretary is often responsible for handling formal mail served to or received at a company's head office. It is therefore vital that the secretary recognises the various formal demands and documents that may be delivered to the registered office and that he takes prompt appropriate action.

Directors are required by law to cooperate with the official receiver or other insolvency practitioner. The company secretary, as an officer of the company, should also cooperate as necessary, particularly regarding the possible handover of statutory registers. The company secretary should ensure that all statutory records are complete and up to date. This is particularly important for the register of members as the shareholders may need to be informed of the company's situation and any holders of partly paid shares (as contributories) may be requested to pay the unpaid balance outstanding on their shares.

Under the CA, each company must maintain a register of charges, even if there are no entries to be made (see Chapter 8). Each charge, which must be kept in the register of charges, must also be filed with the Registrar of Companies within 21 days of creation. When a charge has been satisfied or waived, a Memorandum of Satisfaction or Release must be delivered to the Registrar. These filings must be in order, as any insolvency practitioner will need conclusive evidence of who the company's creditors are and whether their debt is secured and unsecured.

## 9.4 Information available to the public

When a company wishes to enter into a transaction with another company, part of a standard due diligence procedure should be to search *The Gazette* as to whether any insolvency or other proceedings are being brought against the company. *The Gazette* is available online (see Directory) and can be searched by the names of companies, persons or any other key words that might have appeared in notices in *The Gazette*.

The Companies House register of disqualified directors is also available online, and the Registrar maintains, for each company, details of the appointment of administrators or liquidators.

---

**TEST YOUR KNOWLEDGE 7.4**

a What are the grounds for seeking a disqualification order under CDDA 1986?
b What action may be taken against a person who acts as a director whilst disqualified?
c What are the purpose and powers of the IS? What information may be obtained from IS?
d What practical advice and help can a company secretary provide directors in relation to a potential insolvency or dissolution of a company?
e What information can be obtained from the Registrar of Companies and *The Gazette* in relation to insolvency and administration orders?

## **CHAPTER** SUMMARY

■ There are several ways of dealing with companies that have run into financial difficulty. This will often involve an insolvency practitioner taking control of the running of the business.

■ Liquidation of a company can be voluntary (commenced by the company) or compulsory (commenced by a court order).

■ Administration orders are orders of the court and give power to manage to the business to an administrator.

■ The enactment of the EA 2002 has changed the procedures in respect of administration orders. Emphasis is placed on rescuing companies where possible and reduces the right to appoint administrative receivers.

■ Voluntary arrangements can be made which involve binding court agreements on creditors to settle the terms of the debt owed by a company.

■ Companies can be struck off and dissolved if they are no longer required. This can be at the request of the company. However, if the company does not file accounts and other returns, the Registrar may act to strike off a company. Companies, members and creditors can request that company be restored if they have unfinished business with it.

■ Directors of wound up companies who have breached statutory legislation are liable to be disqualified to act as directors for up to 15 years. Persons who have been disqualified cannot act as directors until the disqualification order has expired.

■ Company secretaries should ensure appropriate enquiries are made when appointing a director in case they have been previously disqualified. Appropriate checks should also be made about the name of any company which is being incorporated, in case it is similar to a previously dissolved company.

■ Information about disqualified directors is available from the Registrar of Companies. General guidance for directors about insolvency is available from the IS.

■ A simplified restoration process is available under the CA 2006 by way of administrative restoration.

## PART 2 PRACTICE CASE QUESTIONS

These questions are based on the case scenario outlined at the beginning of Part Two. You will need to refer to content throughout Part Two to provide the answers. The questions may also include material covered in Part One of this study text.

## PART CASE QUESTION 2.1

One of the recent acquisitions of Multiple plc was People's Travel Limited, a travel agent and tourism company. People's Travel owns a small chain of hotels, including one in Burbington-on-Sea, a resort in north-east England. You are approached by a group of hotel owners who want to set up a bureau for visitors and a website which advertises Burbington-on-Sea and takes bookings for hotels, including those owned by People's Travel Limited. The hotel owners will pay the bureau a fee for each booking they receive.

The hotel owners do not want to be involved in the day-to-day running of the bureau, but want to have the final say over its strategy and future direction. They have agreed among themselves that that they will each contribute a small sum to rent an office and hire staff,

but they want to limit their liability for any debts the bureau may incur.

Most of the hotel owners see the bureau as providing a service to them and do not expect a dividend from the bureau. However, some of their colleagues are ambitious and want the bureau to be more enterprising by, for example, running coach trips to neighbouring resorts. It is clear to you that a company needs to be formed. Write a letter to the hotel owners advising them on the types of company available and recommending the type they should choose, explaining how it will meet their objectives. Your letter should also explain the various ways in which as members they can provide the money required to rent an office and hire staff.

## PART CASE QUESTION 2.2

It has been agreed that some of the subsidiary companies of Multiple plc are no longer required and should be struck off. You have been requested to prepare a guidance note appropriate for when the directors of a company wish to apply to strike off the company. The guidance note should cover:

a) the criteria required for a company to be struck off;

b) what authority is required to apply for a striking off and the statutory process of the striking off application;

c) whether any party will be able to object to or withdraw from the striking off and if so, how and why they will be able to do this;

d) the statutory process under which the striking off becomes effective; and

e) what would need to be done in the unlikely event that a company has inadvertently been struck off in error.

Prepare a suitable guidance note for the directors.

# Regulation and disclosure

## ■ LIST OF CHAPTERS

## ■ OVERVIEW

Limited liability is a privilege, and the price for this privilege is the need for publicity and compliance with rules that the information made public is up to date. Chapter 8 describes the company secretary's role in all companies in liaising with and meeting the requirements set by the state as represented by Companies House. It is also important to be familiar with the compliance regime specifically associated with listed and quoted companies, and the with the role of the Panel on Takeovers and Mergers; these are covered in Chapter 6.

This part of the study text also sets out the responsibilities of the company secretary at company meetings. The company secretary has a key role to play in the decision-making processes of the company and its members. It is one of the core duties of the company secretary to ensure the correct procedures are followed at general and board meetings so that decisions are made properly and lawfully. It is also a key responsibility to make sure that decisions are recorded accurately, and that any follow-up documentation is prepared within the appropriate timescales. The procedures and regulations in respect of meetings of the members are very different from those of board meetings. You should ensure that you understand each set of procedures and regulations and know how to apply them correctly. Chapter 9 deals with the organisation and conduct of meetings of the members, and resolutions. Chapter 10 discusses board and committee meetings. In Chapter 11 we look at the secretary's role in preparing the annual report and accounts and the duties and responsibilities of the auditor.

## ■ LEARNING OUTCOMES

After reading and understanding the contents of Part Three, you should be able to:

■ Understand the role of Companies House, the home of the Registrar of Companies, and the CA 2006 provisions relating to it.
■ Know what is required for the annual return.
■ Outline the information required to maintain the statutory registers and where they should be kept.

- Understand the purpose and procedures associated with general meetings, including AGMs and class meetings.
- Know the regulations on general meeting quorums and voting.
- Understand the different types of resolution and when they are used, including the use of written resolutions by private companies.
- Understand the role of the chairman at general meetings, and know what is required of the company secretary before, during and after a general meeting.
- Explain the regulations which govern board meetings, including issues such as notice requirements, voting procedure and the role of the chairman.
- Be familiar with what should be covered at the first board meeting of a newly registered company.
- Understand the main tasks of the company secretary before, during and after the board meeting, including the preparation and keeping of minutes.
- Know the role and membership of the board committees a listed company should establish under the UK Corporate Governance Code.
- Explain the main components of a company's annual report and accounts.
- Know and understand the regulations affecting small and medium-sized private companies and their obligations to prepare and file accounts.
- Apply the disclosure requirements for listed companies.
- Demonstrate a good knowledge of the requirements and procedures for appointing and reappointing auditors, and be familiar with their responsibilities and liabilities.

# PART 3 CASE STUDY

As the Company Secretary of Multiple plc, your core responsibilities include:

a) the maintenance of the company's statutory registers and the timely and correct submission of documents to Companies House;

b) providing company secretarial support for board and committee meetings;

c) organising the AGM and other general meetings;

d) ensuring that the annual report and accounts contains certain statutory information and has been circulated in accordance with applicable statutory and regulatory requirements.

This is not only for Multiple plc, but also for the many subsidiary companies that form part of the Multiple group. You are aware that the company is heavily reliant on your department for the provision of these services. You can only provide these services to a high level of professionalism if your department is properly organised and able to deal with scheduled and ad hoc events quickly and efficiently. This will be a busy year for your department as there will be several matters to attend to and you will need to ensure your department approaches them in a professional way.

# The regulators and disclosure

## ■ CONTENTS

1 Corporate compliance
2 The role and importance of disclosure
3 The role of Companies House
4 Filing returns
5 The annual return
6 Statutory registers

## ■ INTRODUCTION

This chapter is concerned with the regulatory environment for all companies, both public and private, and the company secretary's responsibility for ensuring that the legislation and regulations are followed. We look first at the function and role of Companies House as the keeper of the key information and documents for all registered companies, and its role in making these available to the public. We then look in detail at statutory requirements on all companies in relation to the annual return, the statutory registers and managing records.

## 1 Corporate compliance

We have seen in Chapter 5 that it is a general duty of the company secretary to assist the directors in ensuring that the company complies with the provisions of its Articles of Association. Equally important is the company secretary's responsibility for the safekeeping and maintenance of the company's documentation to ensure compliance with the Companies Acts. This involves the periodic updating of records held by the Registrar of Companies at Companies House, the submission of statutory returns, and the updating and maintenance of statutory registers.

## 2 The role and importance of disclosure

It is accepted that the price of establishing a company as a separate legal entity with limited liability is that it must disclose key information about its affairs. The company secretary has an important part to play in ensuring good disclosure for a company. Good disclosure is not only a statutory requirement, it also shows that a company is being properly managed by the directors and allows third parties to make an informed decision on a company. Good disclosure can also avoid damage to a company, such as fines being imposed for non-compliance with Companies House requirements (see section 3 below), but more importantly, failure to disclose can lead to the reputational damage of companies and directors, and in extreme circumstances, failure to disclose could lead to companies being struck off (see Chapter 7) or directors being disqualified (see Chapter 2). In both these matters it is usually the company secretary who has day-to-day responsibility for making sure appropriate disclosure has been made.

The annual report (see Chapter 11) is one of the key components of company's formal disclosure framework. Many companies also use their annual report as a promotional tool; for example, many listed companies produce elaborate and detailed annual reports which highlight the performance of the company and also address wider issues such as the company's environmental performance. The company secretary is usually responsible for much of the disclosure in respect of the corporate governance controls and for statutory information contained in the directors' report. In addition, the company secretary usually takes responsibility for the formal distribution of the annual report (e.g. to the company's shareholders) and also for maintaining stocks of copies for other reasons (e.g. for marketing or to support a bid tender). Recent legislation has enhanced the role of the annual report for public companies so that they are also required to address the outlook for the company and its strategy, thus giving investors and other interested parties a better view of the prospects for such a company.

More transparent disclosure for listed companies results in a more efficient stock markets (see Chapter 6) as investors and interested parties are able to assess more accurately the value of a company. Even if a company's results and performance are less positive than expected, a company using good disclosure practice will explain why such events have occurred in order to reassure third parties that the business is still under good control. The process for releasing key information to the market is explained in Chapter 6 and it is usually the company secretary who takes responsibility for this.

In many larger organisations, the approach to disclosure must be coordinated between different departments (e.g. Corporate Affairs, Investor Relations and Company Secretariat). A company secretary will therefore need to liaise frequently with these departments and adopt a professional and cooperative way of working. For example, the AGM (see Chapter 9) is quite often taken as an opportunity to communicate company strategy, hence the company secretary will need to liaise with Investor Relations to ensure that this has been planned as an integral part of the meeting.

Company secretaries should not underestimate the time and effort required to ensure good disclosure. This includes having robust procedures to ensure that filing requirements are observed in a timely manner and continuing professional development to ensure that the correct disclosure requirements are known.

## 3   The role of Companies House

Companies House is an executive agency of the BIS, headed by a chief executive and Registrar of Companies, who has overall administrative responsibility. The main office for companies registered in England and Wales is situated in Cardiff; for companies registered in Scotland, the main office is in Edinburgh. The Registrar is accountable to the Secretary of State for the day-to-day running of the agency. There are some 2.5 million limited companies registered in Great Britain. The great majority of them are incorporated as private companies limited by shares; fewer than 1% of the index consists of public limited companies.

### 3.1 Functions

Companies House has a number of functions:

1 *Incorporation of new companies* – This is its primary function. Incorporation documents, in paper or electronic format, are checked by Companies House and, if they are in order, a certificate of incorporation is issued. The certificate of incorporation includes the company's name and unique registration number.

2 *Registration of documents* – Every director has a personal responsibility to ensure that certain statutory documents are delivered to the Registrar as and when required by CA 2006. For example, every company has a legal obligation to provide an up-to-date annual return and, in most cases, to file annual accounts. Filing requirements include details of the company's financial year-end and appointments, resignations and changes in particulars of directors and secretaries. Companies House must be notified of any changes to these core records. Other filing requirements include returns of allotments of shares and changes in the constitution of the company. The great majority of documents lodged with Companies House are for companies incorporated in Great Britain, but returns are also filed for oversea companies with business operations in this country, limited partnerships, limited liability partnerships, European economic interest groupings, open-ended investment companies and newspapers that must be registered under the Newspaper Libel and Registration Act.

Companies House staff check incoming forms to ensure each relevant box contains an entry, that resolutions are in order and accounts are complete. Because of the volume of returns, staff do not check the accuracy of all documents received, and in most cases they do not chase up returns that should have been sent. However, if documents are submitted electronically, the Companies House computer system is able to make some basic checks on the information presented.

3 *Provision of information to the public and monitoring certain statutory compliance* – Virtually all documents registered at Companies House are made available to the public. An essential element of a limited liability company is disclosure of information about it. In dealing with a company that has been given limited liability status, the public must be able to make an assessment of any risks in dealing and doing business with it.

4 *Dissolutions and striking off* – If the Registrar believes that a company is no longer operating, he has the power to remove it from the register. This deprives the company of its legal status. Reinstatement in such circumstances can be costly and time-consuming. Any assets held by the company prior to dissolution become *bona vacantia* and pass to the Crown. The failure by a company to file accounts, annual returns or respond to a communication from Companies House will often result in strike-off action. Companies which no longer require to trade may apply voluntarily for dissolution (see Chapter 7).

5 *Enforcement* – Companies House has considerable powers to enforce compliance with CA 2006. To satisfy the public demand for corporate information and to encourage the timely filing of accounts, penalties are imposed for late filing. If accounts are delivered outside the statutory time limits, the company will be charged a civil penalty calculated on the degree of lateness and whether the company is public or private.

Failure to file is a criminal offence and, on conviction, fines are imposed in accordance with prescribed limits. The fine for non-submission of accounts follows the prosecution of each company director and is set by the court. The civil late filing penalty is payable by the company, and both fines and a penalty could be payable for the same set of accounts delivered late.

The responsibilities that have been given to Companies House under company law are carried out almost exclusively by responding to complaints received. Directors are prosecuted, but the object of the system is to encourage compliance not to impose retribution.

CA 2006 authorises the role of the Registrar. Sections 1060–1120 relate to the Registrar and some key points to note include:

■ The Registrar has powers as to the form, authentication and manner of delivery of documents to Companies House.

■ Section 1075 authorises the Registrar to contact a company in certain circumstances where the documents which have been submitted require correction. The documents may be corrected by the Registrar with the agreement of the company. This avoids the Registrar having to reject a document where there is an error which may be corrected. Section 1076 has similar provisions, allowing a company to provide a replacement document for an original which has not met the appropriate requirements.

■ The Registrar has the power to remove from the register of companies any materials considered to be unnecessary (i.e. information which is not required to meet statutory purposes).

■ Section 1112 creates a new offence of knowingly or recklessly providing false or misleading information to the Registrar. Company secretaries should therefore take great care in checking all information provided to Companies House.

■ The forms for filing with Companies House in respect of CA 2006 are available for download from the Companies House website (see section 4.1 below).

## 3.2 Finding help at Companies House

The Companies House website (see Directory) provides full details on the information required by Companies House, including useful guidance booklets on the regulations for forming and registering, filing and other procedures and some of the statutory forms. They can also be obtained from Companies House's 'WebCHeck' service (which can be accessed via the Companies House website). Basic information on every registered company, including registered office addresses, date of incorporation, accounting reference date and whether they have filed annual accounts and annual returns on time, is available. A full search service, which allows the user to find directorships, forms and resolutions filed at Companies House and other details, is available for a small fee through 'Companies House Direct' service.

Companies House provides a telephone helpline for directors or secretaries who have queries about any documents which must be filed. This is important, as the Registrar is keen to encourage as many companies as possible to remain compliant with their statutory obligations.

Information may also be obtained by post, fax or online or by visiting the main office in Cardiff or the London office. Documents for companies registered in Scotland are held by the Registrar of Companies in Edinburgh.

---

**TEST YOUR KNOWLEDGE 8.1**

**a** What are the main functions of Companies House?
**b** What type of information is available from Companies House?

---

## 4 Filing returns

### 4.1 The forms

Information submitted to Companies House must be on standard forms, although accounts, resolutions and the Memorandum and Articles will be individual in their format (see below). Forms are available from Companies House free of charge and can be obtained in a number of ways:

- downloaded from the Companies House website;
- by post – requests can be made by phone, post or fax (postal charges are also free);
- collected in person from one of the offices of Companies House;
- via approved company secretarial software;
- purchased from firms of legal stationers.

Companies House encourage the use of non-paper forms and hence the easiest and quickest way to obtain them is from the Companies House website.

The forms issued by Companies House under CA 2006 have code letters at the top, together with a short description of the form and a short reference to the relevant section(s) of the Act.

Nearly all forms come in A4 size. Some are single-sided; others extend to several pages. All forms, however, have a box at the top for the company's registered number (the unique number that identifies it). The next box contains the name of the company, exactly as it is registered. The contact details of the presenter are also there in case of any queries, and all forms must be signed and dated. Continuation sheets and other documents have to accompany forms on occasion.

### 4.2 Information submitted on non-Companies House forms

Accounts, resolutions, Memorandums and Articles of Association which are not submitted on Companies House forms should comply with the following:

- Documents must be on plain white paper.
- Paper must have a matt finish.
- Each page must be on A4 paper.
- Each page must have margins of not less than 10 mm.
- Letters must be clear and legible.
- Letters and numbers must be not less than 1.8 mm high.

■ Letters and numbers must be in black.
■ The company number should be prominently displayed, ideally at the top right-hand corner.

These requirements are important because Companies House scans the documents to produce an electronic image. The Registrar is permitted to reject documents that cannot be captured electronically, giving a notice saying why they are unacceptable. An acceptable copy must be delivered within 14 days of the notice, otherwise the original document is treated as not having been delivered. Various Companies House booklets set out the regulations for the quality of non-standard documents.

Documents may also be submitted electronically (see sections 4.3 and 4.5).

## 4.3 Delivery of documents

Until recently every document filed at Companies House was required to have a live signature and be physically delivered. Many documents are still filed in this way. However, it is possible to file documents electronically. This method is increasingly popular and is encouraged by Companies House.

The various ways in which documents can be delivered to Companies House are:

■ *By post* – To Companies House in Cardiff or London. Companies registered in Scotland send their documents to the Registrar's office in Edinburgh.
■ *By courier or personal delivery* – To Cardiff or London. A 24-hour service is provided. Documents are stamped on receipt and can be delivered up to midnight to qualify for that date – helpful when deadlines are close.
■ *Hays document exchange* – Available to those who are registered to use it.
■ *Electronic filing* – Documents may be sent by email via the Companies House website. For more on electronic filing, see section 4.5.

Faxed documents are not acceptable.

### Proof of delivery

Companies House does not routinely acknowledge receipt of paper documents. This could be a problem in light of the late filing penalties. The legal requirement is not that documents are despatched, but that they are received. Companies would do well to cover themselves by sending a stamped addressed envelope with a letter requesting confirmation of receipt. Companies House will endorse the letter and post it back, thereby providing the company with proof of filing. Acknowledgement of receipt is sent before the document is checked and is therefore not confirmation that it has been accepted. Acknowledgements are available for documents submitted electronically.

## 4.4 Authorisation to file

The documents to be filed at Companies House need in the main to be signed by an officer of the company (i.e. a director or company secretary). The forms indicate who should sign – for example, the annual return (form AR01) gives the options of director or secretary. Other forms provide more options, including administrators, auditors, liquidators and other interested parties. The Registrar refers to those who are authorised to file documents as **presenters**.

## 4.5 Electronic filing

### Using approved company secretarial software packages

Electronic filing was introduced for companies registered in England and Wales in 1998 and most Companies House forms can now be filed in this way.

It is attractive to companies and registration agents who are high-volume users and has the added advantage that documents are automatically validated as well as acknowledged. The sender knows very quickly that documents have been accepted and there is no risk of them being returned. Each transmission can contain up to 50 individual documents and invoices for those that are fee-paying are sent out a week later. There are several very good secretarial software packages approved by Companies House.

To replace the signature on paper forms and to comply with the Companies Acts, all documents received via the electronic filing service must be authenticated by or on behalf of the company concerned. Before any documents can be filed electronically the company must notify Companies House in writing of the code that it will use to authenticate documents and the name of the presenter who will present them. Every document filed electronically must bear the relevant company authentication code or it will be rejected. Codes are six-digit numbers and are supplied to Companies House in writing using the company's own notepaper with the electronic filing service application form.

Because there are no signatures in electronic filing, the director or secretary cannot confirm their 'consent to act'. The Companies House solution has been to state that any three of nine personal details will be equivalent to an electronic signature. The personal information may include passport number, mother's maiden name, eye colour or father's first forename. This is based on the theory that the director or secretary is willing and able to reveal this information and indicates that he has consented to act.

## The Companies House Web Filing service

Since 2001, it has been possible to file documents electronically using the Companies House Web Filing service, using much of the same procedures established for those using approved company secretarial software packages. The key points of the Web Filing service are:

- It provides a secure system for any presenter to submit company information via the Companies House website.
- No special software other than standard internet browser software is required.
- Companies must first be issued by post with an authentication code to use web filing.

Each presenter will be issued with a security code to use in combination with the authentication code.

The most popular forms and documents can be filed, including:

- AR01 (annual return);
- AP01–04 (appointment of a director or secretary);
- TM01–02 (terminating appointment as director or secretary);
- CH01–04 (change of particulars for director or secretary);
- AD01 (change in situation or address of registered office);
- SH01 (return of allotments of shares (excluding non-cash));
- AA01 (change in accounting reference date);
- audit exempt abbreviated accounts;
- dormant company accounts (DCA).

Documents filed electronically will be acknowledged and any rejections issued via email (note the difference here: Companies House does not routinely acknowledge receipt if documents have been sent via post). Payment fees for any filed documents (currently the annual return) can be made online using a debit or credit card, or can be settled by way of invoice if an online filing account has been previously established.

Currently Web Filing can be used only for company numbers that begin with '0' or 'SC' (SC companies are those registered in Scotland). Company secretaries should therefore check their registration numbers before attempting to use the service. As each transaction has to be entered separately, high-volume users may find the electronic filing service using company secretarial software packages (summarised above) more appropriate.

## Electronic incorporation

When forming a company electronically, as well as sending the data fields for incorporation to Companies House, the presenters send an attachment with the email which contains the full text of the Memorandum and Articles of Association for the proposed company. This allows Companies House to produce the Memorandum and Articles on the public record as image and microfiche copies in the exact format the presenter requires.

If the incorporation is successful, a certificate is generated in Adobe Portable Document Format (pdf) for electronic return and printing, if required, by the presenter. The public record at Companies House is updated with a full set of documents for the incorporation:

- certificate of incorporation;
- electronic statement of compliance;
- statement of first directors and registered office address;
- Memorandum and Articles of Association.

All the documents generated for electronic incorporations, including the certificate, carry statements to make it clear that the company was incorporated electronically. Any printout of the electronic certificate has the status of a copy of the original authenticated certificate. If at some time an authenticated copy of the certificate of incorporation is needed for admission in evidence in legal proceedings, under CA 2006, s. 1091 the Registrar may be asked to produce a paper copy certified for that purpose.

### The Companies House PROOF service

There has been recent press coverage of companies which have been hijacked by fraudsters changing details of the company's directors and registered office and then using the victim company to obtain goods or services fraudulently on credit. This can leave the legitimate company with an embarrassing problem. In an attempt to deter such fraud, Companies House has introduced the **PROOF service (PROtected Online Filing)**, which is available on Web Filing and company secretarial software packages. To use PROOF, once the company has registered, the Registrar will accept specific forms electronically only if they meet the required authentication criteria. Companies House will reject any paper versions of those forms unless specifically authorised to do so by the company.

---

**STOP AND THINK** **8.1**

Electronic communication has made keeping statutory filing up to date easier. However, it has also made it easier to access information about directors and whether a company's filings are up to date. This increases the pressure on the company secretary to maintain statutory records and ensure that directors are properly advised on their statutory requirements.

---

## 4.6 Time limits and penalties

Filing is compulsory, and there are time limits and penalties for companies that do not meet the filing criteria. The most heavily used forms relating to appointment, resignation and changes in particulars of directors and secretaries must be filed within 14 days of the event. Most general meetings resolutions must be filed within 15 days and annual returns within 28 days of the date to which it is made up. Late filing penalties also apply to the annual accounts and will be imposed not only for non-submission, but also if the accounts are rejected for any reason and not resubmitted in time.

Filing penalties are rigorously enforced, even if the filing is late by only one minute. It is possible to bring a private prosecution for some company law offences, and in 1999 a creditor successfully proceeded against a director for failure to file accounts.

---

**TEST YOUR KNOWLEDGE** **8.2**

a Why is it important for documents to be filed on time?
b What are the benefits of using electronic communications for filing documents with Companies House?
c What are the requirements for documents submitted to Companies House on non-Companies House forms?
d What is PROOF? Why should a company consider it?

# 5 The annual return

All companies must make an annual return each year to show on one document the essential facts about the company for public record. Failure to submit an annual return can lead to a company being struck off.

The annual return is filed on form AR01 and is made up to a specific date – the return date. The return date is not more than 12 months after the previous return, or twelve months after incorporation. The annual return must be submitted to Companies House within 28 days of the relevant return date, together with a filing fee.

Large organisations might have many subsidiary companies and it is often more practical for all these companies to have the same annual return date. There is no restriction on the number of times a company may change its annual return date provided that the next annual return date is not more than twelve months from the previous one.

It is a common misconception that there must be a correlation between the annual return date and the accounting reference date for a company. This is not the case and a company is free to choose any annual return date, independent of the accounting reference date.

Companies House is keen to encourage electronic filing and reduce the use of printed paper. The Registrar has adopted a principle whereby the fee for filing the paper version of the annual return is more expensive than that of the electronic equivalent.

## 5.1 Contents of the annual return

The annual return should include:

- the company number, i.e. its unique identification number given on incorporation;
- the company name in full, as registered at Companies House;
- principal business activities based on the UK Standard Industrial Classification Codes. There are some 500 codes covering business activities and companies are asked for up to a total of four codes to identify their principal business activities. Space is provided for a written description should the codes provided not be sufficient to describe the specific activities of the company. Further information is available from the Companies House website;
- the date of the current return (i.e. the date at which it is made up), not more than one year since the previous one;
- the registered office (i.e. the address notified on form IN01 when the company was incorporated, unless it has been changed by submitting a form AD01);
- the address of the **single alternative inspection location (SAIL)** where statutory registers can be inspected (see section 6.1 below);
- the location of company records. Statutory registers can either be kept at the registered office or at the SAIL address. Confirmation is required as to the location of each register and any changes must be separately notified to Companies House on Forms AD03;
- the company type, which should be indicated by ticking one box only (e.g. a private company limited by shares);
- the company secretary's name and service address;
- the names of the directors and their notifiable details;
- a statement of capital, including details on the class of shares in issue, the amount paid up on each share, the number of shares in issue and the aggregated nominal value. Any particular voting rights attaching to shares should also be disclosed;
- lists of past and present shareholders:
  - private or non-traded public companies are required to provide a full list if one was not included with either of the last two returns. For each shareholder, name, class and number of shares held or transferred and date of any transfer must be shown. The shareholder's address should not be included;
  - for traded public companies, if the shares were admitted to a RIE (such as the Official List) and the company was subject to the disclosure requirements of the DTRs in respect of material shareholders (i.e. disclosure of shareholders with an interest of 3% or more in the company), then since that information is already in the public domain, it is not required to include any further information on shareholders who hold more than 5%. If the

In accordance with
Section 854 of the
Companies Act 2006.

# AR01
## Annual Return

**Companies House**

**A fee is payable with this form**
Please see 'How to pay' on the
last page.

**You can use the WebFiling service to file this form online.**
Please go to www.companieshouse.gov.uk

✓ **What this form is for**
You may use this form to confirm
that the company information is
correct as at the date of this return.
You must file an Annual Return at
least once every year.

✗ **What this form is NOT for**
You cannot use this form to give
notice of changes to the company
officers, registered office address,
company type or information
relating to the company records.

For further information, please
refer to our guidance at
www.companieshouse.gov.uk

## Part 1        Company details

**The section must be completed by all companies.**

→ **Filling in this form**
Please complete in typescript or in
bold black capitals.

All fields are mandatory unless
specified or indicated by *

### A1        Company details

Company number

Company name in full ❶

❶ **Company name change**
If your company has recently
changed its name, please provide
the company name as at the date of
this return.

### A2        Return date

Please give the annual return made up date. The return date must not be a future
date. The annual return must be delivered within 28 days of the date given below.

Date of this return ❷   | d | d | | m | m | | y | y | y | y |

❷ **Date of this return**
Your company's return date
is usually the anniversary of
incorporation or the anniversary
of the last annual return filed at
Companies House. You may choose
an earlier return date but it must not
be a later date.

### A3        Principal business activity

Please show the trade classification code number(s) for the principal
activity or activities. ❸

Classification code 1

Classification code 2

Classification code 3

Classification code 4

If you cannot determine a code, please give a brief description of your
business activity below:

Principal activity
description

❸ **Principal business activity**
You must provide a trade
classification code (SIC code) or a
description of your company's main
business in this section.

A full list of the trade classification
codes are available on our website:
www.companieshouse.gov.uk

**BIS** | Department for Business
Innovation & Skills

CHFP000
10/11 Version 4.2

company was admitted to a RIE and not subject to the disclosure requirements of the DTRs in respect of material shareholders, it will be required to provide a list of shareholders who held at least 5% of the issued shares of any share class. For each shareholder, name, class and number of shares held or transferred and date of any transfer must be shown. The shareholder's address must be included. If the list of shareholders is very large, details may be submitted electronically (for example on a CD-ROM);

■ signature of a director or the company secretary and the date it is signed (not necessarily the date it is made up), but the person signing must be in office on the date it is signed. The date must be within 28 days of the return date;

■ contact details (i.e. name, address and telephone number) of a person (a 'presenter') who can be contacted should there be any queries. This need not be the person who has signed the return.

## 5.2 Completing the annual return

The following practical points usually arise when completing the annual return:

1 Past and present members:
   a) where shares have been converted into stock the amount of stock held and transferred should be shown;
   b) show only the total number of shares held by each member at the date of the return;
   c) it is convenient to arrange issues of shares (e.g. a rights or capitalisation issue) so that the period of renunciation has expired at the date on which the return has to be made. If this is not possible, include the new shares in the summary of the share capital, but annotate the list of members to show the basis of allotments, or provisional allotments, and stating the date on which the period of renunciation will expire. With forward planning it may, alternatively, be easier to amend the annual return date to avoid any such transactions.

2 The annual return can be used to notify amended details of a director or secretary, but appointments of a new director or secretary may only be made on form AP01–04.

---

**TEST YOUR KNOWLEDGE 8.3**

a   When must an annual return be made?
b   How can the annual return date be changed?
c   What information regarding a company's shareholders must be included in an annual return?

---

## 6   Statutory registers

Every company must, under the CA, keep and maintain certain registers that reflect the operation of business. It is the company secretary's responsibility to see that these are kept secure and up-to-date. It is also the secretary's duty to ensure that people who are entitled to inspect the statutory registers have access or receive copies according to the provisions of the Act. The secretary also needs to ensure that improper access (e.g. to board minutes) is not permitted.

Traditionally, companies have kept these records in bound or loose-leaf books, available from legal stationers. The secretary should ensure they are secure. The statutory books and registers may also be kept in electronic form (CA 2006, s. 1135), provided that adequate precautions are taken against falsification (CA 2006, s. 1138) and that they can be reproduced in hard copy form (CA 2006, s. 1135). Special forms are prescribed for notifying the Registrar of the place where registers kept in non-legible form may be inspected. CA 2006 requires that every company keeps the following:

- register of members;
- register of charges;
- books containing the minutes of the company and directors' meetings and resolutions in writing of the members;
- accounting records (see Chapter 11);
- register of directors and a register of secretaries (if applicable);
- if the company is public, a register of interests disclosed.

There are also legal requirements in respect of the register of debenture holders (see below).

## 6.1 Specified locations and inspection

Statutory registers must be kept in specified places where they can be inspected. Unless Companies House has been notified otherwise, the registers should be kept at the registered office. CA 2006, s. 1136 provides the concept of the SAIL. Under this provision, companies may inform Companies House of the specified place other than the registered office where the registers may be inspected. Some of the key statutory registered covered by the SAIL provisions include:

- register of members;
- register of directors;
- directors' service contracts;
- directors' indemnities;
- register of secretaries;
- records of resolutions, etc.;
- contracts relating to purchase of own shares;
- register of debenture holders;
- register of interests in shares disclosed to public company;
- instruments creating charges and register of charges.

The SAIL address must be situated in the part of the UK where the company is registered. There can only be one SAIL address and hence all registers not available for inspection at the SAIL address must be available for inspection at the registered office.

## 6.2 Provision of company information

CA 2006 permits any person to request in writing the particulars of a company. A person may request a company to confirm the address of its registered office, the location where statutory registers may be available for inspection (i.e. any SAIL address) and the type of company records kept at that office or place. The company must provide a written response to the request within five business days of receipt of such a request.

### Inspection of statutory registers

Different provisions under CA 2006 in respect of the inspection of registers apply for private and public companies:

Private companies:

- A person who wishes to inspect registers must give advance notice to the company. The notice must include the time at which the inspection is to start and that time must be between 9:00 am and 3:00 pm. The company is then obliged to allow at least two hours for the inspection.
- The required notice period is two working days where it is during the notice period of a general meeting or during the period of the circulation of a written members' resolution (see Chapter 9). At other times the notice period is ten working days.

Public companies:

- Public companies must make their records available for inspection for at least two hours between 9:00 am and 5:00 pm on each working day.
- There is no need for a person to give advance notice to a public company.

Under the new requirements, some matters in relation to inspection are common to both private and public companies:

- Records need only be made available for inspection on working (i.e. business) days.
- The company is not required to manipulate any register so that it presents information in a different way for the purposes of the person inspecting it.
- The company must permit a person to make a copy of any register but it is not obliged to assist that person in doing so.
- If the company has a soft copy of the register, it has discretion to provide a soft copy on such a request. The company must provide hard copy if requested.

## 6.3 Register of members

As we have seen (section 6.1), the register of members will normally be kept at the registered office. If it is held electronically, the Registrar must be notified of the place where a legible copy may be inspected.

The statutory information (CA 2006, s. 113) to be kept in the register is:

- name and address of member;
- date that person became a member and the date on which that person ceased to be a member, if applicable;
- number and class of share(s) held and cash amount or non-cash consideration paid;
- details where shares have been converted to stock;
- share warrants.

A company with more than 50 members must keep a separate index in the same place as the register to enable easy access to the data (CA 2006, s. 115). An entry relating to a former member of the company may be removed from the register ten years after the date on which he ceased to be a member (CA 2006, s. 121).

Large companies that subcontract the register of members to professional registrars can maintain an online version of their register.

### Registered holders

Only individuals or corporate bodies should be registered as members (see Chapter 13). Names of partnerships, trusts or settlements have no legal capacity and cannot be registered as holders. Instead, the shares should be registered in the names of some or all of the partners or trustees. Usually, the number of joint holders is restricted to four. If documentation is received to register shares in the name of a trust or partnership, this should be rejected.

### Single-member companies

CA 2006 allows companies to be formed with a single shareholder on the register of members or subsequently to reduce the number of shareholders to one. In the case of single-member company, a note should be added to the member's entry in the register, stating that the company has only one member and the date on which the transaction took place (CA 2006, s. 123).

If the membership of a single-member private company subsequently increases, a statement confirming that the company has ceased to have one member should be added in the register of members against the former sole member, together with the date that the number of members increased.

---

**SAMPLE WORDING 8.1**

**Single member in register**

On [date] Mr . . . . . . . . . . . . . . . . . . . . became the sole member of the company.

# Register of Members

**Entered as a member on:** [Date]
**Ceased to be a member on:** [Date]
**Remarks:**

*[Name of company]*

**Name of member:**
**Address:**

**Share class:**

**Nominal value:**

| Date of entry of transaction | Allotment number | Transfer number | Amount paid or agreed to be considered as paid per share | Distinctive share numbers (inclusive) From | To | Certificate number Issued | Cancelled | Number of shares acquired by allotment or transfer | Number of shares transferred | Remaining balance | Remarks |
|---|---|---|---|---|---|---|---|---|---|---|---|

Specimen

## Inspection of the register of members and provision of copies

The provisions in respect of the inspection and provisions of copies of the register of members are contained in CA 2006, ss. 116–119. The register and any index must be open for inspection by any member without charge and by any other person on payment of a fee. As a practical precaution, only copies (i.e. not the original) of documents should be made available for inspection.

The CA 2006 provisions require that inspection is for a 'proper purpose'. Anyone who asks to inspect the register or to be provided with a copy must provide the company with the following information:

- their name and address (or name and address of their organisation);
- the purpose for which the information is to be used;
- whether the information will be disclosed to any other person and if so, the name and address of such other persons and the purposes for which such other persons will use the information.

When a company receives a request for inspection or a copy it must either provide the information within five working days upon payment of the prescribed fee or apply to the court on the basis that the request is not for a proper purpose. If the court rules that there is not a proper purpose for the information, the company will be relieved of its obligation to provide the information. If the court rules that there is a proper purpose, the company must provide the information as requested.

Professional search agents are often found at the offices of larger registrars and the inspection fees are frequently waived. The searcher must extract information as it appears in the register and the company is not required to manipulate the data to enable the searcher to do their job more easily. For example, if the searcher wants a list of all shareholders who live in London, the company is not obliged to provide the data in that format. However, the company may, at its discretion, agree a fee for such a service.

CA 2006, s. 1088 permits an application by a company to the Registrar to make the addresses of its members unavailable for public inspection, if it is considered that the members, former members or subscribers (or a person who lives at the same address) are at serious risk of being subjected to violence or intimidation due to the activities of the company. An application can be made by a company in respect of all the members, or former members, whose addresses were contained in an annual return or a return of allotment of shares delivered to the Registrar on or after 1 January 2003, or as subscribers to the memorandum of association.

## Non-statutory information

It is not uncommon for additional information, such as dividend mandate information, to be kept with the register of members for ease of administration. Any such information does not form part of the statutory register and is therefore not subject to CA regulations. The additional information may, however, be subject to other regulations, such as the Data Protection Act (see section 6.11). Members and the public are not permitted to inspect or obtain copies of non-statutory information relating to members.

## Closing the register and record dates

The CA 2006 does not provide any provision for the closure of the share register for a particular event and this is not common practice. Usual practice is for companies to select a **record date** to determine dividends or other entitlements.

## 6.4 Changes to the register of members

From time to time it will be necessary to make changes to the register. These usually arise as a result of shares being transferred or new shares allotted (see Chapters 12 and 13).

### Change of name

If a member changes name, the share certificate must be submitted, together with evidence of change of name (e.g. a statutory declaration or marriage certificate). On receiving the documents, the appropriate checks should be made (see Chapter 13) and the necessary change(s), including date, made in the register.

## Change of address

Any change of address should be signed by the member if possible. A notification of a change purported to be given by a member of the member's family should never be accepted. Ideally, notifications should give details of the old and new addresses to facilitate identification. The change should be noted in the register.

## Amending the register and rectification

In theory, amendments to the register (known as rectification) can only be made by court order (CA 2006, s.125). Amendments are likely to be necessary only when there has been an error in recording the details of the member, a member who has not agreed to take shares is entered on the register, a member has been omitted in error or where there has been an unnecessary delay in entering transactions on the register.

In practice, minor clerical slips which do not affect the identity of the member can be informally corrected under the authority of a responsible officer, such as the secretary or Registrar. The correction should not overwrite or erase the original entry. There should be a clear record of the person who authorised the change and the reason for it. If the request comes more than three months after the transfer, after the payment of a dividend or it affects the member's identity, there should be no change without recourse to the court. If the company receives a court order to rectify the register, for example as a result of an application by an aggrieved shareholder, the amendments must be made, any incorrect share certificates returned for cancellation and new certificates issued. The court may also order the company to pay damages to the aggrieved party.

Alterations to the register must also be made to any index.

---

**STOP AND THINK 8.2**

The ICSA Registrars' Group best practice recommendation is to allow minor clerical slips on the register of members to be corrected without reference to the court. When would the misspelling of a person's name change from minor to major? Would you correct 'Francis' to 'Frances'?

---

## Overseas branch registers

A company may establish an overseas branch register of members resident in territories where it transacts business. The Registrar should be informed within 14 days of the branch register being established or discontinued, using form AD06–07, which includes details of where the register is to be kept. A duplicate of the branch register should be kept at the same place as the principal register, and be open to inspection in the same way.

A member can request to have his share registered on the overseas branch register instead of the 'main' register.

The branch register may be kept in non-legible form, in which case notification should be made to the Registrar on form AD06–07.

Regulations in respect of overseas branch registers are subject to CA 2006, ss. 129–135. CA 2006 specifies the countries in which an overseas branch register may be established. If a company decides to discontinue with its overseas branch register, it must either be transferred to another overseas branch register or be transferred back to the main register (CA 2006, s. 135).

## 6.5 Register of charges

A register of charges should be kept by every company even if there are no charges to be entered (CA 2006, s. 876). In this context, a charge is a mortgage or a secured loan. It must be open for inspection by any creditor or member of the company free of charge or by any other person subject to payment of the prescribed fee. The register should include:

- a short description of the property charged, or class of property in respect of floating charges;
- the amount of the charge (this may often be expressed as 'all moneys' owed to the charge from time to time);
- the names of the persons entitled to the charge, unless a security to bearer (CA 2006, s. 876).

## 6.6 Minute books

CA 2006, s. 355 provides that every company must maintain a minute book for general meetings and CA 2006, s. 248 provides that every company must maintain a minute book for board meetings. Any such minute, if signed by the chairman of the meeting, is deemed to be evidence of the meeting's proceedings. CA 2006 provides that minutes must be kept for at least ten years.

### Minutes of general meetings and resolutions of members

Minutes of general meetings and resolutions of members passed other than at general meetings must be kept and should be open to inspection by members free of charge. Private companies often keep bound books with the minutes pasted in. The pages are numbered consecutively. It is customary for the minutes to be numbered consecutively too, so that in the first minute book the minutes are numbered 1.1, 1.2, etc., and in the second they are numbered 2.1, 2.2, and so on.

Larger public companies generally use loose-leaf minute books with pages and minutes numbered consecutively. Some companies also compile an index at the back of the minute book referring to items covered by the minutes. Practice varies from company to company; what is important is that there is a clear system of identifying any given minute for each meeting.

In addition to the rights of members to inspect minutes of general meetings, members may demand that copies of general meeting minutes be sent to them. CA 2006, s. 358 states that any member may require a copy of any of the minutes or resolutions upon payment of the prescribed fee.

### Recording decisions by the sole member of a single member company

CA 2006, s. 357 provides that, where the sole member has taken a decision which is usually considered by a company in general meeting, the sole member shall provide the company with a written record of that decision. The written record should be kept in the minute book for general meetings. Failure to comply with this provision is an offence; however, it will not affect the validity of any decision taken.

### Minutes of board meetings

Minutes of general meetings must be kept separate from board minutes since members have the right to inspect the minutes of general meetings, but not of board meetings. There are no statutory requirements for the location of the minute books of board meetings. Model Article 15 (public company Model Article 18) and CA 2006, ss. 248, 355–359 state that minutes must be kept in minute books to record:

- all appointments of directors and officers made by the board;
- all proceedings at meetings of the company, class meetings and board meetings (which must include the names of the directors present).

Minutes of board meetings are dealt with in more detail in Chapter 10.

Minutes are conclusive evidence of decisions taken in general meeting or board meetings. Accurate and concise drafting of minutes is therefore an essential skill for the company secretary. The secretary's duty also extends to preparing minutes promptly after each meeting for approval by the directors, particularly in view of the requirement under CA 2006 to issue minutes of general meetings to members upon request and payment of the prescribed fee.

## 6.7 Register of directors and register of secretaries

Under CA 2006, s. 162, each company must maintain a register of directors, to be kept at the company's registered office or SAIL and under CA 2006, s. 275, each company must maintain a separate register of secretaries, to be kept at the company's registered office. However, since CA 2006 provides that private companies do not have to appoint a secretary unless they choose to do so, it would appear that a 'nil return' is required where no secretary is in place.

### Key points to bear in mind in compiling the registers

■ Include all first names and family name, including title. There is no need to show former names if they have not been used for 20 years or more. The maiden name of a married woman need not be shown unless it has been used for a business purpose in the previous 20 years.

■ A separate register of directors' residential addresses is also required under CA 2006 s. 165. This is because the residential address is 'protected information' which the company cannot disclose. S. 165 also provides that if a director's usual residential address is the same as his service address (as stated in the company's register of directors), the register of directors' residential addresses need only contain an entry to that effect. This does not apply if the director's service address is stated to be 'The company's registered office'. See below for more on a director's service address.

Further information which must be added includes:

■ The country or state or part of the UK in which the director is usually resident.
■ Nationality.
■ Date of birth.
■ The business occupation must be included. If a person is a director of a number of companies, his occupation may be shown as 'director of companies'. If he is a director only of the company to which the register relates, his occupation should be described as 'none' unless he has a business occupation, for example, accountant.
■ Other directorships must include directorships during the previous five years as well as current ones. Directorships of dormant companies or of companies treated as grouped with the company keeping the register need not be included.
■ The appointment of directors or company secretaries and changes in their particulars should be notified to the Registrar on form AP01–04 and form CH01–04 respectively.

### Privacy and confidentiality

The CA 2006 provides directors with some degree of privacy in respect of personal information, in particular their residential address (see above). Under CA 2006, directors are able to provide a service address (i.e. the registered office address) instead of their residential address for the public register held by Companies House. The director's residential address still needs to be supplied to the Registrar, but it will not appear on the public record.

In addition, CA 2006, s. 243 allows directors in certain circumstances to have the benefit of a higher degree of protection in respect of their residential addresses. This is to cater for circumstances where the director (or someone who lives with the director) considers that they are at serious risk of violence or intimidation due to the activities of the company. CA 2006 allows the director's residential addresses to be disclosed in limited circumstances (for example to a specified public authority or to a credit reference agency). However if an application is made to the Registrar of Companies under s. 243, the residential information will not be disclosed to a credit reference agency.

Prior to the enactment of the CA 2006, a director's residential address was a matter of public record. Under CA 2006, s. 1088 an individual whose usual residential address was placed on the public register in respect of a company on or after 1 January 2003 can apply to make the address unavailable for a public inspection by an individual.

It is not necessary to provide a residential address for the register of secretaries (CA 2006, ss. 275–278). A service address may be provided which may be stated as the company's registered office.

## 6.8 Notification of transactions by persons discharging managerial responsibility

The Disclosure and Transparency Rules (DTRs) require **PDMRs** to notify the company of any transactions in the securities of a company admitted to trading on a regulated market (this includes the London Stock Exchange). Other companies have no obligation to comply with the DTRs. A PDMR includes all directors of the company plus the company's most senior management (see Chapter 6 for information on the listed company regime). Company secretaries of listed companies may therefore wish to maintain a register of interests for PDMRs to facilitate reporting requirements under the DTRs.

Under the DTRs, a PDMR must notify the company within four business days of any transaction in respect of the securities of the company. The company will then be obliged to inform the market by releasing an announcement through a RIS as soon as possible and in any case by no later than the end of the following business day after notification by the PDMR.

PDMRs who have interests granted by the company under subscription rights to shares or debentures should ensure that they notify the company if any further grants have been made or of a change in such subscription rights. This includes the granting or exercise of share options under employee share schemes (see Chapter 15). PDMRs are required to make notifications in respect of themselves and any connected person(s), which broadly includes spouse, civil partner, minor children or infant stepchildren and companies in which PDMRs have an interest of 20% or more.

## 6.9 Disclosure of interests in shares for public companies

As any member of the public may own shares in a public limited company, CA 2006 includes regulations which require major shareholders of a public company to make themselves known to that company. There are additional disclosure requirements for quoted public companies which are contained in the DTRs. Furthermore, it is not possible for major shareholders to conceal their identity merely by having a beneficial interest in the shares and registering the legal ownership on the register of members in the name of another person. These provisions are particularly important for listed companies, as share prices can be very sensitive to any speculation that a particular person is building a large shareholding.

### Requisition of information regarding interests in voting shares

Under CA 2006, s. 793 a public company can investigate the true ownership of its shares by sending a written notice to any person whom it knows, or has reason to believe, is interested in the voting shares of the company, asking for information about the identity of the persons interested, the number of shares held and the dates when the interest was acquired. A company can investigate both current shareholdings and shareholdings over the last three years.

The recipient is required to inform the company making the enquiry whether they have or have had an interest, and if so what the nature of the interest is or was. If the recipient fails or refuses to respond, the company is entitled to seek permission of the court to impose restrictions in respect of the shares under investigation. Such restrictions could include withdrawal of voting rights and withholding of dividend payments.

In accordance with CA 2006, s. 808, the responses received from a shareholder under a CA 2006, s. 793 investigation must be recorded in a register of interests disclosed. Company secretaries must ensure the register is kept up to date, as CA 2006, s. 808 requires that the register must be updated within three days of receiving notification from a shareholder. CA 2006, ss. 811–812 provide that the register of interests disclosed must be available for inspection by any person without charge. A copy must be provided to any person on payment of the prescribed fee but this request is subject to the same 'proper purpose' procedures which apply in respect of persons who request a copy of the register of members (see section 6.3 above).

### Disclosure and notification requirements for listed companies

As noted above, there are additional disclosure requirements for quoted public companies as set out in the DTRs. The trigger for notification requirements under the DTRs is in respect of the control of voting rights and/or holding of financial instruments which give an unconditional right or a right exercisable at the holder's sole discretion to acquire shares. The notification requirement is drawn widely to prevent the shareholder avoiding an obligation to disclose their true holding in the company. A person or organisation which has a notifiable obligation must make a notification (using a form prescribed by the FSA) to both the company and the FSA at the same time. If the company is listed, it must also make a notification to the FSA by way of an announcement to the market using a RIS (see Chapter 6). The announcement through a RIS must be made by the end of the working day following the day on which the notification was received. To ensure consistency of information between listed companies, a prescribed pro forma document may be used to make the announcement.

A shareholder must notify the company of the percentage of its voting rights held or the shareholder's holding of financial instruments if the percentage of those voting rights:

- reaches, exceeds or falls below 3%, 4%, 5%, 6%, 7%, 8%, 9%, 10% and each 1% threshold thereafter up to 100% as a result of an acquisition or disposal of shares or financial instruments;
- reaches, exceeds or falls below the above thresholds as a result of events changing the voting rights of the company; for example, if the company were to issue new shares or there was a redemption of shares (see Chapter 12), the percentage of shares held by a shareholder would change as a result.

### STOP AND THINK 8.3

Public companies can take advantage of considerable regulations to find out who its shareholders are. The responsibility for managing the investigative process generally falls to the company secretary, who should provide regular updates to the board about major shareholders. This is important not only to see who may be planning a takeover, but more usually to enable directors to plan discussions with major shareholders to ensure good investor relations.

## 6.10 Register of debenture holders

There is no statutory requirement for a company to have a register of debenture holders. If such a register is maintained, the same principles as those relating to the location of the register of members and the right of inspection apply to the register of debenture holders (CA 2006, ss. 743–748). If the register is in non-legible format, notice of the location where the register is available for inspection must be given to the Registrar of Companies.

It is a common mistake to confuse the register of charges (see section 6.5) with the register of debenture holders.

## 6.11 Data protection

Registers which have to be made available for public inspection are exempt from the provisions of the Data Protection Act 1998 if they only include the information as required by the CA. If any additional information is included, notification under the Data Protection Act will be necessary. In practice, it is often convenient for companies, particularly private companies, to include non-statutory information in the register of members to avoid the expense of maintaining a separate record. For example, the register might include references to dividend mandates, which would include the name of the member's bank and account number. This is not good practice and, if a request for inspection were made, the non-statutory information would have to be removed from the inspection copy.

As the register of members is available for public inspection, a company cannot prevent a third party from obtaining a copy of the register unless it can convince a court that the register is being used otherwise than for a proper purpose. As the definition of 'proper purpose' needs to be further tested in the courts, it is possible that third parties will continue using registers of members as a database for sending unsolicited mail. Shareholders wishing to limit the receipt of such unsolicited mail should contact the Mailing Preference Service (see Directory), a voluntary organisation consisting of major UK marketing organisations. The Mailing Preference Service will remove the shareholder's details from its marketing database on request from the shareholder.

---

### TEST YOUR KNOWLEDGE 8.4

a Where must the registers be kept to comply with CA 2006?
b Who may inspect the register of members?
c How is a company entitled to object to a request to obtain a copy of the register of members?
d At what level of shareholding must a shareholder in a listed public limited company notify the company of their interest? Why?
e Explain the purpose of the Mailing Preference Service.

---

## CASE QUESTION

Each department of Multiple plc is required to prepare an annual budget and operating plan. This sets out the department's requirements for the forthcoming year and for the Company Secretarial department will need to address requirements in respect of statutory compliance. Prepare your first draft of the Company Secretarial department's annual budget and operating plan. It will include what your department needs by way of funding for information technology and staffing support and why funding is required for your department. The budget and operating plan should address the following:

■ the key statutory responsibilities for the company secretarial department for the year;

■ the computerised systems the department will need for the year in order to meet its compliance and governance requirements;
■ why the department will need to keep current staffing levels to maintain the many subsidiary companies within the Multiple group. What would be the implications if such staffing levels were not maintained?
■ Any storage space or special office facilities which may be necessary for the department in the forthcoming year. This should include any security arrangements for confidential materials.

What other key information would be helpful to include in the annual budget and operating plan?

---

## CHAPTER SUMMARY

■ Companies House is responsible for the incorporation and dissolution of companies, for the registration and monitoring of documents and for the provision of this information to the public. Regular filing and communication with Companies House has been enhanced and made easier by the increasing use of electronic communications.
■ All entities incorporated under the Companies Acts must file returns with Companies House. When notifiable events take place they must be notified to Companies House, and as filing is a statutory obligation, there are time limits and penalties for late filing and failure to file.
■ The annual return is a core document and contains the basic details about a company. Every company is required to file an annual return each year, not more than twelve months after the previous return.
■ Every company must keep and maintain statutory registers and the company secretary is responsible for their safekeeping. The statutory registers must be kept at the registered office or at the SAIL which must be notified to Companies House using the appropriate forms.
■ Registers which have to be made available for public inspection are exempt from the provisions of the Data Protection Act 1998 if they only include the information required by the CA. If any additional information is included, notification under the Data Protection Act may be necessary.

- Companies may object to a request to provide a copy of the register of members if the company considers the request has been made for an improper purpose. This will involve an application to the court.
- Major shareholders of a public company have a higher level of disclosure obligation in respect of their shareholdings. Under CA 2006, s. 793 a public company can send written notice to anyone it knows, or has reason to believe, is interested in the voting shares of the company, asking for further information.
- The company secretary is responsible for retention and administration of records.

# Members' meetings and resolutions

## ■ CONTENTS

## ■ INTRODUCTION

This chapter covers the law and regulations governing the conduct of general or members' meetings. This is essential knowledge for the company secretary in ensuring the proper conduct of the meeting itself and advising the chairman when necessary.

The chapter looks at the purpose of the different types of general meeting and covers crucial areas of procedure such as notice, quorum, voting and resolutions. We look in detail at the role of the company secretary before, during and after the meeting in making sure that everything runs smoothly.

## 1 General meetings

General meetings are usually called by the directors. In exceptional circumstances, under CA 2006, s. 306 the court may order a general meeting to be called, held and conducted in the manner in which it sees fit.

The term 'general meeting' includes both annual general meetings and other general meetings. These are sometimes referred to as company meetings or shareholders' meetings.

Private companies are not required to hold an AGM under CA 2006. If the company's Articles specifically require an AGM to be held, this must continue unless and until the Articles are changed. However, a requirement in the Articles for directors to retire and be re-elected at an AGM is not sufficient to require an AGM to be held.

Public companies are required to hold an AGM (CA 2006, s. 336). The AGM must be held within six months of the financial year-end. This requirement cannot be overruled by a company's Articles. If a public company files a form AA01 to shorten its accounting period, it must then hold an AGM within three months of filing the form. Failure to hold an AGM will render the officers of the company liable to a fine.

In common law, for a meeting to be validly constituted, at least two individuals must be present, although it is possible for one person to be treated as a meeting. This will be looked at in more detail later in the chapter.

The general statutory provisions relating to meetings taken from CA 2006 state that:

1 Two members personally present are a quorum unless the company's Articles provide otherwise. For a company with only one member, the quorum is one (CA 2006, s. 318).
2 Any member elected by the members present may be chairman of the meeting subject to the provisions of the company's articles (CA 2006, s. 319).
3 For a company with a share capital, on a poll every member has one vote for each share or one vote for each £10 of stock they hold. For a company without a share capital every member has one vote (CA 2006, s. 284(3)), subject to the company's Articles.
4 For a company with a share capital, members may requisition a meeting if they hold at least 5% of the issued share capital (CA 2006, s. 303 – as amended by The Companies (Shareholder Rights) Regulations 2009). For a company limited by guarantee a meeting may be requisitioned by members holding 5% of the voting rights.

Notice of a company meeting may be given:

a) in hard copy form;
b) in electronic form;
c) by means of a website;
d) a combination of methods (a)–(c) (CA 2006, s. 308).

The notice must:

a) state the time, place and type of meeting (ss. 309 and 311);
b) be sent to all members and directors (s. 310). A member includes anyone entitled to shares by virtue of death or bankruptcy. The auditors and any independent assessor appointed prior to the meeting (see section 9.5 below) must also be sent a copy (s. 502 and s. 348 respectively).

## 2 Notice

Authority to issue a notice convening a general meeting must come from the board. The company secretary has no authority to issue the notice unless instructed to do so by the board, although it is usually the duty of the secretary to prepare it. If the notice has been sent by the secretary, it is usual to find the phrase 'by order of the board' (or a similar phrase) followed by the secretary's name and position. This indicates that the secretary is acting with due authority.

If a notice is issued without proper authority, but every member attends, the notice may still be considered valid. Any objections to the authority must be made as soon as possible; if not, members will be deemed to have acquiesced. Notice may be issued without authority from the directors if the meeting has been ordered by the court or has been validly requisitioned by members.

### 2.1 Period of notice

CA 2006, s. 360(2) sets out the method of calculating 'clear days' for notices of general meetings. This excludes both the day on which the notice is given (i.e. the day that notice is assumed to have arrived) and the day of the meeting.

The period of notice required for all general meetings is 14 clear days, apart from public company AGMs where 21 clear days are required (s. 307).

Under this section the Articles may provide for longer periods of notice, but may not provide for shorter periods.

### 2.2 Delivery

Under the electronic communications provisions of CA 2006, it is no longer necessary to send a hard copy notice of meeting. CA 2006 allows for members to agree to receive the notice electronically, or for them to be deemed to have agreed if they have failed to respond when asked by the company to opt out of delivery by electronic communications.

The rules on delivery for the different methods are as follows:

■ A communication sent by post is deemed to be delivered 48 hours after posting if the company can show that it was properly addressed, prepaid and posted (s. 1147(2)).
■ A communication sent electronically is deemed to be delivered 48 hours after sending if the company can show it was properly addressed (s. 1147(3)).
■ A communication via a website is deemed to be delivered when it is published on the site or when the recipient receives notice of the fact that the information is available (s. 1147(4)). This method of delivery is becoming popular with larger listed companies as it only requires the document to be published in one place. If this method is used, the notice must remain on the website at least until the conclusion of the general meeting.

In calculating deemed delivery, days which are not working days are ignored. These provisions of CA 2006 may be overridden by provisions in:

■ the company's Articles (in relation to communication to members);
■ any document constituting debenture stock (in relation to communication to debenture holders);
■ any agreement with another person (in relation to communications with anyone else).

Evidence of posting on a given day can be confirmed by the date appearing on a postmark. Where mail is posted in bulk for franking, it is sensible to obtain a certificate of posting. If the notice is not put into a post box, it is considered that a letter is posted when it is delivered to or collected by an authorised official of the Post Office and not at the time or date shown on a postmark subsequently impressed on it.

If notices are lost or are accidentally not sent to a member, this does not invalidate the proceedings of the meeting. CA 2006, s. 313 covers non-receipt of a notice.

## Who should receive notice?
The Articles may indicate who is entitled to receive notice of general meetings; but not every member has this right. Preference shares often carry no voting rights and it is possible to issue non-voting ordinary shares. If there is no right to vote, there is usually no right to receive notice or even to attend. However, CA 2006, s. 310(1) states that, unless the Articles otherwise provide, notice of general meeting should be sent to every member.

Some companies publish the notice of the AGM in the same booklet as the annual accounts rather than as a separate document. Every member is entitled to receive a copy of the accounts and therefore a note must be added to the notice to state that it is sent for information only to those members who are not entitled to attend.

The auditors have a statutory right to receive notice, as do the directors, who can also attend and speak even if they are not members. Where there are joint shareholders, notice is usually sent to the person who is named first on the register. If a member has died, notice may be sent to their personal representative if so requested. This also applies to a bankrupt member and his trustee.

## Failure to give notice
No meeting can be validly held unless every person entitled to attend has been given a reasonable opportunity to be present. CA 2006, s. 313 and most Articles provide that accidental omission to give notice of a meeting or non-receipt by a member will not invalidate the proceedings at that meeting. However, once it is shown that some members were not given notice, the onus lies with those claiming the meeting was valid to show that the omission was accidental.

> **STOP AND THINK** 9.1
>
> The importance of proper notice and proper procedure cannot be overemphasised. The dissatisfied shareholder who disagrees with a decision reached by the general meeting will look to invalidate the meeting. As all decisions at an invalid meeting become invalid, proper notice and correct procedure are essential. If you can invalidate the meeting, you invalidate the meeting's decisions.

## 2.3 Consent to short notice

Where it is not possible to give the minimum period of notice required, CA 2006 allows for the statutory period of notice to be waived, but not for dispensing with notice completely. In the case of an AGM for a public company, all those entitled to attend and vote must consent to short notice (s. 337(2)). In practice, this concession is used only by companies with relatively few members as it would be impractical to gain the consent of large numbers. For any other general meeting of a public company, at least 95% of members must agree. For private companies the percentage of members required to agree to shorter notice for any general meeting is 90%. The Articles may specify a higher percentage, but this must not be greater than 95% (CA 2006, s. 307).

Use of the waiver is particularly useful for small public companies where the shareholders are also the directors. The routine business of an AGM can be completed very swiftly with the directors resolving first to convene the AGM and the chairman signing the minutes to that effect, all of which may be done on the same day. If each shareholder attends, their presence at the meeting means that they are each deemed to have received notice.

The company secretary should retain signed consents to short notice as evidence that the meeting was convened validly. These should be kept with the notice convening the meeting or be attached to the relevant meeting minutes.

> **SAMPLE WORDING** 9.1
>
> **Agreement to short notice (plc annual general meeting)**
>
> We, the undersigned, all the members for the time being of . . . . . . . . . . . . . plc, [and in attendance/having a right to attend and vote] at the annual general meeting of that company to be held on ..... 20xx, hereby agree:
>
> a  to accept shorter notice of the said meeting than the period of notice prescribed by section 307(2)(a) of the Companies Act 2006; and
>
> b  to accept copies of the company's accounts less than 21 days before the date of the said meeting as required by section 424(3) of the Companies Act 2006.
>
> Dated this ..... day of ..... 20xx
>
> . . . . . . . . . . . . . . . . . . . . . .
>
> . . . . . . . . . . . . . . . . . . . . . .
>
> (Signatures)

---

> **SAMPLE WORDING 9.2**
>
> **Agreement to short notice (general meeting) of a plc (other than AGM)**
>
> We, the undersigned, being a majority in number of the members together holding not less than 95% of the share capital of . . . . . . . . . plc having a right to attend and vote at the meeting referred to below, hereby agree to a general meeting of that company being held on . . . . 20xx, notwithstanding that shorter notice has been given of the said meeting than the period of notice prescribed by section 307(2)(b) of the Companies Act 2006.
>
> Dated this ..... day of ..... 20xx
>
> . . . . . . . . . . . . . . . . . . . . . .
>
> . . . . . . . . . . . . . . . . . . . . .
>
> (Signatures)

---

## 2.4 Content of notice

The following items should be included in notices of general meetings:

- date, time and place of meeting;
- whether it is an AGM or other general meeting;
- a summary of the business to be transacted;
- the full text of special resolutions (see section 10) that are to be put before the meeting;
- details of any **special notice**;
- an explanation of the members' right to appoint proxies, that they need not be a member of the company (Listing Rules) (see section 9);
- the name and signature of the secretary issuing the notice, including details of the authority;
- any explanatory notes necessary for the member to understand the business being conducted.

In the case of an AGM, routine business, such as accounts, dividends, directors and auditors, are often referred to customarily as **ordinary business**. The same items being considered at any other general meeting become **special business**.

There is no prescribed format for the content of a notice of company general meeting other than to say that statutory provisions and requirements of the Articles must be observed. The notice often forms the basis for a skeleton agenda and should always accurately disclose the purpose of the meeting. If there are special resolutions, they must be described as such.

## 2.5 Other notice contents

The address of the company's registered office should appear. It is now common practice to expand the re-election of directors to show the names of those who will be retiring.

One method of providing information to members before a general meeting is to make documents available for inspection at the company's head office or other suitable address. Other circulars can be sent with the notice, as in the case of a director or auditor being removed from office who may require the company to issue an explanatory memorandum from them to the members.

---

📓 **SAMPLE WORDING** 9.3

**Notice of annual general meeting (private company which has chosen to continue with AGMs)**

. . . . . . . . . . . . . . . . . . LIMITED

NOTICE IS HEREBY GIVEN that THE ANNUAL GENERAL MEETING of the company will be held at [place] on . . .day, 20xx at xx:xx am to transact the ordinary business of the company.

By order of the board,

. . . . . . . . . . . . . . . . . . . . . .

Secretary

(Registered office address)

(Date)

*Note*

1  A member entitled to attend and vote at the meeting is entitled to appoint one or more proxies to attend and vote on his behalf. A proxy need not also be a member.

---

📓 **SAMPLE WORDING** 9.4

**Notice of annual general meeting (public company with listed shares)**

. . . . . . . . . . . . . . . . . . . . . . plc

NOTICE IS HEREBY GIVEN that THE ANNUAL GENERAL MEETING of the company will be held at [place] on day, 20xx at . . . am for the following purposes:

*Resolution 1*: To receive the report of the directors and the audited accounts for the year ended . . . . 20xx.

*Resolution 2*: That the report on directors' remuneration as set out in the annual report for the year to 20xx be approved.

*Resolution 3*: To declare a final dividend of 10 p per ordinary share payable on . . . . . . . . . 20xx to members on the register of members as at the close of business on . . . . . . ,. 20xx.

*Resolution 4*: To re-elect . . . . . . . a director of the company.

*Resolution 5*: To re-elect . . . . . . . a director of the company.

*Resolution 6*: To reappoint . . . . . . . . . the retiring auditors and to authorise the directors to determine their remuneration.

*Resolution 7*: As special business, to consider the following resolution, which will be proposed as a special resolution:

THAT the Articles of Association of the company be altered by deleting the word 'two' in the third line of article 66 and inserting the word 'three' in its place.

*Resolution 8:* That the board be and it is hereby generally and unconditionally authorised to exercise all powers of the company to allot relevant securities (within the meaning of section 551 of the Companies Act 2006) up to an aggregate nominal amount of £. . . . provided that this authority shall expire on . . . . 20xx save that the company may before such expiry make an offer or agreement which would or might require relevant securities to be allotted after such expiry and the board may allot relevant securities in pursuance of such an offer or agreement as if the authority conferred hereby had not expired.

*Resolution 9*: As special business, to consider the following resolution, which will be proposed as a special resolution:

That subject to the passing of the previous resolution the board be and is hereby empowered pursuant to section 571 of the Companies Act 2006 to allot equity securities (within the meaning of section 560 of the said Act) for cash pursuant to the authority conferred by the previous resolution as if section 561 of the said Act did not apply to any such allotment provided that this power shall be limited:

(i) to the allotment of equity securities in connection with a rights issue in favour of ordinary shareholders where the equity securities respectively attributable to the interests of all ordinary shareholders are proportionate (as nearly as may be) to the respective numbers of ordinary shares held by them; and

(ii) to the allotment (otherwise than pursuant to sub-paragraph (i) above) of equity securities up to an aggregate nominal value of £. . . . and shall expire 20xx save that the company may before such expiry make an offer or agreement which would or might require equity securities to be allotted after such expiry and the board may allot equity securities in pursuance of such an offer or agreement as if the power conferred hereby had not expired.

*Resolution 10*: To authorise the company to make donations to EU political organisations and to incur EU political expenditure not exceeding £. . . ., during the financial period ending .. .. . .20xx. In this resolution, 'donations', 'EU political organisations' and 'EU political expenditure' have the meanings set out in the Companies Act 2006.

*Resolution 11*: As special business, to consider the following resolution, which will be proposed as a special resolution: That a general meeting other than the annual general meeting may be called on not less than 14 clear days' notice.

By order of the board,

. . . . . . . . . . . . . . . . . . . . . .

Secretary

. . . . . . . . . . . . . . . . . . . . . . . . . . . . . . . .

(Registered office address)

. . . . . . . . . . . . . . . . . . . . . . . . . . . . . . . .

(Date)

*Notes*

1   A member entitled to attend and vote at the meeting is entitled to appoint one or more proxies to attend and vote on his or her behalf. A proxy need not also be a member.

2   To be entitled to attend and vote at the meeting, and for the purpose of the determination by the company of the number of votes they may cast, members must be entered on the company's register of members at [time and date not more than 48 hours before the time fixed for the meeting] ('the specified time'). If the meeting is adjourned to a time not more than 48 hours after the specified time applicable to the original meeting, that time will also apply for the purpose of determining the entitlement of members to attend and vote (and for the purpose of determining the number of votes they may cast) at the adjourned meeting. If, however, the meeting is adjourned for a longer period then, to be so entitled, members must be entered on the company's register of members at the time which is [number of hours, e.g. 48] before the time fixed for the adjourned meeting or, if the company gives notice of the adjourned meeting, at the time specified in that notice. (A note along these lines is desirable where the company's shares are held in dematerialised form through CREST.)

3   This notice is sent for information only to holders of 6% first mortgage debenture stock 2008/2012 and 7% unsecured loan stock 2007/2015, who are not entitled to attend and vote at the meeting.

## 2.6 Listed companies

The Listing Rules require any circular sent to shareholders of a listed company, including notices of general meetings, to contain:

- a clear and adequate explanation of its subject matter, including enough information for shareholders to be sufficiently informed when voting or taking other actions;
- a notice drawing members' attention to the importance of the document and advising them. if they are in any doubt, on the action to take to consult an appropriate independent adviser;
- where voting is required (except for routine ordinary business), a voting recommendation from the directors;
- a notice advising members that if their shares have been sold or transferred, the circular and any other relevant documents should be passed to the purchaser or transferee.

Increasingly, listed companies are making information available via the internet and/or email. By registering electronically with a company or its registrars, members can be alerted every time a new notice or publication is placed on that company's website. Large companies are now maintaining investor centres containing information of interest to members, including the quarterly results and major announcements, which may be accessed electronically.

Listed companies are also encouraged to comply with the recommendations of the UK Corporate Governance Code (see also the Corporate Governance syllabus and text) concerning AGMs, particularly:

- issuing the notice of the AGM with at least 20 working days' (i.e. excluding weekends and public holidays) notice;
- making constructive use of the AGMs (e.g. by making presentations to private investors);
- publishing the proxy figures.

The implementation of the EU Shareholder Rights Directive also affected listed companies and required minor modification to CA 2006. Key changes included the following:

- The minimum notice period for general meetings other than AGMs increased from 14 to 21 days, unless:
  - the listed company offers the facility for electronic voting for all members; and
  - shareholders have passed a resolution that a general meeting, other than the AGM, may be called on not less than 14 clear days' notice (this resolution is approved by shareholders and would need to be renewed annually).
- Clearer rights for shareholders to ask questions at general meetings and for the directors to provide answers to those questions either at the meeting or by referring the member to the company's website.

## 2.7 Share warrants to bearer

Any company limited by shares may, if authorised by its Articles, issue a warrant stating that the bearer of the warrant is entitled to the shares specified in it (see Chapter 3). Public companies arrange newspaper advertisements for holders of bearer shares giving details of the procedures for receiving dividends and notices. The notice must first be submitted to UKLA for approval. The notice should follow the wording of the notice issued to registered shareholders, with the addition of instruction as to how warrant holders may vote in person or by proxy at the meeting. Private companies with bearer shares will require holders to provide contact addresses at which notices of meetings can be delivered for them.

### CHECKLIST 9.1 AGM notice

✓ Does the notice state it is an AGM and the date, time and place?
✓ Does the notice contain resolutions that can be implemented (i.e. are your resolutions clear)?
✓ Does the notice indicate the authority under which it is being given (usually by you, as company secretary under the authority of the board)?
✓ Does the notice include a reference of the members' right to appoint one or more proxies?
✓ Are special resolutions identified as such? Has the full text of these resolutions been given?

✓ Have sufficient supporting notes been provided, if necessary, to help the member understand the proposed resolutions?

✓ Have you removed items under the heading 'Any Other Business' which would be beyond the notice of the AGM? (CA 2006, s. 311(2) states that the 'general nature of the business to be transacted must be given').

✓ Has the proper notice period been given?

---

**TEST YOUR KNOWLEDGE 9.1**

a  What are the minimum notice periods for general meetings?

b  What are the requisite authorities to consent to holding an AGM and any other general meeting at short notice?

c  Who, other than the shareholders, is entitled to receive notice of general meetings?

d  When is a notice delivered by means of a website deemed to arrive?

e  What are the typical resolutions considered at an AGM?

f  What additional information must be included in the notice of general meeting for listed companies?

g  What corporate governance consideration should listed companies take into account in respect of notice periods?

---

# 3  Annual general meeting (AGM)

## 3.1 Timing and purpose

A public company must hold an AGM within six months of the end of its accounting period (CA 2006, s. 336(1)).

The main purpose of an AGM is for the directors to report on the performance of the company, for the members to question the directors about the company and their conduct of its affairs, and for members to vote on resolutions that have to be put before the meeting (see section 3.2).

Sometimes, because of a change in the company's accounting reference period or because of a problem in preparing the annual accounts, it is not possible to have the accounts ready for submission by the last date on which the AGM must be held. In this case, the meeting must still be held and then adjourned to a date at which the accounts can be presented. Alternatively, the AGM may be held to deal with other business, such as the election of directors, and the accounts dealt with at general meeting at a later date.

## 3.2 The business of an AGM

The routine business of an AGM is as follows:

1  Receive the report and accounts laid before the meeting as required by CA 2006, s. 437.
2  For listed companies, seek approval of the report on directors' remuneration, which appears in the report and accounts (s. 439).
3  Declare the final dividend.
4  Elect the directors who have been appointed since the last AGM and re-elect those who have retired by rotation in accordance with the company's Articles.
5  Appoint, or reappoint, the auditors and determine their remuneration.

Other matters that are commonly dealt with at an AGM include:

■ special resolutions to make any required alterations to the company's Articles;
■ authority to the directors to issue capital as required;
■ authority for the directors to disapply pre-emption rights;
■ authority for the directors to repurchase the company's own shares;

- authority for the directors to offer shareholders the right to receive new ordinary shares instead of cash for all or part of any dividend, if provided for in the company's Articles;
- adoption of employee share schemes or other employee incentive plans using shares of the company;
- approval of political expenditure;
- for listed companies, approval that general meetings, other than AGMs, may be called on not less than 14 clear days' notice (see section 2.6 above).

### CHECKLIST 9.2  AGM planning

✓ Check that the date chosen complies with the statutory minimum 21 days' clear notice.
✓ Check that the date is not more than six months from the end of the accounting period for a plc or, for a private company continuing to hold AGMs, as specified in the Articles.
✓ If the company is listed, check whether the notice period complies with UK Corporate Governance requirement of 20 working days.
✓ Check what else is happening on the chosen date.
✓ If the venue is regularly used, check that it has been booked. If it is a new one, check that is convenient for members to attend at that location.
✓ Check that the board has agreed to convene the meeting and approved the notice of meeting.
✓ Are the annual report and accounts and notice of AGM finalised and printed?
✓ Have you informed interested parties, such as the auditors, institutional investors and the financial and industry sector press?
✓ If the company is listed, do the documentation and arrangements comply with the Listing Rules and the UK Corporate Governance Code?

---

**STOP AND THINK 9.2**

The best way to understand AGMs is to attend some. You will see different styles and approaches, all of which can be acceptable. Choose five leading companies, check the locations, call the company secretary, state that you are studying and ask for an invitation to attend.

---

## 3.3 Circulation of members' resolutions and statements

In addition to the ability of a shareholder to requisition a general meeting (see section 5), shareholders of a public company have the right to add items of business to the agenda of a forthcoming AGM. CA 2006, s. 338 provides that the following may place an item of business on the forthcoming AGM:

- one or more shareholders holding at least 5% of the fully paid up voting capital; or
- not less than 100 shareholders holding shares on which there has been paid up an average sum, per member, of not less than £100.

The requisition must be lodged not less than six weeks before the date set for the meeting, but if the meeting is subsequently set for sooner, the requisition is deemed as being validly served. The procedure is to deposit the signed requisition(s) (stating the object(s) or including any supporting statement) at the registered office. This may be in hard copy or electronic form. In most circumstances the board does not agree with the members' resolution, and it is therefore usual for the board to provide their view on the members' resolution in a statement, together with a recommendation to vote against it. Directors are also at liberty, if they wish, to add a further resolution in response to the requisitioned business. If the request is received before the end of the financial year preceding the meeting, the costs of circulation must be met by the company (s. 340(1)). If the request is received later, it must be accompanied by an amount to cover the expenses of circulation. If not, the directors are not obliged to circulate details of the resolution or any accompanying statement. They are also not required to circulate it if it is considered to be ineffective, defamatory, frivolous or vexatious. Members of private companies may request the circulation of written resolutions (see section 10.4).

CA 2006, s. 314 allows members to request circulation of a statement of up to 1,000 words which relates to a resolution to be proposed at any general meeting or to other business to be dealt with at the meeting. The numbers of members required are as for requesting a resolution to be put to an AGM, however, the request under this section need only be received one week before the meeting. CA 2006, s. 317 provides that the company need not circulate the statement if, on application to the court, it is found that those making it are abusing their rights under s. 314. If the request is received before the end of the financial year preceding the meeting, the costs of the circulation must be met by the company if the request relates to an AGM (s. 316).

---

**STOP AND THINK 9.3**

It is probably a sign that the company is having relationship problems with its shareholders if the shareholders feel it is necessary to requisition a meeting or circulate their own resolution. As part of good corporate governance, the board should understand their shareholders' concerns and be prepared to address them as appropriate.

---

**TEST YOUR KNOWLEDGE 9.2**

a  When must an AGM take place?
b  What is the statutory minimum period of notice for the AGM?
c  What is the main purpose of the AGM?
d  When can the full period of notice of an AGM be dispensed with?
e  What is the procedure for members to put their own resolution to an AGM?

---

# 4  Other general meetings

Meetings of shareholders are referred to as general meetings, apart from the references to AGMs for plcs. General meetings may be convened by the directors at any time and there are no specific requirements about the business to be conducted at such meetings. The term **extraordinary general meeting (EGM)** is not used in CA 2006, although a company's Articles (if written before the introduction of the CA 2006 and Model Articles) may refer to EGMs.

## 4.1  The business of a general meeting

The only business that may be transacted at a general meeting is that specified in the notice convening the meeting. The ordinary or special resolutions to be passed will be in accordance with the CA or as stated in the company's Articles. Examples of resolutions to be passed at a general meeting include:

■ adoption of new Articles;
■ amendments to employees' share schemes;
■ substantial proposed acquisitions or divestments.

## 4.2  When a general meeting is called

Although directors have the discretion to call a general meeting at any time and as often as they wish (CA 2006, s. 302), in practice they will call one only when there is urgent business that cannot be deferred until the next AGM. There are no provisions in the Companies Acts that require general meetings other than AGMs to be held at specific intervals.

In certain circumstances, the directors are required to convene a general meeting on the resignation of an auditor; that is, if an auditor's notice of resignation states that there are matters that should be brought to the attention of the members or creditors. The directors must issue a notice within 21 days to convene a general meeting within 28 days from the issue of notice. The meeting will receive and consider the auditor's explanation of the circumstances prompting his resignation.

A general meeting must be convened by the directors of a public company within 28 days of their becoming aware that the net assets are half (or less) of its called-up share capital. The meeting must be called for not less than 56 days from the date they became aware of the situation and will be for the purpose of considering what steps to take to deal with it (CA 2006, s. 656).

Under CA 2006, s. 306 the court has power to order a general meeting to be convened. The court will not usually interfere in a dispute between directors and shareholders, because the shareholders have the power to call a meeting (see above). The power invested in the court is usually used only in the situation where there is just one member available or willing to attend and there is no other way of obtaining a quorum for the meeting.

## 5   Requisitioned meetings

Under CA 2006, s. 303 members holding not less than 5% of the paid-up capital may requisition the directors to hold a general meeting. The requisition may be in hard copy or electronic form and must be authenticated by the persons requesting it. The requisition must state the general nature of the business to be dealt with at the meeting and may include the text of a resolution to be moved. For a private company, the percentage of members required to make such a request is also 5% if it is more than twelve months since a general meeting has been held which had been called by requisition under s. 303, or in relation to which members had the right to require the circulation of a resolution under either CA 2006, s. 303(3) or the company's Articles. On receipt of the requisition the directors must convene the meeting within 21 days, and the meeting must be held not more than 28 days after the date of the notice of the meeting (CA 2006, s. 304(1)). If the requisition received by the company includes a resolution to be moved at the meeting, the notice of meeting must include notice of the resolution.

In addition to the right to requisition meetings, the cost of circulating members' statements needs to be considered. A company will be required to circulate a statement (not exceeding 1,000 words) regarding resolutions or other business (whether requisitioned by the members or not) if it is requested by

- one or more shareholders holding at least 5% of the fully paid up voting capital; or
- not less than 100 shareholders holding shares on which there has been paid up an average sum, per member, of not less than £100.

Unless it is an AGM and meets the timing requirements (see 3.3 above), members bear the circulation costs unless the company resolves otherwise.

CA 2006, ss. 292–295 provides that for private companies, a requisition can be made for the circulation of a written resolution together with a statement on the resolution. The same 5% shareholding level as above applies. The members requisitioning the business must again deposit or tender a sum to cover the company's expenses in circulating the resolution, unless the company agrees to pay for it. The written resolution and any statement to be sent to all the members may be circulated in hard copy or electronically. The written resolution must be circulated to members not more than 21 days after the obligation arises and must include instructions on how to signify agreement (or otherwise) to the resolution and the date by which it must be passed if it is not to lapse. As with the requisitioning of any other business, the company or any other aggrieved person may apply to the court for an order preventing the circulation of a statement.

CA 2006, s. 305 provides that if the directors do not comply with the requisition of a meeting, the requisitioners, or a group representing more than 50% of the voting rights of all of them, may convene the meeting at any time within three months from the date of deposit of the requisition. As far as possible, the meeting should be convened in the same manner as would be done by the directors. The company secretary should advise the directors to comply with any valid request to requisition a general meeting made by members. The requisitionists have the right to recover their expenses in calling the meeting and CA 2006, s. 305 provides that the company must deduct such costs from the remuneration of the directors.

In practice, if convening a meeting, the directors would circulate the notice to the members with a letter explaining the circumstances in which the meeting was being called and state whether or not they supported the proposals to be considered.

---

**SAMPLE WORDING 9.5**

**Requisition for general meeting**

The Directors,

. . . . . . . . . . . . . . . . . . . . . . plc.

We, the undersigned, being members of . . . . . . . . . plc, holding in the aggregate . . . . . . . ordinary shares of £1 each out of the issued and paid-up capital of . . . . . . . ordinary shares of £1 each, require you, pursuant to section 303 of the Companies Act 2006, to convene a general meeting of the company for the purpose of considering the following resolution(s), which will be proposed as an ordinary resolution(s):

*Resolution(s)*

1 THAT . . . . . . . . . . . . be appointed a director of the company.

. . . . . . . . . . . . . . . . . . . . . . .

. . . . . . . . . . . . . . . . . . . . . . .

(Signatures)

. . . . . . . . . . . . . . . . . . . . . . .

. . . . . . . . . . . . . . . . . . . . . . .

(Addresses)

. . . . . . . . . . . . . . . . . . . . . . .

(Date)

---

**TEST YOUR KNOWLEDGE 9.3**

a Under what circumstances must the directors convene a general meeting other than an AGM?
b When can the full notice period of a general meeting be dispensed with?
c Under CA 2006, s. 304 the directors must convene a general meeting on a member's valid requisition. What is the minimum requirement for the requisition?
d Under what circumstances other than a member's requisition are directors required to convene a general meeting?

---

## 6 Class meetings

A company's Articles usually provide that the capital can be divided into shares of more than one class. Model Article 22 (public company Model Article 43) states:

'Subject to the articles, but without prejudice to the rights attached to any existing share, the company may issue shares with such rights or restrictions as may be determined by ordinary resolution.'

By definition, **class meetings** are meetings of the holders of a class of a company's shares. Meetings must be held whenever the rights of the holder of the class are to be varied as a result of some action proposed to be taken by the company. As the rights are defined in the Articles, any variation must be effected by resolution in general meeting. It is normal to hold a preliminary class meeting and then a full general meeting of the company at the same place, one immediately after the other. Many Articles provide for a preliminary consent to the variation to be obtained from the class, either in writing by the holders of at least 75% of the shares or by **special resolution** passed at a separate meeting of the holders. The latter is usually favoured since the majority need not be 75% of the whole number of shares, but only of votes cast by those present.

Public companies usually discuss any proposed variation of class rights with their institutional shareholders prior to dispatch of the notice of meeting to ensure that the company has their support. It is also useful in ensuring the presence of a quorum.

## 6.1 Convening a class meeting

Unless the Articles provide otherwise, the procedure for convening, holding and passing resolutions at class meetings are the same as for general meetings, except that the right to vote at the meeting is usually restricted to the holders of that particular class of shares. CA 2006, ss. 334 and 335 provide that certain provisions of the Act in relation to meetings do not apply to class meetings. They also provide (s. 334(4)) that a quorum for a variation of class rights meeting shall be two members holding at least one third in nominal value of the shares of that class (excluding any shares held in treasury) and that at an adjourned meeting the quorum shall be one member holding shares of that class.

The Articles will state that a variation is subject to the consent of a certain number of the holders of that class and if the Articles are silent on the matter then CA 2006, s. 630 stipulates that a special resolution is required (or the consent in writing from the holders of at least three-quarters in nominal value of the issued shares of that class). CA 2006, s. 633 gives minority members the right to challenge a decision to vary rights by making an application to the court to have the variation cancelled within 21 days of the resolution being passed. Section 633(2) provides that at least 15% of the dissenting holders of the issued shares concerned who did not consent or vote for the resolution must be party to the application. The court then has to decide whether the variation would unfairly prejudice the shareholders of the class represented. The variation will not have effect until it has been confirmed by the court. The company must file a copy of any court order in respect of the variation with the Registrar of Companies within 15 days of the court order (s. 635).

---

**SAMPLE WORDING 9.6**

**Notice of class meeting**

. . . . . . . . . . . . . . . . . . . . . . . plc.

NOTICE IS HEREBY GIVEN that a SEPARATE CLASS MEETING of the holders of the . . .% second cumulative preference shares in the capital of the company will be held at . . . . . . . . . . . . on . . . day, . . . . . 20xx at . . . . . am (or as soon thereafter as the separate class meeting of the holders of the . . . .% first cumulative preference shares in the capital of the company which has been convened for the same day and place shall have been concluded or adjourned) for the purpose of considering the following resolution, which will be proposed as a special resolution:

*Resolution*

THAT this separate class meeting of the holders of the . . .% second cumulative preference shares in the capital of the company hereby sanctions the passing of the resolution set out in the notice dated . . . 20xx, convening a general meeting of the company on . . . . . . 20xx (a copy of such notice having been produced to this meeting and for the purpose of identification signed by the chairman thereof) and hereby sanctions each and every variation, modification or abrogation of the rights and privileges attached or belonging to the . . . . .% second cumulative preference shares effected thereby or necessary to give effect thereto.

By order of the board,

. . . . . . . . . . . . . . . . . . . . . . .

Secretary

. . . . . . . . . . . . . . . . . . . . . . .

(Address)

. . . . . . . . . . . . . . . . . . . . .

(Date)

*Note*

1  A member entitled to attend and vote at the meeting is entitled to appoint one or more proxies to attend and vote on his or her behalf. A proxy need not also be a member.

> **TEST YOUR KNOWLEDGE 9.4**
>
> **a** Define a class meeting.
> **b** What is the procedure of dissenting shareholders who object to a variation in class rights?

# 7 Agenda

The content and presentation of the agenda for any general meeting should be decided by the chairman in consultation with the secretary. It is sensible for all meetings to have an agenda to act as a directing force on the meeting and to help avoid aimless discussion. An agenda can also prompt advance attention to specific business and give the members a chance to do some preparation and reflection. The accompanying papers and reports to the agenda should be received in time for members to assimilate the data, make comparisons with like statistics and allow thinking time in order to be ready with ideas and views at the meeting.

The chairman's agenda should be slightly different from that circulated to other members as it should have additional brief notes on the background to items (particularly with regard to sensitive issues), information updates and reminders of any previous discussions. This will enable the chairman to conduct the meeting with tact and authority.

---

> **SAMPLE WORDING 9.7**
>
> **Agenda for annual general meeting**
>
> . . . . . . . . . . . . . . . . . . . . . . plc.
> AGENDA for THE ANNUAL GENERAL MEETING to be held at
> . . . . . . . . . . . . on . . . day, . . . . . 20xx
>
> 1 To request that the notice of meeting be taken as read.*
>
> 2 The chairman to address the meeting and to propose:
> THAT the report of the directors and the audited accounts for the year ended
> ..... 20xx now laid before the meeting, be received.
> ............ to second the resolution. **
> The chairman to invite questions and, having replied, to put the resolution to the meeting and declare the result.
>
> 3 The chairman to propose:
> THAT the directors' remuneration report, contained in the annual report and accounts for the year ended ..... 20xx be approved.
> ........... to second the resolution.
> The chairman to invite questions and, having replied, to put the resolution to the meeting and declare the result.
>
> 4 The chairman to propose:
> THAT the final dividend of ..... p per share recommended by the directors be declared payable on ..... 20xx to holders of ordinary shares registered at the close of business on ..... 20xx.
> ........... to second the resolution.
> The chairman to invite questions and, having replied, to put the resolution to the meeting and declare the result.
>
> 5 The chairman to propose:
> THAT the director retiring by rotation, be re-elected a director of the company.
> ........... to second the resolution.

The chairman to invite questions and, having replied, to put the resolution to the meeting and declare the result.

6 ............ a member, to propose:
THAT ............ be reappointed auditors of the company to hold office until the conclusion of the next general meeting at which accounts are laid before the company and that their remuneration be determined by the directors.
............ another member, to second the resolution.
The chairman to invite questions and, having replied, to put the resolution to the meeting and declare the result.

7 The chairman to propose as a special resolution:
THAT the Articles of Association of the company be altered by deleting the word 'two' in the third line of Article 66 and inserting the word 'three' in its place.
............ to second the resolution.
The chairman to invite questions and, having replied, to put the resolution to the meeting and declare the result.

8 The chairman to close the meeting.

*Notes*
\* It is possible, with the meeting's consent, for the notice of the meeting to be taken as read. If this is the case, it will not be necessary to read it, which is particularly useful where the notice or the report is lengthy.
\*\* There is no legal requirement for resolutions to be seconded. Some companies may like members to be able to be involved in this way, others prefer not to have seconders and so save some time, especially if a lot of business is to be transacted.

# 8 Quorum

The definition of a **quorum** is simply the minimum number of persons necessary for the transaction of business. A company's Articles usually specify the quorum for general meetings, but if there is no provision in the Articles, CA 2006 s. 318 will apply (see below).

## 8.1 Quorum for general meetings

CA 2006, s. 318(1) provides that if a company has only one member, the quorum for general meetings is one. If the company has more than one member, s. 318(2) provides that, unless the Articles provide otherwise, two **qualifying persons** present at a general meeting shall be a quorum. However, if the two qualifying persons are both corporate representatives of the same company (appointed under CA 2006, s. 323) or are both proxies for the same member, they do not constitute a quorum. CA 2006, s. 318(3) defines a 'qualifying person' as:

- an individual who is a member of the company;
- a representative of a corporation, appointed under CA 2006, s. 323, for the purposes of that meeting;
- a proxy of a member, appointed for that meeting.

The quorum for meetings may be provided for in the Articles. Model Article 38 (public company Model Article 30), however, simply states that no business (other than the appointment of the chairman of a meeting) may be transacted at a general meeting unless a quorum is present – hence the CA 2006 definition will apply where companies are subject to the Model Articles.

Under common law, a meeting cannot take place if only one person is present, even if that person is present in more than one capacity. Corporate representatives are deemed to be members (not proxies) for the purpose of the quorum and should always be counted, unless they are not eligible to vote.

A company's Articles usually make provision for a procedure to be adopted if a quorum is not present.

Model Article 41 (public company Model Article 33) states that if a quorum is not present within 30 minutes from the time appointed for a meeting, or if during the meeting a quorum is not present, the meeting must be adjourned (see section 9.6 below). The quorum required for the adjourned meeting will be the same as for the original meeting, but companies usually provide in their Articles that if a quorum is not present at an adjourned meeting, the members present shall be a quorum, provided it is not less than two.

## 8.2 Quorum for class meetings

At a class meeting called to consent to an alteration of the rights of a class of shareholders, the quorum is two or more members of the class or their proxies, representing at least one third in nominal value of the issued shares of the class (CA 2006, s. 334(4)). At an adjourned meeting, the quorum is reduced to one member of the class present in person or by proxy and no minimum number or percentage of the shares of the class need be represented. This provision is mandatory and cannot be varied by the Articles. A class meeting of this kind cannot be constituted by one proxy attending on behalf of two or more members, because the provision requires at least two persons to be present. If a quorum is not present at the original meeting, an adjournment of it is compulsory only if the Articles so provide in respect of the class meeting or in respect of general meetings.

At any other class meeting the quorum is that prescribed by the Articles, but if they make no express provision, the quorum is as provided for in CA 2006. s. 318 (see section 8.1).

## 8.3 Failure to maintain a quorum

At common law the quorum should be maintained throughout the meeting. In order to avoid this problem the Articles may provide that a quorum need be present only at the time when the meeting proceeds to business. This was upheld in Re *Harley Baird* (1955), where decisions taken after the number had fallen below the quorum were held to be valid.

## 8.4 Situations when one person can be a quorum

CA 2006, s. 318 states that in the case of a company limited by shares or guarantee and having only one member, one qualifying person present at a meeting is a quorum. In addition, CA 2006, s. 306 provides a solution when there is only one surviving member, or only one member willing to attend meetings: the quorum in these cases can be fixed at one by the court. It is also permissible to have a meeting attended by one person if the company is a single-member private company (see Chapter 8). Private company Articles may provide that the minimum is one and the quorum will be adjusted accordingly to allow the transaction of business by a sole member.

Where more than one person is entitled to attend, the court has the power to authorise the holding of a meeting even though it is known in advance that only one person will be present. This is to deal with a situation where, if a shareholder refuses to attend a meeting, the court will allow the other shareholder to conduct the business of the meeting alone.

---

**TEST YOUR KNOWLEDGE 9.5**

a  In what circumstances may one person constitute a valid quorum?
b  If a quorum is not present at a general meeting, what would you expect to happen?

# 9 Voting

It is an important duty of the chairman of a meeting to ascertain the true sense of the meeting on any question being considered. The chairman may, in the first instance, take a vote on a show of hands, although a poll can be demanded even before this. The chairman calls on those present to vote by raising their hands, first 'For' the resolution and then 'Against'. At this stage each member (present in person or by proxy) has only one vote. A visual count (or if there are many members present a visual survey of the hands raised) is made and the chairman declares the resolution carried or lost. If many members are expected at the meeting, it may be a good idea to issue voting cards to *bona fide* shareholders on arrival. In that way only those who are entitled to vote on a show of hands will be able to do so and this will aid the visual count.

The chairman's declaration of the result is conclusive unless a poll is demanded, and once the entry has been made in the minute book, the validity of the resolution cannot be questioned (CA 2006, s. 320). It is not necessary to minute the number of votes for or against the motion. An ordinary resolution is passed if a simple majority of those voting is attained and a special resolution is passed if not less than 75% of those voting support the resolution.

The necessary majorities for ordinary and special resolutions are discussed later in this chapter.

## 9.1 Further CA 2006 and Model Articles references to voting

It is useful to review the following statutory and Model Articles references concerned with voting:

1. *CA 2006, ss. 288–300* – These sections set out the procedure and provisions in respect of resolutions in writing available for private companies only (see below).
2. *CA 2006, s. 284* – Every member is entitled to one vote on a show of hands (or written resolution for private companies) and one vote for every share in a poll.
3. *CA 2006, s. 286* – In the case of joint holders, the seniority of the member is determined by the order in which they appear on the share register. The first named shareholder is the senior, followed by the second named, and then the third and fourth named (if any). A vote tendered by the most senior member is to the exclusion of any vote cast by the other members.
4. *Model Article 27 (public company Model Article 66)* – A person entitled to a share by operation of the bankruptcy or death of the original shareholder shall have no right to attend the meeting and vote until registered as the holder of the share.
5. *Public company Model Article 41* – No holder can vote if monies are outstanding on the shares (i.e. the shares are partly paid). This does not appear in the private company Model Articles as they stipulate that all shares must be fully paid.

---

**TEST YOUR KNOWLEDGE 9.6**

a   Whose duty is it to ascertain the sense of meeting when votes are cast?
b   What are the differences between a vote on a show of hands and a poll vote?
c   Does the holder of a share warrant have a right to a vote at general meetings?

---

## 9.2 Proxies

Any member who is entitled to vote can appoint another person as his **proxy** to attend and vote in his place (CA 2006, s. 324). Proxy voting simply allows shareholders to use their votes through a third party without the need to attend the meeting. If the company has a share capital, more than one proxy can be appointed. In the case of a company having a share capital, a member may appoint more than one proxy in respect of their shareholding, provided that each proxy represents different shares within that member's shareholding (CA 2006, s. 324). A proxy can speak at the meeting and vote on a show of hands as well as on a poll. A proxy need not be a member of the company. Section 324 also applies to members of a company without a share capital but in this case only one proxy may be appointed.

Other provisions include:

- All notices of company general meetings must display a statement about the right of a member to appoint a proxy (CA 2006, s. 325).
- The shareholder must lodge the appointment of the proxy no later than 48 hours prior to the meeting (CA 2006, s. 327). The 48 hours is calculated only by reference to working days.
- The proxy has a right to demand a poll (CA 2006, s. 329).

If a member has appointed a proxy and then attends and votes at the meeting, his presence will automatically cancel the authority given to the proxy. If a vote is particularly close, the scrutineers must make sure that the same shares (i.e. cast by the member and the proxy) have not inadvertently been voted twice.

## Despatch of proxy cards

If a company is listed, **proxy cards** must be circulated with the notice of the meeting, but this is not obligatory in the case of unlisted public companies or private companies. If they are circulated, by CA 2006, s. 326 they must be issued to all members, not just those who favour the board. Most companies' Articles require that proxies must be lodged at the company's office not less than 48 hours before a meeting. It is illegal for the Articles to provide for a longer period. The Articles may also permit proxies to be lodged between an original meeting and an adjourned meeting. Proxies may be submitted electronically, but only to an address supplied by the company for that purpose (CA 2006, s. 333), for example, emailing a form of proxy to the company secretary's usual email address would not constitute a valid proxy.

The company's office is usually the registered office or some other place specified in the notice convening the meeting. For example, if the company's share registration is carried out by a service registrar at a place other than the registered office of the company, the proxies may be sent to the address of the registrar.

Listed companies should send two copies of the proxy card and circulars to UKLA no later than the date of despatch of the notice. The UK Corporate Governance Code also recommends that proxy forms include a 'vote withheld' box as a voting option.

## Evaluation of proxies

When proxy cards are returned, they must be checked against the register of members and for accuracy of completion. A schedule should be prepared of votes for and against each resolution as quickly as possible to give the board the earliest information as to the aggregate votes cast either way on each motion. Progressive figures are needed daily as these may well determine the course to be adopted at the meeting. Cards that are completed incorrectly should be rejected, but if there is time and the shareholding is substantial, they should be returned to the shareholder for amendment. If the company is listed, the proxy form may reflect the recommendations of the ICSA and the UK Corporate Governance Code (see also the Corporate Governance syllabus and text) by accommodating directions from shareholders to abstain from voting on particular resolutions (see proxy forms below). If this is the case, then votes which have been lodged as abstained will need to be evaluated as appropriate – they should not be included with either the votes 'for' or 'against' the resolution. If a shareholder does not indicate how his vote should be cast, then the proxy will use his discretion as to how they vote, or whether they vote at all. If the chairman is given discretion over proxy votes, he will usually use them to support and vote for the resolution. If the number of proxy votes already lodged in favour of a resolution is in excess of the majority needed, any shareholder who objected to the resolution and called for a poll would be very unlikely to secure a defeat. In these circumstances the chairman of the meeting can disclose the number of proxy votes which have already been lodged in favour of the resolution and invite the objecting shareholder to consider that they would lose on a poll vote. The objecting shareholder may then choose to withdraw their request for a poll.

## Proxy forms

In essence, any approved form will be adequate as a proxy card, although the Articles may specify the form that must be used. Pursuant to the Listing Rules, listed companies should issue the proxy card with the notice in the form of a addressed, stamped postcard or as a page of the AGM documents that can be folded into an envelope size.

One-way proxies appoint a person but do not direct them how to vote. Two-way proxies appoint a person and direct them how to vote. **Three-way proxies** include an option for the shareholder to withhold their vote. Listed companies are required by the Listing Rules to issue three-way proxies so that the member can instruct his proxy how votes are to be cast for each resolution. If no instructions are given by the member, the proxy can vote as he wishes or choose not to vote at all. The chairman of the meeting is usually shown as the default proxy, but that name can be struck out by the shareholder if he wishes to insert the name of a different proxy.

Proxy cards should be as straightforward as possible, requiring only a signature and date by way of execution for an individual. Shareholders who are companies may need to execute the proxy form under seal or require an authorised signatory or director of the company to sign the form.

---

**SAMPLE WORDING 9.8**

**Three-way proxy card**

. . . . . . . . . . . . . . . . . . . . . . plc

FORM OF PROXY FOR USE AT ANNUAL GENERAL MEETING

I/We (block capitals please) . . . . . . . . . . . . . . a member/members of the above-named company, hereby appoint the chairman of the meeting, or . . . . . . . . . . . . . . . as my/our proxy to vote for me/us on my/our behalf at the Annual General Meeting of the Company to be held at 12 noon on . . . . . . . . . . . . . . . the . . . day of . . . . . . . . . . 20xx and at any adjournment thereof.

Signature . . . . . . . . . . . . . . .

Dated . . . . . . . . . . . . . . . . .

Please indicate with an X for each resolution below how you wish your votes to be cast. The 'vote withheld' option below is provided to enable you to abstain on any particular resolution. However, it should be noted that a 'vote withheld' is not a vote in law and will not be counted in the calculation of the proportion of the votes 'for' and 'against' a resolution.

| | For | Against | Vote Withheld | At Discretion |
|---|---|---|---|---|
| **Resolution 1:** To receive the Report and Accounts for the year ended 31 December 20xx | | | | |
| **Resolution 2:** To approve the Report on Directors' Remuneration | | | | |
| **Resolution 3:** To declare a final dividend | | | | |
| **Resolution 4:** To elect . . . . . . . . . director | | | | |
| **Resolution 5:** To re-elect . . . . . . . . . director | | | | |
| **Resolution 6:** To re-elect . . . . . . . . . as auditor and to authorise the directors to fix their remuneration | | | | |
| **Resolution 7:** To authorise the directors to allot securities | | | | |
| **Resolution 8:** To disapply pre-emption rights | | | | |
| **Resolution 9:** To alter the Articles of Association | | | | |

*Notes*

1  A member may appoint a proxy of his own choice. If such an appointment is made, delete the words 'the chairman of the meeting' and insert the name of the person appointed proxy in the space provided. A proxy need not be a member of the company.

2  If the appointer is a corporation, this form must be under its common seal or under the hand of some officer or attorney duly authorised in that behalf.

3  In the case of joint holders, the signature of any one holder will be sufficient, but the names of all the joint holders should be stated.

4  The person appointed as proxy will vote as you have directed in respect of the above resolutions or on any other resolution that is properly put to the meeting. If this form is returned without any indication as to how the proxy shall vote, the proxy will exercise his discretion as to how to vote or whether to abstain from voting.

To be valid, this form must be completed and deposited at the registered office of the company not less than 48 hours before the time fixed for holding the meeting or adjourned meeting (excluding any non-working days).

## CHECKLIST 9.3 **Proxy essentials**

✓ Proxies can vote on a show of hands and on a poll.

✓ Proxies have the right to speak at a meeting and to join in the demand for a poll.

✓ In a company with a share capital (whether public or private) a member can appoint more than one proxy.

✓ In a company without a share capital a member may only appoint one proxy.

✓ One-way proxies appoint a person but do not direct him how to vote; two-way proxies appoint a person and can direct him how to vote; three-way proxies include an option for the shareholders to withhold their votes.

✓ Proxy appointments must be notified to the company; the maximum period in advance the company can require is 48 hours (excluding days which are not working days). Proxies can be revoked at any time before the vote is taken.

## 9.3 Polls

If a motion sponsored by the directors is lost or the sense of the meeting is indeterminate, it is the chairman's duty to ascertain the true sense of the meeting by demanding a poll, a written vote. Many large public companies conduct a poll on each resolution as standard practice as the company considers it better governance to include proxy votes received in addition to the votes of the members who are attending the meeting. The chairman should also consider a poll if the proxy votes received indicate that a different result would be obtained to the vote on a show of hands, if a poll were held.

The Articles cannot exclude the right to demand a poll on all matters except:

■ the election of a chairman; and
■ adjournment.

The ICSA Guidance Note *Voting at General Meetings* provides useful information and advice on preparing and conducting a poll (see Directory).

### Demand for a poll

Model Article 44 (public company Model Article 36) provides that a poll may be demanded:

■ by the chairman of the meeting or by the directors;
■ by at least two persons with the right to vote at the meeting;
■ by a person, or persons, representing not less than 10% of the total voting rights of all the members with the right to vote at the meeting;
■ by a member, or members, representing no less than 10% of the paid-up share capital.

In a private company, Model Article 44 states that a poll must be taken immediately and in such manner as the chairman of the meeting directs. However, in a public company, Model Article 36 allows that all polls (other than on the election of the chairman of a meeting or on an adjournment) may be taken within 30 days of the demand for a poll. In respect of public companies, quite often a poll is held at the conclusion of the meeting as this allows the rest of the proceedings to be transacted without delay. Holding the poll at the end of the meeting also allows a poll to be conducted at the same time as any other resolutions coming before the meeting. Once the meeting has been closed, the chairman will inform the members as to the procedure for conducting the poll.

For the purposes of demanding a poll, the rights of a proxy are considered to be the same as a member. If the chairman holds proxies that are overwhelmingly in favour of the resolution, he may suggest that the demand be withdrawn. If it is not, then the validity of the demand must be ascertained according to the conditions listed above.

## CHECKLIST 9.4 **Preparation for a poll**

✓ Prepare a report of the proxies lodged in favour of the chairman, indicating the numbers for and against the resolution and those who leave it to the discretion of the chairman as to which way to vote.

✓ Prepare a separate list of proxies given in favour of persons other than the chairman.

✓ Try to anticipate the way the meeting might go and whether a poll is likely.

✓ Elect the scrutineers who will be called on if a poll takes place. In smaller meetings, this may be employees of the company. However, in larger meetings the company's auditors or service registrar often act as scrutineer.

✓ Agree the method that the scrutineers will use to report the result.

✓ Prepare ballot papers.

✓ Draft an announcement for the chairman so that if a poll is demanded, he can inform members of the procedure to be followed, or if the poll is to take place at a later date (for public companies only), the date and time for the poll and the procedure to be followed.

### Voting on a poll

There are three methods of voting. The scrutineers are allowed to verify the results and prepare a report and final certificate for the chairman.

The methods are as follows:

1 *Voting lists* – Two sheets laid out on separate tables with the headings of 'For' and 'Against' respectively, where each person voting has to give their name, the number of votes cast and a signature (as member, proxy, authorised representative or corporate body).

2 *Ballot papers* – Individual papers distributed to voters to be completed and handed in.

3 *Electronic voting* – Each shareholder has a hand-held device which they use to cast their vote. The results of the poll (including proxy votes) appear on a large screen in the room after a few moments. When shareholders arrive at the meeting they are given a voting device which records how many shares (and therefore how many votes) they hold. This method can be very useful and efficient for polls at larger company meetings, although it may be rather expensive for smaller companies.

If the poll is conducted immediately after closing the meeting using voting lists, it may involve a large number of people getting up, finding the appropriate list and returning to their seats. This can result in confusion, whereas a poll held on a later date over a two-hour period using the same system will allow voters to come and cast their votes at different times.

Ballot papers do not cause this sort of problem because they are handed out and collected while the members remain seated. If this method is preferred, the requisite number of ballot papers must be prepared before the meeting in case a poll is demanded. If a poll is anticipated, the poll cards can be printed and given to shareholders on arrival. Different colours can be used to indicate members, proxies or corporate representatives.

### Ballot procedure

1 The chairman should inform the meeting of the procedure for the poll, pointing out that that those who have appointed a proxy need not complete a ballot paper unless they wish to alter their vote.

2 Stewards then distribute ballot papers to shareholders.

3 Completed papers are handed to the scrutineers, who will check for completeness and verify holdings.

4 Scrutineers prepare the report and final certificate for the result of the poll for the chairman.

5 If the company is listed, UKLA and the press, if appropriate, should be notified of the result, which should also be put on the company's website (CA 2006, s. 341).

**STOP AND THINK** **9.4**

Compare the advantages and disadvantages of voting on a show of hands compared to a poll vote. Some of the key comparisons are:

- a show of hands is quicker, cheaper and involves less administration;
- on a show of hands, the democracy of a 'one man one vote' principle has been the subject of considerable debate;
- a poll vote allows those shareholders with a greater financial interest in the company (i.e. through a major shareholding) to have more influence than those with a minor interest.

Are there any other comparisons you can think of?

## 9.4 Additional issues for listed companies

The Listing Rules provide that the result of any resolutions passed at general meetings must be released to the Stock Exchange via a RIS. This should be done as soon as possible after the meeting. CA 2006, s. 341, also requires the results of a poll to be made available on the company's website together with additional information such as the date of the meeting and the text or a description of the resolution(s). This should also be placed on the website as soon as practicable after the meeting (but after the release to the Stock Exchange).

The UK Corporate Governance Code also contains recommendations for listed companies:

- where a resolution has been passed on a show of hands, the chairman of the meeting should inform the meeting of the proxy votes lodged, even if a poll vote has not been called;

- the proxy votes lodged should be published on the company's website.

## 9.5 Independent report on a poll

CA 2006, ss. 342–351 introduced new provisions to allow shareholders of a quoted company to require an independent report on a poll. Members holding 5% of the voting rights or 100 members holding shares with voting rights on which an average amount per member of £100 nominal value has been paid up may require the report. The requisition may be in hard copy or electronic form and must be received by the company no later than one week after the poll has been held. On receiving such a request, the directors have to appoint an independent assessor within one week. CA 2006, ss. 343 and 344 give guidance on who may be an assessor and the definition of independence. The independent assessor may be appointed before a general meeting and if so is entitled to attend the general meeting at which the poll is taken, and to attend any subsequent proceeding in connection with the poll. If appointed before the meeting, the independent assessor is also entitled to receive any communications or notices sent to members in respect of the meeting.

The assessor's report must state whether, in his opinion:

- the procedures for the poll were adequate;
- the votes cast were fairly and accurately counted and recorded;
- the validity of proxy appointments was fairly assessed;
- the company complied with CA 2006, ss. 325 and 326 (s. 325 requires a statement about proxy appointment to be included in the notice of meeting; s. 326 refers to company-sponsored invitations to appoint proxies).

The independent assessor has certain rights to information and to attend the meeting at which the poll is taken (if it has not already occurred). Under s. 351 the company must publish on its website the fact that an independent assessor has been appointed and who he is. It must also publish the text of the resolution or state the general nature of the business on which the poll was taken. Once the report is produced this must also be put on the website.

## 9.6 Adjournment

Model Article 41 (public company Model Article 33) deals with adjournment of a general meeting. In the absence of express provision in the Articles, at common law the power of adjournment is vested in the meeting itself. Model Article 41 provides that:

- A general meeting must be adjourned by the chairman if within half an hour of the start time a quorum is not present, or if during a meeting a quorum ceases to be present.
- The chairman of the meeting may adjourn a general meeting at which a quorum is present if:
  - the meeting consents or directs the chairman to do so; or
  - it appears to the chairman of the meeting that an adjournment is necessary to protect the safety of any person attending the meeting or to ensure that the business of the meeting is conducted in an orderly manner.
- If a meeting is adjourned, the chairman of the meeting must:
  - either specify the time and place to which it is adjourned or state that it is to continue at a time and place to be fixed by the directors, and
  - have regard to any directions as to the time and place of any adjournment which have been given by the meeting.
- If the adjourned meeting is to take place more than 14 days later, the company must give at least seven clear days' notice of it to the same persons entitled to receive notice of the original meeting.

All adjournments should be to a time and place that is reasonable in the circumstances.

---

**TEST YOUR KNOWLEDGE 9.7**

**a** What is a proxy? What rights do proxies have?
**b** The Listing Rules require that listed company proxies be 'three-way'. What does this mean?
**c** What voting choices are available to shareholders when completing a proxy card?
**d** Under the Model Articles, who may demand a poll at a general meeting?

---

# 10    Resolutions

## 10.1  Introduction

A **resolution** is the formal way in which a decision is proposed and passed at general meetings.

If a company is listed, two copies of all resolutions passed (other than resolutions concerning ordinary business) must be sent to UKLA immediately they are passed. UKLA will make the resolution available to the public for inspection at a document viewing facility located in their London offices or online via the National Storage Mechanism. CA 2006, s. 30 explains which resolutions which must be filed with the Registrar within 15 days of being passed.

## 10.2  Types of resolution

Four types of resolution may be passed at a general meeting:

1 ordinary resolutions;
2 special resolutions;
3 ordinary resolutions which require special notice;
4 extraordinary resolutions.

## Ordinary resolutions

An **ordinary resolution** is the normal method of securing the members' approval for routine business transacted at general meeting, such as approval of the annual accounts, approval of final dividend and appointment and re-appointment of a director. CA 2006, s. 282 defines it as a resolution passed by a simple majority.

The following can be passed by an ordinary resolution:

- an increase in authorised capital (CA 2006, s. 617) (see Sample Wording 9.9);
- the authorisation of directors to allot shares (CA 2006, s. 551);
- the reappointment of auditors (CA 2006, ss. 485 and 489);
- capitalisation of profits (Model Article 36; public company Model Article 78).

## Special resolutions

A **special resolution** is defined in CA 2006, s. 283. A special resolution must be described as such in the notice of a general meeting and must be passed by a majority of 75% of the votes cast. The notice should set out the exact text of the resolution.

Instances where special resolutions are required include the following, although the Articles can also introduce other instances where special resolutions are required:

- alteration of the Articles (see Chapter 5);
- change of name (CA 2006, s. 77) (see Chapter 5);
- alteration of the company's status by re-registration, for example, from a private to a public company (see Sample Wording 9.10);
- reduction of capital (CA 2006, s. 641);
- purchase of own shares;
- provision of financial assistance for the purchase of its own shares (private companies only);
- disapplication of pre-emption rights (see Chapter 12);
- to wind up voluntarily, in an amalgamation, or by the court (see Chapter 7);
- to sanction the liquidators' sale of company property for shares in another company during a members' winding up (see Chapter 7).

Once passed a printed and signed copy of the special resolution must be delivered to Companies House within 15 days.

---

**SAMPLE WORDING 9.9**

**Special resolution for re-registration of private company as public company**

THAT pursuant to the provisions of sections 90 and 94, Companies Act 2006, the company be re-registered as a public company [with effect from . . . . 20xx or from such other date as may be approved by the Registrar of Companies] and that the Articles of Association of the company be thereupon altered as follows:

a) by deleting the existing article 1 and substituting therefore the following articles to be numbered 1 and 2:
   1 The company's name is '. . . . . . . . . . . Public Limited Company'.
   2 The company is to be a public company;
b) by renumbering the existing articles [.....] as articles [.....] respectively.

## Ordinary resolutions requiring special notice

Special notice is required for certain ordinary resolutions in the following circumstances (CA 2006, s. 312):

- to remove a director by ordinary resolution before the expiration of the director's period of office (see Sample Wording 9.11);
- to fill a casual vacancy in the office of auditor;
- to reappoint as auditor a retiring auditor who was appointed by the directors to fill a casual vacancy;
- to remove an auditor before the expiration of the auditor's term of office;
- to appoint as auditor a person other than a retiring auditor.

Special notice of the intention to propose a resolution must be given by a member or members to the company, irrespective of the number of shares held, at least 28 days before the meeting at which the resolution is to be proposed. CA 2006, s. 312(4) also provides that if, after notice of the intention to move such a resolution has been given to the company, a meeting is called for a date 28 days or less after the notice has been given, the notice is deemed properly given, though not given within the time required. On receipt of such notice, the company must give members notice of the fact that special notice has been given of the intention to propose the resolution in the same way and at the same time as the notice of meeting is given. However, if this is not practicable, the company must give at least 14 days' notice by advertisement in a newspaper with an appropriate circulation or by any other means allowed by its Articles.

No provision is made in CA 2006 for consent to short notice with respect to a resolution requiring special notice. Therefore, such a resolution cannot be passed at a meeting held at short notice.

---

**CASE EXAMPLE 9.1**

**SPECIAL RESOLUTIONS – COUNTING VOTES AT GENERAL MEETINGS**

A special resolution requires a 75% majority of the members present and voting, but how is the vote counted?

In a recent case, 82 members voted for the special resolution and 28 members voted against. The chairman realised that the margin was narrow but made a quick mental calculation: 82 + 28 = 110 and three-quarters of that is 82.5. You cannot have a half of a shareholder so 82 must be sufficient. He declared the special resolution carried by 82 votes to 28.

The chairman was wrong. There were 110 (82 + 28) members present and voting. Three-quarters of 110 is 82.5. The question was not whether half a shareholder could vote but whether 82 was 'not less than 82.5'. Clearly 82 is less than 82.5, so the resolution had not been passed by the requisite majority. The position was complicated by the fact that the chairman had mistakenly declared the resolution carried.

A number of cases support the proposition that if, in the absence of fraud, the chairman of a meeting declares a resolution carried, that declaration is conclusive and the courts will not go behind the declaration and enquire as to the facts. However, in the Citizens' Theatre Limited case it was decided that where the declaration showed on the face of it that the requisite majority had not been obtained – as in this case, where the chairman declared a special resolution 'carried by 82 votes to 28' – such a declaration would not be conclusive.

---

---

**SAMPLE WORDING 9.10**

**Special notice to remove a director**

The Directors,

. . . . . . . . . . . . . . Limited/plc.

I hereby give notice, pursuant to sections 168 and 312, Companies Act 2006, of my intention to propose the following resolution as an ordinary resolution at the next annual general meeting of the company.

*Resolution*

THAT . . . . . . . . . . . . be removed from his office of director of the company.

. . . . . . . . . . . . .

(Signature)

. . . . . . . . . . . . .

(Address)

. . . . . . . . . . . . .

(Date)

---

## Extraordinary resolutions

CA 2006 itself contains no reference to extraordinary resolutions, so resolutions passed under CA 2006 will only be ordinary or special. However, companies which were formed before the introduction of CA 2006 and whose Articles have not been updated may still have references to extraordinary resolutions. The third commencement order which implements the provisions of CA 2006, Part 13 on resolutions and meetings provides that any references in a company's Articles of Association or in any contracts shall continue to have effect. Extraordinary resolutions must be specifically described as such in the notice of a general meeting and the full text of the resolution must be included in the notice.

A majority of at least 75% of the votes cast is required to pass an extraordinary resolution and a signed copy must be delivered to the Registrar of Companies within 15 days of it being passed.

In practice, extraordinary resolutions do not occur very often, except in class meetings. However, care should be taken to check the company's Articles, which may specify that certain types of business must be transacted by extraordinary resolution.

---

**TEST YOUR KNOWLEDGE 9.8**

a What are the main types of resolution? When are they used?
b What is special notice? When is it required?
c What is the requisite majority for passing (i) an ordinary resolution; (ii) a special resolution?

## 10.3 Amendments to resolutions

An ordinary resolution can be amended even if the text has been set out in the notice of the meeting. Model Article 47 (public company Model Article 40) provides that an ordinary resolution to be proposed at a general meeting may be amended by ordinary resolution if notice of the proposed amendment is given to the company in writing not less than 48 hours before the meeting (or such later time as the chairman of the meeting may determine). The proposed amendment must not, in the reasonable opinion of the chairman of the meeting, materially alter the scope of the resolution.

The same Model Article states that a special resolution may be amended by ordinary resolution, if the chairman of the meeting proposes the amendment at the general meeting and the amendment does not go beyond what is necessary to correct a grammatical or other non-substantive error in the resolution.

## 10.4 Resolutions in writing

CA 2006, ss. 288–300 set out comprehensive procedures for private companies to pass resolutions in writing instead of holding general meetings. It is envisaged that in future most small private companies will use this method for dealing with matters requiring a shareholder vote.

A written resolution may be proposed by the directors or members and must be circulated to all those members entitled to vote on it, as well as to the auditors. It is not necessary for all members to sign it. This needs to be done only by the requisite majority for the particular type of resolution. So, for an ordinary resolution only a simple majority of members need to indicate consent and for a special resolution 75% have to agree.

When the resolution is circulated to members they must also be sent information about how to signify agreement and the date by which the resolution must be passed if it is not to lapse (CA 2006, s. 291). A member signifies agreement when the company receives from him, or from someone acting on his behalf, an authenticated document identifying the written resolution to which it relates and indicating his consent. This may be in hard copy or electronic form. The resolution is passed once the required majority of members have signified their consent to it (CA 2006, s. 296).

A written resolution will lapse if it is not passed within 28 days of its circulation date or at such other time as is specified in the Articles (s. 297).

CA 2006, ss. 292–295 set out the procedure by which members of a private company may require the circulation of a written resolution. These are similar to those by which members of a public company may require circulation of a resolution to be proposed at an AGM. This includes the cost of circulating a written resolution, i.e. members are to meet the costs of circulation unless the company resolves otherwise. The company will not be bound to circulate the written resolution unless reasonably sufficient funds have been received to cover the costs of circulation.

Members may also request the company to circulate a statement in respect of the resolution (see section 5 above). Written resolutions may not be used for the removal of a director or auditor from office. A written resolution must be recorded in the company's minute book and the filing requirements with Companies House are the same as they would otherwise be for the different types of resolution. Written resolutions are particularly useful for small private companies and have become a standard method of decision-making, especially for companies with only one member. Under CA 2006, s. 288 public companies cannot pass written resolutions.

**TEST YOUR KNOWLEDGE 9.9**

a When does a written resolution become effective?
b Where should signed written resolutions be kept?
c When is it not possible to use a written resolution?

# 11   The role of the chairman at general meetings

The role of the chairman at a shareholders' meeting is to ensure that the meeting is conducted properly and fairly. The effect of Model Articles 39 and 40 (public company Model Articles 31 and 32) provide the chairman of the company, if appointed, shall be the chairman of the meeting and that any director, regardless of whether he is a member, shall be entitled to attend and speak at any general meeting whether or not he holds shares. Furthermore, the chairman may permit any other person to attend and speak at a meeting even if he is not a member or not entitled to attend or vote.

CA 2006, s. 319 provides that any member may chair a general meeting if he is elected by resolution of the members passed at the meeting. This is subject to the provisions of the Articles about who may chair a meeting. CA 2006, s. 328 contains similar provisions relating to a proxy chairing a meeting.

CA 2006, s. 320 contains provisions regarding the chairman declaring the result of a vote on a show of hands. The other duties and powers of a chairman are under common law as well as the provisions in the Articles. For example, the Model Articles gives the chairman specific powers relating to the conduct of meetings to:

■ demand that a poll be taken and also subsequent consent to a demand for a poll to be withdrawn (Model Article 44; public company Model Article 36);
■ direct the manner, time and place when a poll will be undertaken (public company Model Article 37);
■ rule on any question of the validity of the votes cast at the meeting (Model Article 41; public company Model Article 35).

Part of the duty of the company secretary (see below) is to provide guidance for the chairman of the meeting to ensure compliance with the law and the company's Articles of Association. For example, when preparing the detailed chairman's agenda for a general meeting, it is vital that an opportunity is given for shareholders to raise any questions before a resolution is put to the vote and declared.

Model Article 39 (public company Model Article 31) provides that the chairman of the board be nominated to preside as the chairman at general meetings. If the chairman is not present, another director (e.g. deputy chairman or vice-chairman) should be nominated by the board to take the chair. If neither the chairman nor another director is able or willing to take the chair within ten minutes after the appointed start time of the meeting, then those shareholders present and entitled to vote may choose one of their number to act as chairman and this must be the first item of business for the meeting.

The election of the chairman confers on him all the powers necessary for him to fulfil this role. The Articles of a listed company often give the chairman more extensive powers (e.g. to adjourn without the consent of the meeting).

One area in which the chairman's power is of great importance is the manner in which he deals with unruly shareholders. The chairman is in charge of the meeting and can, subject to the Articles, enforce his decisions on points of order, motions, amendments and questions. The duty of the chairman at a general meeting of a listed company is to ensure that the sense of the meeting is properly ascertained and is expanded to include reporting on the proxy votes which have been lodged prior to the meeting. This is encouraged by both the UK Corporate Governance Code and the ICSA. The chairman should report on the proxy votes lodged for each resolution once the result of a vote on a show of hands has been declared. The ICSA also strongly encourages that a short report stating the proxy votes lodged for each resolution is made available following the meeting to shareholders who attended the meeting and also to other interested parties, for example, by placing the report on the company's website. It is also good practice for the chairman to report on proxy votes lodged so as to ensure that, if the resolution is carried on a show of hands, the result is not at odds with the proxy votes.

**a**   Under the Model Article provisions, how is the chairman of a general meeting determined?
**b**   List two Model Article provisions regarding the powers of the chairman at a general meeting.

# 12   The role of the secretary before, during and after general meetings

## 12.1 The role of the secretary at AGMs

The first job of the secretary is to advise the chairman of the estimated attendance at the meeting so that a room can be booked that will be suitable in terms of size, availability, cost and quality. Members will require a venue that is comfortable, but not so extravagant that they feel their money is being wasted. The secretary is usually responsible for finding, evaluating and hiring an appropriate venue.

### Before the meeting

1 Following approval of the audited accounts, three proof copies of the report and accounts and the notice of the meeting should be signed off. A director must sign the balance sheet; either the secretary or a director must sign the directors' report; and the signature of the auditor is needed on the auditor's report. If the company is listed, the signature of a director or secretary should also appear at the end of the remuneration report within the report and accounts. For the notice, the chairman may sign his statement (if applicable) and the secretary usually signs the notice of the meeting.

2 If the company has a large share register, it is likely that the annual report will be printed externally by commercial printers. Another copy of the annual report and accounts with the names of the signatories should be sent to the company's printers for a final proof prior to the bulk supply being printed for the shareholders.

3 Advise the external registrar (if one is used) of the recommended dividend so that he can prepare the dividend warrants for dispatch to shareholders following approval at the AGM.

4 Arrange with the bankers for a dividend account to be opened so that the money required to pay the dividend can be deposited.

5 Prepare the proxy forms for dispatch with the annual report and accounts and the notice of general meeting. Proxy forms are often provided as either separate cards or a tear-out page in the notice of meeting. They may also be provided electronically via a website.

6 Instruct the printers/registrars of the date when the annual report and accounts, notice of general meeting and proxy form (or notification of their availability on a website if the CA 2006 provisions have been adopted) should be sent to the shareholders.

7 Keep one of the three signed copies of the annual report and accounts with the company's records, send one to the Registrar of Companies and the other to the auditors.

8 Invite the company's solicitors or other appropriate advisers to attend the meeting. The auditors are entitled to attend. Instruct the company's registrars (if applicable) to attend.

9 Check returned proxy forms against the register of members and report the result of the proxy count to the board after the expiry of the deadline for receipt (usually 48 hours before the meeting). For listed companies, a short report of the proxy votes lodged should be prepared for putting on the website and handing out to interested shareholders following the meeting (see section 9).

10 Prepare ballot papers for the event of a poll being demanded.

11 Prepare an agenda (see Sample Wording 9.7) for use by the board. In some circumstances it may be useful to prepare a more detailed agenda for the chairman, together with prepared answers to awkward questions.

12 In a listed company, the chairman sometimes takes the opportunity to update shareholders on the company's recent trading performance, its trading outlook or perhaps on changes in the composition of the board. The secretary should be briefed if such an update will be made because such a statement will have to be released to the market through a RIS. The release of such announcements must be no later than the chairman's address to the meeting.

13 Prepare attendance sheets to register attending shareholders, the press, proxies and representatives.

14 Make the register of members available for inspection in case it is necessary to identify the people attending the meeting, to ensure that only those entitled to be there are present.

15 Make copies of the non-executive directors' letters of appointment (this is a UK Corporate Governance Code recommendation) available for inspection. There is no longer a Listing Rule requirement for directors' service contracts to be available for inspection at the AGM; however, this may be done for the sake of good practice. In any event, the CA requires them to be available for inspection at the company's registered office, so if the AGM is being held there they will need to be available, unless the company has chosen (under CA 2006, s. 228) to hold them somewhere else. As there is no longer a requirement for the company to keep a register of directors' share interests, this need not be available for inspection.

16 Check practical details, for example, catering, layout, security, access and facilities for the disabled, health and safety arrangements, and audiovisual arrangements. These practical details are usually dealt with during a pre-meeting with those responsible for managing the meeting venue.

17 Prepare name cards and/or name badges for the directors and organise proposers, seconders and tellers if required.

## At the meeting

1 Check that all directors are sitting behind their own name cards.

2 Assist/manage the registration process of shareholders or their proxies as they arrive at the meeting – it is necessary to verify the identity of the shareholder or proxy to ensure they are entitled to attend. Similarly, it is necessary to review any letters of appointment or board minutes in respect of a corporate representative, as these do not need to provide any advance warning of their attendance.

3 Check that a quorum is present at all times.

4 Ensure that the number of members/proxies in attendance has not exceeded the room's capacity, to enable everyone to participate in the meeting.

5 Be ready at the chairman's request to read the notice convening the meeting (however, with the consent of the meeting, it may be taken as read).

6 Make sure that the identity of any member who speaks from the floor is known.

7 Be prepared to advise the chairman on any point of procedure. It is customary that the secretary sits next to the chairman of the meeting in order to facilitate this. The secretary should have to hand a copy of the company's Memorandum and Articles of Association, the latest annual report and the notice of meeting, in order to assist in handling queries.

8 Assist the chairman and any tellers in counting the votes on a show of hands.

9 Assist with the setting up of a poll if one is demanded and advise the chairman on whether it can be taken immediately (i.e. if the secretary has anticipated the poll and has prepared the necessary documentation) or whether it should be taken at a later date – public companies are permitted under the Model Articles to take the poll within 30 days of the demand being made.

## After the meeting

1 Send copies of any special resolutions or other resolutions specified by CA 2006, s. 30, signed by the chairman, to the Registrar of Companies within 15 days of the resolution being passed.

2 Complete the necessary arrangements and procedures for the routine (e.g. appointment of directors) and non-routine business (e.g. alteration of the Articles) and send the appropriate copies of special resolutions and statutory forms to Companies House.

3 Make the necessary arrangements for the dividend to be paid if the payment date is some time after the meeting.

4 Promptly prepare the minutes of the meeting. CA 2006, s. 358 obliges a company to provide the minutes of a general meeting to any member within 14 days of receiving such a request. Section 358 also provides that the minutes be available for inspection by members at the company's registered office or at such other place as may be specified in regulations (yet to be passed).

5 If the company is listed, the results of the votes must be announced to the Stock Exchange via an RIS. The results of proxy votes lodged ahead of the meeting should be made available on request and placed on the company's website. If a poll has been held, the result should be announced to the market and put on the company's website (CA 2006, s. 341).

## 12.2 The role of the secretary at other general meetings

The role of the secretary before, during and after any other general meeting is similar to that at the AGM. However, as it is unlikely that the annual report will be received or a dividend approved, these elements of the secretary's role can be ignored. For listed companies, the results of each resolution at any other general meeting must be announced to the market via a RIS.

---

**TEST YOUR KNOWLEDGE** **9.11**

a It is good practice to have available the registers and spare copies of the agenda at the AGM. What other documents and forms should be ready for use at the AGM?
b List the duties to be performed by the secretary during the AGM.
c List the duties to be performed by the secretary after the conclusion of the AGM.

---

# 13 Minutes

It is a statutory requirement under CA 2006, s. 355 that companies record the proceedings at all general meetings. CA 2006, s. 248 contains similar provisions for the proceedings of meetings of directors (i.e. of the board and its committees).

The minutes must be signed by the chairman; his signature is *prima facie* evidence that the meeting has been properly constituted and conducted. Failure to comply with keeping minute books will make the company and every officer liable to a daily default fine (see chapter 8).

Minutes are the written record of business transacted at a meeting and of the decisions reached. They are the permanent record of the proceedings. Although there is no statutory format for minute writing, they should be clear, concise and free from ambiguity. All relevant dates and figures should be stated (e.g. by stating monetary or other limits) and should not be left ill-defined. Minutes must be impartial.

No alterations should be made to minutes, except to correct obvious errors. This should be done before signature, the alterations being initialled by the chairman. Once signed, minutes may not be altered and any subsequent revisions should be dealt with by an amending minute at a subsequent meeting.

AGM minutes are approved at the next board meeting after the AGM. It is not necessary for them to be approved by shareholders at the next AGM.

## CHECKLIST 9.5 **Writing minutes**

✓ Minutes must be:
  - objective;
  - clear;
  - concise;
  - complete.
✓ Minutes should be written:
  - impersonally;
  - in the past tense.
✓ Minutes should contain:
  - the name of the company (company number);
  - the type of meeting;
  - the day and place of meeting;
  - those present or in attendance and apologies received;
  - details of relevant discussion;
  - the full terms of resolutions adopted.

## 13.1 Location and inspection of minutes

A company is required to keep the minutes of its general meetings at its registered office and make them available for inspection by the members (CA 2006, s. 358).

Members have a right to inspect the minutes of general meetings and to be supplied with a copy of any minutes within 14 days of making the request. A company may levy the prescribed fee for providing a copy based on the number of words. As this is likely to be a small amount in practice most companies will not bother to charge it.

The rights of members to inspect minutes are confined solely to minutes of general meetings and they have no right to inspect the minutes of board meetings. For this reason it is good practice to keep separate books for board meeting minutes and general meeting minutes. Each board committee will usually also have its own minute book.

## CASE QUESTION

The AGM of Multiple plc will be held next week and you are in a planning session with the chairman of the company. The business to be conducted is routine, but there is also a proposal to amend the Articles of Association. The following matters are discussed which require action from you:

■ The chairman is worried about demonstrators and environmental activists attending the AGM who object to the way Multiple conducts its business. What arrangements need to be made and issues considered in view of this?

■ Many shareholders are expected to attend, although it is not possible to predict accurately in advance the numbers attending. What is being done to plan for this and to accommodate attending shareholders? The chairman would also like you to brief him on the advantages and disadvantages of using a poll or a show of hands to conduct voting. If a poll were conducted, what would be the best way to do this given the large numbers of shareholders expected?

■ Some shareholders are expected at the meeting to request that two extra resolutions be added to the end of the meeting as 'any other business'. What issues need to be considered in advance? Prepare a script for the chairman to handle such a request being made.

■ The chairman is keen that the company completes all necessary actions after the AGM has been held. Prepare a checklist (including timescales) of all the steps and actions which will be completed by the secretarial department following the AGM.

## CHAPTER SUMMARY

■ All public companies are required to hold an AGM. Private companies are not required to hold an AGM unless there is a specific requirement for this in their Articles.

■ Generally, the AGM must be held within six months of the end of the financial year. A general meeting (i.e. not the AGM) can be called at any time, for a specific purpose, although there are certain circumstances where directors are required to convene a general meeting (e.g. if members requisition it).

■ Notice periods for general meetings are strictly regulated and it is essential that the proper procedures are followed.

■ The agenda acts as a driving force for the meeting. The content and the presentation for the agenda should be decided between the chairman and the secretary.

■ For a meeting to be valid, there must be a quorum.

■ Proxies may be appointed to represent a member by attending, speaking and voting at a meeting. Listed companies are required by the Listing Rules to issue three-way proxy cards, enabling the proxy to vote on each individual resolution and to give the proxy direction on how to vote.

■ There are four types of resolution for decision-making: ordinary, extraordinary, special and ordinary with special notice.

■ Private companies may pass shareholder resolutions in writing by the same majority as would be required if the resolution were passed at a meeting. The proposed resolution must be sent to all eligible members and the auditors. If they are not passed within a specified time, they will lapse.

■ The secretary organises the practical arrangements as well as preparing and issuing the documents for the meeting. After the meeting, he is responsible for ensuring that resolutions and changes to the board of directors are filed with Companies House, notified to UKLA (if applicable for listed companies) and for preparing minutes of the meeting.

# Board meetings and committees

**10**

## ■ CONTENTS

## ■ INTRODUCTION

This chapter looks at the key tasks in planning, organising and conducting board meetings.

## 1  Meetings of the board

Directors collectively form a board, with each director having an equal say in matters of company business and policy and with one vote each at meeting. The Articles contain provisions relating to board meetings. For example, Model Article 13 (public company Model Article 14) provides that the chairman may have a casting vote in addition to his own. Model Article 16 (public company Model Article 19) also provides that, subject to the other Articles, the directors have discretion to make further rules about how board meetings are conducted. Many companies adopt a board procedures manual to cover how board meetings are conducted. It is important to note that there are many differences in the procedures used at board meetings compared to general meetings.

Board meetings do not have to be held at fixed intervals, but in practice it makes sense to set a timetable so that recurrent events (e.g. the approval of annual accounts) can be prepared in advance. Larger companies should have regularly scheduled meetings so that the board can consider the financial and trading position of the company at appropriate intervals.

The chairman will normally instruct the company secretary to convene a meeting, but any director, acting independently or by instructing the company secretary, can call a board meeting (Model Article 9; public company Model Article 8). There is no automatic right for a director who cannot attend to appoint a proxy. However, the Model Articles for public companies provide for the appointment of alternate directors (public company Model Articles 25–27) (see Chapter 2).

## 2  Chairman

The duties of the chairman are largely the same whether at general meetings or at meetings of directors. Less formal meetings of directors are not as likely to call on the chairman to exercise control over the proceedings.

The Articles should cover the appointment of the chairman and, in some cases, deputy or vice-chairman. Model Article 12 for a public company provides for the appointment of a chairman, deputy chairman or assistant chairman. However, in keeping with the desire to simplify arrangements for private limited companies, the equivalent Model Article for a private company (Model Article 12) does not provide this flexibility. Both Model Articles provide that the directors may elect a chairman of their meetings and determine the period for which the chairman is to hold office. Usually, the person appointed chairman of the board will also take the chair at general meetings of the company (Model Article 39; public company Model Article 31) and will be regarded as chairman of the company.

It is important to keep a clear record of who the chairman is and the terms of appointment. Disputes can arise if there is not a regular chairman, particularly if the Articles give the chairman a casting vote. A written record is important as Model Article 12 (public company Model Article 12) requires no particular formality for the resignation of the chairman.

Minutes of each board meeting should clearly state who has assumed the position of chairman of the meeting. If the appointed company chairman is unable to attend (e.g. due to illness) or is unwilling to chair the meeting within ten minutes of the time set for the meeting, Model Article 12 (public company Model Article 12) allows the other directors to appoint a fellow director to assume the chair for that meeting.

The duty of the chairman is to manage the board meeting. He should seek the views of the other directors and facilitate the discussion of each agenda item. Following the discussion, the chairman should ascertain, if required, whether the board approves the agenda item concerned (see section 6). If any matter has an equal number of votes for and against from the directors voting, Model Article 13 (public company Model Article 14) provides the chairman with a casting vote to resolve the matter.

# 3   Notice

While the CA is very explicit on the notice required for AGMs, there is no provision in the Act regarding notice for directors' meetings. Under common law directors must be given reasonable notice. For some companies, reasonable notice would be a week; in others it might be much shorter. Even if there is a fixed timetable for regular meetings it is still sensible to issue reminders, sending a copy of the agenda at the same time. Model Article 9 (public company Model Article 8) states that notice must be given to each director but need not be in writing – hence notice can be given orally or by telephone. The Model Articles also provide that if directors will not be participating in the same place, the notice must include how it is proposed that the directors should communicate with each other during the meeting (See Sample Wording 10.1).

If adequacy of notice is disputed, then business transacted at the meeting can be declared invalid.

---

**SAMPLE WORDING 10.1**

**Notice of board meeting**

. . . . . . . . . . . . . . . . . . . . . . LIMITED/plc

. . . . . . . . . . . . . . . . . . . . . . . . . . . . . .

(Address)

To: . . . . . . . . . . . . . . . . . . . . . .

(Date) . . . . . . . . . . . . . . . . . . . . .

Dear Sir,

I have to inform you that a meeting of the directors of the company will be held at . . . . . . . . . . . . . .
. . . . . . . . . . . . . . . . . . . . . . . . . . . . . . on . . . . . . . . . . . . . . . . . . . . . . day, . . . . . . . . . . . . . . . . . . . . . .
20xx at . . . . . . . . . . . . . . . . . . . . . am (GMT)

It is anticipated that directors participating in the meeting will not be in the same place. Pursuant to the Company's Articles, it is proposed that a teleconferencing system be used so that directors can communicate with each other during the meeting. Details of the teleconference are:

. . . . . . . . . . . . . . . . . . . . . . . . . . . . .

BUSINESS

. . . . . . . . . . . . . . . . . . . . . . . . . . . . .

. . . . . . . . . . . . . . . . . . . . . . . . . . . . .

Yours faithfully,

. . . . . . . . . . . . . . . . . . . . . . . . . . . . .

Secretary

---

**TEST YOUR KNOWLEDGE 10.1**

a  When should board meetings be held?
b  How much notice is required?
c  What are the Model Article requirements regarding the chairman of a board meeting?

## 4  Agenda

Items are placed on the agenda in the order in which they will be discussed at the meeting. Supporting papers should be referred to by page numbers or some other referencing system in order to keep the agenda as concise as possible.

The agenda and supporting papers should ideally be issued to the directors about one week before the meeting to provide adequate opportunity for the directors to study them before the meeting.

---

**STOP AND THINK 10.1**

The procedures adopted to issue agendas and board papers vary from company to company. For example, some companies send papers by email or allow directors to access them via a secure website as this reduces circulation costs and the directors receive their papers quickly. However, some directors prefer to receive hard copies bound or in a folder rather than having to print them out themselves. What is important is that a reliable and efficient system is adopted tailored to the needs of the directors. The secretary should therefore be proactive in facilitating this process.

The secretary should also take into account the security of agendas and papers sent, particularly where the papers are dealing with confidential matters (or price-sensitive matters for listed companies). The use of recorded delivery for documents sent by post or password protection for computer documents should be considered.

---

Agendas vary according to the type of meeting and the type of business to be discussed, etc. However, a typical agenda will include the following:

■ apologies for absence;
■ minutes of the last meeting, circulated with the agenda;

- matters arising from the minutes;
- business of the present meeting – presentations, reports, resolutions, etc.
- any transactions that need to be conducted;
- any other business;
- date of the next meeting.

Any other business is usually the last item on the agenda, but can be contentious if the business raised does not give the directors enough time to consider the merits of the proposal. Because of this, some chairmen refuse to put matters under this heading to the vote until the next meeting.

It is helpful to number minutes and resolutions sequentially to help with cross-referencing when the minutes are written up.

---

**SAMPLE WORDING 10.2**

**Agenda for board meeting for a listed company**

. . . . . . . . . . . . . . . . . . . . . . plc
Agenda for board meeting to be held at . . . . . . . . . . . . . . . . on . . . . . day . . . . . 20xx

**1 MINUTES**
The chairman to sign the minutes of the board meeting held on Tuesday, 24 March 20xx.

**2 MATTERS ARISING**
To discuss any matters arising from the previous meeting.

**3 TRADING REPORT**
To review the company's trading performance since the last board meeting, including major contracts awarded or lost and market overview and update.

**4 FINANCIAL REPORT**
To review the company's financial position and performance since the last board meeting.

**5 ACQUISITIONS AND DIVESTMENTS**
To consider for approval proposals to: acquire XYZ Limited for £1.5 million in cash; dispose of the ABC Limited (a wholly-owned subsidiary) for £4 million in cash.

**6 STRATEGY DISCUSSION**
To receive a strategy presentation on emerging market opportunities in the Far East and to discuss what strategic action, if any, the company should take.

**7 SHARES AND STOCK TRANSFERRED**
To produce transfer audit reports dated . . . . . and . . . . . 20xx from the company's registrars and to resolve:
THAT share transfers Nos.. . . . . to . . . . . inclusive and loan stock transfers Nos. . . . . . to . . . . . inclusive be approved.
THAT the sealing and issue of share certificates Nos. . . . . . to . . . . . inclusive and loan stock certificates No's . . . . . to . . . . . inclusive be confirmed.

**8 DOCUMENTS EXECUTED UNDER SEAL**
To produce the seal book and resolve:
THAT the affixing of the common seal of the company to the documents set out against items Nos. . . . . . to . . . . . inclusive in the seal book be confirmed.

**9 DATE AND VENUE OF NEXT MEETING**
To confirm that the next scheduled meeting of the Board will be held at 10.30 am on Tuesday, 7 July 20xx in the board room of the company's registered office.

**10 ANY OTHER BUSINESS**
To consider any other business and to declare the meeting closed.

## 4.1 Agenda for the first board meeting

The first board meeting of a newly formed company must deal with several non-recurrent items before the company can carry on its business. The company's first directors are those listed in the form IN01 submitted for the company's registration. The first meeting of those directors constitutes the first board meeting and should be held as soon as possible after incorporation.

The following items will form part of the agenda for the meeting:

- *Certificate of Incorporation* – This should be produced by the company secretary and its receipt recorded.
- *Appointment of first directors* – This is a formality to be recorded in the minute book.
- *Appointment of the chairman of the board*.
- *Appointment of the secretary* (for a public company but optional for a private company) – This is a formality as the secretary will have been named in the registration documents.
- *Appointment of company's solicitors*.
- *Appointment of company's brokers*.
- *Appointment of company's bankers* – Usually by reference to a standard form of resolution, supplied by the bank).
- *Appointment of company's auditors*.
- *Submission and adoption of a design for the common seal* (if required) and the establishment of rules for its use.
- *Consideration for the raising of capital* – Deciding on the method used will entail the preparation of subsequent documents such as draft underwriting contracts.
- *Formal instructions to the secretary* – This will involve appointing the various officers and dealing with further requirements such as the bank's need for specimen signatures, etc.

There may be other matters which it may be appropriate to consider at the first board meeting, including:

- *Change of accounting reference date* – The directors may decide a date different from the end of the month in which the company was incorporated.
- *Allotment or transfer of shares* – Further shares may be allotted or transferred, particularly where the company was acquired off the shelf in which case the shareholders will be the formation agents.
- *Change of registered office* – This may be necessary if the company was acquired off the shelf.
- *Informing HM Revenue & Customs of the formation of the company* – within three months of incorporation. Standard HM Revenue & Customs forms are available for this purpose.

---

**SAMPLE WORDING 10.3**

**Agenda for first board meeting**

. . . . . . . . . . . . . . . . . . . . . Ltd
Agenda for board meeting to be held at . . . . . . . . . . . . . . . on . . . . . day . . . . 20xx

1. Produce the certificate of incorporation and a print of the Memorandum and Articles of Association as registered.

2. Note that the first directors of the company named in form IN01 are . . . . . . . . . . . . . . . . . . . . . . and . . . . . . . . . . . . . . . . . . . . .

3. Resolve:
   THAT . . . . . . . . . . . . . . . . . . . . . be appointed chairman of the board.

4. Note that the first secretary of the company named in form IN01 is . . . . . . . . . . . . . . . . . . . . . and resolve:
   THAT the appointment of . . . . . . . . . . as secretary be confirmed at a salary payable from . . . . . 20xx at the rate of £ . . . . . per annum, such appointment being terminable by . . . . . months' notice in writing given by either party to the other at any time.

5. Resolve:
   THAT the situation of the registered office of the company, namely . . . . . . . . . . ., be confirmed.

6. [optional] Resolve:
   THAT the seal, of which an impression is affixed in the margin hereof, be adopted as the common seal of the company.

7. Consider opening a bank account with . . . . . . . . Bank plc and, if thought fit, resolve:
   [Resolutions in accordance with bank's printed form for opening an account.]

8. Consider the appointment of auditors and resolve:
   THAT . . . . . . . . . . . be appointed auditors of the company to hold office until the conclusion of the first general meeting at which accounts are laid before the company.

9. Produce and read to the meeting notices dated . . .. 20xx given by . . . . . . . . . and . . . . . . . . . pursuant to section 185 of the Companies Act 2006.

10. Produce a form of application dated . . . . 20xx from . . . . . . . for 98 shares of £1 each in the capital of the company at a price of £1 per share, together with cheques for a total of £100, being payment in full for the said 98 shares and for the 2 shares taken by the subscribers to the Memorandum of Association.
    Resolve:
    a THAT 98 shares of £1 each, fully paid and numbered from 3 to 100 inclusive, be allotted to . . . . . . . . . . .
    b THAT the under-mentioned share certificates drawn in respect of subscribers' shares and the allotment made by resolution (a) hereof be approved and that the common seal be affixed thereto:
    No. 1: 1 share numbered 1
    No. 2: 1 share numbered 2
    No. 3: 98 shares numbered from 3 to 100 inclusive

11. Resolve:
    THAT all the shares of the company in issue shall henceforth cease to bear distinguishing numbers.

12. Resolve:
    THAT the company files the necessary return(s) with HM Revenue & Customs in respect of the notification of the company's incorporation.

13. Any other business.

14. Dates for future board meetings.

**TEST YOUR KNOWLEDGE 10.2**

What should be the main items on the agenda for the first board meeting of a newly registered company?

**STOP AND THINK 10.2**

The company secretary is responsible for preparing the agenda for any board meeting in a logical manner. For example, the board should not consider whether to pay a dividend until it has reviewed the financial position of the company. The company secretary should work with the chairman to ensure the agenda is logical and also in an order which suits the way in which the chairman will run the meeting.

# 5  Quorum

The quorum required for board meetings is generally fixed by the Articles. Model Article 11 (public company Model Article 10) provides that the quorum may be fixed by the directors, and unless so fixed shall be two; it allows alternate directors to be counted. The quorum must be disinterested, i.e. it must comprise directors who are entitled to vote on a particular matter before the meeting. A quorum must be present for each item of business, but if a director has an interest in a contract, he will not be permitted by the Articles to vote on it and may not be counted for the purposes of the quorum for that item of business.

Where the number of directors falls below that fixed as the quorum (e.g. if a company has only two directors, and one resigns or dies) Model Article 11 (public company Model Article 11) allows the continuing directors or sole remaining director to continue for the purpose of filling vacancies or calling a general meeting.

Generally speaking, it is preferable to fix a low quorum because doing so eases the conduct of the board's business. However, this needs to be balanced with the governance point that there must be enough directors present to give any matter proper consideration.

The quorum for board meetings may also affect the quorum for committees of the board where the Articles provide that the regulations governing proceedings at board meetings shall also apply to committees (see section 10).

The company secretary should assess the quorum of the meeting at the beginning of the meeting and again as necessary if any directors leave the meeting or if the directors are considering a matter in which a director is interested. It is the secretary's responsibility to advise the chairman of the meeting if there is a problem with the quorum. If the meeting becomes inquorate, the secretary should advise the chairman to adjourn the meeting immediately until the correct quorum is available.

## 5.1  Video conferences and telephone meetings

Recent cases have questioned whether directors participating in board meetings by video conference or conference telephone can be counted in the quorum and vote. Some companies have amended their Articles expressly to provide for holding board meetings by telephone and state that any director who is able to speak and be heard by each of the other directors present shall be deemed to be present in person. The common law concept of a meeting is the simultaneous transfer of views or a meeting of minds at a particular point in time.

The courts are willing to adapt long-established legal principles in order to allow technology to be used to facilitate meetings and tend to impose less stringent rules on meetings of directors than meetings of members. Model Articles expressly provide that a directors meeting may be held when all the directors are not in the same place. Model Article 10 (public company Model Article 9) permits the directors to decide where the meeting is to be treated as taking place, which may be where any of the directors taking part in the meeting are located. It has been customary for directors to consider that the chairman's location is the location where the meeting is being held.

---

**STOP AND THINK 10.3**

Think about the benefits of using video and telephone meetings. For example, a global business may need to convene a board meeting at short notice when directors are in different locations throughout the world. Participation via video or telephone would be better than being unable to attend. Cost savings on travel and accommodation should also be taken into account.

# 6   Resolutions and voting

The rules on voting at meetings of the board are based on common law, but are subject to modification by the company's Articles. Board meetings are usually much less formal than general meetings and decisions are normally reached by consensus rather than being put to a vote. When a resolution is put to a vote, each director has one vote, unless the Articles provide otherwise. Questions are decided on a majority of votes cast for or against the resolution, although the chairman is often given a second or casting vote in the event of a deadlock (Model Article 13; public company Model Article 14). Some Articles require a special majority for certain types of business and most restrict the right to vote if a director has a personal interest in the matter under consideration.

Voting is normally conducted on a show of hands, but should take account that some directors may have more votes than others (e.g. if they are acting as an alternate for a director who is absent) and voting papers can be used if the chairman finds it difficult to calculate the number of votes for and against on a show of hands.

If the chairman has a casting vote, this must be provided for in the Articles and must be used only when there is a deadlock. The chairman is not obliged to use his casting vote and, if he does, he is not bound to use the casting vote in the same way as his original vote. There are two guiding principles:

1  As adopted by the Speaker at the House of Commons: that the casting vote should be used to preserve the status quo.
2  More commonly used: that the casting vote should be used in the best interests of the company.

Directors have a right to have their opposition to a resolution recorded in the minutes and this has the effect that they will not be liable for the consequences of that transaction.

It is good practice at meetings when a consensus has been reached for the chairman to summarise what has been agreed. This prevents directors from leaving the meeting with different opinions as to what was decided and helps the secretary when preparing the minutes. If the chairman tries to move on to the next item without summarising the last decision, the secretary should ask him to provide this summary so that it can be properly recorded.

---

**STOP AND THINK 10.4**

Not every item of business considered by a board requires a formal resolution and vote. Sometimes an item may be presented as an update and the board will simply note the progress made. This is a good example of how the agenda and business of a board meeting varies from the agenda and business of a general meeting.

---

# 7   Resolutions in writing

Articles frequently allow directors to act without holding a meeting if they are unanimous. Model Article 8 provides that a resolution in writing, signed by all the directors (or otherwise agreed to in writing) entitled to receive notice of a meeting of the board, shall be as valid and effective as if it had been passed at a meeting properly called and held.

Public company Model Articles 17 and 18 have additional requirements in respect of directors' resolutions in writing. Notice of a proposed written resolution must indicate the time by which it is proposed that the directors should adopt it. Even if the last director who signs the resolution does so after the stipulated time, the resolution becomes adopted by the board.

If it is convenient, written resolutions could be a single document, signed by each director. Otherwise a separate copy of the resolution could be sent to each director for signature. The document(s) signed by the directors should be inserted in the minute book. As unanimous consent is required, the resolution becomes effective from the date of the last signature. Written resolutions of the board therefore override the usual requirement of that a simple majority is required to approve a board resolution.

Provision may be made for using electronic communications – and hence no signatures – subject to any terms and conditions the board may decide.

---

**SAMPLE WORDING 10.4**

**Resolution in writing**

. . . . . . . . . . . . . . . . . . . . . . LIMITED/plc

Pursuant to the authority given by Article . . . . of the company's Articles of Association, we, the undersigned, all the directors for the time being of . . . . . . . . . . . . . . . Limited/plc [entitled to receive notice of a meeting of directors], hereby resolve:

THAT


Dated this . . . . . . . day of . . . . 20xx.

. . . . . . . . . . . . . . . . . . . . .

. . . . . . . . . . . . . . . . . . . . .

(Signatures)

---

## 7.1 Alternate directors

The position of alternate directors needs to be considered when preparing board resolutions in writing. The Model Articles for public limited companies only provide for alternate directors and these provide that a resolution signed by an alternate director need not also be signed by his appointer, and vice versa. However, alternate directors are entitled under the public company Model Articles to receive all notices and written resolutions, even if they are not required to sign or agree them (see Chapter 2).

---

**TEST YOUR KNOWLEDGE 10.3**

a What is the quorum required for board meetings? What procedures should be followed if the number of directors falls below the required quorum?
b What are the Model Articles provisions in respect of voting in board meetings?
c Is a simple majority sufficient to pass a resolution in writing?
d When does a resolution in writing become effective?

# 8 Minutes

Minutes should be prepared by the secretary and circulated in draft form to the directors for comment. They should be included in the papers for the next meeting and, if approved, signed by the chairman. Any amendments or alterations to the minutes should be summarised at the beginning of the next set of minutes, for example:

'subject to minute no. .. . . . being amended to read . . . . . . . . . . . . . . . .
. . . . . . . . . . the minutes of the last meeting were approved and signed'.

Once signed, minutes are evidence of the proceedings of the relevant meeting.

The effect of CA 2006, ss. 248 and 355–359 and Model Article 15 (public company Model Articles 18 and 19) is that minute books must be kept for all meetings of the board, board committees, written resolutions, general meetings and decisions of a sole shareholder. The names of the directors present must be included in the minutes of that meeting. If a director leaves the meeting at any point or rejoins it, this should be recorded in the minutes. It should be clear from the minutes who chaired the meeting and that a quorum was present.

Directors and auditors have a right to inspect all minutes at any time, but members, creditors and the public cannot inspect, or take copies of, minutes of directors' meetings. There are no statutory requirements as to where the minutes of board meetings must be kept, but it is usual to find them at the registered office or at the principal place of business. CA 2006, s. 248 requires minutes of directors' meetings held on or after 1 October 2007 to be recorded and kept for ten years.

## 8.1 Writing minutes

Preparing minutes is a skill. Minutes must reflect accurately what was decided, giving sufficient detail yet remaining concise. The preferences of the chairman will be paramount in the way the minutes are presented, but all minutes must include the following basic elements:

- name of the company;
- place where the meeting was held;
- day and date of the meeting;
- names of those present and in attendance;
- apologies for any absences;
- approval of any previous minutes;
- record of the proceedings; if appropriate a numbering system should be used for each substantive item of business;
- chairman's signature.

The record of the proceedings should include the text of any resolutions put to the meeting and the result of any vote. All papers presented to the meeting must be clearly identified and retained for as long as the minutes themselves. Records of any written resolutions should be entered in the minute book. This is particularly important if there is only one director who is the sole member making written resolutions regarding the company.

In certain circumstances, it may be helpful to prepare draft minutes ahead of a board meeting. This may be helpful where certain formalities or formal resolutions need to be observed and it will be helpful for directors to focus on these as part of their decision-making. However, these minutes should always be in draft and subject to the actual discussion of the directors, and such minutes in advance would be unsuitable in most cases where directors are debating issues.

**SAMPLE WORDING 10.5**

**Minutes of board meeting for a listed company**

. . . . . . . . . . . . . . . . . . . . . plc

BOARD MEETING

held at on . . . . . . . day, . . . . . 20xx.

Present:

. . . . . . . . . . . . . . . . . . . . .    . . . . . . . . . . . . . . . . . . . . . (in the chair) } Directors

. . . . . . . . . . . . . . . . . . . . .    . . . . . . . . . . . . . . . . . . . . . Secretary

. . . . . . . . . . . . . . . . . . . . .    . . . . . . . . . . . . . . . . . . . . . Chief Accountant (Item 6)

1   The chairman signed the minutes of the board meeting held on . . . . . 20xx and of the . . . . . . . . . .
. . . . . . committee meeting held on . . . . . 20xx, copies having been circulated to the directors.

2   Transfer audit reports dated . . . . . 20xx from the company's registrars were produced and it was
resolved:
    **a**   THAT share transfers Nos. . . . . . to . . . . . inclusive and loan stock transfers Nos. . . . . . to . . . . .
inclusive be approved.
    **b**   THAT the sealing and issue of share certificates Nos. . . . . . to . . . . . inclusive and loan stock
certificates
Nos. . . . . . to . . . . . inclusive be confirmed.

3   The seal book was produced and it was resolved:
THAT the affixing of the common seal of the company to the documents set out against items
Nos. . . . to . . . inclusive in the seal book be confirmed.

4   There were produced and considered:
    **a**   list of bank balances at . . . . 20xx and forward cash statement for the six months to . . . . 20xx;
    **b**   financial statement at . . . . 20xx.

5   . . . . . . . . . . . . . . . . . . joined the meeting.

6   There were produced and discussed a proof print of the report of the directors and the accounts
for the year ended . . . . 20xx together with a draft of the chairman's statement to be circulated
with the report and accounts, the notice of meeting and form of proxy.
It was resolved:
    **a**   THAT the sum of £xxxx be transferred from the profit and loss account to the general reserve
account.
    **b**   THAT, with reference to minute No. 5 of the seventh annual general meeting held on . . . . 20xx,
the remuneration of the auditors be fixed at £xxxx.
    **c**   THAT the report of the directors, the chairman's statement and the audited accounts for the
year ended . . . . 20xx including the final dividend of xx p per share recommended therein
(making a total dividend of xx p per share for the year) be approved and that, subject to
approval by the company in general meeting, such dividend be paid on . . . . 20xx, to
shareholders registered at the close of business on . . . . 20xx.
    **d**   THAT the signature of the balance sheet by any one director on behalf of the board be
authorised.
    **e**   THAT the signature of the directors' report by the secretary on behalf of the board be
authorised.
    **f**   THAT the signature of the remuneration report by the chairman of the remuneration committee
on behalf of the board be authorised.
    **g**   THAT the eighth annual general meeting of the company be convened and held on . . . . . day,
. . . . 20xx at . . . . . . . . . . . . . . . . . . . . at XX am, to transact the ordinary business of the   .
company and that the secretary be authorised to issue notice accordingly, together with a form
of proxy in accordance with the proof print submitted to and approved by this meeting.

> **h** THAT the company's bankers, . . . . . . . . Bank plc, be requested to open dividend account No.
> . . . . in the name of the company and be authorised to honour warrants dated . . . . 20xx drawn
> on the said account bearing the facsimile or autographic signature of the secretary without
> other signature thereto.
>
> It was resolved:
>
> THAT the secretary be authorised to release forthwith to the Stock Exchange and to the company's
> press agents a preliminary announcement of the results for the year ended 20xx in the form
> produced to and approved by this meeting.
>
> 7  The question of office hours was discussed and it was decided that with effect from . . . . 20xx the
> office should close each day at XX pm instead of at YY pm . . . . dissented from this decision and
> asked that his dissent be recorded in the minutes.
>
> 8  The company secretary noted that the date of the next meeting was . . . . . 20xx.
>
> 9  There being no further business, the chairman declared the meeting closed.
>
> . . . . . . . . . . . . . . . . . . . . .
> Chairman

## 8.2  Keeping the minutes

In a private company where the directors and shareholders are one and the same, the minutes are often kept at the back of the company registers (usually a bound book into which the pages of minutes are firmly attached). When outside shareholders are involved it is advisable to keep minutes of board meetings and minutes of general meetings separate because shareholders do not have the right to inspect minutes of board meetings. Larger companies often keep their minutes in loose-leaf binders, but all the pages should be consecutively numbered so that it is easy to see at a glance if any pages have been removed.

Security is important. The minute books should be stored in a fireproof, locked cabinet or safe to prevent any physical damage or unauthorised alterations. As documents are usually prepared on a word processor it is also necessary to password-protect computer files containing the minutes and supporting documents. Care should be taken when sending such documents via email to prevent unauthorised access. Some larger organisations make an electronic copy of the signed minutes so that in the event of loss or damage of the original signed minutes, a copy of the signed minutes are available.

# 9  The role of the secretary before, during and after board meetings

The company secretary plays a central role in the preparations for and management of board meetings. He is also responsible for any administration arising from the meeting.

### Before the meeting
1  Prepare the notice of the board meeting when instructed by the directors. This should include date, time, venue, agenda and draft proposed resolutions.
2  Send the notice to directors and any company managers or professional advisers who are invited. Advise branches, departments or other parts of the company responsible for producing papers or information for board meetings.
3  Prepare the agenda for the meeting, setting out the full text of any formal resolutions to be passed. The company secretary should review a draft agenda with the chairman prior to issuing it.
4  Circulate the agenda, formal resolutions, reports, financial statements and any other documents that are to be considered at the meeting. It is wise to keep a few spare copies for the meeting.

5 Check that the boardroom is prepared, for example:
  a) there are sufficient chairs for the attendees;
  b) the room is at a comfortable temperature, well lit and ventilated;
  c) audiovisual equipment is working properly;
  d) refreshments are available as appropriate;
  e) name plates have been set out (if appropriate) to assist in the positioning of directors and attendees around the table (it is customary that the secretary sits next to the chairman of the meeting);
  f) writing paper and pens have been laid out to allow directors to make notes.
6 Check that a quorum will be reached. If any director is unable to attend, advise the chairman accordingly.
7 Take to the meeting:
  a) a copy of the Articles of Association;
  b) the directors' attendance book (if appropriate);
  c) the minute book;
  d) a copy of the CA;
  e) the agenda and other necessary documents (plus spare copies).

## At the meeting

1 Record the names of the directors and others present and report apologies for absence(s).
2 If the company uses directors' attendance books (i.e. a non-statutory register used to confirm director attendance at meetings), arrange for this to be signed by each attending director.
3 Check that a quorum is present and ensure it is maintained throughout the meeting, particularly if there are any items to be considered in which any director has an interest.
4 Take accurate notes, minute the decisions and note any further actions.
5 Record late arrivals or early departures of any directors and the attendance of anyone who has been invited to attend for particular items.
6 Give advice on request about procedure, or rules and regulations governing the meeting. It is appropriate for the secretary to intervene in the meeting (unless he is also a director) only if the board is proposing to do something contrary to the company's Articles, or that is unlawful.
7 Keep track of progress against the agenda. Advise the chairman if any agenda items have been overlooked.
8 Arrange to have people brought into the meeting who have been invited when appropriate.
9 At the end of the meeting, make sure that any papers which form part of the company's records are cleared away, and in particular ensure that any confidential reports or letters are removed.

## After the meeting

1 If the company is listed, announce to the market via an RIS any decision to declare or recommend a dividend, to make an issue of shares or debentures or any decision relating to issues such as payment of a fixed dividend or interest payment or any other decision which is required to be announced under the DTRs.
2 Notify departments, branches and relevant personnel of decisions that affect them.
3 Comply with any filing necessary at Companies House.
4 Make a note of any item that has been deferred to make sure it is not overlooked.
5 Prepare the minutes in draft form from the notes taken.
6 The precise procedure for the circulation of minutes will vary from company to company. However, it is usual to send a copy of the draft minutes to the chairman and CEO in the first instance, then to every director present at the meeting, asking for comments by a given date. The minutes are then distributed in their final form to all directors. If a director makes a comment about the wording of a particular minute, the alteration should be agreed by the chairman, who should mention the amendment at the next board meeting.
7 Produce a final set for approval and signature by the chairman at the next meeting.
8 File a copy of the meeting agenda and supporting papers. Destroy unused spare copies.
9 Enter any minutes approved and signed in the company's minute book.

---

**a** What are the statutory and Model Article provisions in relation to minutes of meetings?

**b** Are there any statutory requirements as to the location of board minutes?

**c** What would be good practice in respect of the keeping of minutes? For how long should they be kept?

**d** What are the key tasks for the company secretary before, during and after the board meeting?

**e** Apart from the specific papers relating to the meeting, what should the company secretary take to the meeting?

# 10 Committees

It is common for larger companies to establish committees for specific purposes, either on a temporary or a permanent basis. For example, a permanent committee may be set up to deal with approving share transfers and new certificates, or a committee could be set up specifically to fill a staff vacancy and would be disbanded once the vacancy was filled.

Committees of directors may be appointed only by a resolution of the board, which should specify its membership and duties, together with any conditions on the exercise of their powers and limitation on duration. The company's Articles usually provide that the regulations governing board meetings should also be applied to the procedures at committee meetings.

## 10.1 Listed companies – committees required under the UK Corporate Governance Code

Under the UK Corporate Governance Code listed companies are expected to establish and maintain three principal committees: the audit committee, remuneration committee and nomination committee.

### The audit committee

- Should consist only of independent NEDs.
- Should not include the chairman of the board (except for listed companies outside the FTSE 350, where the chairman of the board may be included where he was considered independent on appointment).
- Should have one member who has significant relevant and recent financial experience.
- Is responsible for reviewing all aspects in connection with the financial reporting of the company and all aspects of internal control.
- Makes recommendations to the board on the AGM resolutions to appoint or reappoint the auditors. The committee will also recommend removal of auditors. In addition, the committee ensures that the auditor remains independent of the company so that the audit report provided in the annual accounts is not compromised (see Chapter 11).

### The remuneration committee

- Should consist only of independent NEDs.
- May include the chairman of the board.
- Is responsible for reviewing the remuneration packages for executive directors, including their salary, share options and pensions.

### The nomination committee

- Should consist of a majority of independent NEDs.
- May be chaired by the chairman of the board, unless it is considering the appointment of his successor.
- Evaluates the balance of skills, experience and knowledge on the board and, based on this evaluation, prepares a role description and person specification for a particular appointment.

■ Is responsible for recommending to the board the appointment of new directors and for reviewing whether existing directors should have their terms of appointment extended or renewed.

The UK Corporate Governance Code recommends that the terms of reference for the audit, remuneration and nomination committees be made available on request and recommends that each company posts the terms of reference on their company website. Guidance on standing committee terms of reference can be found in the relevant ICSA Guidance Notes on the ICSA website (see Directory).

Only directors can be appointed members of board committees, unless the Articles provide otherwise. This means that there is no provision for non-directors (including the company secretary, unless he is also a director) to be appointed as voting members of committees, but they may have the right of attendance.

Model Articles 5 and 6 reflect these arrangements by providing that:

■ only directors may delegate powers to a person or committee on terms the directors think fit;
■ the proceedings of a committee shall be governed by the Articles insofar as they relate to the proceeding of board meetings.

However, the Articles of many listed companies allow individuals other than directors to be members of board committees, subject to certain limits, for example that the number of non-director members must not exceed the number of directors who are members.

It is possible to delegate to a committee consisting of only one director, but in practice committees usually number two or more. It is also possible and sometimes practical to appoint post-holders rather than named individuals.

## 10.2 Committee powers and duties

The powers delegated to a committee must be stated in the original resolution forming that committee. Where a committee is established to deal with specific contracts it is necessary to state explicitly that it has power to appoint the relevant professional advisers and incur any necessary costs in carrying out its duties. Committees established solely to make recommendations to the board do not need such powers.

Standing committees need more formal rules because they are established permanently to perform certain duties on a regular basis. The formal rules are usually contained in the terms of reference, which are approved by the board. The company secretary is usually responsible for drafting terms of reference and he should be pro-active in ensuring the board reviews and amends them as necessary, for example, if the composition of the board changes.

Model Articles 5 and 6 (public company Model Articles 5 and 6) state that directors may delegate any of their powers to a person or committee on such terms and conditions as they think fit. Any committees must follow the procedures which are used by the board to take decisions (as far as applicable) but this does not prevent the board from making further provisions on how the committee shall be operated.

## 10.3 Appointing a committee chairman, voting, quorum

It is usual for the board to specify a committee quorum (see Sample Wording 10.6) and to nominate the committee chairman (who need not be the company chairman), especially for standing committees. It is important that the extent of any delegated powers is specified in the committee's terms of reference.

---

**SAMPLE WORDING 10.6**

**Specimen board resolutions to appoint committees**

THAT, pursuant to Article no. . . . of the company's Articles of Association, Messrs. A, B and C (any two of whom shall be a quorum) be appointed a committee with the power to . . . . . . . . . . . . . . . . . .

THAT, pursuant to Article no. . . . of the company's Articles of Association, any two directors be appointed a committee to take such action and to complete all documents necessary for the purpose of . . . . . . . . . . . . . . .

**TEST YOUR KNOWLEDGE** **10.5**

Describe the roles and membership of the board committees a listed company should establish and maintain under the UK Corporate Governance Code.

## CASE QUESTION 1

The chairman of the company explains that a new director is expected to be appointed shortly by the board. As part of the induction pack, the chairman would like for you to include a briefing note on the arrangements for board meetings and the key committees of Multiple plc. Prepare a suitable briefing note for the proposed new director.

## CASE QUESTION 2

As part of its expansion, Multiple plc will require two new subsidiary companies to be incorporated. One will be Plenty plc and the other Scarce Ltd. As several other new subsidiary companies are expected to be formed shortly you have decided to prepare a set of template minutes for the first board meeting of a company.

The template minutes will include matters which need to be considered for both a public limited company and a private limited company so that the preparer of the minutes can delete any inapplicable wording. Prepare the template minutes.

## CHAPTER SUMMARY

- Board meetings are an essential part of the management of a company. They do not have to be held at fixed intervals, but it is good practice to have a regular timetable.
- There are many differences in the procedures of board meetings compared to general meetings; for example, there is usually no fixed notice period to convene a board meeting.
- The person who is chairman of the board is generally regarded as chairman of the company.
- The secretary should draft the agenda and review it with the chairman prior to dispatch. Board papers should be issued to allow the directors sufficient time to review them ahead of the meeting. The agenda and supporting papers should be organised in the order in which they will be discussed.
- The first board meeting of a new company is an important milestone at which specific matters must be covered.
- The quorum for a board meeting is usually specified in the Articles. Making use of technology such as videoconferencing allows directors to be counted as 'present' even if they are at a different location.
- Resolutions of the board are usually carried on a simple majority; however, board resolutions in writing require unanimous consent.
- The company secretary is responsible for the safekeeping of minute books.
- The company secretary plays a central role in the preparations for and management of a board meeting, and any administration arising from it.
- Committees can only operate under express authority of the board. In order to comply with the UK Corporate Governance Code, listed companies are expected to appoint a remuneration committee, audit committee and a nomination committee as standing committees.

# Annual report and accounts, and auditors

## 11

## ■ CONTENTS

1 The annual report and accounts
2 Duty to keep accounting records and prepare accounts
3 Preparation, laying and delivery of accounts
4 Summary financial statements
5 The directors' report and business review
6 Listed company disclosure
7 Preliminary announcements, half-year reports and interim management statements
8 Auditors

## ■ INTRODUCTION

Every company with limited liability is required to deliver accounts to the Registrar of Companies. This chapter summarises the legal requirements concerning the preparation and publishing of the annual accounts and accompanying reports. Although the compilation of the annual report is not the prime responsibility of the company secretary, he is likely to act in a coordinating role in consultation with the company's internal and external advisers; the preparation of material for inclusion in the directors' report is an important part of this role.

Also covered in this chapter are preliminary announcements and half-year reports, and the duties and responsibilities of auditors.

## 1 The annual report and accounts

The Companies Acts require all companies to keep two kinds of accounts: original books of account or accounting records in which transactions are entered as they occur (CA 2006, s. 386) and annual accounts showing the results of the company's business activities during the period to which they relate and the company's assets and liabilities at the end of that period (CA 2006, s. 394).

**Statutory accounts** are individual or group accounts, which must be filed with the Registrar of Companies. These may be either full accounts (submitted by most companies) or abbreviated accounts which qualifying small and medium-sized companies may deliver (see section 3.4).

**Non-statutory accounts** are any balance sheet or profit and loss accounts of a company dealing with a complete financial year, other than as part of its statutory accounts. This includes data in newspaper advertisements and prospectuses, employee accounts, preliminary announcements and, to the extent that they include comparative information relating to a complete financial year, interim accounts.

It is important to understand the difference in meaning of the following terms:

- *Laying accounts* – Means circulating them to shareholders for consideration at a general meeting (CA 2006 s. 437).
- *Delivering accounts* – Means filing them with the Registrar at Companies House (CA 2006, s. 441).
- *Publishing accounts* – Means publishing, issuing, circulating or otherwise making them available for public inspection in a manner intended to invite the general public, or any class of members of the public, to read them (CA 2006, s. 436).

## 2 Duty to keep accounting records and prepare accounts

The requirement on companies to keep and regularly publish proper accounts showing their assets and liabilities and the results of carrying on their business activities goes a long way to protect directors, shareholders and creditors alike. The main benefits are:

- providing information to directors about a company's financial position so that they may better plan its future activities and avoid committing irregularities, such as the payment of dividends out of capital or borrowing beyond the limits set for them by the Articles;
- enabling shareholders to judge whether the company's affairs are being competently managed, whether the company's profits to its turnover and its net assets are adequate, whether the recommended dividend is sufficient and to ascertain whether the value of their shares is higher/lower than a valuation based on the company's assets, earnings and dividends;
- enabling creditors to judge whether the company will be able to pay its debts and whether they may safely extend further credit to it;
- enabling customers to ascertain whether the company is of sufficient financial standing, prior to becoming a client of the company;
- if a company is wound up, providing information from which the liquidator can see what assets he may realise, and what claims against the company he has to meet.

Accounting records must be kept at the registered office or any other place the directors may decide. They should be open to inspection by the officers of the company at all times.

The auditors have right of access to the books, accounts and vouchers (CA 2006, ss. 499–500), but there is no statutory right of access for members or the general public. CA 2006, s. 499 provides auditors with the statutory right to require directors and employees to provide them with information necessary to enable them to carry out the duties of auditor. Officers (directors, managers and the secretary) are liable to penalty for default in keeping accounts (CA 2006, s. 387).

The records must be kept for at least three years by a private company from the date on which they are made and for six years by a public company (CA 2006, s. 388). Companies may have their own document retention policies in excess of this length.

### 2.1 Accounting reference period

The period covered by the accounts is known as an accounting reference period and ends on an accounting reference date. On incorporation, a company's first financial year begins on the first accounting reference period and ends with the last day of that period or such other date, not more than seven days before or after the end of that period, as the directors may determine (CA 2006, s. 390). Subsequent financial years are also permitted to have the accounting period to end up to seven days before or after the end of that period.

In the case of a newly incorporated company, the accounting reference date is the last day of the month in which the anniversary of incorporation falls (CA 2006, s. 390), unless the directors resolve at incorporation to select another date (see below). The first accounting reference period must be a period of more than six months and less than 18 months, beginning with the date of incorporation and ending with its accounting reference date. The accounting reference date does not need to be the same as the annual return date (see Chapter 8).

### Change of accounting reference date

CA 2006, s. 392, provides that the accounting reference date may be changed, subject to the regulations above, so that the first accounting period is not less than six months or longer than 18 months. Changes to the accounting date should be notified to the Registrar of Companies on form AA01. The following rules apply:

1 You may not change a period for which the accounts are already overdue.
2 You may not extend a period beyond 18 months unless the company is subject to an administration order.

In accordance with Section 392 of the Companies Act 2006.

# AA01
## Change of accounting reference date

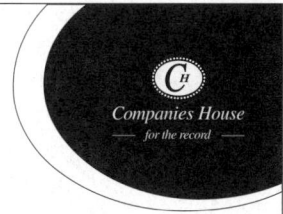

*Companies House*
*— for the record —*

**You can use the WebFiling service to file this form online.**
Please go to www.companieshouse.gov.uk

✓ **What this form is for**
You may use this form to change the accounting reference date relating to either the current, or the immediately previous, accounting period.

✗ **What this form is NOT for**
You cannot use this form to
- change a period for which the accounts are already overdue; or
- extend a period beyond 18 months unless the company is in administration.

For further information, please refer to our guidance at www.companieshouse.gov.uk

**1**   **Company details**

Company number   ☐ ☐ ☐ ☐ ☐ ☐ ☐ ☐

Company name in full

→ **Filling in this form**
Please complete in typescript or in bold black capitals.

All fields are mandatory unless specified or indicated by *

**2**   **Date of accounting reference period**

Please enter the end date of the current, or the immediately previous, accounting period. ❶

Accounting period ending on   [d][d] [m][m] [y][y][y][y]

❶ **Date of period you wish to change**
The current period means the present accounting period which has not yet come to an end.

The immediately previous period means the period immediately preceding your present accounting period.

**3**   **New accounting reference date ❷**

...fere.ce r... be
→ **Shortened**. Please complete 'Date shortened so as to end on'.
→ **Extended**. Please complete 'Date extended so as to end on'.

Please enter the date the accounting reference period has been shortened to.

Date **Shortened** so as to end on   [d][d] [m][m] [y][y][y][y]

**or**   Please enter the date the accounting reference period has been extended to.

Date **Extended** so as to end on   [d][d] [m][m] [y][y][y][y]

❷ **New accounting reference date**
If you wish to move the end of your current, or immediately previous, reference period to an earlier date, please insert the required date in the box marked 'Shortened'.

If you wish to move the end of your current, or immediately previous, reference period to a later date, please insert the required date in the box marked 'Extended'.

You cannot change a period for which the accounts are overdue.

You cannot extend a period beyond 18 months unless the company is in administration.

3 You may not extend periods more than once in five years unless:
   a) the company is in administration; or
   b) you have the specific approval of the Secretary of State (a copy of the approval will need to be sent to the Registrar of Companies); or
   c) you are extending the company's accounting reference period to align with that of a parent or subsidiary undertaking established in the EEA; or
   d) the form is being submitted by an oversea company.

There is no limit on the number of times a company may shorten its accounting reference period, or a minimum length of a shortened period.

Listed companies must issue an announcement through an RIS immediately on any change of accounting reference date, and if the accounting period is extended beyond 14 months will be required to issue an additional interim report.

The accounting reference date for any company can be checked by contacting the Registrar by telephone or by using their website (see Directory). The website also shows the deadline by which the accounts must be filed.

---

**STOP AND THINK 11.1**

When a company is being incorporated from new, it is important for the company secretary to draw the accounting reference date to the attention of the directors. They will need to consider what would be the most appropriate accounting year for the business. This is particularly important given the limitations on extending the accounting reference period.

---

**TEST YOUR KNOWLEDGE 11.1**

a Where should accounting records be kept?
b Why is it important for companies to prepare and publish annual accounts?
c How is the accounting reference date set for a company on incorporation? What are the restrictions on a company changing its accounting reference date?

---

## 3 Preparation, laying and delivery of accounts

### 3.1 Timing

Accounts must be laid before a general meeting (for public companies and any private companies which have opted to continue holding annual general meetings) and delivered to the Registrar of Companies:

- within six months after the end of the relevant accounting reference period (see section 2.1) for a public company (CA 2006, s. 442); or
- within nine months after the end of the relevant accounting reference period for a private company (CA 2006, s. 442). However, any private company which has opted to continue holding general meetings at which accounts will be laid will need to consider the impact of this – for example, the AGM must be held within six months of the end of the financial year.

The Registrar issues a reminder to the registered office of the company 6–8 weeks before the time due for accounts filing to advise the company that the filing deadline is approaching.

Listed companies are required by the DTRs to publish their annual financial report no later than four months after the year-end. The annual financial report must be available to the public for at least five years following publication and two copies should be sent to UKLA's Document Viewing Facility. Listed companies are also required to issue half-year financial reports within two months of the period end. All listed companies have the option of considering whether they wish to announce their preliminary full year results. (See Chapter 6 for information on these obligations.)

If the accounts are the first accounts of the company and cover a period of more than twelve months, the time limit is nine or six months from the first anniversary of the incorporation of the company or three months from the end of the financial year, whichever expires later.

### Late filing penalties

If the accounts are delivered to the Registrar outside the periods laid down, the company is subject to a late filing penalty (CA 2006, s. 451), levied by the Registrar. The penalty arises automatically and appeals against the penalty are accepted in exceptionally restricted circumstances only, such as a personal tragedy affecting a sole director.

The penalties are calculated on a sliding scale according to how late the accounts are received. Penalties for public limited companies are greater than those for private limited companies. The Companies House website (see Directory) has full details on penalties, how to avoid them and commonly asked questions about appeals against penalties.

---

**STOP AND THINK 11.2**

A good company secretary will have a diary system to act as a reminder of when accounts need to be filed with the Registrar. Although it is the duty of directors to ensure accounts are filed on time, secretaries should remind directors of the filing dates to ensure preparation of the accounts has not been overlooked.

Do not wait until the last moment to file accounts. Last-minute problems, such as a postal strike, are not valid excuses for late filing and a penalty will be levied. Company secretaries should work closely with directors on preparation of the accounts, and if it is clear that the accounts will be late, the company secretary should advise the directors to consider whether an application should be made to the Registrar for an extension (which is usually for an additional 28 days). Any application for an extension must be made as soon as possible and in any case prior to the filing deadline. If the filing deadline has been missed, the company secretary should advise the directors to consider maintaining regular contact with the Registrar, who has limited discretion to defer prosecution for a short time if there has been a genuine unforeseen circumstance.

---

## 3.2 Preparation

The form and content of the accounts are set out in CA 2006, s. 396, which details the information required in the profit and loss account, balance sheet and any other information required. There is an overriding requirement that the accounts give a true and fair view of the company's financial state. If there is reason to depart from the statutory provisions, it should be noted.

The accounts must also be prepared according to applicable international accounting standards in force as varied from time to time.

### Parent companies

If a company is a parent company, it must prepare group accounts complying with CA 2006, s. 404, which requires the accounts of the parent company and the subsidiary companies to be prepared on a consolidated basis. The accounts should consist of a balance sheet for the parent company, a consolidated balance sheet for the group of companies and a consolidated profit and loss account for the group of companies. If the subsidiary carries out a substantially different activity from the parent, and consolidating the results would obscure the true and fair view, the directors can decide not to consolidate (CA 2006, s. 405).

## Abbreviated accounts

A company which qualifies as a small company (see sections 3.4 and 8.8) may file **abbreviated accounts** with the Registrar consisting of:

- an abbreviated version of the balance sheet, together with abbreviated notes and a statement immediately above the signature(s) of the director(s) that they have relied on the exemptions available to the company as a small company;
- a special auditor's report (unless the company is also claiming audit exemption) stating that the requirements for qualifying as a small company have been met.

Full accounts must be prepared and issued to shareholders; they should include a copy of the special auditor's report. There is no requirement for a profit and loss account or a directors' report to be included in abbreviated accounts.

A company which qualifies as medium-sized (see section 3.4) may file abbreviated accounts with the Registrar consisting of:

- the full balance sheet, together with notes and a statement immediately above the signature(s) of the director(s) that they have relied on the exemptions available to the company as a medium-sized company;
- a profit and loss account, which can be abbreviated and does not need to disclose turnover;
- a special auditor's report stating that the requirements for qualifying as medium-sized have been met, a copy of which should be included in the full accounts issued to shareholders;
- directors' report.

There are further exemptions for small companies and small groups relating to the director's report and full accounts submitted to shareholders.

## 3.3 Circulation

Under the Companies Acts, copies of the full accounts must be sent to all members of the company, all debenture holders and everyone entitled to receive notice of general meetings at least 21 days prior to the general meeting at which they are to be laid before the members, unless all members agree otherwise (CA 2006, s. 423). However, the following needs to be noted under CA 2006, s. 424:

- private companies do not need to hold an AGM (see Chapter 9). If a private company does not hold an AGM, it must circulate its accounts not later than the end of the period for filing accounts and reports, or if earlier, the date on which it actually delivers its accounts or reports to Companies House.
- a public company must circulate its accounts at least 21 days before the relevant general meeting (referred to as the 'relevant accounts meeting' in s. 424).

Copies may be circulated electronically or made available on the company's website provided members are notified that the accounts are available to view online. CA 2006, s. 430 also requires publicly quoted companies to put the annual report and accounts on the company website as soon as possible following publication, and to ensure that it can be accessed at least until the next annual report and accounts are published. As has been noted above, listed companies are required to lodge two copies of the accounts with UKLA's Document Viewing Facility.

In addition to the obligation to circulate annual accounts to members and debenture holders, CA 2006, ss. 431–432 require a company to provide a further copy of the accounts to members and debenture holders on request. This must be provided within seven days and without charge. Companies should also refer to their Articles as to whether they are obliged to provide additional copies to joint holders. CA 2006 provides that all notices should be given to the joint holder whose name appears first in the register of members in respect of the joint holding and that such notice is sufficient for all joint holders.

Traditionally, the meeting at which a company lays its accounts before shareholders is the AGM, but the Act allows for them to be laid at any general meeting. In practice, it is unwise for a company's Articles to stipulate that the accounts are to be laid before the AGM, since circumstances could arise which make that impossible.

As well as the statutory circulation list, the company secretary often maintains a mailing list of other persons who may wish to receive the annual accounts (e.g. the bank or a major supplier). The company secretary should also retain a small stock of spare annual reports throughout the year to deal with any requests for additional copies from shareholders, debenture holders or interested parties. This is particularly relevant where a company has taken advantage of the provisions under CA 2006, Part 13. These provisions allow companies to use electronic communications as a default method to communicate with shareholders. This allows companies to make electronic copies of its accounts available to shareholders as a first choice (unless a shareholder otherwise objects). However, a shareholder may at any time request a paper copy of the annual accounts.

**STOP AND THINK 11.3**

The company secretary should ensure that the register of members and debenture holders (if any) is as up to date as possible prior to the circulation of the annual accounts. Any queries regarding recent changes of addresses of members should be carefully noted and special care should be taken to ensure members who have recently changed address actually receive the annual accounts.

## 3.4 Exemptions

### Small and medium-sized companies

Companies defined as small and medium-sized may deliver abbreviated accounts to the Registrar. The intention is to reduce the administrative burden of many companies of preparing their annual accounts and to permit more companies to benefit from certain tax allowances. The legislation also brings the UK into line with the maximum threshold levels available under applicable EU directives.

To qualify as a small company, at least two of the following conditions must be met:

- annual turnover must be £6.5 million or less;
- the balance sheet total must be £3.26 million or less;
- the average number of employees must be 50 or fewer.

To qualify as a medium-sized company, at least two of the following conditions must be met:

- annual turnover must be £25.9 million or less;
- the balance sheet total must be £12.9 million or less;
- the average number of employees must be 250 or fewer.

If the company is a parent company, it cannot qualify as a small or medium-sized company unless the group headed by it is also small or medium-sized.

Generally, a company qualifies as small or medium-sized in its first financial year, or in any subsequent financial year, if it fulfils the conditions in that year and the year before. If the company ceases to be small or medium-sized, the exemption continues for the first year that the company does not fulfil the conditions. The exemption continues uninterrupted if the company reverts to being small or medium-sized the following year.

### Small and medium-sized groups

A parent company may qualify for exemption providing none of its member companies is a public company, a banking or insurance company or an authorised person under FSMA 2000. To qualify as a small group, at least two of the following criteria must be met:

- aggregate net turnover must be £6.5 million or less;
- the aggregate net balance sheet total must be £3.26 million or less;
- the aggregate average number of employees must be 50 or fewer.

To qualify as a medium-sized group, it must satisfy at least two of the following conditions:

- its aggregate net turnover must be £25.9 million or less;
- the aggregate net balance sheet total must be £12.9 million or less;
- the aggregate average number of employees must be 250 or fewer.

## Unlimited companies

Unlimited companies do not have to file a copy of their accounts with the Registrar unless at any time during the period covered by the accounts the company was:

- a subsidiary or a parent of a limited undertaking; or
- a banking or insurance company (or the parent of such a company); or
- a qualifying company in terms of the Partnerships and Unlimited Companies (Accounts) Regulations 1993; or
- operating a trading stamp scheme.

A company will be regarded as a qualifying company if it is a member of a partnership governed by the laws of any part of Great Britain and all the other members of the partnership are either limited companies, limited liability partnerships or unlimited companies, or a Scottish firm, each of whose members is a limited company.

Pursuant to CA 2006, Part 13, a private company is not required to hold AGMs and hence would not lay accounts before the members in general meeting (see Chapter 9).

## 3.5 Delivery of accounts

The company secretary should arrange for the following signatures:

- *Directors' report* – Signed by the company secretary on behalf of the board or by a nominated director.
- *Balance sheet* – Signed by a nominated director.
- *Auditor's report* (if any) – Signed in the name of the senior statutory auditor (CA 2006, ss. 503–504).

At least three original signed sets of accounts should be prepared. The original signed version should be delivered to the Registrar within the statutory time allowed. The auditors will usually also require original signed accounts and an original set should be retained by the company.

Certain companies may have to deliver additional items to the Registrar as part of the annual accounts:

- If the company is a parent of a group, the accounts will have two balance sheets, one for the parent company and another consolidated balance sheet for the whole group. The company secretary should ensure that the director signs both balance sheets; and
- If the company is listed (see section 6), a nominated director or the company secretary should also sign the directors' remuneration report on behalf of the board.

Delivery of accounts is necessary even if the company is **dormant** (see section 8) and has not traded throughout the year.

The Registrar has strict requirements as to the acceptable quality of documents to be received, for example, the text in the annual accounts must be greater than the stipulated minimum size and the company registration number should appear on the front page. The secretary should check that the annual accounts meet these requirements before obtaining the signature of the director and auditor.

The Registrar of Companies now also accepts the electronic filing of accounts. Accounts which are exempt from audit and accounts for dormant companies (see section 8 below) can be filed via Companies House's **Web Filing Service**. The service is not currently available for:

- Accounts which require an audit;
- Group accounts;
- Public Limited Companies;
- Limited Liability Partnerships;
- Private Companies Limited by Guarantee (having no share capital); and
- Community Interest Companies.

Once accounts are submitted via the Web Filing Service, Companies House will send emails to confirm receipt and to confirm if the data has been accepted or rejected. This service provides several advantages for directors, accountants and company secretaries. For example, once registered, a reminder will be emailed when accounts are due. The service also has inbuilt templates and checks to check for errors, which should help to reduce the incidence of rejections. Another useful feature of the service is that accounts can also be filed with HM Revenue & Customs at the same time.

## 3.6 Liability for statements in accounts and reports

CA 2006 contains provisions to explain the directors' and company's liability for statements made in accounts and reports. CA 2006, s. 393 requires directors not to approve accounts unless they are satisfied that they give a true and fair view of the assets, liabilities, financial position and profit or loss of the company.

### Directors' liability under CA 2006, s. 463

Section 463 is in relation to the directors' report, directors' remuneration report and summary financial statements. It provides that a director will be liable to compensate the company for any loss it suffers as a result of any untrue or misleading statement or omission. This requires the director's actual knowledge of the untrue or misleading statement or omission, or recklessness as to the matter. Note that s. 463 provides that the liability is owed to the company and to no other person (e.g. a shareholder).

### Issuers' liability for reports and statements published under the Disclosure and Transparency Rules (CA 2006, s. 1270)

These provisions are in relation to companies whose securities are traded on a regulated market (including companies listed on the London Stock Exchange) and amend the provisions of FSMA 2000. The provisions relate to the publication of annual financial statements, half-year statements and interim management statements. Under s. 1270, a company is liable to investors who acquire securities of the issuer (i.e. the company) and suffer a loss as a result of an untrue or misleading statement or omission in a report. As with s. 463, knowledge or recklessness is required, but the scope s. 1270 is wider than s. 463 as it applies to PDMRs; this includes all directors and some of the most senior managers in the company. Although the liability is owed only from the company to an investor, other statutory sanctions continue against a company (e.g. market abuse).

CA 2006 does not provide a direct route for an aggrieved shareholder to take direct action against a director for deliberate or reckless misleading or untrue statements or omissions. Instead, an investor will need to claim against the company under s.1270. If the claim is successful, the company will be obliged to compensate the investor, and the company itself will then have to claim against the director under s. 463.

In addition, in respect of companies whose securities are traded on a regulated market, each annual or half-year report must include a responsibility statement made by the persons who are responsible within the issuer. This is usually the whole board, but if it is only one or some of the directors, they must be named in the report for this purpose.

---

**✎ TEST YOUR KNOWLEDGE 11.2**

a What are abbreviated accounts and when can they be filed? Who should receive a copy?

b What criteria must a company meet to qualify as a small or medium-sized company?

c By when must a public company and a private company file its annual accounts with the Registrar of Companies? What are the statutory timescales in respect of the circulation of annual accounts to members?

d Explain the provisions of CA 2006, ss. 463 and 1270.

As a practical step, company secretaries should ensure that a robust process of verification is in place prior to the release of information covered by ss. 463 and 1270. This will ensure that appropriate managers and directors have reviewed the information and have confirmed it as correct, complete and reasonable prior to its release.

# 4   Summary financial statements

Subject to its Articles of Association, all companies may choose to issue a **summary financial statement** to shareholders instead of the full accounts (CA 2006, s. 426). This may be made available electronically (e.g. on a website) or sent by email to those who have requested it.

The summary financial statement regulations avoid overwhelming private investors with detailed and complex annual accounts. It also saves companies with large shareholder bases substantial costs in printing and posting annual accounts.

The summary financial statement accounts to be prepared, laid and delivered must include the following (CA 2006, ss. 427–428):

- a profit and loss account, or, in the case of a company not trading for profit, an income and expenditure account, made up to the accounting reference date;
- a balance sheet as at the same date;
- a summary directors' report;
- a report by the auditors;
- a consolidated profit and loss account and balance sheet, where required (in this case, a profit and loss account for the company alone is not obligatory);
- if the company is listed, a summary report on directors' remuneration (see section 7).

There are detailed statutory requirements on the method of ascertaining the wishes of members regarding the receipt of full accounts.

## CHECKLIST 11.1  Producing summary financial statements

✓ The company must have ascertained that the shareholder does not want to receive the full accounts. This may be accomplished by sending the shareholder a reply-paid card which requests the shareholder to opt in to receive the full accounts. If the shareholder fails to reply, it is assumed that the shareholder is willing to receive the summary financial statement.
✓ The period allowed for the laying and delivery of accounts must not have expired.
✓ The summary financial statement should be approved by the board and the original copy signed on their behalf by a director whose name must be stated on the copies issued to shareholders.
✓ The summary financial statement must be derived from the annual report and accounts and must state that it is only a summary of the full accounts (CA 2006, ss. 427–428).
✓ As a minimum, the summary financial statement should include:
  – specified summary extracts from the directors' report;
  – a summary profit and loss account;
  – earnings per share information;
  – a summary balance sheet;
  – comparative amounts;
  – a statement by the company's auditors of their opinion of whether the summary financial statement is consistent with the full accounts and complies with the CA and the Regulations;
  – a summary report on directors' remuneration (for listed companies).
✓ The statement must also include, in a prominent position, a declaration that the summary financial statement does not contain sufficient information to allow as full an understanding of the results of the group (or company, if it is not required to prepare group accounts) and the state of affairs of the company and group (if applicable) as would be provided by the full annual accounts and report.
✓ A statement should be included informing shareholders of their right to receive a copy, on request, of the full accounts without charge.
✓ The requirements of CA 2006, s. 435 relating to the publication of non-statutory accounts do not apply to summary financial statements.

The documents that comprise the annual report of the directors on the affairs of the company, together with the accounts and auditor's report, have other papers annexed. These may include:

- the chairman's statement, a business review and general information about the company;
- a financial calendar giving information about proposed dividend payment dates and other matters of interest;
- the directors' remuneration report (see section 6.5).

# 5 The directors' report and business review

## 5.1 The directors' report

The secretary plays an important role in preparing material for the directors' report. The directors' report must be attached to the accounts (CA 2006, s. 423), except in the case of small companies issuing abbreviated accounts (see section 3.2).

The auditors are required to comment in their report if any information given in the directors' report is not, in their opinion, consistent with the company's accounts (CA 2006, s. 496). A summary of the statutory requirements of the directors' report (for non-banking companies) is as follows (these are provided primarily for CA 2006, ss. 415–419):

- *Principal activities* – details are required for the company and its subsidiary undertakings and any significant changes to those activities during the year.
- *A review of the development of the business of the company and its subsidiaries during the year and of their position at the year-end* – This could include significant items such as the development of new products or markets, acquired or discontinued operations, or major capital projects.
- *An indication of likely future developments in the business of the company and its subsidiaries and an indication of any activities of the company and its subsidiaries in research and development.*
- *Results and dividends* – The recommended dividend must be disclosed.
- *Any difference in the market value of land since the balance sheet date.*
- *The names of directors of the company at any time during the year* – It is usual to state the dates of appointment or retirement and it is helpful to include changes in directors since the end of the year and rotation of directors at the AGM. It is sensible to provide biographical details of the directors proposed for election or re-election (age, other directorships and experience relevant to the company's affairs) to enable shareholders to make an informed decision. For a listed company, the chairman and members of the audit, remuneration and nomination committees should also be identified.
- *Details of any charitable or political donations in excess of £2,000 made during the year.*
- *Acquisition of the company's own shares* – Particulars of own shares purchased or acquired or made subject to charges or liens during the year. Details are required of the number and nominal value of the shares purchased, the percentage of the relevant called-up capital, the aggregate consideration paid and the reasons for the purchase.
- *A statement on the company's policy for disabled employees* – Required for a company which employs more than 250 people. Many listed companies make this disclosure voluntarily when the parent company is small or non-trading.
- *A description of the action taken during the year to introduce, maintain or develop arrangements to:*
  - provide employees systematically with information affecting them as employees;
  - consult them, or their representatives, regularly on decisions likely to affect their interests;
  - encourage employees' involvement through share schemes or other means; and
  - achieve a common awareness among all employees in a company employing on average more than 250 people in the UK of the financial and economic factors affecting the company's performance. Many listed companies make this disclosure voluntarily when the parent company is small or non-trading.
- *A statement of whether the company has any branches outside the UK but within the EU.*

- *Supplier payment policy* – If the company is listed or is a large private company which is a subsidiary of a listed company, it should be stated if it is the company's policy to follow any code or standard on payment of suppliers and the place where information about the standard can be obtained. Details should also be given of the year-end trade creditors expressed as a number of days. The method of calculation is specified in detail and is based on the amount invoiced by suppliers in the year.
- *Auditors* – A statement concerning the reappointment of auditors is customary but is not a statutory requirement.
- *Audit information* – A statement that, to the best of their knowledge, there is no relevant information of which the auditors are unaware and that the directors have taken action to make themselves aware of such information. Companies which are exempted from an audit (see section 8) are not subject to this provision.
- *Indemnity arrangements* – Companies which have indemnity arrangements with their directors (see Chapter 2) need to disclose such indemnities. Any indemnity agreements must be made available for inspection by shareholders.

### Approval and signature

The directors' report should be approved by the board and signed by a director or the company secretary on the board's behalf. The name of the signatory should be stated. The copy of the directors' report delivered to the Registrar should contain an original signature (CA 2006, ss. 444–447).

## 5.2 The business review

CA 2006, s. 417 requires all but small companies to include a **business review** in their directors' report. In addition to the existing disclosure for the directors' report, the business review requires:

- a fair review of the business of the company;
- a description of the principal risks and uncertainties facing the company;
- a balanced and comprehensive analysis of:
  - the development and performance of the business during the financial year,
  - the position of the company at the end of that year, consistent with the size and complexity of the business;
- financial key performance indicators to assist an understanding of the development, performance or position of the business. Where appropriate, non-financial key performance indicators should also be disclosed on issues such as environmental or employee matters. Key performance indicators must be measurable – for example, if the company plans to reduce energy consumption by 10%, the key performance indicator should show the percentage reduction achieved so far. Medium-sized companies need not comply with the requirement to produce non-financial key performance indicators;
- a general duty to promote the success of the company (CA 2006, s.172) (see Chapter 2) is imposed on directors, which needs to be taken into account and reflected when drafting the business review;
- CA 2006 also provides an exemption from disclosing impending matters which are in the course of negotiation if such disclosure would be prejudicial to the company's interests.

Companies are not required to disclose information about a person if that disclosure would, in the directors' opinion, be seriously prejudicial to the interests of the company.

Quoted companies reporting under CA 2006 are required to include an enhanced business review in the directors' report (see section 6.3).

Many companies already disclose much of the information required for the business review in different sections of their annual report. To avoid repetition, some companies will include cross-references in their business review to where the required information can be found in the annual report.

Sample Wording 11.1 is an example of a directors' report. It shows content and format only. It should not be assumed that it contains all the possible items required by law or that all the matters mentioned below are the subject of express requirements.

**SAMPLE WORDING** **11.1**

**Directors' report (private company)**

. . . . . . . . . . . . . . . . . . . . . Limited

REPORT OF THE DIRECTORS for the year ended 31 December 20xx.

Directors: . . . . . . . . . . . . . . . . . . . . .

Directors: . . . . . . . . . . . . . . . . . . . . .

The company is a retail confectioner and tobacconist and traded satisfactorily throughout the accounting period.

The accounts for the year ended 31 December 20xx show a net profit of £ . . . . . . . after charging all expenses and taxation. Adding thereto the unappropriated profit of £ . . . . . . . brought forward there remains an unappropriated profit of £ . . . . . . . to be carried forward. No dividend will be paid for the year.

**Directors' responsibilities**

UK company law requires the directors to prepare accounts for each financial year, which give a true and fair view of the state of affairs of the company and of the profit and loss for that period. In preparing those accounts, the directors are required to:

• select suitable accounting policies and then apply them consistently;

• make judgements and estimates that are reasonable and prudent;

• follow applicable accounting standards, subject to any material departures disclosed or explained in the accounts;

• prepare the accounts on the going concern basis unless it is inappropriate to presume that the company will continue in business.

The directors are responsible for maintaining adequate accounting records which disclose with reasonable accuracy at any time the financial position of the company and enable them to ensure that the accounts comply with the Companies Act 2006. They are also responsible for safeguarding the assets of the company and for taking reasonable steps for the prevention and detection of fraud and other irregularities.

**Auditors**

The company is not required to hold annual general meetings. Subject to the receipt of any objections as provided under statute or the company's Articles of Association, the company is relying on the provisions for the deemed reappointment of XYZ as auditors as provided in CA 2006, s. 485.

As far as the directors are aware, there is no relevant audit information of which the auditors are unaware and the directors have taken all steps that he or she ought to have taken as a director in order to make themselves aware of such audit information.

By order of the board

. . . . . . . . . . . . . . . . . . . . .

Secretary

. . . . . . . . . . . . . . . . . . . . .

(Address)

. . . . . . . . . . . . . . . . . . . . .

(Date)

. . . . . . . . . .

# 6   Listed company disclosure

## 6.1  Listing Rules requirements

Listed companies are required to disclose detailed additional information in their annual accounts as provided for in the Listing Rules and the DTRs. The latter require companies to publish their accounts no later than four months after the year-end.

### Listing Rules: key requirements for accounts

The Listing Rules require listed companies to include the following in their accounts:

■ An explanation of differences of 10% or more between published forecasts or estimates and actual results.

■ Details of directors' interests in shares updated to within one month prior to the date of the notice meeting and distinguishing between beneficial and non-beneficial interests.

■ Details of substantial shareholdings, defined as holdings of 3% or more of the company's capital. The disclosure relates to any class of capital which may vote in all circumstances at general meetings of the company.

■ Details of any shareholders' authority for the purchase of own shares still valid at year-end. The names of the sellers must be given for all purchases made, or proposed to be made, by the company during the year other than through the market or by tender or partial offer to all shareholders. For purchases, or options or contracts to make purchases, entered into since the year-end, information in respect of purchases during the year must be given.

■ Details of equity or equity-linked securities issued for cash.

■ Key contracts or agreements: (i) contracts with controlling shareholders – 'contracts of significance' between the company or a subsidiary and a controlling shareholder, and (ii) key contracts which have a significant effect upon the change of control of the company.

■ A statement of compliance in respect of the UK Corporate Governance Code (see section 6.4).

■ A report on directors' remuneration (see section 6.5).

■ A statement that the business is a going concern with supporting assumptions or qualifications as necessary. This statement is sometimes found with the corporate governance disclosures (see section 6.4) or it can be included in the operating and financial review, where it can be placed in the context of a discussion of the financing of the company.

■ A statement of directors' responsibilities for preparing the accounts is required. If the statement does not meet the minimum requirements, the auditors must include similar details in their report. The auditors must include in their report a statement that they have reviewed the disclosures made in accordance with the Listing Rules and DTRs and state whether, in their opinion, the company has complied with the disclosure requirements.

## 6.2  Directors' report

A sample directors' report for a listed company is shown in Sample Wording 11.2 as an example of content and format. It should not be assumed that it contains all the possible items required by law. Listed companies are required to have their annual accounts posted on their websites and you are strongly encouraged to view a selection in order to gain a better impression of current disclosure.

**SAMPLE WORDING** 11.2

**Directors' report (holding company with listed shares)**

. . . . . . . . . . . . . . . . . . . . . plc.

REPORT OF THE DIRECTORS for the year ended . . . . 20xx.

The directors submit their report and the audited financial statements of . . . . . . . . plc for the year ended 20xx.

**Business and principal activities**
The group's principal activities are . . . . . . . . . . . . . . . . . . . . . . During the year under review the company disposed of its interests in . . . . . . . . as part of its strategy to focus on its core businesses. A detailed review of the development of the business and future strategies is provided below and can also be found on pages [....] to [....] of this report.

**Dividends**
The directors recommend a final dividend of 6.06 p net per ordinary share to be paid on . . . . . . . . . . 20xx to those members on the register at the close of business on . . . . . . 20xx. Together with the interim dividend of 3.5 p net paid on . . . . . . . 20xx, the total ordinary dividend for the year would amount to 9.56 p net (12.75 p gross) per ordinary share.

**Transfers to reserves**
The profit attributable to ordinary shareholders amounted to £. . . .million, which after dividends of £ . . . . . million, resulted in a transfer to reserves of £ . . . . . million.

**Directors**
The names of the directors of the company are shown on page [....].[1]

Mr [    ] was appointed a director on . . . . . . . . . . 20xx and will seek election at the forthcoming annual general meeting.

Mrs [    ] and Mr [    ] retired from the board on . . . . . . . . . . 20xx.

Mr [    ] and Mr [    ] retire by rotation at this year's annual general meeting and each, being eligible, will offer himself for re-election. Both have contracts of service with the company which can be terminated by not more than one year's notice.[2]

**Transactions with directors**
At . . . . . . . . . . 20xx there subsisted a contract between . . . . . . . . . . Limited and the company for the leasing to the company of its headquarters premises at an exclusive rent of £ . . . . per annum. Mr . . . . . . . . controls 90% of the share capital of . . . . . . . . . Limited. No other director has or had a material interest in any contract or arrangement to which the company or any subsidiary is or was a party.

**Directors' and officers' liability insurance and indemnity agreements**
The company has purchased insurance to cover directors' and officers' liability as permitted by the Companies Act 2006. There are no indemnity agreements for any director.

**Corporate governance**
The board considers that it has complied throughout the year under review with the requirements of the UK Listing Authority relating to the UK Corporate Governance Code (see separate report).

**Directors' responsibilities**
The directors are required by UK company law to prepare financial statements for each financial year which give a true and fair view of the state of affairs of the company and the group as at the end of the financial year and of the profit and loss for that period. In preparing the financial statements, suitable accounting policies have been used and applied consistently, and reasonable and prudent judgements and estimates have been made. Relevant accounting standards have been followed. The directors are responsible for maintaining adequate accounting records, for safeguarding the assets of the group and for preventing and detecting fraud and other irregularities.

**Annual General Meeting**

The 20xx AGM will be held at [location] on Tuesday, 14 June 20xx at 10.00 am. A notice of the AGM is enclosed with this Annual Report.

**Purchase and cancellation of own ordinary shares or shares held in treasury**

Details of the company's own ordinary shares which have been purchased and either cancelled or held in treasury are provided in Note X to the Accounts.

**Contracts of significance**

There were no contracts of significance during the financial year. There were no significant agreements to which the company is party which take effect, alter or terminate on the change of control in the company following a takeover bid.

**Related party transactions**

There were no related party transactions during the financial year.

**Share capital, rights and obligations attaching to shares**

The structure of the company's share capital and changes to the share capital during the financial year is shown in Note X to the Accounts. Rights attaching to the company's ordinary shares are set out in the company's Articles of Association (the 'Articles'). Further details of the rights and obligations attaching to shares are provided on pages [. . .]–[. . .].

**Research and development**

[Statement regarding research and development activities]

**Supplier payment policy**

Group operating companies are responsible for agreeing the terms and conditions under which business transactions with their suppliers are conducted and it is our policy to comply with those terms and to make suppliers aware of them. A copy of the company's terms and conditions with its suppliers is available from the registered office at . . . . . . . . . . . . . . . . . . . . . . . . . . . . 31 December 20xx, the company had an average of xx days purchases outstanding in trade creditors.

**Contributions for political or charitable purposes**

The company and its subsidiaries made the following contributions during the year:

For political purposes (to the . . . . . . . . Party): £ . . . .

For charitable purposes: £ . . . .

A resolution is sought at each annual general meeting to approve all expenditure for political purposes.

**Employees**

The average weekly number of employees during the year in the UK was . . . .

The aggregate remuneration paid to employees was £ . . . . million. Further information concerning employees is given on page xx.

The company has continued its policy of giving disabled people full and fair consideration for all job vacancies for which they offer themselves as suitable applicants, having regard to their particular aptitudes and abilities. Training and career development opportunities are available to all employees and we continue to endeavour to retrain any member of staff who develops a disability during employment with the company.

It is group policy that there should be effective communication with all employees who, subject to practical and commercial considerations, are consulted and involved in decisions that affect their current jobs or future prospects. Individual businesses use management briefing at all levels, together with consultative committees and other methods of consultation. An Employee Report was issued to all employees, with a specific insert relating to their own part of the business.

The company operates an Employee Benefit Trust (EBT) for the purpose of operating its employee share schemes and the EBT will, from time to time, hold ordinary shares in the Company for the purpose of satisfying awards under employee share schemes. In respect of any shares held by the EBT, the EBT may vote in respect of those shares.

**Assets**

A professional valuation of the company's properties was made at ...... 20xx, and the valuation of £ .... million has been incorporated in the accounts of the company. The directors do not have any intention of making any sales of the properties held for long-term use in the company's business. Provision has therefore not been made for any liability to taxation on capital gains which would arise if the properties were sold at their revised values.

**Substantial interest**

On 20xx ........ Limited had an interest in .... shares of £1 each in the ordinary share capital of the company representing ..... % of the capital.

**Income and Corporation Taxes Act 1988**

The company is not a close company, as defined by the Income and Corporation Taxes Act 1988.

**Branches**

The company has branches in Paris, Bonn and Madrid.

**Auditors**

A resolution to reappoint the retiring auditors, .............., and to authorise the directors to fix their remuneration will be proposed at the annual general meeting.

The directors have taken action to make themselves aware of any relevant information which would be of relevance to the auditors. As far as the directors are aware there is no relevant audit information of which the auditors are unaware.

**Business review**

The following reviews the business of the company for the financial year:

[fair review of the business of the company]

- [description of the principal risks and uncertainties facing the company]
- [analysis of:
  - the development and performance of the business during the financial year, and
  - the position of the company at the end of that year.]

[Main trends and factors likely to affect the future development or performance of the business]
[Environmental matters]
[Employees, including any information about policies and the effectiveness of such policies]
[Social and community issues, including any information about policies about the effectiveness of such]
[Key contractual and other arrangements essential to the business]

**Key performance indicators**

[Key performance indicators regarding the business, environmental matters and employee matters]

**Going concern**

After making enquiries, the directors confirm that they have a reasonable expectation that the company has adequate resources to continue in operational existence for the foreseeable future. For this reason, the going concern basis continues to be adopted in preparing the financial statements.

By order of the board

. . . . . . . . . . . . . . . . . . . .

Secretary

. . . . . . . . . . . . . . . . . . . .

(Address)

. . . . . . . . . . . . . . . . . . . .

(Date)

. . . . . . . . . .

*Notes*

1. The Listing Rules requires the identity of the directors, together with a short biographical note on each, to be shown in the report and accounts. Listed companies, therefore, usually provide biographical details for each of the directors on a separate page.
2. A company must state in the directors' report whether any director proposed for re-election is subject to a service contract. If the directors do not have service contracts, this must be stated.

## 6.3 Enhanced business review

Quoted companies reporting under CA 2006 are required to include an enhanced business review within their directors' report to include additional information. This should explain the development, performance or position of the company's:

- main trends and factors likely to affect the future development or performance of the business. This means there is a statutory requirement to include an element of forward looking disclosure for quoted companies;
- environmental matters, including any information about policies in relation to such matters and the effectiveness of them;
- employees, including any information about policies in relation to such matters and the effectiveness of them;
- social and community issues, including any information about policies in relation to such matters and the effectiveness of them;
- key contractual and other arrangements essential to the business. An exemption is available if the disclosure of such information would be seriously prejudicial to the other party and contrary to the public interest.

## 6.4 Statement on corporate governance

Listed companies are required to disclose in their annual report whether they have complied with the provisions of the UK Corporate Governance Code for the year under review. They are also required to describe how they have applied the principles of the UK Corporate Governance Code. Any non-compliance with the Code principles must be explained. Usual practice is for the company to produce a separate corporate governance report in the annual report or to include corporate governance disclosure within the directors' report. (The UK Corporate Governance Code is covered in more detail in the Corporate Governance syllabus.)

As a result of certain EU directives listed companies are required to include a corporate governance statement in their annual report, which confirms the corporate governance code which is applicable to the company. The statement must include appropriate disclosures in respect of audit committees and other corporate governance arrangements. A listed company which is already making disclosures in accordance with the Code will satisfy the Directives' requirements.

## 6.5 The directors' remuneration report

The Directors Remuneration Report Regulations 2002 and CA 2006 require quoted companies to produce detailed information regarding all aspects of directors' remuneration (CA 2006, ss. 420–422). This underpins and extends the disclosure obligations of the Code, the Listing Rules and the DTRs. In summary, quoted companies are required to produce a directors' remuneration report containing at least the following:

- membership of the remuneration committee and the name of any person who has advised or assisted the committee, including any director who is not a member of the committee;
- a forward-looking statement on remuneration policy, covering:
  - a detailed summary and explanation of any performance criteria for long-term incentive and executive share option schemes for each director;
  - details of relevant companies for comparison;
  - details and explanations of the policy governing contract and notice periods for executive directors and compensation on termination of directorships;
  - the duration of contracts with directors and termination payments;
- a performance graph showing shareholder return (i.e. growth in share price plus dividends or other distributions) over the past five financial years, as compared to the performance of a recognised index or comparator group of companies;
- detailed reports on service contracts for each person who served as a director of the company in the financial year, including contract dates and expiry dates, and provision for compensation in the event of early termination;

- remuneration paid to each director during the year, including bonuses and taxable benefits (e.g. company cars and expense accounts). This should be shown in the form of a table along with the total remuneration paid to each director in the previous year so that shareholders can make a comparison;
- any significant award made in the financial year to anyone who was not a director at the time of the award, but had previously been a director of the company;
- details (shown in tabular form) of any shares, debentures, share options or interests in any other long-term incentive schemes held for each director;
- details of any short-term incentives such as annual bonus plans;
- a description of the general rights for each director under any company pension scheme with details on the value of each director's pension during the year;
- a description of any services provided by a director to a third party, together with disclosure of any sums paid to such third parties.

The company secretary is generally the best placed to draft the disclosure regarding directors' service contracts, interests in shares and long-term incentives. The company's auditors also need to audit much of the information in the directors' remuneration report and their audit opinion to the accounts will include a statement that they have done so. The directors' remuneration report must be approved by the board and signed by a director or the secretary on behalf of the board.

Quoted companies must move an ordinary resolution at the meeting where the reports and accounts are laid to approve the directors' remuneration report for the financial year. The resolution is advisory in nature. This means that members are not permitted to reject it, but can express their concern if they do not agree with the remuneration policy and practices of the company.

---

### TEST YOUR KNOWLEDGE 11.3

a  State three requirements in the Listing Rules in connection with the preparation of accounts.

b  What must a directors' report contain?

c  What information must be contained in the business review?

d  Which type of company is required to provide an enhanced business review? What additional information must be provided?

e  What should the directors' remuneration report contain?

f  Who must receive the directors' remuneration report?

---

## 7 Preliminary announcements, half-year reports and interim management statements

### 7.1 Preliminary announcements

To ensure that information reaches the market in an orderly manner, many listed companies prepare a preliminary announcement of their annual results ahead of the publication of the annual report. Listed companies are not obligated under the listing regime to issue a preliminary announcement. However, if a company does choose to do so, it must comply with the Listing Rules, which require that the preliminary announcement must be released as soon as it has been approved by the board. However, they do not stipulate precisely when a preliminary announcement must be released, but as the annual report for a listed company must be published within four months of the financial year-end, the preliminary results would obviously need to be announced within that period.

The preliminary announcement is one of the most important routine announcements a company makes during the year, as there is usually great interest in the company's annual performance and prospects. Under the Listing Rules, board decisions regarding dividends, profits and other matters requiring announcement should also be announced without delay once they are agreed.

The contents of the announcement must have been agreed with the auditors and must be consistent with the annual report and accounts to be published shortly thereafter. The preliminary announcement should contain, as a minimum:

■ a summary profit and loss account or statement of income with prior year comparative figures for all the above – dividend information should be included;
■ balance sheet and a cash flow statement, other financial statements along with any significant additional information necessary for assessing the results being announced.

## 7.2 Half-year reports and interim management statements

### Half-year reports

Listed companies are required by the DTRs to prepare a half-year report on the activities and profit and loss for the first six months of each financial year. The half-year report must contain, as a minimum, a table of figures containing the same items as those set out above for preliminary annual announcements. The comparative figures in this case will be those for the corresponding half-year period in the preceding financial year. The report must also include any other significant information enabling investors to make an informed assessment of the trend of the group's activities, any declaration of interim dividend and, if appropriate, a reference to the group's prospects in the current financial year.

The accounting policies and presentation applied to the half-year figures must be consistent with the latest published accounts unless they are to be changed in the subsequent annual accounts. Where this is the case, the new accounting policies and presentation should be followed. The changes and the reasons for them should be disclosed in the half-year report. The accounts must be subject to review by the auditors prior to release.

The DTRs require that the half-year report be published as soon as possible and in any event within two months of the end of the period to which it relates. After board approval, it must be published by notifying a RIS without delay. It is not necessary to send the half-year report to shareholders.

The half-year report must also include a responsibility statement made by the issuer (CA 2006, s. 1270 and DTRs) (see section 3.6).

### Interim management statements

The Disclosure and Transparency Directive requires quoted companies to produce two interim management statements during the year. The first must be issued in a period between ten weeks after the beginning and six weeks before the end of the first six months of the company's financial year. The second must be issued in a period between ten weeks after the beginning, and six weeks before the end, of the second six months of the company's financial year. As this broadly equates to a quarterly process, quoted companies which already produce quarterly results are not required to issue interim management statements.

The interim management statement is in respect of the relevant period between the beginning of the company's six-month period and the date of publication of the statement. The interim management statement must include:

■ an explanation of material events and transactions that have taken place during the relevant period and its impact on the financial position of the company;
■ a general description of the financial position and performance of the company during the period.

---

a What is the difference between the annual report and the preliminary announcement?
b What are the timing requirements in respect of the release of (i) the preliminary announcement, and (ii) the half-year report?
c What are the publication requirements in respect of the half year report?
d What are the required contents of an interim management statement? Are all companies required to release an interim management statement?

---

**STOP AND THINK** **11.4**

The preparation of the annual report and accounts requires significant input from and preparation by the company secretary. There are other types of annual reports that companies produce which also require input from the company secretary – for example, many larger organisations produce an annual report on the company's corporate responsibility performance. Although such reports may follow voluntary codes or other statutory requirements, these are not annual report and accounts within the meaning of the CA 2006 and so their content will differ. Such reports are outside the scope of this study text, however, companies' reporting on their corporate social responsibility is covered in more detail in the Corporate Governance syllabus.

# 8 Auditors

The auditor makes an independent report to a company's members as to whether its financial statements have been properly prepared in accordance with the Companies Acts. The report must also say if a company's accounts give a true and fair view of its affairs. Every company which is not exempt (see below) or dormant must appoint an auditor. Failure to appoint or reappoint auditors makes the company and all responsible officers liable to a fine. If the members fail to appoint or reappoint auditors, the company must within seven days give notice to the Secretary of State who has the power to appoint an auditor for the company if necessary.

## 8.1 Eligibility

To be eligible for appointment as a company auditor, the person or firm must be a member of a recognised supervisory body (RSB). The Act stipulates that no person may be appointed as an auditor of a company if he is an officer or employee of that company, or a partner or employee of an officer or employee of the company. Five supervising bodies are recognised as having rules designed to ensure that auditors are of the highest professional competence:

1 The Chartered Accountants Institute of England and Wales.
2 The Chartered Accountants Institute of Scotland.
3 The Chartered Accountants Institute of Ireland.
4 The Association of Chartered Certified Accountants.
5 The Association of Authorised Public Accountants.

If an auditor becomes ineligible during his term of office, he must give notice to the company in writing and vacate office immediately, together with a statement of the circumstances to be brought to the attention of the members and creditors. In these circumstances, the Secretary of State will require the company within 21 days to engage the services of someone who is eligible. That person must either:

■ audit the relevant accounts again; or
■ review the first audit and report and state whether a second audit is necessary.

## 8.2 Appointment

The directors may appoint the first auditor of the company. The auditor holds office until the end of the first meeting of the company at which its accounts are laid before the members. At that meeting the members of the company can reappoint the auditor or appoint a different auditor to hold office from the end of that meeting until the end of the next meeting at which accounts are laid.

CA 2006 abolishes the requirement for private companies to hold an AGM; thus provisions for the deemed reappointment of auditors have been included in CA 2006, s. 485. For private companies which do not hold an AGM, the auditor's period of office is deemed to run between the end of 28 days following the circulation of the annual accounts to the corresponding period in the following year. The auditor is deemed to be reappointed unless 5% of members (or such lower number as prescribed in the company's Articles) object by giving notice to the company (CA 2006, s. 488).

Directors may also appoint an auditor to fill a casual vacancy brought about by the death or resignation of a previous auditor.

## 8.3 Resignation

If an auditor wishes to resign from office he must give notice in writing to the company at its registered office (CA 2006, s. 516), together with a statement declaring whether or not there are any circumstances connected with his resignation that he considers should be brought to the attention of the members or creditors (CA 2006, s. 519). If there are no circumstances to be brought to the attention of the members, the company should file a copy of the notice, but not the statement, with the Registrar of Companies within 14 days. The directors will then fill the casual vacancy.

If the auditor does disclose circumstances that should be brought to the members' attention, a period of 21 days must elapse to allow the company or any other aggrieved person to apply to the court to restrain publication (CA 2006, ss. 520–521). If an application is to be made to the court, the court must be satisfied that the auditor is not abusing its rights to secure needless publicity for defamatory material. If no application to court is made, the auditor must file a copy of his statement with the Registrar in the following seven days.

Unless it has applied to the court for an order restraining publication, the company must send a copy of the statement to all those entitled to receive a copy of the accounts within 14 days of receipt. The auditor is then entitled to:

- circulate to members a statement of reasonable length which is not defamatory of the reasons for his resignation;
- requisition a general meeting at which he may explain the reasons for his resignation;
- attend and speak at the meeting, which must be convened within 21 days of the requisition and held within 28 days of the notice convening the meeting.

If the company is listed, auditors will be required in every instance to make a statement explaining the circumstances of their ceasing to hold office and this statement must be deposited at the company's registered office (CA 2006, s. 519).

## 8.4 Removal

If a company wishes to change its auditor, the usual procedure is to request the auditor to resign voluntarily (see section 8.3); the directors then fill the casual vacancy. The matter could be left until the existing auditor retires at the next general meeting and the meeting could then proceed not to re-appoint the existing auditor but appoint the new auditor in his place (see Sample Wording 11.3).

---

**SAMPLE WORDING 11.3**

**Resolution (company in general meeting) for removal of auditors**

THAT . . . . . . . . . . . . . . . be removed from office as auditors of the company with immediate effect [and that . . . . . . . . . . . . . . . be appointed auditors of the company in their place to hold office until the conclusion of the next general meeting at which accounts are laid before the company and that their remuneration be fixed by the directors].

---

**CHECKLIST 11.2 Removal or non-reappointment of auditor**

✓ Special notice must be given to the company of the proposed resolutions (CA 2006, s. 511) (see Sample Wording 11.4). The same procedure applies whether the proposed resolution is to remove the current auditor or to appoint any auditor other than the retiring auditor.

✓ Copies of the special notice must be sent immediately by the company to the auditor proposed for removal, the auditor to be appointed or to the auditor who is not being reappointed, as appropriate.

✓ The auditor proposed to be removed or not reappointed may make representations in writing to the company and may ask the company to circulate the representation to the shareholders (CA 2006, s. 511).

✓ The company must comply with the request, and state in the notice of meeting that the representation has been made. If it is too late to include the representation with the notice of the meeting, it must still be sent out to all shareholders who received the notice, or if it is still too late, the auditor may require the representations to be read out at the meeting.

✓ An auditor who has been removed is also entitled to receive notice of, and attend and speak at, the meeting at which the resolution for his removal or non-re-appointment is to be considered.

---

**SAMPLE WORDING 11.4**

**Form of special notice**

To: The Directors

. . . . . . . . . . . . . . . Limited/plc . . . . . . . . . . . . . . . [Date]

I give notice under sections 510 and 511 Companies Act 2006 of my intention to move the following ordinary resolution at the next annual general meeting of the company:

RESOLUTION
[Set out text of appropriate resolution, e.g. Sample Wording 11.3 (resolution for removal of auditors)]

(Signed) . . . . . . . . . . . . . . .

*Note*
The notice of the relevant general meeting should make reference to receipt of the special notice, e.g.:

To consider the following resolution, special notice having been received of the intention to propose the resolution as an ordinary resolution:

RESOLUTION
[Set out text of resolution.]

### Procedure where auditors are removed or not reappointed

If the need for a change of auditor is more pressing, the company may, by ordinary resolution, remove an auditor before his retirement. The vacancy arising from the removal is usually filled by the company in general meeting, but it may also be filled by the directors. Notice of the removal should be given to the Registrar on form AA03.

## 8.5 Remuneration

The remuneration of auditors, including expenses, is fixed by the company in general meeting. In practice it is usual for the meeting to give authority to the directors to fix the remuneration of the auditors. This resolution is often combined with the resolution reappointing the auditors for the coming year.

The amount of remuneration and expenses must be stated in a note to the company's annual accounts (CA 2006, s. 494). Companies are also required to disclose any remuneration received by an auditor for non-audit services, such as financial or taxation services. All the regulations apply to benefits in kind as well as to payments in cash; where there are any such benefits, their nature and their monetary value must be disclosed. Payments to auditors for non-audit fees have become an increasingly important aspect of corporate governance following the accounting scandals in Enron and WorldCom. The UK government, shareholders and corporate governance institutions became concerned that where the auditor of a company also performs a substantial amount of non-audit work for that company, his independence and objectivity could be compromised. Additional disclosure is therefore required by the company on the fees payable to the auditor and on the processes which are used to ensure that the auditor's independence and objectivity are not compromised. CA 2006, ss. 493–494 contain provisions which give the Secretary of State authority to require companies to disclose additional information regarding the terms of an auditor's engagement, remuneration, performance of duties and provision of non-audit services to the company.

## 8.6 Rights, duties and liabilities

The primary duty of the auditor is to report to the members on the statutory accounts of the company, copies of which are to be laid before the company in general meeting. Sometimes it may be necessary for the auditor to report on more than one set of accounts if they have been produced late, or if the company has shortened its accounting period. In the case of private companies electing to dispense with the annual appointment of auditors, the auditor will be required to report on accounts sent to the members and others during his term of office.

The auditor is in a contractual relationship with the company, which implies an obligation to perform work with skill and care. A similar duty is owed in tort as well as an obligation to comply with statutory duties.

Other functions include:

- reporting on non-disclosure of information regarding directors' and employees' emoluments and substantial contracts with directors or loans to directors;
- considering whether the information given in the directors' report is consistent with the corresponding accounts;
- auditing interim accounts;
- making statements in connection with the re-registration of a private company as a public company (see Chapter 4);
- reporting in connection with a private company purchasing its own shares;
- giving a statement of opinion in a summary financial statement (see section 4) considering the consistency of the summary statement with the annual report and account and auditors' reports;
- giving an audit opinion in respect of certain parts of the directors' remuneration report which listed companies are required to produce (see section 6.5).

### The rights of the auditor

When the auditor is preparing his report he must carry out whatever investigations are appropriate to state whether proper accounting records have been maintained and confirm that the company's accounts are in agreement with those records. If this is not the case, the auditor must state this in his report. It is an offence for any officer of a company to give false information or explanations, or to make a statement that he knows to be misleading or deceptive when questioned by the auditor (CA 2006, s. 501).

The auditor has certain statutory rights of access to the information he needs to carry out his duties. These include:

- a right of access at all times to the company's books, accounts and vouchers and to ask the directors and officers for information or explanations as he deems necessary to perform his duties (CA 2006, s. 499);
- entitlement to attend any general meetings and to receive all notices and other communications relating to general meetings, at which he may also speak if there are any matters concerning him as auditor. For private limited companies, the auditor is also entitled to receive copies of any proposed shareholder written resolutions together with applicable supporting documentation (CA 2006, s. 502);
- subsidiaries of companies incorporated in Great Britain must give the auditor any information or explanations he requires to perform his duties in respect of the parent company;
- in the case of a parent company with a subsidiary incorporated outside Great Britain, the parent company must obtain any information or explanations requested by the auditor that he deems reasonable.

## Rights of the auditor under the Companies (Audit, Investigations and Community Enterprise) Act 2004

Following the Enron and WorldCom scandals, the Companies (Audit, Investigations and Community Enterprise) Act was enacted in 2004 in order to increase the powers of auditors and improve the quality of financial reporting. These powers have been incorporated into CA 2006. Key points relating to the preparation and production of accounts are:

- auditors have power to request information from a director or employee and it is a criminal offence not to cooperate with auditors or to supply them with misleading information;
- directors are required to certify that they have not withheld any relevant information from the auditors of the company; and that the accounts do not contain any untrue or misleading information;
- the Financial Reporting Review Panel has power to review accounting practices;
- audit firms are subject to professional standards and codes of conduct;
- the BIS has power to investigate companies and to require access to company premises to aid investigations.

## Liabilities of the auditor

Auditors are required to act honestly and with reasonable care and skill in discharging their duties. An auditor is liable to the company for any loss resulting from negligence or default in the performance of his duties, although the court may grant relief in certain circumstances (e.g. where the auditor has acted honestly and reasonably).

If proper accounting records have not been kept or the books do not reflect the true position, the auditor must state this.

An auditor's liability is unlimited. This has led to concerns that an audit firm could go out of business were it to be found liable in a court, which could lead to reduced competition in the marketplace, particularly among the larger audit firms. CA 2006, ss. 534–538, therefore, provide that the liability of auditors may be limited. Any such limitation would need the approval of the company and its shareholders by way of ordinary resolution. The details of the limitation would be set out in a liability limitation agreement, which can reduce the extent of liability to no less than such an amount which is fair and reasonable taking into account the auditor's responsibilities and contractual obligations and the professional standards expected of him.

The liability limitation agreement must be disclosed in the annual report and accounts of the company and the agreement will be in relation to the acts or omissions of the auditor for the relevant financial year. Shareholders have the right to revoke the agreement by ordinary resolution. This will have the effect of removing the limitation of liability for any acts or omissions following the date of revocation.

CA 2006, s. 507 introduces two new offences for auditors:

1 knowingly or recklessly causing an auditor's report to include misleading or deceptive information;
2 knowingly or recklessly omitting information in the auditor's report which is required by CA 2006.

### Shareholder rights to raise audit issues

CA 2006, s. 527 provides shareholders of a quoted company the right to have a statement placed on the company's website ahead of a general meeting at which the accounts are to be considered. The statement shall be in relation to the audit of the accounts or any issue surrounding an auditor who has ceased to hold office. In order for the statement to be placed on the company's website, it must be requisitioned by members representing at least 5% of the total voting rights or by 100 members holding paid up shares on average sum per member of not less than £100.

## 8.7 The auditor's report

Each set of accounts which is required to be audited must contain a report from the auditors (CA 2006, s. 495), which must contain the following statements:

- That, in the opinion of the auditors, the annual accounts have been prepared in accordance with CA 2006.
- That a true and fair view has been given in respect of:
  - the balance sheet, the state of affairs of the company as at the end of the financial year;
  - the profit and loss account of the company for the financial year;
  - for group accounts, the state of affairs of the group as at the end of the financial year, the profit and loss for the financial year, and the undertakings included in the consolidation as a whole so far as concerns the members.

The auditor's report must include the names and signatures of the auditors. The copy of the accounts submitted to Companies House must have the auditor's report signed by the auditor (see section 3.5). If the auditor is a firm, the name and signature of the senior statutory auditor must appear in the auditors' report on behalf of the firm (CA 2006, s. 504).

## 8.8 Audit exemptions

### Small companies

Private companies with a turnover of £6.5 million or less and having a balance sheet total of no more than £3.26 million are exempt from the requirement for an annual audit provided that the company has not during the year been:

- registered as a plc;
- a parent company or a subsidiary;
- subject to the regulatory regimes specified in CA 2006, s. 478 such as banking and insurance companies, registered insurance brokers, FSA-authorised persons or appointed representatives, trade unions or employers' associations.

Becoming exempt from the audit requirement does not automatically terminate the appointment of existing auditors, but it is reasonable to ask the existing auditors to resign. If a company loses its exemption – for example, it grows beyond the turnover threshold or becomes part of a group – the directors may appoint auditors at any time prior to the next general meeting at which the accounts are to be laid before the members. The auditors will hold office until the conclusion of that general meeting.

Even if a company meets the audit exemption requirements, it is necessary to bear in mind that the purpose of auditors is to provide some measure of reassurance to members that the accounts are a true and fair reflection of the business. For this reason, CA 2006, s. 476 provides that any member or members holding at least 10% of the nominal value may, by notice in writing deposited at the registered office of the company no later than one month before the end of the current financial year, require the company to obtain an audit of its accounts for that year.

In accordance with
Section 512 of the
Companies Act 2006.

# AA03

## Notice of resolution removing auditors from office

Companies House
*for the record*

| ✓ **What this form is for**<br>You may use this form to give notice of a resolution removing an auditor. | ✗ **What this form is NOT for**<br>You cannot use this form to give notice that an auditor has resigned. | For further information, please refer to our guidance at www.companieshouse.gov.uk |

### 1   Company details

| | |
|---|---|
| Company number | |
| Company name in full | |

→ **Filling in this form**
Please complete in typescript or in bold black capitals.

All fields are mandatory unless specified or indicated by *

### 2   Date of resolution *

Date of resolution   d d m m y y y y

### 3   Auditor's details *

| | |
|---|---|
| Firm/Partnership/Individual removed from office | |
| Building name/number | |
| Street | |
| Post town | |
| County/Region | |
| Post code | |
| Country | |

### 4   Date of removal *

Date of removal   d d m m y y y y

### 5   Signature

Signature   X   X

This form may be signed by:
Director ❶, Secretary, Person authorised ❷, Administrator, Administrative receiver, Receiver, Receiver manager, Charity Commission receiver and manager, CIC manager.

❶ **Societas Europaea**
If the form is being filed on behalf of a Societas Europaea (SE) please delete 'director' and insert details of which organ of the SE the person signing has membership.

❷ **Person authorised**
Under either section 270 or 274 of the Companies Act 2006.

**BIS** | Department for Business
Innovation & Skills

CHFP000
05/10 Version 4.0

## Audit exempt companies: filing requirements

Unaudited accounts may be delivered to the Registrar in the form of an abbreviated balance sheet and notes containing the following statements above the director's signature:

1 For the year ended [date] the company was entitled to exemption under CA 2006, s. 477.
2 Members have not required the company to obtain an audit in accordance with CA 2006, s. 476.
3 The directors acknowledge their responsibility for:
   a) ensuring the company keeps accounting records which comply with CA 2006, s. 386; and
   b) preparing accounts which give a true and fair view of the state of affairs of the company as at the end of the financial year, and of its profit or loss for the financial year, in accordance with the requirements of CA 2006, ss. 394–396, and which otherwise comply with the requirements of the Companies Act relating to accounts, so far as applicable to the company.
4 The accounts have been prepared in accordance with the special provisions of the CA relating to small companies.

If the company chooses, it may deliver the unabbreviated accounts prepared for its members. The same statements must appear on the unabbreviated balance sheet.

## Dormant companies

Dormant companies must deliver accounts and all other required returns to the Registrar. Under CA 2006, s. 480 they automatically qualify for audit exemption provided they have no significant accounting transactions during the year (i.e. transactions that should be entered into the company's accounting records). If this is the case, the company needs only prepare and deliver an abbreviated balance sheet and notes to the Registrar.

The following transactions are not regarded as significant transactions, and will not affect a company's claim for dormant status:

■ payment for shares taken by the subscribers to the Memorandum and Articles of Association;
■ fees paid to the Registrar of Companies;
■ civil penalties imposed by the Registrar (e.g. late filing penalties);
■ attending to statutory matters (e.g. an amendment to the Articles of Association, change in registered office, or a change in director).

Any other transactions which are entered into the company's accounting records, such as bank/interest charges, will disqualify the company from claiming dormant status. If a company ceases to be dormant, subject to other possible audit exemptions, it will need to appoint auditors again.

Companies House form AA02 reduces the administrative burden of preparing accounts for dormant companies by providing spaces for balance sheet entries and a special declaration by the directors which confirms:

■ the directors' responsibility for preparing accounts;
■ that the company qualified as dormant for the period.

Dormant companies may be required for a variety of reasons – for example, to protect a trading name (see Chapter 4). The duty of a director in managing a dormant company is therefore no less than the duty for managing a trading company in that accounts and any other returns must be filed on time. A company can remain dormant for any length of time, provided the necessary returns and payments are sent to the Registrar. However, it may be voluntarily dissolved if there appears to have no purpose. A dormant company cannot be struck off or dissolved simply because it is not trading (see Chapter 7).

In accordance with
Section 444 and 448 of
the Companies Act 2006.

# AA02
## Dormant company accounts (DCA)

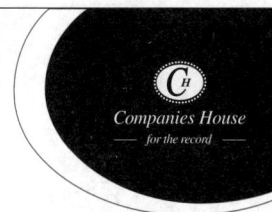

Companies House
*for the record*

**You can use the WebFiling service to file dormant company accounts online.**
Please go to www.companieshouse.gov.uk

✓ **What this is for**
You may use the AA02 'Dormant company accounts' (DCA) for accounting periods beginning on or **after** 6th April 2008. Please read the guidance in Section 6 before completion.

✗ **What this is NOT for**
You cannot use the AA02 if the accounting period begins before 6th April 2008.

For further information, please refer to our guidance at www.companieshouse.gov.uk

---

**1**    **Company details**

Company number

Company name in full

→ **Filling in the DCA**
Please complete in typescript or in bold black capitals.

All fields are mandatory unless specified or indicated by *

---

**2**    **Date of balance sheet**

Date of balance sheet     | d | d | | m | m | | y | y | y | y |

---

**3**    **Accounts**

| | Current Year | Previous Year |
|---|---|---|
| Called up share capital not paid | £ | £ |
| Cash at bank and in hand | £ | £ |
| **Net assets** | £ | £ |

**Issued share capital**

Ordinary shares [        ] of [ £        ] each

| | | |
|---|---|---|
| Shareholders' fund | £ | £ |

---

**Statements**

For the below year ending the company was entitled to exemption from audit under section 480 of the Companies Act 2006 relating to dormant companies.

For the year ending     | d | d | | m | m | | y | y | y | y |

Director's responsibilities:
- The members have not required the company to obtain an audit of its accounts for the year in question in accordance with section 476.
- The directors acknowledge their responsibilities for complying with the requirements of the Act with respect to accounting periods and the preparation of accounts.

These accounts have been prepared in accordance with the provision applicable to companies subject to small companies' regime.

☐ Please tick the box if during the year the company acted as an agent for a person.

---

**BIS** | **Department for Business Innovation & Skills**

CHFP000
05/10 Version 4.0

---

TEST YOUR KNOWLEDGE **11.5**

**a** What is the procedure when an auditor resigns?

**b** Who is responsible for the appointment and reappointment of auditors?

**c** What is the procedure for the deemed reappointment of an auditor where a private company does not hold annual general meetings?

**d** When is the remuneration of auditors fixed? Who fixes their remuneration?

**e** What rights must be granted to an auditor?

**f** What criteria must a company meet in order to be exempt from audit?

**g** Can members of an audit-exempt company require it to have its accounts audited?

**h** What sort of company might use form AA02? Why might it be useful?

---

## CHAPTER SUMMARY

- A company is required to keep and regularly publish proper accounts showing its assets and liabilities. Auditors have the right of access to the accounting records, but there is no statutory right for the general public to do so. The directors are liable to penalties for failure to keep accounts.

- Accounts should be laid before a general meeting (for public companies and private companies opting to continue to hold AGMs) and delivered to the Registrar of Companies within six months of the end of the financial year end for a public company and nine months for a private company. Listed companies must publish their annual accounts within four months the financial year-end. Listed companies have the option of issuing preliminary annual results and must issue half-year reports and interim management statements.

- All limited companies, including dormant companies, must deliver signed accounts to the Registrar. Limited companies which qualify as small or medium-sized may file abbreviated accounts.

- The accounts usually must include a directors' report, which should include principal activities, a business review, an indication of likely future developments, results and dividend, and names of directors at any time during the year. If the company is listed, the chairman and members of the audit, remuneration and nomination committees should be included.

- Listed companies have additional obligations arising from the Listing Rules and the DTRs, principally the requirement to publish a statement of how the company has applied the principles of good governance from the UK Corporate Governance Code, together with an explanation where the principles have not been applied and why. In addition, listed companies should include a statement that the business is a going concern, and must also produce a directors' remuneration report with their accounts.

- Auditors are appointed annually, unless the company is private and does not need to hold AGMs. Auditors should be suitably qualified.

- An auditor's primary responsibility is to report to the members on whether he considers the company accounts have been prepared in accordance with applicable legislation and are a true and fair view of the business over the period.

- The auditor's report must state that the balance sheet and profit and loss account represent a true and fair view of the company's state of affairs.

- Private companies may be exempt from the requirement for an annual audit provided they meet the exemption requirements. Instead, they may file an abbreviated balance sheet and statements from the directors acknowledging their responsibility for keeping accounting records and preparing accounts. Dormant companies are generally exempt from auditing requirements.

# PART 3 PRACTICE CASE QUESTIONS

These questions are based on the case scenario outlined at the beginning of Part Three. You will need to refer to content throughout Part Three to provide the answers. Note that some questions may also include material covered in Parts One and Two of this study text.

## PART CASE QUESTION 3.1

The Finance Director of Multiple plc has asked you to assist him in advance of the board meeting which will consider the company's annual report and accounts. You have agreed to prepare the following:

■ a note detailing which sections of the annual report and accounts will require to be signed and by whom, together with the appropriate filing requirements. The note should also describe the CA requirements with regard to the entitlement to receive copies of the annual report and accounts; and

■ a short note on the purpose and requirements of producing the directors' report within the annual report and accounts. This will include a checklist of the typical subject headings found in the directors' report section of a listed company's annual report and accounts.

Prepare the matters requested above.

## PART CASE QUESTION 3.2

Today is the day of the AGM for Multiple plc, which was due to start at 10.00 am in the Grand Hall. A number of complications arise at the meeting:

Due to traffic congestion only one shareholder, Ms Timely, arrived on time. She notes that she was the only shareholder present for ten minutes after the meeting was due to start, before other shareholders arrived. Ms Timely also notes that the chairman has not arrived, despite the fact that the meeting should have started ten minutes ago. Ms Timely queries whether the meeting can still proceed, given the delay of the shareholders and of the chairman, and asks for an explanation of the provisions in the company's Articles regarding the situation.

The meeting eventually starts following the arrival of the chairman of the meeting. Mr Moan, who is a joint shareholder with his wife, claims that the meeting is invalid as he did not receive his copy of the AGM notice. Mr Moan states that the only reason he knew of the meeting is because a friend mentioned it to him yesterday. The chairman has given Mr Moan assurances that the notice was posted to all shareholders over a month ago and that the meeting is valid. Mr Moan asks what the circumstances are under which the company can claim that the meeting is indeed invalid given his apparent non-receipt of notice.

Due to recent flooding, only half of the Grand Hall is available for use. The chairman realises that the remaining space is inadequate as several shareholders are outside the meeting unable to enter. The chairman asks you if he has the power to adjourn the meeting, and if so, whether he could adjourn the meeting to 3.00 pm the same day to the Royal Hotel, which is nearby.

Provide the advice as requested above.

## PART CASE QUESTION 3.3

It is now a few weeks later and you are at a board meeting of Multiple plc. There are a couple of items in particular which require resolving:

First, the remuneration committee has recommended that the proposed new CEO be appointed with a six-year fixed-term service contract; in this way they believe stability in the top management can be achieved. As the committee believes that many shareholders will not approve of such a long service contract, the committee proposes to keep the matter confidential. The finance director is unhappy with both the length of the service contract and the committee's plan to keep matters quiet and has queried whether there are any CA or Listing Rules requirements with regards to the approval, disclosure and inspection of the proposed service contract.

Second, the matter of how to deal with an apparent equal split of directors' votes with regard to a new project with New Street Consultants Ltd has arisen. The finance director supports the project and claims that two of the NEDs, who are absent from the meeting, have appointed him as their alternate. One of the alternate appointments is in writing whilst the other, according to the finance director, was made during a telephone conversation with the absent NED half an hour before the start of the meeting. The chairman claims that it is 'one man one vote' and in any case does not believe that either alternate appointment is valid. The chairman, who is against the new project, has also accused the chief executive of wishing to vote in favour because he has a substantial shareholding in New Street Consultants Ltd. The chairman claims that if the matter is deadlocked by votes, the board's only choice is to continue discussing the matter until at least one director changes their decision.

The chairman has threatened to resign if all the directors do not stop their constant disagreements. All the other directors, with the exception of the director of human resources, have stated that if the chairman resigns they too will resign as shareholder confidence in the company would collapse.

Provide advice to the following:

a) the finance director in respect of the specific queries raised on the proposed new chief executive's service contract;

b) the chairman on (i) the validity of the votes already cast; (ii) the validity of the alternate appointments and their voting entitlement; and (iii) the remedies available to him under the Company's Articles on the event of a voting deadlock; and

c) the director of human resources on the constitutional problems if he was left as the sole director of the company and the options that would be available to him.

# Shares

## ■ LIST OF CHAPTERS

## ■ OVERVIEW

This final part covers the detailed work of the secretary as registrar and as an administrator of employee share schemes.

Chapter 12 looks at shares and share capital, including allotment of shares and capital events, such as alteration of share capital and redemption and purchase of own shares.

We have already seen that the register of members is a statutory document which must be kept up to date, reflecting the changes brought about by transfer and transmission of shares, corporate capital events or changes in personal circumstances of the shareholders. Chapter 13 reviews the procedures and best practice involved in implementing changes to the register, emphasising the importance of checking the accuracy of documents being presented.

Chapter 14 summarises the statutory position on dividends and the procedures associated with paying dividends.

Finally, Chapter 15 reviews the main types of employee share schemes and the role of the secretary in establishing and administering such schemes.

## ■ LEARNING OUTCOMES

After reading and understanding Part Four, you should be able to:

- Explain the different classes of shares.
- Understand the procedure and regulation on allotment and issue of shares, and the procedure and regulation for altering capital.
- Apply the procedure and regulation on transfer and transmission of shares, and maintenance of the register of members.
- Demonstrate the procedures for registering documents relating to shares and members.
- Understand the purpose and application of the CREST system.
- Explain the statutory provisions in respect of dividend payments, including the relevant Model Articles and the role of the external registrar.

- Apply the procedures required to pay a dividend, including the format and content of the dividend warrant and tax voucher and supporting arrangements such as mandates and the Bankers' Automated Clearing System (BACS).
- Know what is required if the board resolves to offer scrip or dividend reinvestment plan (DRIP) dividends.
- Explain the different types of employee share scheme available and the tax implications.
- Be able to assist in establishing and administering an employee share scheme.
- Understand the advantages and disadvantages for employers of running an employee share scheme.
- Recognise the additional requirements for employee share schemes in listed companies.

# PART 4 CASE STUDY

As Multiple plc becomes larger, volume of share-related transactions will increase; this relates not only to transfers of existing shares but also the allotment of new shares. Discussions at recent board meetings have focused on issuing shares to finance the acquisition of new business opportunities and also creating employee share schemes to continue motivating employees to perform well. The company is also keen to reward its shareholders for investing in the company and is looking at ways of adding more facilities to the dividends it pays to shareholders. As company secretary of Multiple plc you are aware that all of these matters will require the contribution of your department in order to help the company move forward in achieving its targets.

As Multiple plc is listed on the London Stock Exchange, you have outsourced maintenance of the share register for the listed company to Accurate Registrars Limited. The share registers in respect of the subsidiary companies of Multiple plc are managed internally by your direct reports. In order to ensure the best possible service to the shareholders of Multiple plc you hold frequent meetings with Accurate Registrars to ensure a high standard of service is maintained.

# Shares and share capital

■ **CONTENTS**

■ **INTRODUCTION**

This chapter outlines the financial structure of a company in relation to share capital and the secretary's responsibility for ensuring the correct procedures are followed for the issue and allotment of shares. The regulations here are particularly important for listed companies. We also look at the alteration of share capital, including the treatment of treasury shares.

This chapter covers the changes in the procedures concerning share capital brought about by CA 2006.

## 1 Introduction to shares and capital

Every company limited by shares needs to decide how the share capital of the company will be divided. It is left to the company to decide what rights will attach to its shares.

### 1.1 Classes of share and share rights

A share is defined as:

> 'a fixed and indivisible section of the capital of a company, a part allotted or owned, a division, section or portion'.

Some companies have more than one class of share. If a company does have more than one class, it is good practice to set out the different classes with their respective rights in the Articles of Association. The rights attaching to shares typically relate to voting rights and rights to receive dividends or capital and whether shares can be redeemed.

In more detail, the various classes of shares include:

■ *Ordinary shares* – If a company has only one class of share, they are de facto ordinary shares. Ordinary shares rank after preference shares (see below) for the purposes of dividends and return of capital, but carry voting rights not normally given to holders of preference shares. These are the company's risk capital and the directors must decide whether to declare a dividend to be paid out of the **distributable profits**. Ordinary shareholders stand to gain or lose the most on a winding up, depending on the surplus assets available. It is now not uncommon for companies to divide their ordinary shares into 'A' and 'B' ordinary shares with different rights attached to each.

■ *Preference shares* – Typically these carry a preferential right to a fixed dividend and usually rank higher in priority than other classes of shares in a winding up. If a company has a distributable profit, a dividend may be paid on preference shares. The fixed rate of dividend is often expressed as a percentage and is deemed to be **cumulative**, unless stated otherwise. This means that, should a company fail to pay the dividend, it will accrue to the shareholder and become payable, together with the next dividend due, at the next payment date. Preference shares may have restricted voting rights and usually carry no further right to participate in profits beyond the applicable dividend rate.

- **Redeemable shares** – Under Model Article 22 (public company Model Article 43), a limited company may issue shares which can be redeemed by the company at their nominal or par value at some stated date in the future. CA 2006 s.684 provides that private companies are able to issue redeemable shares unless their articles provide otherwise, whereas public companies must have authorisation in their articles. At the time of issue, there must also be shares in issue which are not redeemable to avoid the possibility of the entire issued share capital being redeemed, leaving the company with no shareholders. The actual amount of repayment will be the nominal value regardless of the market value. Redeemable shares offer a certain amount of protection to the investor, and companies might welcome them because the investor will not stay with the company forever. Once there are sufficient distributable profits, the redeemable shares may be redeemed and control of the company can revert to those who controlled the company before the investor joined.

- *Debentures and loan stocks* – **debentures** are effectively loans to the company by investors who receive interest, usually at a fixed rate. These are not strictly a class of share, but are frequently referred to when looking at a company's financial structure. Debentures are secured loans on the assets of the company and rank ahead of the payment of dividends on both preference and ordinary shares. Interest on debentures must be paid even if the company does not have sufficient distributable reserves; failure to pay may lead to an event of default. Debentures also rank ahead in repayment of capital in a liquidation. Debentures do not carry voting rights.

- *Founder shares* – **Founder shares** are sometimes issued to the founders or promoters of a company and usually carry enhanced rights over other classes of share. For example, founder shares can have proportionately increased voting rights and an entitlement to surplus profits over a specified level.

- *Deferred shares* – **Deferred shares** commonly carry very few rights. As their rights are deferred to the ordinary shares, they usually carry no right to vote or participate in a distribution. They usually have the right of repayment of their capital value in a winding up.

CA 2006 provides certain default share rights. Section 285 states that, subject to any specific rights or restrictions which may apply, every member who is present in person, or any corporation that is represented in person at a general meeting, is entitled to one vote on a show of hands (or one vote in respect of a written resolution for a private limited company), and one vote for every share held in the case of a poll. Public company Model Article 71 provides that all dividends should be declared and paid pro rata to the amounts paid up on the shares (this provision does not apply to private company Model Articles, which envisage that all shares will be fully paid up).

CA 2006, s. 630 provides that class rights may be varied either in accordance with the provisions set out in the Articles of Association or where the Articles contain no such provisions, by special resolution. A written resolution is permissible for private companies. CA 2006, s. 637 requires the Registrar to be supplied with particulars of the variation within one month of the variation. CA 2006, s. 633 allows the right of class members to object to a variation. Holders of not less than 15% of the issued shares of the particular class (provided they did not support the resolution) may apply to the court to have a variation cancelled. The application must be made within 21 days of the resolution being passed and any variation cannot come into effect until the court has made its ruling. The court will consider whether the variation would unfairly prejudice the shareholders of that class and then make its ruling, a copy of which must be filed by the company with the Registrar within 15 days. It is also possible to protect class rights from variation by utilising the 'entrenchment' provisions of CA 2006, s. 22 (see Chapter 5).

## Warrants

A **warrant** is a document entitling the holder to subscribe for equity capital of a company at some future date(s) at a price determined at the time the warrant is issued. A warrant should not be confused with a share warrant to bearer, which is a document evidencing title to shares which have already been issued (see Chapter 3). Warrants may be listed and traded on the London Stock Exchange and in practically all cases are registered in the same way as shares, although they do not constitute a part of the company's share or loan capital, and no dividends or interest is payable.

Warrants may be issued only if the Articles allow it and a register of warrant holders may be maintained in a similar way to the register of members (see Chapter 8). As there are no statutory provisions governing warrants, the procedures regarding transactions, such as transfer, inspection of register, requests for copies of the register and the despatch of the annual report and accounts to warrant holders, need to be included in the terms of issue of warrants. Transfers of warrants are subject to stamp duty in the same way as transfers of shares (see below).

## 1.2 Capital

### Issued capital

Issued capital is the company's total capital which has been issued and taken up by the members. It is expressed in terms of its nominal rather than actual value. For example, a company which issues 250 shares, has an issued share capital of £250 (i.e. 250 shares × £1), if they are fully paid.

### Paid up capital

Shares are not always paid for in full at the time they are taken up. In the example above, the company could issue 250 shares where payment is due in two equal parts. This would mean its **paid up capital** is £125 (i.e. 250 shares × 50p), with the balance due at some point in the future.

### Share premiums

A **share premium** is the difference between the issue price of a share and its nominal value. For example, if the nominal value of a share is £1 and it is issued for £1.50, the premium is 50p. When a company states its share capital, only the nominal amount of the shares is included. The amount of any share premium is credited to a share premium account (CA 2006, s. 610), the use of which is restricted to:

- paying up unissued shares to be allotted to members as fully paid shares;
- writing off the expenses and/or commissions paid by the company on an issue of those shares.

The share premium account is treated as paid up share capital of the company.

### Nominal value

Issued shares are ascribed a nominal or par value. However, once a company has begun trading, the actual value of the shares will vary according to the company's performance and demand for the shares, the nominal value does not change. The nominal value of a share may therefore not be representative of its true value.

**TEST YOUR KNOWLEDGE 12.1**

a What are the main classes of shares?
b Are there any limits to the number of shares which a company may issue?
c How is a share premium calculated? What are the possible uses of a company's share premium?

# 2 Allotment of shares

The CA states that:

'shares in a company are taken to be allotted when a person acquires the unconditional right to be included in the company's register of members in respect of the shares'.

Allotment takes place formally when authority to enter the name of the allottee in the register of members is given. This follows the formal resolution by the directors to allot shares. The term 'issue' is not defined by statute, but is used to cover the process where new shares pass to a shareholder. In practice, the two words are often used interchangeably, with no real distinction being made.

It is common practice for the power of allotment to be delegated by ordinary resolution to the directors or to incorporate that power into the Articles of Association.

## 2.1 Procedure prior to allotment

The allotment of shares has to be carefully planned and managed. The following is a summary of the procedure:

- check the directors are authorised to allot the shares;
- check that the allotment is in proportion to members' existing holdings;
- send allotment application forms to those applying for shares;
- process allotment application forms and payments for shares;
- board resolves to allot shares;
- send out share certificates;
- file forms at Companies House (e.g. form SH01).

In further detail, the company secretary should follow these main points of procedure.

### Authority to allot shares

Check that the directors are authorised to allot shares (CA 2006, ss. 549 and 551). If they are not, pass the appropriate resolution(s) at a general meeting (see Sample Wording 12.1). The authority must state the maximum number of shares which may be allotted and the date on which the authority will expire, which must be not more than five years from the date of incorporation of the company or the date on which the relevant resolution is passed.

The authority is usually given by ordinary resolution. Any resolution renewing an earlier authority must specify an expiry date within five years of the date of the renewal resolution and state the amount of securities that may be allotted (or the amount remaining to be allotted). If the company is likely to make frequent allotments, the company secretary should consider proposing to the directors to add a resolution at each AGM giving directors authority to allot shares.

A copy of any resolutions giving authority to allot must be filed with the Registrar (CA 2006, s. 30) and should be attached to any copies of the Memorandum and Articles.

---

**SAMPLE WORDING 12.1**

**Resolution giving directors authority to allot shares**

THAT with effect from the time of the passing of this resolution the directors be unconditionally authorised, pursuant to sections 549 and 551, Companies Act 2006, to allot relevant securities (as defined in that Act) up to a maximum amount of £ XXXX [in accordance with the provisions of Article XX of the Articles of Association of the company] at any time or times during the period of five years from the date hereof and at any time thereafter pursuant to any offer or agreement made by the company before the expiry of this authority.

---

## Pre-emption rights

It is common for the Articles to provide that if new shares are to be issued, they must be offered to existing shareholders first, in proportion to their existing holdings. This can be done by:

- a provisional allotment letter (see Sample Wording 12.4) in which the shareholder is informed that shares have been provisionally allotted to the shareholder; or
- a letter of rights which invites the shareholder to apply for a specified number of shares.

If the company is listed, UKLA requires that any new issues of shares for cash should first be offered to existing holders as a **rights issue** (see section 3). If there is no provision in the Articles, CA 2006, s. 561 provides pre-emption rights for existing shareholders in proportion to their existing holdings, including holders under employee share schemes.

## Disapplication of pre-emption rights

A private company may disapply pre-emption rights permanently by its Articles (CA 2006, s. 561). In addition, for private companies with only one class of share, there is no time limit on the authorities to allot under CA 2006, s.550 and hence there is no expiration limit for disapplication of pre-emption rights for such companies.

Private and public companies can disapply pre-emption rights for a specific allotment provided:

- the company passes a special resolution; and
- the directors give a statement which accompanies the notice of the meeting to propose the special resolution in which they give:
  - the reasons for making the recommendation,
  - the amount to be paid to the company in respect of the allotment,
  - the directors' justification of that amount.

If the company is listed, the time limit on the disapplication is six months after the date of the financial year end or until the next AGM, whichever is earlier.

## Expected consideration

Take into account the consideration (payment) the company expects to receive for the allotment, especially any special arrangements for non-cash consideration (see section 2.3).

## Application form

Once the matters described above have been dealt with, a standard application form should be prepared for distribution (see Sample Wording 12.2).

---

**SAMPLE WORDING 12.2**

**Form of application for shares (suitable for a private company)**

To the Directors, . . . . . . . . . . . . Limited

I enclose a cheque for £100, being payment in full for 100 shares of £1 each in . . . . . . . . . . . . Limited, and I hereby apply for and request you to allot such shares to me. I agree to take the said shares subject to the constitution of the company and I authorise you to enter my name in the register of members as the holder of the said shares. Dated this . . . . . . day of . . . . . . . 20xx.

Signature:

. . . . . . . . . . . . . . . . . . . . . . .

Name in full:

. . . . . . . . . . . . . . . . . . . . . . .

Address:

. . . . . . . . . . . . . . . . . . . . . . . . . . . . . . . . . . . . . . . .

---

> **STOP AND THINK 12.1**
>
> For smaller private companies, especially where the shareholders and the directors are the same people, it is possible to arrange the allotment of shares on a single day. This may be appropriate when the directors/shareholders have already informally agreed to the transaction or when the allotment of shares is required urgently (e.g. to provide additional capital to the business). The process involves:
>
> - convening a board meeting where the board will consider a form of application of shares already prepared by the shareholders;
> - if necessary, convening a general meeting at short notice to abolish the authorised share capital and/or to give the directors authority to allot shares;
> - the receipt by the board of a consent to short notice by the shareholders;
> - adjourning the board meeting to hold the general meeting;
> - holding the general meeting to pass the necessary resolutions;
> - reconvening the board meeting to note the resolutions just passed at the general meeting and for the board to resolve the allotment of the shares.
>
> This process cannot be used for large or listed companies. Under CA 2006, private companies may use written resolutions instead of the general meeting and (if allowed by the Articles) instead of the board meeting as well.

### Listed companies

Listed companies are required to send shareholders an explanation in connection with a resolution proposing to grant the directors authority to allot shares which must include:

- a statement of the maximum amount of shares that the directors will have authority to allot and the percentage that amount represents of the issued share capital;
- a statement by the directors as to whether they have any present intention to exercise the authority and, if so, to what purpose;
- a statement as to when the authority will lapse.

It is common for listed companies to pass a special resolution as part of the routine business at the AGM to disapply pre-emption rights up to a specified limit. However, listed companies must recognise the pre-emption guidelines of institutional shareholders such as those published by ABI and NAPF. These guidelines recommend that:

- a resolution be passed for annual disapplication of pre-emption rights, not exceeding 5% of issued share capital;
- no more than 7.5% of issued share capital may be subject to disapplication of pre-emption rights within any rolling three year period.

## 2.2 Allotment procedure

1  On receipt of the completed application form and remittance, share certificates (see Chapter 13) should be prepared.
2  The board should pass a resolution to allot the shares and to authorise the issue of share certificates (see Sample Wording 12.3). The resolution should be passed as soon as possible since, until the application is accepted by notification of allotment to the applicant, he is free to withdraw the application.
3  The share certificate should be sent to the applicant with formal notification of the allotment. All letters of allotment must be posted simultaneously, and for listed companies, letters of allotment should be serially numbered and initialled by a responsible official.
4  The necessary entries should be made in the register of members.
5  A return of allotments (on form SH01) should be filed with the Registrar within one month of the date of allotment. CA 2006, s. 554 requires a company to register an allotment of shares as soon as practicable and in any event within two months after the date of the allotment.

Shares allotted may be paid up in money or in money's worth, including goodwill and know-how, but a public company may not accept services to the company as payment.

In accordance with
Section 555 of the
Companies Act 2006.

# SH01
## Return of allotment of shares

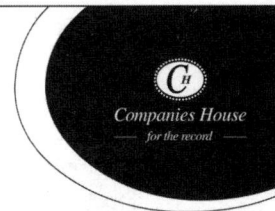

Companies House
*for the record*

**You can use the WebFiling service to file this form online.**
Please go to www.companieshouse.gov.uk

✓ **What this form is for**
You may use this form to give notice of shares allotted following incorporation.

✗ **What this form is NOT for**
You cannot use this form to give notice of shares taken by subscribers on formation of the company or for an allotment of a new class of shares by an unlimited company.

For further information, please refer to our guidance at www.companieshouse.gov.uk

## 1   Company details

Company number   ☐☐☐☐☐☐☐☐

Company name in full

→ **Filling in this form**
Please complete in typescript or in bold black capitals.

All fields are mandatory unless specified or indicated by *

## 2   Allotment dates ❶

From Date   [d][d] [m][m] [y][y][y][y]

To Date   [d][d] [m][m] [y][y][y][y]

❶ **Allotment date**
If all shares were allotted on the same day enter that date in the 'from date' box. If shares were allotted over a period of time, complete both 'from date' and 'to date' boxes.

## 3   Shares allotted

Please give details of the shares allotted, including bonus shares.
(Please use a continuation page if necessary.)

❷ **Currency**
If currency details are not completed we will assume currency is in pound sterling.

| Class of shares (E.g. Ordinary/Preference etc.) | Currency ❷ | Number of shares allotted | Nominal value of each share | Amount paid (including share premium) on each share | Amount (if any) unpaid (including share premium) on each share |
|---|---|---|---|---|---|
| | | | | | |
| | | | | | |
| | | | | | |

If the allotted shares are fully or partly paid up otherwise than in cash, please state the consideration for which the shares were allotted.

**Continuation page**
Please use a continuation page if necessary.

Details of non-cash consideration.

If a PLC, please attach valuation report (if appropriate)

**BIS** | Department for Business Innovation & Skills

CHFP000
03/11 Version 5.0

---

> ### SAMPLE WORDING 12.3
>
> **Board resolution for allotment of shares**
>
> A form of application from applying for 100 shares of £1 each was produced and the receipt of £100, being payment in full therefore, was reported.
>
> Resolved:
>
> a) THAT 100 shares of £1 each, fully paid and numbered from . . .to . . . inclusive be allotted to . . . . . . . . . . . . . . . . . . .
>
> b) THAT the said 100 shares shall henceforth cease to bear distinguishing numbers.
>
> c) THAT the sealing and issue of share certificate No . . . for 100 shares of £1 each, fully paid, drawn in respect of the said allotment, be authorised.

## Restrictions on allotment

CA 2006, s. 578 states that there shall be no allotment in a public company unless:

■ shares are subscribed in full;
■ the offer is made on terms that the shares subscribed for may be allotted in any event or if specified conditions are met (for example, that the allotment will be carried out if the issue is under subscribed).

Any other allotments carried out contrary to s. 578 carry the following consequences:

■ they are voidable at the instance of the applicant;
■ directors are personally liable to compensate the company and applicant for losses suffered due to irregular allotment.

Shares may not be allotted at a discount (CA 2006, s. 580). In the event of contravention of this provision, the allottee is liable to pay to the company the amount of any discount (with interest).

Public companies are not permitted to allot shares as fully or partly paid up (as to nominal value or any premium) other than in cash if the consideration for the allotment is or includes an undertaking which is to be or may be performed more than five years after the date of allotment (CA 2006, s. 587). Shares taken by a subscriber to the Memorandum of Association of a public company must be paid up in cash (CA 2006, s. 584).

Public companies cannot allot unless at least 25% of the share's nominal value of £50,000 (or the equivalent in euros) minimum is subscribed. They require cash on allotment, but a non-cash consideration is acceptable, provided it has been independently valued, a copy forwarded to the Registrar of Companies on form SH01 and approved by ordinary resolution of the company (CA 2006, ss. 599 and 601).

## Letters of renunciation

Allottees are permitted to renounce shares allotted to them in favour of another person by completing a letter of renunciation. Listing Rules regulations require:

■ a form of renunciation which must appear on the back of the allotment letter;
■ allottees must be given the facility to split the renunciation;
■ the renunciation periods must not exceed six weeks for fully-paid shares and one month for partly paid shares.

Listed companies usually use documentation which is in a standardised format. Form X is typically the renunciation form offering the provisional allottee the ability to renounce his right to the shares specified in the provisional letter of allotment to the person named in Form Y. Form Y is the registration application form giving the details of the person in whose name the shares are to be registered.

**SAMPLE WORDING** 12.4

**Renounceable letter of allotment (private company)**

. . . . . . . . . . . . . . . . . . . . . LIMITED

A. FULLY PAID LETTER OF ALLOTMENT

Dated . . . . . . . . . . . . . .

Dear Sir/Madam,

I am writing to inform you that you have been allotted . . . . . . . . . . . . . Ordinary Shares of £xx each in the capital of the company. Pursuant to an Ordinary Resolution passed on the day of . . . . . 20xx, these shares are credited as fully paid and will rank *pari passu* with the other existing Ordinary Shares in the capital of the company. If you wish to retain all the shares comprised herein you need do nothing with this Letter of Allotment. If you wish to dispose of all the shares comprised in this letter, you should complete the Letter of Renunciation attached hereto and hand this letter to the renouncee before the . . . . . . . . . . . . day of 20xx.

The registration application form, also attached hereto, must be completed and signed by the renouncee (if any) and returned with this letter to the registered office not later than . . . . . . . . . . . . to be exchanged for a share certificate. Unless this letter is returned, duly renounced, on the . . . . . . . . . . . . day of 20xx, the certificate for the shares will be automatically issued in your name.

Yours faithfully

. . . . . . . . . . . . . . . . . . . . . . .

Secretary

B. LETTER OF RENUNCIATION

To the Directors of . . . . . . . . . . . . . . . . . . . . . . LIMITED

I/We hereby renounce my/our right to all the shares specified in the Letter of Allotment in favour of the person(s) signing the Registration Application Form.

Dated this . . . . . . . . . . . . day of . . . . . 20xx

Signed . . . . . . . . . . . . . . . . . . . . . . . . . . . . . . . . . . . .

C. REGISTRATION APPLICATION FORM

To the Directors of . . . . . . . . . . . . . . . . . . . . . . LIMITED

I/We accept the shares of £ . . . . each in the above named company renounced by the Letter of Renunciation and I/we request registration in the under-mentioned names and in the amounts indicated below, subject to the constitution of the company.

Signed

. . . . . . . . . . . . . . . . . . . . . . . . . . . . . . . . . . . . . . . . . .

Name

. . . . . . . . . . . . . . . . . . . . . . . . . . . . . . . . . . . . . . . . . .

Address

. . . . . . . . . . . . . . . . . . . . . . . . . . . . . . . . . . . . . . . . . .

## 2.3 Shares allotted for non-cash consideration

A public company may not allot shares either fully or partly paid up for a payment other than cash, unless the consideration has been valued by an appointed valuer within the six months prior to the allotment, and a copy of the valuation sent to the proposed allottee (CA 2006, ss. 593–597). The valuation report must be made by an independent person who would be qualified to be an auditor of the company.

The valuer's report must state:

■ the nominal value of the shares being allotted for a consideration other than cash;
■ the amount of any premium payable on the shares;
■ the consideration which has been valued and the method used to value it;
■ the amount of the nominal value of the shares and any premium treated as paid up for a consideration other than cash.

A copy of the report should be sent to the Registrar of Companies when the return of allotments form SH01 is filed (CA 2006, s. 597).

### Procedure

A formal contract is drawn up for the transfer of the non-cash consideration to the company and for the allotment of the shares in consideration of the assets. The contract should be sent to the Registrar with the return of allotments. If there is no written contract, particulars of the agreement must be set out on form SH01.

Where allotments of shares are made by way of share exchange in a takeover bid there are exemptions to the procedure, and also where the shares are allotted under a capitalisation issue by the capitalisation of reserves.

Private limited companies do not need to have non-cash consideration independently valued. Directors can apply their own valuation, if this is acceptable to the allottee.

## 2.4 Calls and instalments

Calls on shares arise when, under the terms of the issue, only part of the nominal amount of each share is payable at the time of allotment and the remainder is to be paid at a later date or dates.

Where shares are not fully paid on application, the usual practice is for the balance to be payable by instalment(s) due on a fixed date(s). Following receipt of all required payments for any shareholding, a fully paid share certificate will be issued in exchange for the receipted allotment letter or letter of acceptance.

If a shareholder fails to pay the remaining balance, the partly paid shares are at risk of forfeiture (see section 4.3).

## 2.5 Listed companies: allotment exemptions

Companies with a full listing on the London Stock Exchange must arrange for any newly issued securities to be admitted to the official list and to trading on the exchange (see Chapter 6) before they can be dealt in. In normal circumstances, a prospectus is required to support the issue of new shares. However, when a company is issuing a relatively small number of securities over a specified period, there are exemptions.

### Exempt applications

A formal application is used typically when a specific number of shares is to be allotted on a certain event, for example, if an acquiring company were to purchase another company by offering a set amount of the acquirer's securities. Another exemption is a block listing application, where the company wishes to set aside a block of shares which may be issued in the future, for example, where options to acquire shares are to be granted under employee share schemes (see Chapter 15) or where shares are to be issued under scrip dividend plans (see Chapter 14).

Documentation for the formal application must be submitted to UKLA at least two business days ahead of the date the company wishes the securities to be eligible to commence trading. These documents are known as the 48-hour documents and the process is outlined in Checklist 12.1.

### CHECKLIST 12.1 Formal application for allotment of shares

✓ Complete an application for admission to securities to the official list.
✓ Complete an application for admitting the securities to trading for the London Stock Exchange.
✓ Provide an explanatory letter stating the number of shares to be issued, the date securities are to be traded and the reason for the issue of shares.
✓ Pass a board resolution confirming the allotment of shares.
✓ Prepare a letter to the London Stock Exchange confirming that the securities due for allotment have not been offered to the public.
✓ Prepare a standard Stock Exchange announcement in respect of the admission of securities to the official list and for trading on the London Stock Exchange.

A similar process, using a variant of the above forms, must be followed for block listing applications. If a company has made a block listing application, it must provide information to UKLA every six months confirming the actual number of securities which have been issued in the past six months in accordance with the block listing application.

Fees are payable on both types of exempt application and the sum due is based on the value of securities being admitted. The applications are usually reviewed by UKLA on each business day and the company is informed once their application has been accepted.

### STOP AND THINK 12.2

Where applicable the formal application and block listing application exemptions streamline the process and reduce the costs of issuing securities. The secretary must be proactive in planning when the company is likely to need to issue securities so that applications can receive authorisation by the board and approval by UKLA in good time.

### TEST YOUR KNOWLEDGE 12.2

a What are pre-emption rights? How might they be disapplied?
b What is a letter of renunciation?
c Which form is used to notify return of allotments to the Registrar of Companies? When must the form be submitted?
d What is the procedure for the allotment of shares for a non-cash consideration?
e When might a block listing application be used? What are the benefits?

## 3  Rights issues

A rights issue is an issue of shares to the existing shareholders pro rata to their existing holdings. Companies use them to obtain additional funding from the company's shareholders, rather than obtain working capital by borrowing from banks or other financial institutions.

### CHECKLIST 12.2  Rights issue

✓ Check that the directors have been authorised under CA 2006, s. 551 to allot additional shares. If they are not, authority must be sought via an ordinary resolution of the members.

✓ The directors must resolve to increase the company's issued share capital by a rights issue and to issue the provisional allotment letters to the shareholders.

✓ If the company is listed, it is likely to be required under the Prospectus Rules (see Chapter 6) to issue a prospectus.

✓ Letters of renunciation must also be sent if it is the intention that existing shareholders can renounce their entitlement to third parties. (The Articles should be checked to ensure no pre-emption rights on allotment are infringed, and any such rights overridden by special resolution.) If renunciations rights are not offered, the shareholder would still have the ability to refuse to take up the rights issue.

✓ Once the closing date for acceptance is reached, the directors resolve to allot those shares taken up.

✓ Update the register of members.

✓ Prepare appropriate share certificates and issue to shareholders.

✓ File forms SH01 with the Registrar of Companies within one month and file copies of the resolutions within 15 days.

The following key issues may affect the timetable:

■ If there are shareholders to whom the company cannot send rights (e.g. shareholders resident in foreign jurisdictions where participation in the rights issue might breach local legislation), a special resolution will be required adding two weeks (i.e. sufficient time to convene a general meeting) unless such a resolution has been passed routinely at the AGM. The usual process for ineligible shareholders in foreign jurisdictions is to sell their rights and to forward any cash proceeds to them.

■ Rights issues must be kept open for shareholders to accept for at least 14 days (CA 2006, s. 562). To ensure that the rights are sent to as up-to-date a list as possible, a shareholders' register should be obtained near to the date of despatch. The company secretary should take care and responsibility for ensuring the register of members is up to date for the transaction.

■ If a shareholder does not take up his right and does not renounce it, the shares that would have been allotted to him can be sold in the market at the end of the rights issue process. Any surplus funds in excess of the rights price, less brokerage expenses, are returned to the shareholder. A shareholder who takes no action during a rights issue is often referred to as a 'lazy shareholder'.

### 3.1  Rights issues and listed companies

If a company is listed, it may be required by the Prospectus Rules (see Chapter 6) to issue a prospectus in relation to the rights issue. As a prospectus contains detailed information about the company, this may take some time to prepare and listed companies should factor this into their planning.

The price at which shares are offered under a rights issue is critical in much the same way as an original offering (see Chapter 6). In order to encourage the success of a rights issue, shares are usually offered at a discount to the prevailing market price. This does not disadvantage any shareholders as all shareholders are being made the same offer in proportion to their existing shareholding. A discount rate of 20% off the market price is not unfamiliar. Some listed companies may offer a much higher discounted rights issue price; this is known as deep discounting.

The price of the shares being offered, the prevailing market conditions, the performance of the company and demand for the company's shares will all be important factors in launching a successful rights issue for a listed company. Brokers and banks offer underwriting services during a rights issue and the appetite for offering underwriting (and sometimes the commission charged) is dependent in part on the matters mentioned above.

## 3.2 Other types of share issues

- *Open offers* – Existing holders may be invited to subscribe for securities but the benefit of the right cannot be sold or assigned.
- *Capitalisation or bonus issues* – The directors can arrange for fully paid shares of the same class to be allotted free of charge to existing holders in proportion to their holdings. No new capital is raised by the company and holders can keep or sell all or part of their allotment (the shares are usually issued on renounceable certificates). The market price of the shares falls roughly in proportion to the increase in the company's issued share capital. A bonus issue is often perceived as a sign of confidence of the company's fortunes and strong financial position.
- *Exchanges and conversions* – New securities can be listed as a result of existing securities being exchanged for, or converted into, new securities.
- *Exercise of options or warrants* – Some securities carry rights for the holder to subscribe cash for further securities which are then allotted when the rights are exercised.
- *Other issues* – Shares issued under employees' share schemes, for example (see Chapter 15).

---

**STOP AND THINK 12.3**

The secretary has an important role in corporate strategic planning. The secretary should be aware of any forthcoming transactions that may involve the issue of new shares, particularly with regard to allowing sufficient time for any general meetings which may be required.

---

**TEST YOUR KNOWLEDGE 12.3**

a What is a rights issue?
b How long does a rights issue have to remain open to shareholders?
c Why do companies launch rights issues?

---

# 4 Alteration of capital

Most company secretaries will be involved at some time in a change to the share capital of a company. This might include:

- the consolidation of shares;
- the subdivision of shares;
- cancellation of unissued stock;
- conversion of stock into shares;
- redenomination of share capital;
- reduction of capital.

The power to authorise alteration of the share capital must come from the company's Articles. If there is no provision, the Articles must be altered by special resolution in general meeting.

The resolutions to authorise alteration of the Articles and to alter the capital can be put at the same meeting, with the second conditional on the first being approved. A reduction in share capital is strictly regulated because it may reduce the available funds the creditor can look to for payment (see section 4.5).

## 4.1 Consolidation, subdivision and redenomination of shares

### Consolidation

In a **consolidation** shares of a low nominal value are aggregated into a smaller number of shares of an increased nominal value. For example, five shares of 10p each would be consolidated into one share of 50p. Consolidation does not often arise, but it can be convenient if a company has issued a large number of ordinary shares which have a low nominal value or as part of a complex reorganisation of the company's share capital.

The procedure is similar to increasing the share capital, except that the register of members should be rewritten to show the holdings of each member in the new denomination. Existing share certificates should be cancelled and new ones issued with a notice stating that the consolidation has taken place. Notification on form SH02 should be sent to the Registrar of Companies within one month.

Some holdings may not consolidate into an exact number of new shares, causing those members to 'lose' that fraction of their holding. If the company is listed, the fractional shares should be aggregated, sold on the market and the proceeds distributed to the appropriate members, subject to a minimum amount. In unlisted companies, arrangements have to be made for the fractions to be sold to someone (for example, the chairman), at an agreed price.

---

**SAMPLE WORDING 12.5**

**Ordinary resolutions to consolidate shares and sell fractions**

THAT the 10,000 shares of 25p each in the capital of the company be consolidated and divided into 2,500 shares of £1 each.

THAT the aggregate of the fractions of a share of £1 arising on such consolidation be sold through the company's brokers and that the proceeds thereof be distributed pro rata to the members entitled thereto.

---

### Subdivision of shares

Subdivision of shares is where shares of a high nominal value are divided into a larger number of shares of lower nominal value. For example, one share of £1 each would be divided into four shares of 25p. Subdivision is therefore the opposite of consolidation and is usually effected to make the shares more marketable. It is also known as splitting shares.

The procedure is the same as that for consolidation, except that fractions of shares do not arise. The same form SH02 must be used to notify the Registrar within one month of the resolution being passed. The register of members needs to be rewritten to show the shares held in the new denominations, and existing share certificates should be cancelled and replaced.

In accordance with
Section 619, 621 & 689
of the Companies Act
2006.

# SH02

## Notice of consolidation, sub-division, redemption of shares or re-conversion of stock into shares

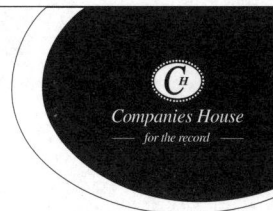

Companies House
*for the record*

✓ **What this form is for**
You may use this form to give notice of consolidation, sub-division, redemption of shares or re-conversion of stock into shares.

✗ **What this form is NOT for**
You cannot use this form to give notice of a conversion of shares into stock.

For further information, please refer to our guidance at www.companieshouse.gov.uk

### 1  Company details

Company number

Company name in full

→ **Filling in this form**
Please complete in typescript or in bold black capitals.

All fields are mandatory unless specified or indicated by *

### 2  Date of resolution

Date of resolution   d d m m y y y y

### 3  Consolidation

Please show the amendments to each class of share.

| Class of shares (E.g. Ordinary/Preference etc.) | Previous share structure | | New share structure | |
|---|---|---|---|---|
| | Number of issued shares | Nominal value of each share | Number of issued shares | Nominal value of each share |
| | | | | |
| | | | | |
| | | | | |

### 4  Sub-division

Please show the amendments to each class of share.

| Class of shares (E.g. Ordinary/Preference etc.) | Previous share structure | | New share structure | |
|---|---|---|---|---|
| | Number of issued shares | Nominal value of each share | Number of issued shares | Nominal value of each share |
| | | | | |
| | | | | |
| | | | | |

### 5  Redemption

Please show the class number and nominal value of shares that have been redeemed. Only redeemable shares can be redeemed.

| Class of shares (E.g. Ordinary/Preference etc.) | Number of issued shares | Nominal value of each share |
|---|---|---|
| | | |
| | | |
| | | |

---

> **SAMPLE WORDING 12.6**
>
> **Ordinary resolution to subdivide shares**
>
> THAT the 5,000 shares of £1 each in the capital of the company be subdivided into 20,000 shares of 25p each.
>
> Using the above subdivision as an example:
>
> 5,000 shares × £1 nominal value each = £5,000
>
> which is the same authorised share capital as:
>
> 20,000 shares × 25p nominal value each = £5,000.
>
> The total share capital of the company is not affected by a consolidation or subdivision.

## Redenomination of shares

A limited company having a share capital may redenominate its share capital (or any class of shares) into another currency by ordinary resolution (CA 2006, ss. 622–628). Details of the conversion into the other currency must be prepared, for example the prevailing exchange rate to be used on a particular date as set out in the proposing resolution. The day or period set for the exchange rate must be within 28 days before the resolution is passed. Notice of a redenomination must be given to the Registrar within one month, accompanied by the appropriate Statement of Capital. CA 2006, ss. 626 permits a company, within three months of the redenomination, to reduce its share capital for the purposes of rounding the nominal values into values which, in the directors' opinion, would be more suitable. The reduction can be for no more than 10% of existing nominal value and the reduction must be passed by a special resolution and the Registrar must be notified within 15 days of its passing.

## 4.2 Cancellation of unissued shares

The need for cancellation does not often arise, but can occur following a scheme of arrangement after the repurchase of its own shares by the company or where the company has a class of shares, none of which has been issued.

---

> **SAMPLE WORDING 12.7**
>
> **Resolution to cancel unissued shares**
>
> That the 1,000 shares of £5 each in the capital of the company which have not been taken or agreed to be taken by any person be cancelled and that the share capital of the company be diminished by £5,000.

An ordinary resolution must be passed at a general meeting and the procedure is similar to that for the consolidation of shares.

Cancellation of unissued shares should not be confused with reduction in the share capital, which is a more formal procedure and a significant event in the life of the company (see section 4.5).

## 4.3 Forfeiture

When shares have been partly paid, the balance outstanding on them can be called at any time by the directors or in accordance with any pre-planned schedule of payments. Any shares on which a call has been made but the holder has not paid, or when payment is overdue, can be forfeited. In practice this happens rarely; if it does go ahead, procedures must be strictly adhered to. It would be wise to seek legal advice early in the process. Model Articles 52–62 for a public company set out the basic approach. There are no equivalent regulations for a private company as the private company Model Articles provide that all shares shall be fully paid.

### Procedure

1 If a call remains unpaid, the directors should write to the member(s) requiring payment of all outstanding amounts within 14 days and stating that if this is not met, the shares are liable to forfeiture. Joint shareholders are jointly and severally liable to pay the outstanding balance.
2 If the call remains unpaid, the share may be forfeited by resolution of the directors. The directors should also consider whether the shares are to be transferred to another person or whether there are provisions in the Articles that need to be followed (see below).
3 If the member cannot or will not pay the call, he may wish to surrender the shares and it is usual to ask for the share certificate to be returned.
4 Details of the forfeiture must be entered in the register of members. Forfeited shares may be sold or cancelled. If the shares are being sold, the Model Articles authorise the directors to execute the stock transfer form in place of the shareholder who has forfeited (i.e. in place of a transferor).
5 Any dividends or other distributions owing but not paid are also forfeited. A member whose shares have been forfeited ceases to be a member as soon as the register of members is updated. He is, however, still liable for any amounts unpaid. If the shares are reissued, the original member is no longer liable once the full amount has been received by the company from whatever source.

## 4.4 Conversion of shares into stock

In practice, conversion of shares into stock rarely occurs since there is no advantage in having a company's capital in this form. Prior to CA 1948, companies preferred to have stock rather than shares to avoid having to give each share a distinguishing number. The 1948 Act abolished the need for numbering shares where they are fully paid and as a result there are very few companies that have capital in the form of stock. Under CA 2006 it is not possible to convert shares into stock, although it will remain possible to reconvert stock into shares.

If it does happen, the procedure is the similar to that for the consolidation of shares. The ordinary resolution should specify the units of stock that are to be transferred and the register of members must be updated to take account of the change.

## 4.5 Reduction of issued capital

Reduction in capital is a much more formal procedure because the reduction may affect the company's ability to repay its creditors. CA 2006, s. 641 allows a private limited company having a share capital to take advantage of a simpler process to reduce its share capital by special resolution supported by a solvency statement. In any other case (including public companies) a special resolution and confirmation by the court is required (CA 2006 ss.645–651). In respect of private companies limited by shares, such a company may not reduce its capital if as a result of the reduction there would no longer be any member holding shares other than redeemable shares.

CA 2006, ss. 642–644 provides a capital reduction procedure for private companies, which allows the share capital to be reduced using a directors' solvency statement.

There are three circumstances in which capital can be reduced:

1 The company is reorganising and has more capital than it needs.
2 The company is cancelling the amount uncalled on shares issued.

3 The company has lost capital through wastage of assets with the result that nominal capital no longer reflects the company's value.

The solvency statement required by s. 643 is that each of the directors are of the opinion that there is no grounds on which the company could be found to be unable to pay its debts. The statement must confirm the directors' opinion that the company will be able to pay its debts as they fall due over the next year. The statement must be made not more than 15 days before the special resolution to pass the reduction. The special resolution, solvency statement and a Statement of Capital must then be delivered to the Registrar within 15 days of the passing of the special resolution. A reduction of capital becomes effective upon registration by the Registrar.

Where confirmation of the capital is required by the court (CA 2006 ss.645–651), a detailed record should be kept of each stage of the process as the secretary will have to make an affidavit confirming that the procedures, such as date of the issue of notice, and the date and timing of the meeting, have been carried out correctly. The secretary and the chairman will also give affidavit evidence on other matters in support of the petition by the company to the court, depending on the nature of the reduction.

The company's legal advisers should be involved at an early stage, because it will be their responsibility to prepare the documentation for the court.

## Procedure where confirmation is required by the court

1 The board takes the decision to propose a reduction in capital.
2 They convene a general meeting with notice containing the exact wording of the special resolution to be considered (see Sample Wording 12.8).
3 If the special resolution is passed, a copy is filed with the Registrar within 15 days; for listed companies two copies are sent to the UKLA.
4 The company applies to the court for an order confirming the reduction.
5 The court will settle a list of creditors entitled to object and ascertain their wishes.
6 The court then takes such action as it thinks fit to settle the claims of any dissenting creditors.
7 The court has the power to direct the company to add the words 'and reduced' to its name, and state the reasons for the reduction. If the company is a plc and authorised share capital falls below the £50,000 minimum (or equivalent if denominated in euros), the company must be re-registered as a private company, using form RR08.
8 The court can then confirm the reduction.
9 On completion of the court proceedings the following are delivered to the Registrar of Companies:
   a) the court order; and
   b) if applicable, a replacement clause for the capital clause in the Memorandum (called the minute) approved by the court.
   The reduction takes effect from the date of the registration (CA 2006, s. 649).
10 The Registrar will issue a certificate as to the registration of the order and minute which is conclusive evidence. This is published in *The Gazette*.
11 If applicable, the company makes suitable alterations to the share certificates.

---

**SAMPLE WORDING 12.8**

**Special resolution to reduce capital**

That the capital of the company be reduced from £10,000 divided into 10,000 shares of £1 each (which have been issued and are fully paid up) to £5,000 divided into 10,000 shares of 50p each and that such reduction be effected by returning to the holders of the said shares paid-up capital to and that such reduction be effected by returning to the holders of the said shares paid-up capital to the extent of 50p per share and by reducing the nominal amount of each of the said shares from £1 to 50p.

## 4.6 Effect of alterations of capital on voting rights

When considering any alteration of capital, the effect on the existing voting rights of shareholders should be taken into account to ensure that voting rights among the different classes of shares remain in the same proportion. If they are affected by the alteration of capital, it will be necessary to change them to restore the previous position. In this case, separate class meetings must be held to obtain the consent to change.

## 4.7 Serious loss of capital in a public company

CA 2006, s. 656 imposes an obligation on the directors of a public company to convene a general meeting on becoming aware that the net assets of the company have fallen to, or below, the value of half of its called-up share capital. The directors are under a duty to call such a meeting within 28 days of any of their number becoming aware of the situation and the meeting must be held not later than 56 days after that time.

The purpose of the meeting is to consider whether any action should be taken to deal with the situation, and if so, what. No matter may be considered at the meeting apart from those measures unless it would have been permissible under the rules applicable to general meetings. It appears, therefore, that if remedial measures are called for which cannot be taken by the board, the general meeting can only express an opinion about what is needed to resolve that a further meeting shall be held to take remedial action, for example, to resolve on proper notice to reduce capital or even to resolve on winding up.

---

**TEST YOUR KNOWLEDGE 12.4**

a  What is meant by (i) consolidation of shares; (ii) subdivision of shares?
b  Why is reduction in share capital significant?
c  What procedure should be followed by the board in respect of the forfeiture of shares?

---

# 5  Redemption of shares

It was noted in section 1 that redeemable shares are intended to be repurchased by the company at some point in the future. This section looks at how this is achieved.

Redeemable shares cannot be redeemed unless they are fully paid, and can only be paid for out of distributable profits or out of a fresh issue of shares made for the purpose.

As a general rule, companies are prohibited from giving financial assistance for the purchase of their own shares, although certain exemptions are given to private companies. In certain circumstances private companies can fund the purchase out of capital but this is not available to public companies. Public companies may benefit from certain limited exceptions as set out in CA 2006, s. 678 where the giving of assistance is only incidental to some larger purpose of the company.

It is usual for redeemable shares to be redeemed at a certain date. As a result it is often necessary to make annual purchases. This is done by:

■ buying on the open market, which is particularly advantageous if the price is lower than the redemption value; or
■ by arranging a random draw ('drawing'). The arrangements for making drawings are complex and expensive.

If purchases are made on the market, the company's brokers will be instructed to purchase the number of shares required for the annual instalment of redemption. If the price is favourable, the company may continue to make market purchases to cover future instalments.

Any shares redeemed must be reported in the company's next annual report and accounts.

## 5.1 Procedure for drawing

In summary, shareholders holding redeemable shares are selected at random to have their shares redeemed. A circular is sent to the shareholders concerned informing them that their shares will be redeemed. The register of members is then amended to show the redemption and payment in respect of the redemption is sent to the shareholder. Form SH02 must be filed at Companies House reflecting the redemption.

Looking at the procedure in further detail:

1 Prepare a complete listing of relevant shareholders at the record date.
2 Depending on the number of shares to be repurchased, break down the holdings into parcels of, say, 5,000 shares. Each parcel is allocated a unique reference number.
3 Prepare a schedule showing the allocation of the parcels. Where a holding is not an exact multiple of 5,000, the balance is consolidated into composite parcels.
4 Prepare tickets for each parcel showing the reference number.
5 Arrange a date for the drawing. Any special requirements in the Articles should be observed, for example the drawing is often required to be held in the presence of a solicitor, notary public or other scrutineer.
6 If the company is listed, advise UKLA of the date of drawing, the record date, the number of shares to be drawn and the redemption price.
7 Prepare the following documents:
   a) a formal notice to be sent to holders whose shares have been drawn for redemption, informing them that the drawing has taken place and notifying them of the number of shares to be redeemed;
   b) a circular to be sent to shareholders whose shares have been drawn for redemption detailing procedure;
   c) payment advice.
8 The drawing should be made in the presence of at least three people: one person to draw and two to cross-check the unique numbers against the list of shareholders.
9 Listed companies should notify UKLA after the drawing has taken place, confirming the number of shares which are still in issue and will remain listed.
10 Send the formal notice prepared under 7a above to all shareholders whose holdings have been drawn.
11 About three weeks before the date the redemption monies are due, send the circular prepared under 7(b) enclosing forms of payment authority and discharge for their signature.
12 Open a redemption account at the bank, and transfer the necessary funds to cover the cheques to be issued.
13 Check the returned forms of payment authority before cheques are despatched with the payment advice. The cheques should be sent to arrive on the due date.
14 Send reminders to shareholders who have not returned their forms.
15 Debit the shareholders' accounts in the register of members with the number of shares redeemed.
16 Send notice of the redemption to the Registrar on form SH02 within one month of the redemption.

## 5.2 Procedure following market purchase

1 Notify UKLA of the number of shares purchased and the number still outstanding.
2 Pay the brokers for the shares on the relevant settlement date.
3 If the shares have been purchased cum div (see Chapter 14), make sure that the holdings concerned are deleted from the dividend list as no dividend will now be payable.
4 Update the register of members by debiting the shareholders' accounts with the number of shares redeemed.
5 File form SH02 at Companies House.

## 6 Purchase of own shares

CA 2006, s. 690 gives power to limited companies and to companies limited by guarantee with a share capital to purchase their own shares. This includes any redeemable shares for which specific authority must be given by the company's Articles (see Model Article 22; public company Model Article 43). CA 2006, ss. 690–691 also provide that the power to purchase own shares is subject to any restriction in the company's articles and that a company may not purchase its own shares unless they are fully paid. Where a company purchases its own shares, the shares must be paid for on purchase (however an exception applies on redemption of redeemable shares, where CA 2006, s. 685 provides that the shareholder and company may agree that payment for redeemable shares may be made at a later date). There are a number of circumstances where it might be useful for a company to purchase its own shares, not least for small and medium-sized companies where the unmarketability of unquoted shares can be a burden.

Other circumstances include:

- buying out a dissident shareholder who could harm the company's business;
- sale by the estate of a deceased shareholder;
- purchasing the shares of a proprietor who is retiring;
- buying back shares to reduce the chance of a takeover bid;
- purchase of own shares to hold in treasury (see below).

Following the purchase, there must be at least one member of the company holding non-redeemable shares. Only fully paid shares can be repurchased by the company.

As a general rule, companies are prohibited from giving financial assistance to purchase their own shares, although some exceptions are given to private companies in CA 2006, ss. 678–683. In certain circumstances private companies can fund the purchase out of capital (CA 2006, s. 709). This is not available to public companies.

The procedures involved in a purchase of own shares are complex and must be followed carefully. Failure to follow statutory procedures could result in the purported purchase being void. Both the company and any members contemplating participating in a buy-back should take specialist taxation advice.

The requirements for purchases by a company of its own shares are contained in CA 2006, s. 693–701. They are either:

- 'off-market', where the purchase is either not on a RIE (see Chapter 6) or subject to a marketing arrangement; or
- 'market', where the purchase is both on a RIE and subject to a marketing arrangement.

### 6.1 Procedure for off-market purchase

1 Off-market purchases must be authorised by special resolution of the members. The purchase may also be made under a 'contingent purchase contract', that is, a contract under which a company may become entitled or obliged to buy its own shares, which has previously been authorised or is conditional on receiving shareholder approval. The maximum authorisation period for such purchases is five years.
2 A copy of the proposed contract of purchase, or written memorandum, must be available at the company's registered office for inspection by the members for at least 15 days prior to

the date of the meeting where the special resolution is to be considered. The contract or memorandum must include the names of the members holding the shares that are to be purchased.

3 Due to a conflict of interests, shareholders affected by the proposed contract may not vote on the special resolution.

4 A copy of the special resolution must be submitted to the Registrar within 15 days of its approval.

5 When the shares have been purchased, a completed form SH03 must be returned to the Registrar within 28 days of the delivery of the shares to the company. The repurchase of shares is subject to stamp duty (see below) and the form must be first stamped by HM Revenue & Customs to confirm that the appropriate stamp duty has been paid.

## 6.2 Procedure for market purchase

The requirements are less stringent for market purchases as such shares are by definition purchased at arm's length. However, listed companies must comply with the relevant sections of the Listing Rules.

1 UKLA must be notified as soon as possible after a decision to propose the purchase of own shares.

2 Listed companies quite often have a provision to make a purchase of their own shares as a standing item at each AGM. The authority sought from shareholders to make the purchase of own shares usually lasts until the next AGM, where it is normally renewed.

3 Although an ordinary resolution is necessary, institutional shareholder bodies have requested that the authority be sought by special resolution, stipulating the maximum number of shares that may be purchased and the maximum and minimum purchase prices.

4 The company should not purchase shares at any time when the directors would not be free to do so on their own account under the Model Code.

5 Details of any purchases must be notified to a RIS no later than 7.30 am on the business day following the purchase.

6 Form SH03 should be sent to HM Revenue & Customs Stamp Office with a cheque for the required amount of stamp duty (payable at 0.5% on the consideration, rounded up to the nearest £5, subject to a minimum threshold of £1,000). Once the form has been stamped it will be returned to the company, which must then file it with the Registrar within 28 days of the delivery of the shares to the company.

A copy of the contract or memorandum for purchasing shares must be kept at the registered office and must be available for inspection by the members without charge. Details of own share purchases must be reported in the next directors' report. Listed companies are required to disclose details of any shareholders' authority for the purchase of own shares still valid at the year-end. Own shares repurchased are cancelled, unless they are held in treasury (see below), and the issued share capital of the company is reduced accordingly.

## 6.3 Listed companies

### Additional points that listed companies need to consider

Listed companies must explain (usually in their circular convening the general meeting at which authority to purchase its own shares is being sought) the reasons why directors consider the opportunity for the purchase to be in the best interests of the company and its shareholders.

Where general authority to purchase its own shares is sought annually, provided there are no unusual features to the authority been sought and the Listing Rules are being complied with, it is not necessary to submit the circular or proxy card in advance to the UKLA for approval.

Institutional shareholder guidelines restrict the amount of its own shares which a company may repurchase to 10% of the issued share capital.

In accordance with
Section 707 of the
Companies Act 2006

# SH03
## Return of purchase of own shares

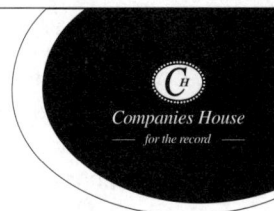

Companies House
*for the record*

✓ **What this form is for**
You may use this form to give notice of a purchase by a limited company of its own shares.

✗ **What this form is NOT for**
You cannot use this form to give notice of a purchase by an unlimited company of its own shares.

For further information, please refer to our guidance at www.companieshouse.gov.uk

---

**1**     **Company details**

Company number    [ ][ ][ ][ ][ ][ ][ ][ ]

Company name in full

→ **Filling in this form**
Please complete in typescript or in bold black capitals.

All fields are mandatory unless specified or indicated by *

---

**2**     **Shares purchased for cancellation**

The section below should be completed by public limited companies (PLC) only.

| Class of shares (E.g. Ordinary/Preference etc.) | Number of shares purchased | Nominal value of each share | Date that the shares were delivered to the company | Are these qualifying shares? ❶ | Maximum price paid for each share | Minimum price paid for each share |
|---|---|---|---|---|---|---|
| | | | / / | ☐ Yes | | |
| | | | / / | ☐ Yes | | |
| | | | / / | ☐ Yes | | |
| | | | / / | ☐ Yes | | |
| | | | / / | ☐ Yes | | |

Please show the aggregate amount paid on shares purchased for cancellation.

Total aggregate amount

For HM Revenue and Customs Stamp Office only

❶ **Qualifying shares**
Qualifying shares are shares eligible to be placed into treasury.

---

**BIS** | **Department for Business Innovation & Skills**

CHFP000
05/10 Version 4.0

## 6.4 Treasury shares

As an alternative to purchasing and cancelling their own shares, a plc may hold purchased shares in treasury provided they are quoted on the London Stock Exchange or AIM or its securities are traded on equivalent recognised exchanges within another EEA state in Europe. Any other type of company cannot hold treasury shares.

The shares may be purchased in the market or via an off-market transaction (see above). The company must finance such purchase out of distributable profits; it must not fund the purchase of the treasury shares out of a fresh issue of new shares. Following the acquisition of treasury shares, the company effectively becomes a member of itself.

### Authority to acquire shares

An ordinary resolution is required to approve a company purchasing its own shares for holding in treasury; many companies will be able to use their existing shareholder authority to make such purchases. However, existing resolutions should be carefully reviewed, particularly in relation to whether the resolution covers the cancellation of repurchased shares or their use in employee share schemes. Best practice is that the explanatory notes accompanying the shareholder circular should explain whether the company intends to cancel any shares purchased or to hold them in treasury.

In addition to the requirement to pass an ordinary resolution, a check will need to be made against the Articles of Association to determine whether there are any provisions prohibiting the holding of treasury shares. As the Regulations do not override existing provisions in the Articles, a special resolution may be required to remove any prohibitive provisions.

### Use of treasury shares

Once the necessary resolution(s) has been passed, the company may acquire its own shares and hold them in treasury. The company then has three options about how to use the treasury shares, which may be used in any combination:

1 *Sell the treasury shares in the market* – Treasury shares sold must be offered to existing shareholders on a pre-emptive basis, in much the same way as newly issued shares are offered. However, these pre-emptive rights can be disapplied in the same way as for new issued shares (i.e. by special resolution). Guidelines issued by ABI recommend that listed companies may seek authority to disapply pre-emption rights in respect of no more than 5% of the issued share capital; this will include both new issued shares and treasury shares sold into the market. Whilst the purchase of shares to be held in treasury will have the usual rate of ad valorem stamp duty payable (see Chapter 13), the sale of treasury shares will not attract stamp duty.

2 *Cancel the treasury shares* – The procedure provided above would be used to cancel the shares and to reduce the issued share capital accordingly.

3 *Transfer the treasury shares to satisfy the exercise of share options or grant of shares under an employee share scheme* – Treasury shares may be transferred to satisfy shares required under an employee share scheme (see Chapter 15). Many companies have established an employee trust to facilitate the award of shares under employee share schemes and companies will need to evaluate whether it is necessary or desirable to retain the trust or use treasury shares instead. As with the new issue of shares, treasury shares transferred to satisfy employee share schemes are not subject to pre-emption rights and therefore do not count towards any limits for the disapplication of pre-emption rights (see above).

### Holding shares in treasury

Whilst shares are held in treasury:

■ If at any time the treasury shares are no longer qualifying shares (e.g. the company is no longer a listed company), the company must immediately cancel all outstanding treasury shares.

■ The number of treasury shares held must be disclosed in the annual report and accounts.

■ If the number of treasury shares changes, this must be notified to the market (under the DTRs) at the end of the month in which the change occurs.

- The shares remain listed with the relevant stock exchange. This carries ramifications:
  - it is not necessary to seek a fresh listing application if the treasury shares are sold or transferred to satisfy an employee share scheme; and
  - treasury shares cannot be sold or purchased if that were to breach the Model Code in respect of dealing in shares during a close period (see Chapter 6).
- If any of the treasury shares are redeemable shares, then such shares will be cancelled on the date of redemption.
- Treasury shares must be excluded for certain purposes, most notably:
  - they do not rank for dividends or other distributions of assets;
  - the company cannot vote the treasury shares at general meetings or attend general meetings by reason of holding treasury shares;
  - treasury shares must be excluded from participation in a rights issue;
  - treasury shares must be excluded for the purposes of calculating any notifiable interests of major shareholders (i.e. shareholders who own 3% or more of the voting rights of a company). They must similarly be excluded from the calculation of the 30% threshold in respect of a takeover bid for a quoted company (see Chapter 6). The secretary will therefore need not only to adopt a proactive approach to monitoring the number of shares held in treasury but also make any necessary adjustments to the applicable reportable shareholding percentages in respect of major shareholders and potential bidders.
- A company will, however, be permitted to allow treasury shares to be eligible in the allotment of bonus shares provided the shares are fully paid.
- The acquisition of treasury shares must be reported to the Registrar on form SH03 within 28 days of the date of acquisition. Similarly, if treasury shares are sold, cancelled, redeemed or transferred for the purposes of an employee share scheme, the Registrar must be informed on form SH04 or SH05 within 28 days of such an event.

### STOP AND THINK 12.4

Listed companies may need to spend a considerable amount of time considering whether treasury shares will be beneficial for them. Much of the responsibility for introducing and administering treasury shares will fall to the secretary. A careful review of many systems (e.g. to ensure treasury shares are excluded from dividend payments, monitoring the usage of the disapplication of pre-emption rights, the timing of sales and purchases to avoid closed dealing periods) will be required by the secretary.

The secretary should also consider the practical aspects of dealing with shares in treasury. For example, it may be administratively beneficial for the treasury shares to be held in CREST to facilitate possible frequent disposals and acquisitions of shares.

### CASE QUESTION

As part of Multiple plc's expansion, consideration is being given to gaining extra funding through its share capital. Two matters are due to be considered at the forthcoming board meeting:

- The company has 5 million partly paid shares and the board would like to call the outstanding payment. The board would like to you to prepare a note setting out the procedures, timescales, documents and announcements which may be required. *

- The board is considering issuing shares via a rights issue. Again they would like a note setting out the procedures, timescales, documents and announcements which may be required.

* Reviewing Chapter 13 may also be helpful in preparing this note.

Prepare the required notes for the next board meeting.

---

┌─────────────────────────────────────────────────────────────────────┐
│ ✎  **TEST YOUR KNOWLEDGE** 12.6                                       │
│                                                                       │
│ **a** Why might a company want to purchase its own shares?            │
│ **b** What is an off-market purchase?                                 │
│ **c** What are the institutional shareholder guidelines in respect of the amount of own shares a │
│   company may repurchase?                                             │
│ **d** What actions should be taken if this percentage level is exceeded? │
│ **e** How might a company make use of its treasury shares?            │
└─────────────────────────────────────────────────────────────────────┘

## **CHAPTER** SUMMARY

■ A share is a fixed and indivisible section of the capital of a company. There are several different classes of shares and these carry specific rights as designated in the Articles of Association.

■ Issued capital relates to shares which has been issued, taken up and outstanding.

■ Allotment of shares is one of the core duties of the company secretary. He should take care at the outset to ensure that the directors are authorised to allot the shares and that due care is taken of the provisions for any pre-emption rights. Allottees may renounce any shares allotted to them in favour of another person; this should be anticipated.

■ Issues of shares can include rights issues, bonus or capitalisation issues, exchanges and conversions.

■ At some point it may be necessary for the company to alter its capital structure (e.g. by creating new shares). If there is no provision to do this in the Articles they can be altered by special resolution. Other alterations to capital include consolidation or subdivision of shares, cancellation of unissued shares and reduction of issued capital. A public company must convene a general meeting as soon as it becomes aware that the net assets of the company have fallen to, or below, the value of half its issued share capital.

■ A company may redeem or purchase its own shares out of distributable profits. In special circumstances, a private company may purchase shares out of capital but this option is not open to public companies. Companies listed on the London Stock Exchange or trading shares on AIM may purchase their own shares and hold them in treasury.

In accordance with
Section 730 of the
Companies Act 2006.

# SH05

## Notice of cancellation of treasury shares by a public limited company (PLC)

*Companies House*
*— for the record —*

✓ **What this form is for**
You may use this form to give notice of a cancellation of treasury shares in a public limited company.

✗ **What this form is NOT for**
You cannot use this form to give notice of a sale or transfer of treasury shares for a public limited company. To do this, please use form SH04.

For further information, please refer to our guidance at www.companieshouse.gov.uk

---

**1**    **Company details**

| | |
|---|---|
| Company number | ☐☐☐☐☐☐☐☐ |
| Company name in full | |

→ **Filling in this form**
Please complete in typescript or in bold black capitals.

All fields are mandatory unless specified or indicated by *

---

**2**    **Treasury shares cancelled**

| Class of shares (E.g. Ordinary/Preference etc.) | Number of shares cancelled | Nominal value of each share | Date(s) shares were cancelled |
|---|---|---|---|
| | | | / / |
| | | | / / |
| | | | / / |
| | | | / / |
| | | | / / |
| | | | / / |
| | | | / / |
| | | | / / |
| | | | / / |
| | | | / / |
| | | | / / |
| | | | / / |
| | | | / / |
| | | | / / |
| | | | / / |
| | | | / / |
| | | | / / |
| | | | / / |
| | | | / / |
| | | | / / |

---

**BIS** | Department for Business Innovation & Skills

CHFP000
05/10 Version 4.0

# 13 | Share registration

## ■ INTRODUCTION

We saw in Chapter 1 that the company secretary is responsible for the registrar function within the company, either directly or through an outside agency. In Chapter 8 we covered the requirements for maintaining the statutory registers, including the register of members. This chapter describes a further duty of the registrar: share registration. We look at the procedures required for registering shareholders, the issue of share certificates and how to manage common situations, such as the death of a member, which require the registration of legal documents and notices.

## 1 Transfer of shares

A shareholder has a right to transfer shares to whomever he pleases, although the right to transfer may be restricted by the Articles of Association.

Under the Stock Transfer Act 1963, a proper instrument of transfer must be delivered to the company. There are two standard forms:

1 stock transfer form;
2 CREST, which causes the shares to be **dematerialised** into the transferor's broker's CREST account (see below).

In practice, the stock transfer form will be used when dealing off-market, and CREST will be used if the shares are dematerialised.

### 1.1 Transfer procedure

If a private transaction takes place in shares of both a private company and a public company, the member wishing to dispose of his holding (the transferor) completes stock transfer form J30 and passes it, with the relevant share certificates, to the purchaser (the transferee) in exchange for the agreed price.

The transferee enters his name and address on the stock transfer form, dates it and has it stamped at a HM Revenue & Customs Stamp Office (see Directory). The transferee is liable for any stamp duty payable (see section 4).

The transferee does not have to sign the stock transfer form provided the shares are fully paid. If the Stamp Office is not satisfied that the consideration represents the full value of the shares being transferred, it will ask for the basis of the valuation to be supported by documentary evidence. Once the Stamp Office is satisfied, it will imprint a stamp onto the stock transfer form. The stamp clearly shows how much stamp duty has been received, or, if no duty is payable, the fact that it has been adjudicated as such.

If the transferor and/or transferee are members of CREST and hold or intend to hold the shares concerned in dematerialised form under CREST, the relevant CREST procedures will apply (see below).

The stamped stock transfer form is returned by HM Revenue & Customs to the transferee. The stamped transfer and share certificates are then forwarded to the company by the transferee for registration. When the company receives the stock transfer it should check the documents carefully, update the share register, cancel the old share certificate and issue a new one to the transferee.

The procedure in more detail is:

1 Check that the details of the transferor and of the shareholding transferred agree with the share certificate and the register of members. Pay special attention to whether the whole or only part of the shareholding is being transferred.

2 If the company has several classes of shares in issue, check that the shares transferred are fully and correctly described. A separate transfer form should be completed for each class of shares being transferred.

3 If the shares transferred are partly paid, check that the amount shown as paid up on each share on the share certificate has been correctly entered on the transfer. If the company has recently called up a further amount on its shares, no transfer should be accepted until the due date of payment of the call unless the call has been previously paid. If the shares are partly paid, ensure that the transferee has executed (signed) the stock transfer form in addition to the transferor.

4 The share certificate accompanying the transfer should be the original issued by the company. If a duplicate share certificate has been issued, this must be surrendered to the company prior to registration.

5 Check that the transfer has been duly executed by the transferor or by his attorney. If the transferor's agent (e.g. broker, accountant or bank) is handling the share transfer process, the agent's stamp usually appears on the stock transfer form in the space provided. The presence of the agent's stamp should give additional comfort to the secretary/registrar that the signature of the transferor is genuine and this would help reduce the incidence of forged transfer fraud.

6 If the shares are held in joint names, all holders should execute (sign) the stock transfer form.

7 The company's registration records should be checked to ensure that the holding is free from any lien or restraint on transfer.

8 Check that the transfer has been stamped by HM Revenue & Customs and that the stamp duty (see below) payable is appropriate for the value of the transfer.

9 If all these points are in order, the transfer should be entered in the register of members, debiting the number of shares transferred in the transferor's account and crediting the account (new or existing) in the name of the transferee.

10 The old share certificate should be cancelled and a new certificate issued in the name of the transferee. If only part of the holding covered by the share certificate lodged is being transferred, prepare a balance certificate in the name of the transferor. The cancelled certificate should be endorsed with details of how the shares have been dealt with.

11 The transfer should be approved at a board meeting and authority given for the new certificate(s) to be sealed. If the company has in its Articles restrictions on transfer of shares or clauses giving pre-emption rights in connection with transfers, check that the transfer does not contravene any such provisions.

12 The transfer and cancelled share certificate should be filed.

13 The new certificate should be sealed by the company (or executed by it under CA 2006, s. 44) and sent to the transferee if he lodged the transfer personally or to any agent who may have lodged it on his behalf. Any balance certificates should be sent direct to the transferor or his agent. Certificates must be ready within two months of the date on which the transfer was lodged (CA 2006, s. 776). Where the company is listed, certificates should be issued within three business days of the lodgement of the transfer for registration.

A core duty for the company secretary is to monitor share movements and transactions on the register of members to identify any likelihood of stake-building in the company's shares by a potential takeover bidder (see Chapters 1 and 6). A public company is also entitled under

**STOCK TRANSFER FORM**

(Above this line for Registrars only)

**J30**

Certificate lodged with the Registrar

Consideration Money £ . . . . . . . . . . . . . . .

(For completion by the Registrar/Stock Exchange)

| Full name of Undertaking. | |
|---|---|
| Full description of Security. | |

| Number or amount of Shares, Stock or other security and, in figures column only, number and denomination of units, if any. | Words | Figures |
|---|---|---|
| | | ( units of ) |

Name(s) of registered holder(s) should be given in full; the address should be given where there is only one holder.

If the transfer is not made by the registered holder(s) insert also the name(s) and capacity (e.g., Executor(s)) of the person(s) making the transfer.

In the name(s) of

Account Designation (if any)

**PLEASE SIGN HERE** ⇨

I/We hereby transfer the above security out of the name(s) aforesaid to the person(s) named below *or to the several persons named in Parts 2 of Brokers Transfer Forms relating to the above security:*

Delete words in italics except for stock exchange transactions.
Signature(s) of

1. . . . . . . . . . . . . . . . . . . . . . . . . . . . . . . . . . . . . . . .

2. . . . . . . . . . . . . . . . . . . . . . . . . . . . . . . . . . . . . . . .

3. . . . . . . . . . . . . . . . . . . . . . . . . . . . . . . . . . . . . . . .

4. . . . . . . . . . . . . . . . . . . . . . . . . . . . . . . . . . . . . . . .

A body corporate should execute this transfer under its common seal or otherwise in accordance with applicable statutory requirements

Stamp of Selling Broker(s) or, for transactions which are not stock exchange transactions, of Agent(s), if any, acting for the Transferor(s).

Date . . . . . . . . . . . . . . .

Full name(s) and full postal address(es) (including County or, if applicable, Postal District number) of the person(s) to whom the security is transferred.

Please state title, if any, or whether Mr., Mrs. or Miss.

Please complete in typewriting or in Block Capitals.

Account Designation (if any)

I/We request that such entries be made in the register as are necessary to give effect to this transfer.

| Stamp of Buying Broker(s) (if any) | Stamp or name and address of person lodging this form (if other than the Buying Broker(s) ) |
|---|---|
| | |

Reference to the Registrar in this form means the registrar or registration agent of the undertaking, not the Registrar of Companies at Companies House

JFL0020 / Rev 5.3  03/2008

company law to require a company it has reason to believe has an interest in its voting shares to give full details of their holdings (see Chapter 8).

## Blank transfers

When the shareholder completes a stock transfer form but leaves the name of the transferee blank, this is called a **blank transfer**. This usually happens when the shares are used as a form of security for a bank loan. The completed form and share certificate are then deposited with the creditor (usually a banker). If the shareholder fails to repay the loan, the creditor completes the form and the shares are transferred to him.

## Forged transfers

A forgery is an invalid attempt to transfer shares and is void; no rights can be created. If it becomes apparent that shares have been transferred under a forged transfer:

- The true owner must be restored to the register of members and compensated for any lost dividends.
- The transferee must be removed from the register.
- If the transferee has already sold to another (a second transferee), the issue of a share certificate to that person will stop the company from denying his title; the second transferee will be able to sue for damages, but he must still be removed from the register of members.
- The company may claim compensation from the person who lodged the transfer.
- The transferee can claim compensation from the forger.

In some circumstances it may not be possible to make a successful recovery of losses from the forger. Companies and company registrars can therefore insure against losses caused by forged transfers under the Forged Transfers Acts 1891 and 1892.

---

**STOP AND THINK** **13.1**

Company secretaries should regularly review the amount of cover provided under any forged transfer insurance. The appropriate level of cover should reflect the capitalisation of the company.

---

## Refusal to register

Checks should be made as to whether there is any reason why the transfer should not be registered, for example, if the transferee is known to be an infant (particularly in the case of partly paid shares), a person of unsound mind, a bankrupt or an entity that is not a body corporate. Transfers that are unacceptable for any of these reasons should be refused registration under the powers given to directors by the general law or in the Articles of Association, even though the shares may be fully paid (Chapter 3 gives additional coverage on further restrictions on membership).

Private company Model Article 26 contains an unqualified right for directors to refuse to register any transfer. Public company Model Articles 63 and 64 provide that the directors may refuse to register the transfer of a share where:

- the share is not fully paid;
- the transfer is not lodged at the company's registered office or such other place as the directors have appointed;
- the transfer is not accompanied by the share certificate or such other evidence as the directors may require;
- the transfer is in respect of more than one class of share; or
- the transfer is in favour of more than four transferees.

Remember, however, that shares in listed companies must be freely transferable, so in practice directors are not generally in a position to restrict or refuse to register a transfer.

Refusal to register must be exercised in the interests of the company and must be positively effected by a resolution of the directors. It is not sufficient merely to take no action on a transfer. Notice of refusal to register must be given to the proposed transferee as soon as possible and in any event within two months of the date on which the transfer was lodged (CA 2006, s. 771 and Model Article 26 (public company Model Article 63)). If the company successfully refuses to register the transfer, the existing member holds the shares in trust for the transferee, who continues to own the equitable interest in the shares while the legal title remains with the vendor.

---

**TEST YOUR KNOWLEDGE 13.1**

**a** What is a stock transfer form?
**b** What is a blank transfer?
**c** What checks need to be made when registering a transfer?
**d** When might a transfer be refused?
**e** Why should companies consider forged transfer insurance?

---

## 2   Share certificates

Companies are required to issue share certificates to shareholders within two months after an issue of shares or the date when the transfer documents have been received by the company (CA 2006, ss. 769 and 776). The issue of share certificates is a core duty of the company secretary. A share certificate should contain at least the following basic information:

- a certificate serial number;
- the name and number of the company;
- the name of the registered holder exactly as it appears in the register of members;
- the number and description of the shares to which the certificate relates, including a statement as to the extent to which the shares are paid up;
- the date of the certificate.

Every member is entitled to one or more certificate(s) free of charge for all the shares of each class held (Model Article 24, public company Model Article 46). Each certificate should be sealed with the seal or executed under signature. The company is not bound to issue more than one certificate for joint holders. If a certificate is lost (see below) or destroyed, the company may require any evidence and indemnity necessary to protect itself from exposure of fraudulent use of the lost or stolen certificate. This does not apply if the certificate is defaced and returned to the company for reissue.

Keep in mind that a share certificate is only *prima facie* evidence of a holding and the person in possession of a certificate may not necessarily be the holder of the shares. The register of members provides the definitive evidence of a holding.

The company secretary usually retains a store of blank certificates for issue at a later date. These should be kept in a locked cabinet to prevent unauthorised access or stored in a secured place on a computer system.

### 2.1 Listed company requirements

Listed companies must also comply with the detailed requirements of the Listing Rules, for example, the certificate must state the country of incorporation and the authority under which the company is incorporated. If the shares have preferential rights, these should be detailed on the reverse of the certificate. For security reasons, the number of shares should be shown twice in the certificates of listed companies, either once in figures and once in words, or once in figures and once in figures contained in boxes referring to millions, hundreds of thousands, tens of thousands, thousands, hundreds, tens and units.

---

**SAMPLE WORDING 13.1**

**Certificate for ordinary shares**

ORDINARY SHARES

Certificate no._____No. of shares

. . . . . . . . . . . . . . . . . . . . . . . . . . . . . . plc

(Incorporated under the Companies Act 2006)

(Registered in England and Wales No. 1234567)

THIS IS TO CERTIFY that . . . . . . . . . . . . . . . . . . is/are the Registered Holder(s) of . . . . fully paid Ordinary Shares of 10 pence each in the above-named company, subject to the Articles of Association of the Company.

Executed by . . . . . . . . . . . . . . . . . . . . . . plc

this . . . . . . . . . . day of . . . . . . . . . . 20xx*

(Signed) . . . . . . . . . . . . . . . . . . . . . . (Director)

. . . . . . . . . . . . . . . . . . . . . . . . . . . (Secretary/Director)

T. No . . . . . .

No transfer of the shares (or any portion thereof) comprised in this certificate can be registered without the production of this certificate.

Exd. . . . . . . . . . . . . . . . . . . . . . . . . . . . . . . . . . . . . . . . . . . . . . . . . . . . . . . . . . . . . . . . . . . . . .

*Certificates may instead be executed by impressed seal (common seal or securities seal), rather than by signature under CA 2006, s. 44, in which event the Articles will usually provide that certificates may be sealed without the need for signature. In this event the execution clause will instead read:

Given under the [common] seal of the Company this . . . . . . . . . . day of . . . . . . 20xx

---

## 2.2 Lost certificates

Once the company secretary has been informed by a member, or his representative, that a share certificate may be lost, the procedure is as follows:

1  Note in the register that a particular certificate is reported missing. Ask the member to conduct a thorough search for the missing certificate.
2  Once it has been confirmed that the certificate is definitely lost, ask the member to execute an indemnity guaranteed by the bank or insurance company to protect the company against the fraudulent misuse of the lost certificate. The bank or insurance company will usually charge the shareholder a fee for this indemnity. It is also not unusual for the company to request that a statutory declaration regarding the circumstances of the certificate's loss to be executed by the shareholder.
3  On receipt of the indemnity, issue a duplicate share certificate, marked 'Duplicate'.
4  Enter the details of the original certificate on the 'stop list'.
5  Ask the member to return the lost certificate if it is subsequently found.

## 2.3 Request for certification

Certification occurs when a member wishes to split the shares represented in one certificate or to sell shares to more than one person in one transaction. This is necessary because it is not possible to provide a share certificate to accompany the stock transfer form for more than one transferee at the same time.

The procedure is as follows:

1 The member lodges the share certificate and the transfer form with the company.
2 The company endorses the transfer form with the words 'certificate lodged' and returns it to the member. The transferee is obliged by CA 2006, s. 775 to accept the endorsement of the company in lieu of the share certificate.
3 On return of the transfer form, the company issues the appropriate share certificates: one certificate representing the number of shares transferred and a balance certificate representing the number of shares retained by the seller.

---

### TEST YOUR KNOWLEDGE 13.2

a What information should be shown on a share certificate?
b What is the procedure when a member loses his share certificate?
c Why is certification necessary?

---

## 3 Registration of documents

The registrar should establish reliable systems for checking and recording the documents received. For example, all documents received for registration must indicate clearly the particular shareholding concerned and the full name and address of the shareholder as registered. Where joint shareholders are concerned, the names in the document should be in the same order as they appear in the register of members. If there is any discrepancy between name(s) in the register and names in the document, a declaration of identity should be obtained before the document is registered.

Documents lodged for registration should be photocopied and given a serial number. This should also be included in any entry in the register of members to enable cross referencing in future.

### 3.1 Transmission of shares

Transmission of shares occurs when ownership changes other than by ordinary transfer, such as on the death, insolvency or insanity of the member. A stock transfer form does not need to be completed and there is no stamp duty to be paid as no payment is made.

### Member's death

CA 2006, s. 773 provides that an instrument of transfer may be executed by a personal representative on behalf of a deceased person.

CA 2006, s. 774 provides that any document produced to the company that is by law sufficient evidence of **grant of probate** or **letters of administration** is acceptable. There is no need to request a copy of the death certificate provided a **grant of representation** has been received. This is because the grant will include the confirmation that the person has died. Although the legal title to the shares passes automatically to the executor, the name of the deceased must remain on the register of members until the appropriate documentation has been produced.

The grant of probate must be an office copy bearing the impression of the seal of the court. Once this has been received, the procedure outlined in Checklist 13.1 applies.

# CHECKLIST 13.1 Member's death: grant of probate

✓ Check that there is a complete match between the deceased's name in the probate and the registered shareholder in the company.

✓ Check whether the deceased had more than one shareholding (e.g. one in his own name and another in joint names).

✓ Check for any other matters that may affect the transmission of shares (e.g. a recent bankruptcy order).

✓ Check that the share certificate has been returned and if not, ask for it to be sent.

✓ Keep a photocopy of the grant of probate.

✓ Enter the date of registration of the probate with the name and address of the executor(s) named in the probate in the account of the deceased in the register of members, annotating with the word 'deceased' after the name of the shareholder.

✓ Annotate the share certificate with the fact of death, the date of registration of the probate and the name(s) of the executor(s).

✓ Endorse the probate and the share certificate with the company's registration stamp and return them to the person who lodged them with the company. It is helpful to enclose a new dividend mandate form for completion, revoking any existing instructions.

When a person dies without making a will, or where the person named in the will is unable to act, letters of administration are granted by the court appointing a person to administer the estate. The procedure for registering letters of administration is similar to the procedure above. For example, where a person dies without a valid will and leaving no relatives, a grant of administration is made appointing the Treasury Solicitor to administer the estate. Where a sole or surviving executor dies without having named an executor, or a sole or surviving administrator dies, in either case without having completed the distribution of the original deceased's estate, the court will appoint a person to administer the estate.

Once the grant has been accepted by the secretary/registrar, the personal representative(s) may address a letter of request to the company to enter their names in the register of members as holders of the shares or to register the shares in the name of a third party (e.g. the person named in any valid will). The method of dealing with the shares is determined by the Articles (Model Articles 27–29; public company Model Articles 65–68). There is no prescribed form for the letter of request, but as a practical measure the company should have its own template version to send to the personal representative, which should be signed by all executors or administrators. The letter should be registered by the company (unless the Articles prohibit it) if a grant of representation for the shareholder has already been registered.

Once a letter of request has been registered by a company, neither a grant of probate nor any subsequent grant of administration may be registered by the company.

If a member's death occurs just before a general meeting, the secretary should review the company's Articles to see if a personal representative can attend. Model Article 27 (public company Model Article 66) does not give personal representatives the right to attend or vote at general meetings, although this does not prevent the representative from receiving notice.

When the value of an estate is less than £5,000 and the shareholding is not large, the company may apply the simplified procedures under the Administration of Estates (Small Payments) Act 1965. Where the deceased's personal representative is applying to have the shares transferred to them without grant of probate, they must produce:

- the death certificate;
- the share certificate;
- a statutory declaration which states the claimant's relationship to the deceased and the reasons for claiming the deceased's shares (this will need to be sworn in the presence of a solicitor); and
- a letter of indemnity, usually backed by a third party guarantee.

If the secretary/registrar is in doubt as to whether the simplified procedure is applicable, the usual process of seeking grant of representation should be requested.

### Member's death in joint shareholdings

If one of two or more joint shareholders dies, the principle of survivorship applies and the surviving holder(s) will have full powers to deal with the joint shareholding. A certified copy of the death certificate is required to evidence the death. The register of members should be amended by crossing out the name of the deceased holder so that the surviving (joint) holder(s) remain. The copy of the death certificate should be recorded and validated by the company's registration stamp, the share certificate endorsed and validated, and the documents returned to the sender. If the deceased was the first named holder in the joint holding, the second named holder shall become the first, the third named holder shall become the second, etc.

The secretary should be aware of the restrictions in public company Model Article 65, which state that nothing shall release the estate of a deceased member from any liability in respect of any share which had been jointly held. There is no equivalent article in the private company Model Articles as they envisage that all shares will be fully paid.

### Member's insolvency

Under IA 1986, an individual becomes bankrupt when the court makes an order against him. A trustee is then appointed to administer the estate of the bankrupt person. The shareholding remains in the name of the bankrupt shareholder until a letter of request is received from the trustee in bankruptcy. The shares held by the bankrupt are usually sold to raise money for the creditors, but may also be registered in the name of a third party (i.e. a creditor).

If the shares are partly paid, the trustee may disclaim them as 'onerous property'. If the bankrupt is a joint holder, his interest passes to the trustee and not the remaining holders.

### Member's mental disorder

The Court of Protection may declare a person mentally unfit under the Mental Health Act 1983. A court order is issued giving specified powers to a receiver. The receiver is entitled to deal with the shares according to the powers granted under the court order and the secretary/registrar should ensure that the court order is inspected carefully to ensure the receiver does not act outside of those powers.

## 3.2 Power of attorney

Under the Power of Attorneys Act 1971, an agent (the attorney) can be given the power to act on someone's behalf. A power of attorney may be specific (i.e. for a particular purpose) or general (i.e. for a specified period of time). A general power of attorney is often used when the principal (the 'donor') is ill, going abroad or where a trustee delegates his power.

The Mental Capacity Act 2005, which applies only in England and Wales, enables individuals to grant a lasting power of attorney even if they should lose their capacity. In order for the powers to come into effect they must first be registered with the Public Guardian (see Directory) which maintains a register of Lasting Powers of Attorney (LPA) and Enduring Powers of Attorney (EPA).

Enduring Powers of Attorney, created under the Enduring Powers of Attorney Act (EPAA) 1985, remain valid, but if the donor of the power has become incapable, must be registered with the Public Guardian before they can be used.

The power should be executed as a deed. The individual should sign the document, making it clear that the document is executed as a deed (e.g. by using the words: 'Signed by . . . . . . . . . . . . . . as a deed'). The signature should be witnessed by an independent witness.

When a power of attorney is received for registration, the procedure outlined in Checklist 13.2 should be followed.

## ✅ CHECKLIST 13.2 **Power of attorney**

✓ Check that it is in the correct form and has been executed properly.

✓ Check that there is complete match between the donor of the power and either a registered shareholder or a person in the process of acquiring shares, evidenced by, for example, a stock transfer form or a renounced allotment letter.

✓ Check that the power is an original or a copy certified as genuine by a solicitor or stockbroker.

✓ If the power was set up under EPAA 1985, check that there is documentary support that it has been registered with the Public Guardian.

✓ Photocopy the complete power for the company's records.

✓ Check whether the appointment is joint, in which case establish whether the attorneys must act together ('joint') or may act individually ('joint and severally'). Check also whether the registered address of the shareholder might have changed.

✓ Note when the power becomes effective and any expiry date or expiry event.

✓ Stamp the power with the company's registration stamp and return it to the sender.

Every time a document executed by the attorney is lodged with the company, cross-check it with the copy of the power to ensure validity. The secretary should also check for any limitations on the power and should also check for any specified time period within which the power will lapse.

---

### 👤 STOP AND THINK **13.2**

Company secretaries often provide advice to shareholders on practical queries. When advising shareholders, company secretaries should remember that a power of attorney can be used to authorise another person to act on the shares without the need for a share transfer. This may provide a practical solution for a shareholder's query.

---

### 📝 SAMPLE WORDING **13.2**

**Form of general power of attorney (pursuant to Powers of Attorney Act 1971, s. 10)**

This general Power of Attorney is made this . . . . . day of. . .20xx by A.B. of . . . . . . . . . . . . . . . . . . . . . .

I appoint C.D. of . . . . . . . . . . . . . . . . . . . . . . . . . . . . . . . . . . . . . . . . .

[or C.D. of . . . . . . . . . . . . . . . . . . . . . . and E.F. of . . . . . . . . . . . . . . . . . . . . . . . jointly or jointly and severally] to be my attorney(s) in accordance with section 10 of the Powers of Attorney Act 1971.

IN WITNESS WHEREOF I have hereunto set my hand and seal the day and year first above written.

Signed, sealed and delivered by the above-named A. B. in the presence of:

. . . . . . . . . . . . . . . . . . . . . . . . . . . . . . . . . . . . . . . . . . . .

A power of attorney may be ended in the following ways:

- the power was created for a fixed time period or event;
- the power is revoked at any time by the donor;
- the donor dies; or
- the donor becomes mentally ill (however an enduring power of attorney would not be revoked in this case).

When a power is revoked or lapses, the copy of the power should be suitably marked and moved to a lapsed file.

## 3.3 Court orders

The registrar's department will have to deal with a number of court orders. The most frequent orders and the effect of each of them are summarised below:

1 *Stop notice* – Under the Charging Orders Act 1979, a stop notice is a set of documents stamped by the court with which a company must comply. The stop notice will consist of at least two documents: (i) a Notice; and (ii) an Affidavit provided by the person who wishes to lodge the notice. A stop notice is an instruction from the court restraining the company from accepting any transfer from the person named in the transfer for a period of 14 days. Stop notices can also be applied to dividend payments. If after 14 days no further instructions have been received, the company can proceed to register the transfer of shares. A note should be made in the register of members that restrictions have been placed on the holding. If during the 14-day period attempts are made to transfer the shares or the dividend is due to be paid, a notice should be sent to the person who lodged the stop notice.

2 *Bankruptcy order* – This is an order to vest the shares in a trustee after the member has been declared bankrupt. After verifying and registering the documents, all further communications should be addressed to the trustee, or as directed by him.

3 *Protection order* – A receiver may be appointed by order of the Court of Protection to manage the income of a person who is deemed incapable because of mental disorder.

4 *Liquidation* – The company will require a copy of the court order in a compulsory winding up. In a voluntary winding up, copies of the resolution to wind up and the appointment of the liquidator will be required.

5 **Charging order** – This is a court order charging the shareholder's shares for the benefit of his creditors, in other words, the shares are sold to pay the debts. The order is in two parts. First, an interim provisional order is made which acts a stop notice. If settlement of the debt is made, the order will be discharged. If settlement is not made, the order is may be made final or absolute, which authorises the sale of the shares.

6 **Vesting order** – A court order requiring a change of owner of the shares, usually applied when removing a trustee from the register of members.

7 **Third party debt order** (previously known as a garnishee order) – A court order which can apply to income generated from assets, which in the case of shares will apply to dividends. Dividends from the shares will be applied for the benefit of the shareholder's creditors, in other words, the dividends are ordered to be paid to the shareholder's creditors. As with a charging order, third party debt orders are made in two parts. However, the third party debt order itself cannot effect the transfer of shares to another person. Nor can a third party debt order prevent the shareholder from selling the shares whilst the third party order is in effect.

On receipt of any of the above documents the secretary/registrar should take the steps outlined in Checklist 13.3.

### CHECKLIST 13.3 Secretary's actions on receiving a court order

✓ Check that the document received is an original or 'office copy' provided by the court, bearing the seal of the court. Photocopies of documents are not acceptable.

✓ Make sure the details of the court documents agree with the details on the register of members. If in doubt, seek clarification of the identities.

✓ Make a careful check in case the same shareholder is on the register of members more than once (e.g. once in their sole name and again in a separate entry as part of a joint holding).

✓ Carefully review the scope of the powers claimed under the court order.

✓ Review any effective dates, if applicable, contained in the court order and ensure any action is taken in good time.

✓ Make appropriate notes against the register of members.

✓ Review the company's corporate calendar so that you are ready to take any appropriate action ahead of an impending event, for example, a dividend record or payment date.

All court orders should be acted on as soon as they are received.

## 3.4 Other matters relating to ownership

Other situations that can occur are listed briefly below:

■ *Notices to joint holders* – CA 2006, Part 6 of Sch. 5 (communications by a company) provides that all notices and other communications may be sent to the first name on the register and notice so given shall be sufficient notice to all the joint holders. Companies do have the discretion of sending communications to each joint holder and the Model Articles are silent on the matter. Transfers, however, require signatures from all the joint members.

■ *Dividend payments to joint holders* – Model Article 31 (public company Model Article 72) provides that dividend payments to the first named holder of a joint holding is good discharge of the payment.

■ *Change of name* – The member must submit the share certificate, together with evidence of change of name (e.g. marriage certificate or deed poll). The documents provided must be originals, or the office copy or a photocopy certified by an acceptable third party, such as a solicitor. If the shareholder is a corporate shareholder, they should provide the certificate of incorporation to evidence the change of name (see Chapter 8). The secretary/registrar should take a copy of the appropriate evidence and return originals to the member. The register of members should then be amended. The share certificate can be recalled and amended to show the change of name and sent back to the member. Alternatively, it may be recalled and retained by the company and a replacement certificate issued in the new name.

■ *Change of address* – Changes should be signed by the member if possible. A notification of a change purported to be given by a member of the member's family should never be accepted. Ideally, notifications should give details of the old and new addresses to facilitate identification. On receiving notification of a change of address, it is sensible to review any recent mailings to the shareholder, in case they have been sent to the wrong address.

■ *Nominee shareholders* – CA 2006, s. 126 prohibits the entry of a trust onto the register of members in the case of companies registered in England and Wales. A company cannot, therefore, recognise a beneficial interest under a trust. This situation is commonly dealt with by placing nominee information against the name of the legal holder, for example 'X Nominees Limited, A/C Jane Smith'.

■ *Minors* – The Model Articles do not contain a prohibition against minors becoming members of a company, but it is not good practice to accept a minor as a member in his own name. One reason is because complications can arise regarding the contractual capacity of the minor, especially if the shares are partly paid. The usual course of action is to request that the shares be registered in the legal name of a responsible adult (e.g. a parent or guardian), with the name of the holding showing an account in respect of the minor. For example, 'Harold Williams' [i.e. the adult] A/C James Williams' [i.e. the minor].

- *Designated account* – If a bank is holding a number of shares for different clients, it can request that its single holding be split into different accounts, designated to represent each of its clients, for example, Standard Bank No. 1, Standard Bank No. 2. This ability to separate accounts is available to all members.
- *Statutory declarations* – These include declarations of identity and declarations of usage, and must be in a form as stipulated by the Statutory Declarations Act 1835. A statutory declaration must be sworn in front of a solicitor.
- *Failure to notify contact details* – Public company Model Article 80 provides that if a company sends two consecutive documents to a member over a period of at least twelve months and each of those documents is returned undelivered, that member ceases to be entitled to receive notices from the company. The member must then provide the company his new address or other means of contacting the holder as permitted by the company (e.g. email) or in statute. There are no equivalent provisions in the Model Articles for a private company.

---

**STOP AND THINK 13.3**

The importance of accuracy when making changes related to share ownership cannot be overemphasised. Company secretaries should ensure that they have appropriate processes in place to ensure register amendments have been thoroughly checked.

---

**TEST YOUR KNOWLEDGE 13.3**

a  What is the difference between transfer and transmission of shares?
b  What is the procedure for registering the death of a member?
c  Explain the difference between a grant of probate and letters of administration? What is the collective description for both of these terms?
d  What steps are required on a member's death in a joint shareholding?
e  What checks should be made when a power of attorney is received for registration?
f  What usually happens to the shares held by a member upon his insolvency?
g  What are the two parts of a charging order?
h  What documents should be requested upon the change of name of a member?

---

## 4  Stamp duty and stamp duty reserve tax (SDRT)

### 4.1 Stamp duty charge

Sales of shares or stock or marketable securities attract stamp duty ad valorem (according to the value of the transaction), currently at the rate of 0.5% of the value payable by the transferee. Stamp duty is not payable for instruments executed where the consideration of the transaction is £1,000 or less (the previous threshold was £5). Where transfer is subject to stamp duty, a rounding charge applies to the next £5.

### 4.2 Exemptions

The reverse of the stock transfer form (see above) contains two certificates, one of which must be signed if the transfer is exempt from ad valorem stamp duty. The following are the most common instances which will qualify for one of the two exemptions:

- Where the consideration for the transaction does not exceed £1,000. The person signing the certificate must confirm that the transaction does not form part of a larger transaction or series of transactions which would in total exceed £1,000 (this is necessary to prevent the avoidance of stamp duty payment).

■ Transfers which were previously subject to a £5 fixed duty, such as transfers between nominees and declarations of trust.

■ Where there is no monetary consideration (e.g. on shares transferred as a gift or transfers between spouses).

■ Shares which have been transferred by way of transmission, such as on bankruptcy or insolvency of the shareholder, as part of a divorce settlement/ dissolution of a civil partnership, or on shares transmitted following the death of a shareholder.

■ Cancellation or sale of treasury shares which have previously been purchased by the company (see chapter 12).

Where the transfer being made is claiming the benefit of stamp duty exemptions, the secretary or registrar should make a careful check that the certification on the reverse of the stock transfer form has been properly completed. Where the transfer qualifies for stamp duty exemption, the stock transfer form is not sent to the HM Revenue and Customs Stamp Office as part of the transfer process.

Where a large company with many subsidiaries wants to transfer shares from one subsidiary company to another, it would not be appropriate for stamp duty to be paid on the full value of the shares transferred as the shares still remain within the same group of companies. Parent companies may, therefore, take advantage of the provisions of the Finance Act 1930, s. 42 which will allow them to apply to the stamp office to exempt the transfer of shares from stamp duty.

An exemption to stamp duty may also apply to certain transactions where the offeror company is acquiring the offeree company in a share for share transaction.

The person responsible for maintaining the company's register of members is legally responsible for ensuring that all transfers accepted for registration are duly stamped, or certified as exempt.

## 4.3 Stamp duty reserve tax (SDRT)

SDRT is a separate tax with its own rules, procedure and collection machinery. It is charged at the rate of 50p per £100 on share transactions which do not attract stamp duty, including Stock Exchange transactions settled through CREST. Transactions involving renounceable letters of allotment and transaction closed within a short period of time attract reserve tax.

---

✎ **TEST YOUR KNOWLEDGE** **13.4**

a  Under what circumstances are share transfers usually exempt from stamp duty?
b  In which circumstances is stamp duty reserve tax applicable?

---

Unlike stamp duty, the tax applies to the agreement to transfer (whether oral or written) and does not depend on the execution of a written instrument of transfer for a charge to arise. The tax charge arises on the date the agreement is made or becomes unconditional and the tax is payable seven days after the end of the month in which the charge arises, except where the tax is accounted for by special arrangement between the stamp office and operators of electronic transfer systems and exchanges.

SDRT (at 1.5%) also applies to transfers to certain nominees (lists are published by HM Revenue & Customs) where, for example, the shares are to be held as cover for American Depositary Receipts. Both stamp duty and SDRT legislation provide for penalties for late payment and interest may also be charged.

# 5   CREST and the dematerialisation of shares

CREST is the settlement system for most listed equities and other traded financial instruments and is a recognised clearing house. It was established in order to bring securities trading in the UK and Eire up to the best international standards by making securities settlement faster, cheaper and more secure by using less paperwork. CREST is a voluntary system, giving investors the choice of holding their securities in certificated form or in dematerialised accounts. Certificated form is more expensive to hold and transfer, reflecting the additional administrative work involved in handling share certificates. Settlement within CREST occurs on a 'delivery versus payment' basis; that is, at the point the buyer acquires title to the securities, the buyer's bank guarantees to pay the seller's bank, who in turn becomes obliged to pay the seller. Delivery versus payment helps to provide additional confidence in the market that trades will be settled and shares transferred on time.

## 5.1 The CREST players

- At the centre is the CREST processing system, owned and operated by Euroclear, which facilitates the following:
  - authenticating and matching instructions from parties who wish to settle a transaction;
  - amending records of account holdings and recording associated payment obligations;
  - roviding information for settlement banks and registrars to allow legal title and payment to be moved;
  - calculating and collecting stamp duty and SDRT (see above) and subsequent payment to HM Revenue and Customs;
  - monitoring the behaviour of members and maintaining industry standards.
- A participant is an organisation having a formal relationship with CREST and includes members, registrars, receiving agents, payment banks, regulators, HM Revenue & Customs and information providers.
- A user is a participant with the technical capacity to input into CREST who may act on behalf of one or more participants, which may include themselves.
- A member is a participant who holds stock in accounts within the CREST system and who appears on the company register as the legal owner of the securities. They must:
  - have a contract with a bank who in turn has a contract with CREST;
  - be a user; and
  - accept the terms and obligations of CREST.
- A sponsored member is an institution that has the same rights and responsibilities as a member, but relies on a sponsoring user to interface with CREST. This will allow a CREST participant to have separate nominee companies appear on company registers with the participant as user and the nominee companies as sponsored members. In addition, within each membership and sponsored membership account, a number of separate identities (designations), called Member Accounts, can be established. This enables members or sponsored members to operate individual client holdings.
- Payment banks are those participants who guarantee payment for transactions delivered to their customer through CREST, although actual settlement takes place outside CREST.
- Participants and users must adhere to strict performance and security requirements of the CREST system, which are set out in operating manuals.

## 5.2 How CREST works

CREST provides an interactive Windows package. The process is as follows:

1 *Input* – Two CREST members agree a transaction and the settlement instructions are input by their users.
2 *Matching* – CREST authenticates and matches the settlement instructions.
3 *Settlement* – When the time for settlement is reached, CREST will:
   a) adjust buyers and sellers securities accounts to reflect movement of stock;
   b) adjust cash memorandum accounts;

c) amend payment obligations of member's payment banks;

d) send a register update request (RUR) to the registrar; and

e) mark the transaction as 'settled'.

4 *Registration* – The registrar responds to the RUR within two hours by amending the register to reflect the members' accounts within CREST.

The Stock Exchange operates **rolling settlement** three working days after the bargain is struck (T + 3). This applies to certificated and dematerialised shares. In order to ensure that they can meet the requirements of T + 3 settlement, active private investors are more likely to hold shares in a nominee. This results in the underlying shareholder losing direct contact with the company unless specific arrangements were made by the nominee. CA 2006, ss. 145–153 addresses this problem by providing for nominees to decide whether they wish to send requests to receive information from underlying shareholders directly to the company. If the nominee decides to send the requests to the company, the company is obliged to send the information (e.g. the annual report) direct to the underlying shareholder.

The functionality of CREST has increased since its introduction, reflecting its popularity with institutions, registrars and other users. Additional services provided now include:

- settlement of money market instruments and a wide range of international securities;
- corporate actions, including electronic proxy voting;
- support in the administration of large-scale new share issues;
- electronic dividend payments, electronic tax vouchers and other electronic dividend election instructions.

## 5.3  Becoming eligible for CREST

Almost all listed securities participate in CREST. A newly listed company will need to consider the settlement of transactions in CREST. The following points should be noted:

- A board resolution is sufficient to make securities eligible for CREST. Statutory provisions provide that this may override any prohibitive provisions in the Articles of Association. However, it is still good practice to review the Articles and to make necessary amendments at the first available opportunity.
- Notice of the board resolution must be given to every member of the company within 60 days of it being passed.
- A copy of the board resolution must be sent to the Registrar of Companies within 15 days of its passing and must be appended to the Articles of Association.

## 5.4  CREST and the registrar

The principal role of the registrar when looking at share transfers and transmissions is the reconciliation between CREST holdings and those of the registrar. This involves:

- responding rapidly to register update requests (see above);
- daily reconciliation of total CREST holdings for each security;
- daily reconciliation of each stock account which has been adjusted with the registered accounts, to ensure all transactions have been properly communicated;
- periodic reconciliation of all balances.

In response to market-makers' concerns about the visibility of their settled positions, CREST provides and runs a member of CREST called CREPON. This member, acting as a pooled nominee, holds stock for those who wish to operate their own accounts directly, but who do not wish to appear on the register. CREPON provides market-makers with the same facilities that are available to normal CREST members, but ensures their holdings appear as a single entry on the register.

## 5.5  Dematerialisation of shares

CA 2006 has provisions which allow for the mandatory dematerialisation of shares. These provisions have not been enacted and would only be likely to be enacted following consultation with companies, registrars, nominees and shareholder interest groups. The provisions allowing mandatory dematerialisation arise as a result of calls within the securities industry to stop issuing share certificates as evidence of share ownership and also to streamline the share transfer process without the need for share certificates.

---

**TEST YOUR KNOWLEDGE** **13.5**

**a**  In relation to CREST, what is (i) a participant; (ii) a user; and (iii) a sponsored member?
**b**  What is rolling settlement?
**c**  What is the role of the registrar in relation to CREST?

---

## CASE QUESTION

As explained earlier, the share register of Multiple plc is maintained by Accurate Registrars Limited. As company secretary of Multiple plc you wish to hold regular meetings with Accurate Registrars to ensure they are providing a high level of service in respect of the maintenance of the register. In view of this:

**1**  Prepare an agenda for the regular meetings with Accurate Registrars which will cover (a) all of the topics you need to discuss to ensure the register of members is being maintained appropriately, and (b) useful management information in respect of the share register.

**2**  What levels of service would you expect from Accurate Registrars? Prepare a list which shows the target times in which you want Accurate Registrars to deal with the various matters which may arise maintaining the register of members.

## CHAPTER SUMMARY

- Shares are transferred using a stock transfer form unless the parties concerned are members of CREST. Care must be taken that the transfer is executed according to regulation and best practice, and that any likelihood of fraud is minimised. Every effort should be made to ensure that the register of members is accurate. The secretary should also be aware of share movements to alert the board to the possibility of stake-building.

- Transmission of shares and other registrations are also a key part of the company secretary's role. All documentation provided for registration should be carefully checked and in case of doubt further evidence should be requested.

- The company secretary may be the person to whom court orders are delivered. He must ensure that they are dealt with promptly.

- Share certificates are *prima facie* evidence of a holding. The register of members provides definitive evidence as to who are the members.

- A power of attorney can be used to authorise another person to act on the shares without the need for a share transfer.

- Unless exempted, the transfer of shares will attract stamp duty or stamp duty reserve tax. The conditions for exemption can be found on the stock transfer form.

- CREST is the paperless settlement system for public quoted equities. It provides institutional investors and active private investors the opportunity to trade shares more efficiently and with less administration.

# Dividends

## ■ CONTENTS

## ■ INTRODUCTION

In whatever way dividends are paid to members – whether in cash or in assets – the company secretary is responsible for making the arrangements. This chapter concentrates on the procedures necessary to ensure that the process goes smoothly. We start by looking at the Model Articles and then follow these into practice.

The second half of the chapter looks at scrip and DRIP dividends and we conclude with the role of the external registrar in paying dividends.

## 1  What are dividends?

Companies have an implied power to distribute profits to members, subject to any limitations in the Articles of Association. A company may not make a distribution except out of distributable profits available for the purpose (CA 2006, s. 830). These are defined as a company's accumulated realised profits less its accumulated realised losses. **Dividend** payments may not be made out of capital, which must be maintained so that the company can meet its liabilities due to creditors. Statutory provisions in respect of distributions are contained in the CA 2006, Part 23, ss. 829–853.

A company's Articles set out the rights of different classes of shareholder to receive dividends. Model Article 71 for a public company provides that, subject to any rights attached to shares, dividends are declared and paid according to the amounts paid up on the shares; partly paid shareholders usually receive dividends pro rata to the amount that they have paid up on the shares. There is no equivalent provision in the Model Articles for a private company as it is envisaged that all shares will be fully paid.

Cash dividends are either paid as:

- a **final dividend**, after the end of the financial year, based on the final audited accounts for the year; or
- an **interim dividend**, before the end of the financial year.

Public companies must ensure that the proposed distribution does not reduce the net assets of the company to less than the aggregate of the company's called-up share capital and its undistributable reserves. Shareholders do not usually have a right to receive a dividend unless shares of a particular class carry a fixed dividend. A dividend is declared and paid at the directors' discretion. The decision whether a distribution can be made is determined in conjunction with the company's relevant accounts (CA 2006, s. 836) – normally the last audited accounts (CA 2006, s. 837).

If the accounts show that there are insufficient distributable profits to make a distribution, the directors must refer to interim accounts. These must be prepared to such a standard that they would enable a reasonable judgement to be made. The interim accounts prepared by a public company must comply with the rules for preparing annual accounts; they do not need to be audited, but they must be filed with the Registrar of Companies. There are no rules concerning the format of interim accounts for a private company, nor is there any filing requirement. Thus private companies can use suitable management accounts to support a dividend payment in such circumstances. Similar requirements relate to public companies that propose to make a distribution during their first financial year. In such cases, the accounts ('initial accounts') must be accompanied by an auditor's report.

At a board meeting where a dividend payment is proposed, the secretary should offer guidance to the directors to ensure the discussion includes a review of the relevant accounts. When preparing board minutes of the discussion, explicit reference must be made that the directors reviewed relevant accounts prior to approving or proposing the dividend payment.

## 1.1 Dividend regulations

The payment of dividends is regulated by CA 2006, Part 23. The Model Articles provide additional regulations:

1 *Declaration* – A company may declare dividends by ordinary resolution. Members may resolve to decrease the amount recommended by directors, but may not declare a dividend that exceeds the amount recommended by the directors (Model Article 30; public company Model Article 70).

2 *Interim dividend* – These are paid between general meetings and do not need the approval of shareholders. The power to pay interim dividends is usually delegated to the directors, who must be satisfied that the payment is justified by sufficient distributable profits (Model Article 30, public company Model Article 70).

3 *Right to receive dividends* – Subject to any rights attached to shares, dividends are declared and paid according to the amounts paid up on the shares for which the dividend is paid (public company Model Article 71).

4 *Payment* – This is usually made by **dividend warrant** (essentially, a cheque). Since 1973, no tax has been deducted from dividends, which are paid at the rate declared. Before the abolition of advance corporation tax (ACT) in April 1999, the company was required to pay a sum equal to the tax credit to the Inland Revenue (now HM Revenue & Customs). The abolition of ACT does not mean that tax credits are abolished. They are now reduced from a quarter of the net dividend (20% of the gross) to one ninth (10% of the gross).

5 *Joint holders* – Dividend warrants are usually issued in the name of and sent to the first person on a joint holding. This is good discharge for the company profits (Model Article 31, public company Model Article 72). It is therefore up to the other joint holders to claim their share of any dividend from the first named holder.

6 *Interest* – No interest is payable on dividends unless the shares carry an express right (Model Article 32, public company Model Article 74). This means that if the dividend remains outstanding, the member is unlikely to be able to claim any interest to which the company may have received the benefit.

7 *Unclaimed dividends* – Any dividend not claimed within 12 years of the date due for payment can be forfeited and is no longer owed by the company (Model Article 33, public company Model Article 75).

8 **Scrip dividends** (see section 3) – These are shares issued fully paid to shareholders instead of a cash dividend. They are different from bonus issues as the shareholder is usually given the choice of electing to take shares or cash.

## 1.2 Illegal dividends

Problems with illegal dividend payments can arise in many cases because public companies have failed to file interim accounts at Companies House, as may be required prior to the payment of a dividend.

There are no criminal sanctions for breaches of the CA relating to the payment of dividends. The civil consequences of receiving an unlawful dividend are covered in CA 2006, s. 847.

A director who is a party to an unlawful distribution could be liable to the company for breach of duty if he is misapplying its funds. A shareholder is entitled to assume in the absence of any evidence to the contrary that the dividend was properly paid from realised profits.

---

**CASE EXAMPLE 14.1**

**Illegal dividends**

An investment trust found that it had paid dividends that were technically illegal because of non-filing of interim accounts for the previous ten years. It therefore asked shareholders to pass a special resolution to sanction the distributions and to authorise the company to execute deeds of waiver releasing shareholders and the directors from any liability. The directors and their associates abstained from voting and HM Revenue & Customs permission had been obtained confirming that the dividends would continue to be treated as having been paid at the time of the original payment. Non-UK-based shareholders were advised to consult their own professional advisers.

It was held in the Precision Dippings case that shareholders could not retrospectively validate an illegal dividend; however, the route taken by the investment trust seems to achieve similar aims. If such a resolution were to be passed and it was later found that the company was facing solvency problems at the date of the resolution, the validity of the deeds of waiver might be open to challenge. However, the investment trust took extensive legal advice before involving the shareholders.

---

The initiative in paying dividends rests with the directors because they declare them and approve the accounts on which they are based. Accordingly, the directors are liable if a dividend is distributed unlawfully. If, however, the directors relied on the accounts and it later appeared that assumptions or estimates used were unsound, they would not be liable. Any member of a company can apply to the court for an injunction to restrain the company from paying an unlawful dividend, but if members knowingly receive an improperly paid dividend, the company is entitled to recover those monies from the shareholders (CA 2006, s. 847).

---

**STOP AND THINK 14.1**

Investors and city analysts take a keen interest in the dividend policy of a listed company. Dividends often act as an indication of the fortunes of a company and it is not uncommon for a company's share price to fall if the dividend payout is not maintained. There is therefore real pressure on directors of listed companies to maintain dividend payouts, but this can never be at the expense of making illegal payments.

---

**TEST YOUR KNOWLEDGE 14.1**

a  What is the difference between a final dividend and an interim dividend? What authority is required before each can be paid?
b  How are partly paid shareholders dealt with in respect of dividends?
c  What are a company's obligations in respect of issuing dividends to joint holdings?
d  Do shareholders need to approve an interim dividend payment?
e  What is a dividend warrant?
f  What is the liability of a director who has made an illegal dividend payment? Are there any grounds for defence?

## 2 Declaring and paying dividends

### 2.1 Procedure for declaring the dividend

It is helpful to set out a plan and timetable of events and use it as a checklist to ensure that everything necessary is done in a timely fashion.

### CHECKLIST 14.1 Declaring a dividend

✓ Check the Articles of Association of the company for any special provisions. Model Article 30 (public company Model Article 70) provides that a company may declare dividends by ordinary resolution.

✓ If an interim dividend is proposed, hold a board meeting to propose a resolution to declare a dividend (see Sample Wording 14.1). Shareholders do not need to approve an interim dividend payment.

✓ Final dividends must be recommended to the shareholders for their approval in general meeting. Private companies may dispense with AGMs (see Chapter 9) and will either convene a general meeting, retain their AGM so that the final dividend can be approved or pass a written resolution of the members.

✓ The dividend payment can have a considerable impact on a listed company's share price. Decisions by the board of a listed company on dividends (usually decided and announced at the same time as annual or half-year results) must be notified to a RIS without delay pursuant to the DTRs (see Chapter 6).

---

### SAMPLE WORDING 14.1

**Dividend resolutions**

1 Interim dividend (directors at board meeting)[1]

THAT an interim dividend for the year ended . . . . 20xx of . . . . p per share of the ordinary shares of £1 each of the company be [declared payable] [paid][2] on . . . . . . . 20xx to shareholders registered at the close of business on . . . . . . 20xx.

2 Final dividend (company in general meeting).

THAT a final dividend for the year ended . . . . 20xx of . . . . p per share [making, with the interim dividend of . . . . p per share already paid, a total dividend for the year of . . . . p per share] on the ordinary shares of £1 each of the company, be declared payable on . . . . . . . 20xx to shareholders registered at the close of business on . . . . . . 20xx.

*Notes*
1 An appropriate description of the relevant accounts which were reviewed should be provided.
2 Appropriate form of wording to be used dependent on provisions of Articles.

---

### 2.2 Paying the dividend

The company secretary is responsible for making dividend payments, either directly through an in-house department or through the company's registrar. Again, the importance of forward planning must be emphasised.

### Record date

Because the register of members changes constantly, it is necessary to select a date at which the register is fully updated. At the close of business on the record date the register is printed or copied to a separate computer file and this copy provides the basis for compiling a dividend list to show the amounts to be paid to each shareholder. The record date should be agreed in the resolution to declare a dividend (see Sample Wording 14.1).

For listed companies, the London Stock Exchange publishes a schedule of recommended record dates together with associated ex-dividend dates and the latest date by which an announcement in respect of the dividend may be made. Listed companies are expected to follow these recommended dates in order to preserve an orderly market.

To avoid doubt with shareholders, dealings in large companies are expressed in terms of cum div (the buyer takes the dividend) or ex div (the seller keeps the dividend). The aim is to reduce the number of instances where a shareholder has disposed of all or part of a shareholding, but the transfer has not been registered by the time of the record date. The chosen record date is included in the announcement of a forthcoming dividend for a listed company and dealings are done on an ex div basis from the stated date. Otherwise the purchaser would have to claim the dividend from the seller.

## Dividend warrants

The dividend warrant authorises the company's bank to pay the dividend when it is presented by the member's bank. The bank should have been previously supplied with a specimen of the completed form of warrant to facilitate checking and to deter fraud. As warrants are paid, the company's bank should send them to the company (or registrar) with a covering schedule so that they can be checked against the dividend list. They should be kept for a time in case a problem with evidence of payment arises at a later date.

## Electronic tax vouchers

Tax vouchers can be sent by electronic means (e.g. by email) under the Income and Corporation Taxes (Electronic Certificates of Deduction of Tax and Tax Credit) Regulations 2003.

Companies need to decide whether to offer this service; and shareholders need to opt in to receive it. The default position for both companies and members is to continue to use paper tax vouchers. Shareholders can withdraw their consent at any time and opt to receive paper vouchers instead.

Sufficient security must be built into the system so that shareholders cannot amend the electronic tax voucher and sufficient functionality must be provided so that the electronic tax voucher can be stored in electronic format and also be printed on paper.

As with electronic communications for other shareholder documentation (e.g. the annual report), the company should check that its Articles contain no prohibitive provisions before deciding whether to offer electronic tax vouchers.

Consider the benefits of the introduction of electronic tax vouchers. Previously, companies and registrars were frustrated that they could pay dividends electronically, but that they still had to incur the additional expense of sending tax vouchers in hard copy. Sending a tax voucher electronically reduces the risk of it getting lost in the post. Electronic tax vouchers are also supported by the government as they will help to encourage e-business, reduce business costs and therefore make the UK market more competitive.

## DIVIDEND SHEET

# Dividend Sheet

COMPANY ..........................................................................................................

DIVIDEND TYPE ........................................ DIVIDEND No. ...........................

PAYABLE TO ......................................................................................................

AMOUNT PER SHARE ........................................................................................

| Name (and Address) | Share-Holding | Tax Credit | Amount of Dividend | Warrant Number | BACS/ Bulk Ref No. | Warrant Cashed |
|---|---|---|---|---|---|---|
|  |  |  |  |  |  |  |
|  |  |  |  |  |  |  |
|  |  |  |  |  |  |  |
|  |  |  |  |  |  |  |
|  |  |  |  |  |  |  |
|  |  |  |  |  |  |  |
|  |  |  |  |  |  |  |
|  |  |  |  |  |  |  |
|  |  |  |  |  |  |  |

## DIVIDEND TAX VOUCHER

PAYMENT No.
001

TAX VOUCHER
• .............. PLC
ORDINARY SHARES OF £1 EACH FULLY PAID

ISIN CODE
GB0001234567

| HOLDING | TAX CREDIT | DIVIDEND PAYABLE |
|---|---|---|
|  | £ | £ |

14-SEPT-05
WARRANT No.
123456

This voucher should be kept. It will be accepted by HM Revenue & Customs as evidence of tax

FINAL DIVIDEND ON
ORDINARY SHARES.
RATE: 7.0 PENCE PER SHARE
YEAR TO 3 1-DEC-04
TO HOLDERS
REGISTERED ON 30-APR-05

## CHECKLIST 14.2 **Paying the dividend**

✓ Ensure a bank account has been credited with funds to make the dividend payment. Consider opening a special account for this purpose.

✓ Ensure the register of members is up to date on the record date so that the dividends may be correctly despatched. For example, ensure that all transfers, transmission documents, probates, changes of address, mandates and other documentation have been processed.

✓ Prepare dividend warrants and **dividend tax vouchers** for printing. An electronic version of the dividend tax voucher should be prepared for shareholders who have elected to receive electronic communication.

✓ Prepare envelopes for posting.

✓ Compile a dividend sheet which records the amount of dividend and tax credit for each shareholder. If the system is computerised, the dividend record sheet and the warrants will be produced at the same time. Certain shares (for example, shares held in treasury; see Chapter 12) do not rank for dividend and any dividend entitlement must therefore be waived. **Dividend waivers** should therefore be included in the list.

✓ Check that the overall total of the number of shares on which the dividend is paid agrees with the company's issued capital.

✓ Distribute the warrants and tax vouchers at the appropriate time. Distribute tax vouchers by electronic means to shareholders who have opted for electronic communication. Liaise with the company's bank as the warrants are presented for payment.

## 2.3 Unclaimed dividends

The active life of a warrant is displayed on the warrant itself and is usually 6–12 months, after which it becomes stale in much the same way as a cheque. Significant numbers of shareholders fail to clear their dividend warrants and companies have adopted various strategies to cope with this. If lines of enquiry produce no results and the board has so resolved, the company ceases to be liable to pay the dividend after twelve years, even if the relevant warrant is then presented.

If the company is listed and a member fails to cash his warrant for three consecutive payments, the company can stop posting them. In addition, if at least three dividends have not been claimed during a period of twelve years and the shareholder is untraceable, the shares can be forfeited.

Sometimes warrants are returned to the company because the shareholder has moved and left no forwarding address. The company could try to trace the shareholder, for example, through the bank where the shareholder previously collected his dividend. In other cases, warrants can be lost in the post or just disposed of by a present occupier, in which case they are neither returned nor presented for payment. In this instance, write to the shareholder at the known address to try to ascertain whether the warrant did not reach the correct address or has been overlooked. If the warrant has been lost, the company should issue a duplicate, first obtaining an indemnity from the shareholder against the risk that the missing warrant may be subsequently presented (see Chapter 13).

If the shareholder has died, the warrants should be retained until probate or letters of administration have been received. The warrants can then be reissued to the deceased's estate (see Chapter 13).

It is good practice to maintain an outstanding dividend register for those warrants not cashed.

## 2.4 Dividend mandates

In order to minimise the risk of dividend warrants going astray a member can issue standing instructions (an 'evergreen' instruction) or a dividend mandate to the company so that payment goes straight into a designated bank account.

The ICSA has produced a standard form of mandate which companies are encouraged to use, with detailed guidance notes.

Changes in a member's details will require a new mandate – for example, if the member changes bank account, or the shareholding is closed and subsequently reopened. Many companies encourage the use of mandates because it reduces their administrative burden.

## DIVIDEND MANDATE

# Request for Payment of Interest or Dividends

Please complete in BLOCK CAPITALS using black ink and return in accordance with the instructions overleaf

**A** Name of Company in which shares are held

Shareholder Reference Number (if known)

**B** Full name and address of the first named holder (see note 1 below)

Name

Address

Postcode

Account Designation (if any)

Daytime Telephone Number

**C** Full name(s) of any other holders (Including Deceased if applicable)

Name

Name

Name

Deceased (if Applicable)

**D** Signatures

This form must be signed by ALL the registered holders, executors and administrators

Signature (1)

Signature (2)

Signature (3)

Signature (4)

When completed on behalf of a corporate body, each signatory should state the representative capacity e.g. Company Secretary, Director.

Date

Please pay future interest or dividends for the above company directly to the following or to any other bank or building society which that organisation may instruct

**E** Name of Bank, Building Society or person

**F** Full address, including postcode

Notes
1. Where shares are in the name of a deceased holder, instructions signed by the executor(s) or administrator(s) should indicate the name of the deceased.
2. Payment in accordance with these instructions discharges the company and registrar from any further liability.
3. The registrar reserves the right to require additional confirmation of the signature.

Branch sort code

Account number

Building Society Reference or Roll Number (if applicable)

**G** Stamp of Bank/Building Society

If the holder is a corporate body the stamp of the bank or building society is required. For personal shareholders the stamp is required where payment is being made other than to the sole or first named holder. The branch stamp is required to confirm that the signature(s) in box D is that of the shareholder(s) or an authorised signatory.

This form is approved by the Institute of Chartered Secretaries and Administrators

### The Bankers' Automated Clearing System (BACS)

Dividend mandates are usually paid directly into the shareholder's bank accounts via **BACS**. This is an electronic payment system used by many companies to make payments directly to banks and building societies. Details of dividends, together with bank sort codes and account numbers, are transmitted to BACS in electronic form by the company at least three days before the dividend payment date. Tax vouchers can be sent to each shareholder either through the post (with each dividend payment or through a consolidated annual tax voucher), or electronically (see section 2.2).

BACS removes some of the risks and brings cost savings, with shareholders' funds being cleared for use on the due date. It reduces the opportunity for fraud and prevents such problems as shareholders forgetting to notify the company of a change of address.

Where a company proposes to use BACS for the first time to distribute dividend payments, the Articles of Association should be checked to ensure that they do not provide that payment be made only by cheque or warrant. In this case, the Articles would have to be amended by special resolution in general meeting (or by written resolution for private companies).

## 2.5 Dividend payments to share warrant to bearers

A share warrant to bearer is a negotiable instrument which entitles the holder of the warrant (i.e. the bearer) to the number of shares stated on the warrant. As there is no register of members for share warrants to bearer, it is not possible to follow the procedures outlined above for registered shareholders. Instead, the share warrant will include dividend coupons which the bearer must surrender to the company for payment of dividends. Appropriate records of dividend coupons returned must be maintained.

---

**TEST YOUR KNOWLEDGE 14.2**

a  What is the record date?
b  What do the terms ex div and cum div mean?
c  Who makes the decision to pay a final dividend?
d  How can a company deal with the problem of unclaimed dividends?
e  How does BACS work in relation to dividend payments?
f  What are the benefits of a dividend mandate?

---

## 3  Scrip dividends

The company's Articles can provide for shareholders to elect whether they receive dividends in the form of shares (scrip dividends) instead of cash. New, fully paid-up shares are issued, allowing the shareholder to build up his holding in the company without incurring brokerage expenses and stamp duty. It has the added advantage to the company that money otherwise distributed in cash as dividends can be retained in the business. The value of shares is still taxed as a distribution of income and therefore the shareholder must still be provided with a tax voucher as evidence of tax deducted. For listed companies, the price of the shares is arrived at by taking the average of the middle market quotations for five business days, commencing on the date when the shares are first quoted as ex div on the Stock Exchange.

If a company has power by its Articles simply to pay dividends or if its Articles are silent on the matter, it may distribute dividends only in the form of cash. Issuing shareholders with scrip dividends results in an allotment to shareholders otherwise than in proportion to their existing shareholding (i.e. to only those shareholders who wish to receive the scrip). For this reason shareholder authority should be sought.

## CHECKLIST 14.3  **Scrip dividend**

✓ Make sure the company's Articles allow the directors to offer shareholders the right to elect to receive shares instead of a cash dividend.

✓ If necessary, pass an ordinary resolution at general meeting to give the board power to offer shares instead of cash for all or part of any interim or final dividends.

✓ Entitlement will still be to those members whose names appear on the register at the record date.

✓ Set the price for the shares (see above), calculated by the directors with reference to recent share issues or market prices.

✓ Prepare a circular letter to be sent to shareholders giving the price of the new shares and explaining what action is needed if they wish to elect to take shares instead of cash.

✓ Prepare the form of election to accompany the circular with the following information:
  – number of shares held on dividend record date;
  – maximum number of shares on which election may be made;
  – number of shares on which the dividend will be paid;
  – maximum number of new shares to be issued;
  – number of shares that the shareholder wishes to elect for (if this is fewer than the maximum).

✓ Prepare special dividend warrants to show the number of elected shares and the number of non-elected shares on which the normal cash dividend will be paid.

✓ Update the register of members, prepare new share certificates and file form SH01 (see Chapter 12).

✓ Issue tax vouchers.

✓ If the company is listed, apply to UKLA and the Stock Exchange for the new shares issued as scrip dividends to be listed and admitted to trading (see Chapter 6).

Scrip dividends are optional. Each time a dividend is paid, shareholders must elect whether to receive cash or shares. However, it is possible for shareholders to sign scrip dividend mandates to instruct that all future dividends be in the form of shares until countermanded under an evergreen scrip dividend scheme. If there is a balance of cash that does not make up the multiple required for a new share, the cash balance can be paid to the shareholder, or carried forward and added to the next dividend payment. The total is then used for the purpose of the scrip dividend on that occasion and any further balance of cash carried forward again. Naturally, the use of an evergreen scheme reduces administration costs for the company and is more convenient for the shareholder.

Companies may also encourage shareholders to take up the scrip dividend option by offering enhanced scrip dividends where the value of the shares being offered exceeds the value of the cash payment. Prior approval from HM Revenue & Customs is required for enhanced scrip dividends.

---

### TEST YOUR KNOWLEDGE **14.3**

**a**  What is a scrip dividend?
**b**  What are the advantages of a scrip dividend (i) to the member; (ii) to the company?
**c**  What is an evergreen scrip dividend scheme? What are its advantages?

---

## 4   Dividend reinvestment plans (DRIPs)

**DRIP dividends (DRIPs)** are where the company offers a facility to a shareholder to use the dividend to purchase additional shares on the stock market. The shares are purchased on the day the dividend is paid at the current market price, but have the advantage of lower dealing costs because it is a bulk purchase. Stamp duty is still payable on the purchase of shares. A tax voucher must also be issued in respect of the tax credit. The difference between scrip and DRIP is that with

DRIP the shares received are already in issue, whereas with scrip new shares are issued to the shareholder. As the shares are not new there is no dilution of the company's share capital, but the cash saved on dividends is not retained in the company for its benefit as in the case of a scrip. Again, if there is a cash balance, this is carried forward and added to the next dividend. As there is no disapplication of pre-emption rights, DRIPs do not require shareholder approval before they can be operated, but can be agreed by simple board resolution. DRIPs can be made evergreen in much the same way as scrips.

## 5 Consolidated dividends service

Registrars have always offered a dividend service but the leading registrars now offer a consolidated dividends service for listed companies. This is an online service designed to streamline the dividend payment process for CREST participants with designated accounts (see Chapter 13). It allows information to be downloaded electronically instead of receiving paper tax vouchers.

There are a number of key benefits:

1  There is no longer the need to deal with large volumes of cheques and tax vouchers, a great saving on administration.
2  Dividend payments are reconciled electronically before the payment date, thereby allowing quicker payment and improved efficiency.
3  A single tax voucher is issued per dividend, simplifying book-keeping.
4  Data are secure because the software used encrypts the data transferred between the user's computer and the registrar's computer.

CREST participants register for the consolidated dividends service and a dividend mandate is applied by the registrar to all CREST member accounts for the participants. This is done each time a dividend is paid so that any new accounts are picked up at the dividend record date. A few days before the dividend date the registrar produces a computer file containing a breakdown of payments due to each member account and a total which represents the full payment to the CREST participant.

An email is then sent to the account holder advising that the file can be downloaded. This allows the participant to be fully reconciled to the estimate of member payments and avoids the need for a clerical check against a paper list.

---

**TEST YOUR KNOWLEDGE 14.4**

a  What are the differences between scrip dividends and DRIP dividends?
b  What is the consolidated dividends service?

---

**CASE QUESTION**

As company secretary of Multiple plc, you hold a meeting with the Head of Investor Relations about making the best use of the company's website to provide helpful information to the company's shareholders about the services available to them. The Head of Investor Relations asks you what information should be put on the website (i) about the services provided to shareholders generally, and (ii) specifically about dividend information and services.

Research the websites of leading FTSE100 listed companies. Make a list of the typical and helpful information about shareholder services and dividends. Prepare a proposal for the Head of Investor Relations as to what information about shareholder services and dividends should be placed on Multiple plc's website.

## CHAPTER SUMMARY

■ Companies have an implied power to distribute profits to members, subject to any special provisions in the Articles.

■ Dividends are paid at the discretion of directors. Final dividends must be authorised by passing an ordinary resolution. Shareholders cannot increase the level of dividend proposed by directors.

■ Dividends are paid out of distributable profits, not out of capital. Directors must review relevant accounts to ensure there are sufficient distributable profits before approving or proposing a dividend payment.

■ Payment of dividends is regulated by CA 2006, Part 23 and Model Articles 30–35 (public company Model Articles 70–77) provide further guidance.

■ A record date must be set to determine the members who are eligible to receive payment. For listed companies the Stock Exchange publishes recommended record dates and related ex div dates to minimise complications so that both buyer and seller are aware which party will receive any forthcoming dividend.

■ Once the decision to pay the dividend and the rate is passed, dividend warrants and tax vouchers should be prepared which should be cross-checked with a dividend record sheet. The overall number of shares on which the dividend is paid should equal the company's issued capital.

■ Most larger companies use an automated system for paying dividends, where members complete a dividend mandate, designating a bank account where the money is to be paid. This is recommended by ICSA and avoids the complications of dividend warrants being lost or going astray.

■ Scrip and DRIP dividends can be issued instead of cash so that shareholders can increase their shareholding.

■ Listed companies registered with CREST can take advantage of the consolidated dividend service, an online service intended to streamline the payment process, allowing information to be downloaded electronically instead of receiving paper tax vouchers.

# Employee share schemes

**15**

## ■ CONTENTS

## ■ INTRODUCTION

Many companies have introduced employee share schemes in an attempt to boost individual performance and increase staff loyalty by providing an opportunity for employees to participate in the financial future of the company. This chapter outlines the most common types of employee share scheme, including those approved by HM Revenue & Customs, and how they operate. We also look briefly at additional matters for listed companies.

## 1 What is an employee share scheme?

An employee share scheme is defined in CA 2006, s. 1166 as a scheme for encouraging or facilitating the holding of shares or debentures in the company by or for the benefit of:

- bona fide employees or former employees of the company or group of companies; or
- the spouses, civil partners, surviving spouses, surviving civil partners or children or stepchildren under the age of 18 of such employees or former employees. (Stepchildren include equivalent relationships arising through civil partnership under the Civil Partnership Act 2004.)

Successive governments have held the view that it is good to encourage the public to invest in shares generally, and in particular for employees to invest in shares in the company for which they work. The schemes available are designed to give employees the opportunity to acquire shares in the company, sometimes on favourable terms, in savings-related share option schemes, share incentive plans, company share option plans or long-term incentive plans. Their aim is to create a performance incentive by offering employees the chance to benefit from the growth of the company, and in doing so to encourage employee loyalty and retention. This aim is further supported by making tax relief available to both companies and those participating in HM Revenue & Customs-approved schemes.

## 2 Common terms used in employee share schemes

There are many specialised terms used in the management and administration of share schemes. Before looking at the most popular types this section explains the more common terms:

1 *All-employee schemes and discretionary schemes* – In an all-employee scheme the company intends all, or substantially all, of its employees to participate in the savings-related scheme or the share incentive plan (SIP) (see below) are all-employee schemes, for example. By contrast, in a discretionary scheme the company intends that only a selected group of employees, usually defined by their seniority, business function or duration of service to the company, will participate, for example, a company share option scheme (see below).

2 *'Bad' or voluntary leaver* – If an employee ceases to work for a company, their right to any benefit under an employee share scheme usually depends on the circumstances under which they leave. Most schemes contain provisions which control the amount of benefit available for employees who leave. It is common practice for schemes to stop or limit any benefit to employees who resign voluntarily or are dismissed for misconduct – the bad or voluntary leavers. Good or involuntary leavers include those who leave for reasons of ill health or are made redundant. Most schemes contain provisions which allow all or some benefits under the scheme to be made available to these participants. These benefits are also usually available to the personal representatives of any participant who dies while in employment.

3 *Dilution* – The shares used to satisfy employee share schemes are either new shares issued from the company's unissued but authorised share capital or existing shares purchased by the company for the purposes of the scheme. Where new shares are used, the number of shares is sometimes expressed as a percentage of the issued share capital; this is known as **dilution**. For example, if a company has an issued share capital of 10 million shares and wishes to grant share options over 100,000 shares from its unissued shares as part of an employee share scheme, this would equate to a dilution of the issued share capital of 1%.

4 *Exercise* – The process by which the participant takes up his right under certain schemes to convert an option (see below) into a share in the company.

5 *Exercise period* – The window of opportunity in which participants may exercise their option or claim their incentive. For example, in an HM Revenue & Customs-approved company share option plan (CSOP), options may generally be taken up in the seven-year period between the third and tenth anniversaries of the date of grant. This is the **exercise period**.

6 *Exercise price or option price* – This is the price at which a share option may be exercised. The price is usually set at the time of grant in relation to the prevailing market price or by using a formula which takes the market price into account. For example, if a company awards an employee with a share option under an HM Revenue & Customs-approved CSOP when the price of a share is £1, this will also be the exercise price. If, when the employee decides to exercise the share option, the share price has risen to £1.50, they will still be able to purchase the share at the exercise price of £1.

7 *Grant* – The process by which the company awards the participant an option, share or other incentive.

8 *'In the money' option* – When the market value of a share at the point of exercise is greater than the exercise price, this is informally referred to as an **'in the money'** option to reflect the worth of the option. The opposite of 'in the money' is **'underwater'**, which is when the market value of the share is less than the exercise price. For example, an employee who has a share option with an exercise price of £1 per share is unlikely to exercise the option if the market price is only 75 p per share, as the option is more expensive than purchasing shares at market price.

9 *HM Revenue & Customs-approved scheme* – Any employee share scheme designed and administered according to HM Revenue & Customs requirements.

10 *Lapse* – Most options or incentives granted have a finite period during which benefits may be available. Once the benefit is no longer available under any circumstances it is considered to have lapsed.

11 *Maturity* – See vest (16 below).

12 *Option* – The right granted by the company giving the participant in the scheme an opportunity, but not an obligation, to acquire shares in the company at a price or a formula fixed at the outset. The process of converting the option into a share is called 'exercising an option'. Participants are not shareholders until they exercise an option and receive a share.

13 *Performance condition* – Some employee share schemes require that certain conditions must be met before the option, share or other incentive can be exercised or received. These

conditions usually relate to achieving minimum corporate performance levels, for example, a certain level of earnings per share of the company or a certain level of total shareholder return (i.e. the amount of increase in the company's share price plus dividends or other distributions).

14 *Scaleback* – Some all-employee share schemes have a maximum number of options or shares which are available to employees on any one invitation. In the event that participants have applied for more options or shares than are available, the number of options or shares will be reduced to no more than the maximum permitted.

15 *Scheme rules or plan rules* – Each employee share scheme should be governed by a comprehensive set of rules which are generic and govern the key features of the scheme. If any queries arise under an employee share scheme, the scheme rules must be reviewed in order to provide the solution. In some circumstances the grant of an option, share or other incentive may be accompanied by an agreement which provides additional detail as outlined in general terms in the scheme rules (see section 9.2).

16 *Vest* – Most employee share schemes provide for a minimum waiting period before the option, share or other incentive is available to the participant, in whole or in part. The point at which the benefit becomes available is referred to as vesting.

17 *Vesting period* – The minimum period until which the option, share or other incentive is available to the participant, in whole or in part.

---

**TEST YOUR KNOWLEDGE 15.1**

a How is a share scheme defined under the CA?
b What is the difference between a 'good leaver' and a 'bad leaver'?
c Explain (i) a discretionary scheme; (ii) an all-employee scheme.
d What is the significance of operating an HM Revenue & Customs-approved scheme?
e What is the difference between the terms 'in the money option' and 'underwater option'?

---

## 3 Share incentive plans (SIPs)

If a SIP is offered, it must be offered to all full-time and part-time UK resident employees; minimum employment service requirements may be set, but these must not exceed 18 months. Any employee who has a material interest in the company cannot participate in a SIP.

As SIPs are operated as HM Revenue & Customs-approved schemes, they must follow HM Revenue & Customs requirements. However, the SIP concept is flexible, allowing some latitude for the company to create a plan to suit its particular circumstances.

### 3.1 Key points

SIPS offer:

■ an opportunity for all employees to hold shares in their company;
■ free shares up to an annual limit of £3,000;
■ **partnership shares** bought by employees up to £1,500 annually;
■ the choice for the employer to give **matching shares** to match partnership shares;
■ freedom for companies to use a combination of free, partnership and matching shares;
■ a tax-efficient way of accumulating shares.

Each of these points is discussed below.

### 3.2 Free shares

■ An annual limit of up to £3,000 value in shares may be allocated by the company free of charge to employees, regardless of their salary and with no liability to tax or NICs.

- There are variations in the method that free shares may be distributed among the workforce, but the distribution must be based on individual, divisional or corporate targets and must not be designed to focus rewards on highly paid individuals.
- If the employee voluntarily leaves the company within three years of the award of free shares, the company has the discretion to provide that the shares can be forfeited. Special forfeiture exemptions apply for involuntary leavers who leave prior to three years.

### 3.3 Partnership shares

- Employees may elect to save up to £1,500 per annum or 10% of their annual salary (whichever is the lower) to purchase additional shares ('partnership' shares). A minimum saving level may be set which must not be more than £120 per annum.
- One benefit of purchasing partnership shares is that the employee purchases them from pre-tax and pre-NIC earnings, i.e. the price of purchasing partnership shares is deductible from the employees' tax and NIC liability calculations, thus reducing the employee's taxable income.
- An employees' accumulated savings over a 12-month period can be used to purchase company shares. There is no minimum holding time for partnership shares.

### 3.4 Matching shares

- These are free shares that are given by the company to employees in a ratio, not to exceed 2:1, to partnership shares. The maximum allocation by the company is £3,000 per annum, or 20% of the employees' annual salary, whichever is lower.
- Matching shares must be offered on the same terms to all employees.
- If the employee leaves the company voluntarily within three years of the award of matching shares, the company has the discretion to provide that matching shares can be forfeited. Special forfeiture exemptions apply for involuntary leavers who leave within three years.

To encourage further participation by employees, HM Revenue & Customs regulations permit dividend payments of up to £1,500 per annum arising from dividends paid on the shares held in a SIP to be reinvested to acquire further shares ('dividend shares').

All the shares in the SIP are held in a trust on behalf of the employees. The shares in the SIP must be fully paid and irredeemable. Free and matching shares must be held in the plan for at least three years and for a maximum of five years. Partnership shares can be taken out of the plan immediately. When employees leave, all their shares come out of the plan.

### 3.5 Tax implications

It is an HM Revenue & Customs requirement that all shares in the SIP are held in a trust based in the UK.

Employees do not pay income tax or NIC on the value of the free, matching or partnership shares provided they keep them in the SIP for at least five years.

If employees take shares out of the SIP prior to three years from grant, income tax and NIC are payable on the market value of the shares at the time they are taken out. There is no income tax on dividend shares reinvested provided those shares are held in the plan for at least three years. If free or matching shares are taken out of the plan between three and five years after grant, income tax and NIC are charged, based on the lower of the value of the shares when they were first awarded (or salary used to purchase the shares for partnership shares), or when they are taken out. No capital gains tax is payable on any increase in value if the shares are kept in the plan until they are sold while the shares stay in the plan. After three years, shares withdrawn from the SIP and immediately sold are not subject to capital gains tax. If the sale is not immediate, capital gains tax may be payable on any difference between the current value and the value when the shares were withdrawn.

If an employee leaves involuntarily, HM Revenue & Customs guidelines provide that the employee is exempt from income tax and NIC.

Companies can take advantage of corporation tax relief for their costs in setting up and running the plan, and there is further relief for companies acquiring shares on behalf of employees. Companies also obtain relief equal to the value of the gross salary of partnership shares purchased by employees.

---

**TEST YOUR KNOWLEDGE 15.2**

**a** What are the three elements of share awards under a SIP?
**b** What are the tax implications for employees participating in a SIP?

---

# 4 Savings-related schemes (sharesave schemes)

## 4.1 Key points

■ Savings-related schemes provide an opportunity for all employees to buy shares in their company at a discounted price.
■ Employees can save up to £250 per month via a savings contract to buy shares. The savings contract can be for three, five or seven years.
■ The savings are kept at a bank or building society until the savings contract matures.
■ Tax exemptions are available when employees exercise their options.

Each of these points will be looked at in further detail below.

## 4.2 Savings contract and exercise of options

These are often referred to as **Save As You Earn (SAYE)** or sharesave schemes. Sharesave schemes are operated as HM Revenue & Customs-approved schemes and are open on an all-employee basis to both full-time and part-time employees. A sharesave scheme must be offered to all qualifying participants on equal terms. HM Revenue & Customs approval cannot be given to any sharesave scheme which has an employment qualifying service of five years or greater. Sharesave schemes cannot be offered to employees or directors of close companies who own or control 25% or more of the shares.

Under the scheme, employees are given an option to buy a fixed number of shares in the company. The option price is set by reference to the market value of the shares at the time of grant, but the employer has the discretion to discount the option price by up to 20%. For example, if the market price of a share is £1 on the date of grant, the company may grant the options at an option price of between 80p and £1. The same option price must be offered on the same terms to all employees.

In order to pay the option price, employees enter into a contract to save with a 'savings carrier' (NS&I, a bank or building society) for a period of either three or five years and the employee can save between £5 and £250 per month, At the end of this period, the employee will receive a tax-free bonus which will be added to the accumulated savings. Employees who take out a five-year option also have the opportunity to decide whether to take the proceeds after the fifth anniversary and exercise their option to buy or leave the savings for another two years (during which they will not be required to make any further contributions) to earn an additional tax-free bonus.

At the end of the savings period, participants usually have six months to exercise their options, after which the options lapse. Participants who have left involuntarily before the end of the savings period may use the savings accumulated until the time they leave the company to purchase the shares at the option price and usually have six months in which to exercise this. In the case of a participant's death, the personal representative may have up to twelve months to exercise the option from the date of death.

Employees do not have to exercise their option. For example, if the prevailing share price has fallen below the option price (i.e. is underwater), they can simply take the savings from the SAYE contract plus their bonus and use the money as they see fit.

## 4.3  Tax implications

An employee in an approved savings-related scheme does not pay income tax or NIC on the bonus or interest received under the savings contract, or on the benefit from being able to buy shares at a favourable price, or on any increase in the value of shares between when the option was granted and when it is exercised. The same applies to participants who exercise their option prior to the end of the savings period due to leaving the company on involuntarily. If the participant is able to exercise the option after having left voluntarily he will be subject to income tax on the benefit.

The usual rules of capital gains tax apply when the shares are sold.

## 4.4  Sharesave and SIP: a comparison

There is nothing to prevent an employer from offering both a sharesave and a SIP. Secretaries should be prepared to advise employers on the relative merits of each scheme, taking into account factors such as:

- Savings made under the SIP are prior to tax and NIC, making the SIP more tax-efficient than the sharesave scheme for both the employees and the employer (the employer is also entitled to claim a deduction).
- SIPs offer more flexibility in design than sharesave schemes.
- Sharesave schemes offer a lower risk to employees. If the options become underwater, employees can continue saving through the SAYE contract, receive a tax-free bonus at maturity and allow the sharesave option to lapse. As the SIP involves the purchase of shares, the possibility of adverse movements in the share price increases the risk profile.
- Sharesave schemes are simpler to understand than the SIP.

# 5   Profit-sharing schemes

HM Revenue & Customs approval status for profit-sharing schemes was withdrawn in favour of SIPs (see above). No new schemes received HM Revenue & Customs approval after April 2001. An employer may still choose to establish or continue to operate a profit-sharing scheme as a bona fide share scheme, but any awards of shares under such scheme after the end of December 2002 will not be HM Revenue & Customs approved and do not therefore have available the tax reliefs previously provided.

The purpose of a profit-sharing scheme is to give all employees a common target of achieving at least a certain level of company profit for the year. If the profit target is achieved, a formula is used which determines a proportion of the profits which is set aside for the profit-sharing scheme. The proportion of the profits is then used to subscribe for the employing company's shares or to purchase the shares in the market. The shares are then held in a trust for a qualifying period (usually two or three years) before they can be released to the employee. No performance conditions usually apply in the qualifying period as the performance was met at the outset by the company achieving the target profit level. The employer would need to consider when drafting the scheme rules whether the participant should have a beneficial interest during the qualifying period (e.g. be eligible to receive any dividends or to vote via proxy at general meetings) bearing in mind that there could be tax implications in giving participants the benefit of a beneficial interest.

As there are no HM Revenue & Customs approved requirements for profit-sharing schemes, the tax treatment will vary according to the structure of the scheme. However, most employers favour a SIP as there are tax reliefs available for both employer and employee.

**a** How do the tax benefits of the SIP compare to the sharesave scheme?

**b** What are the main features of a sharesave scheme?

**c** Why was HM Revenue & Customs approval withdrawn for profit-sharing schemes? Can such schemes still be operated?

# 6 Company share option plans (CSOPs)

Unlike a sharesave scheme and SIP, a **company share option plans (CSOP)** is usually discretionary in that employers select managers to participate. CSOPs are sometimes also referred to as executive share option plans (ESOPs).

## 6.1 Key features

■ Employees can receive up to £30,000 worth of tax-approved options.

■ The options can be exercised between three and ten years after grant.

These will be looked at in more detail below.

## 6.2 Discretionary participation

CSOPs are often operated on a discretionary basis, frequently as executive share option schemes for the benefit of managers and other senior employees. The company grants selected employees an option to purchase shares in the company at a future point, subject to the provisions in the scheme rules. The expectation is that the value of the shares will increase over time and that when the option is exercised, the participant will be able to purchase the shares at the option price, which will be lower than the prevailing share price. The excess of the share price over the option price is therefore the employee's 'gain'. The vesting of options granted under a CSOP is usually subject to the achievement of one or more performance conditions, normally measured over a period of three years.

## 6.3 HM Revenue & Customs requirements

In order to receive and maintain HM Revenue & Customs-approved status, the following matters must apply to the operation of the CSOP:

■ Participation must be limited to employees (including full-time executive directors) of the company. The scheme cannot be offered to any employee or director owning or controlling 25% or more of a close company (or who has had such an interest at any time during the past year).

■ Options must be granted at no less than the fair market value of the underlying shares. For listed companies, this is usually the quoted market value at the time of grant. Non-listed companies may require an accountant or auditor to determine a fair value for the shares.

■ Options must not be transferable or pledged as a security.

■ The shares must be fully paid and are usually ordinary shares (i.e. they have no special rights or restrictions).

■ If the company has more than one class of shares, the class under which the CSOP is offered should not be controlled by directors or employees, or by a holding company.

■ The options may be exercisable for a period of between three and ten years. Special circumstances may apply for the exercise of options prior to three years in the event of involuntary termination of employment, change of control of the company or the exercise of options by personal representatives on behalf of a deceased participant.

■ There is a limit of £30,000 on the aggregated market value of options granted per participant. This value is determined at the time of grant. For example, if the participant receives 10,000 options at fair market value at an option price of £2 per share, the value of the options for HM Revenue & Customs purposes is £20,000. Any options granted above the £30,000 limit will form part of an unapproved plan under which income tax is payable upon exercise of the option (see below).

## 6.4 Tax implications

For HM Revenue & Customs-approved CSOPs, income tax is not chargeable when the option is granted, and there is no income tax or capital gains tax liability on the increase in value of the shares between the grant and the exercise of the option. There is no income tax charge on the disposal of shares, but capital gains tax may arise when the shares are sold. For the employer, the costs of establishing and maintaining a CSOP are deductible against the company's profits for the determination of the company's tax liabilities. For unapproved CSOPs, an income tax liability may arise at the time of grant where the option price is less than the fair market value of the underlying shares.

## 6.5 Exercise process

Once the option vests, the participant will have an opportunity to exercise the option. The participant will need to provide the exercise price for the number of options which he wishes to exercise. This may be achieved by the participant immediately selling some shares to cover the exercise price, which can then be met by a short-term loan (often provided by the company or the stockbrokers who place the share sale) or by an undertaking to the company to pay the exercise price. Alternatively, participants may choose to provide the cost themselves in the form of a cheque or bank transfer.

---

### WORKED EXAMPLE 15.1

Employee A wishes to exercise 10,000 options under an HM Revenue & Customs-approved CSOP at an option price of £2 per share, when the market price of a share is £2.50. He will need to raise £20,000 (i.e. 10,000 options × £2 per share) and produce the option certificate entitling him to exercise the 10,000 options. However, the underlying value of the shares he will acquire is £25,000 (that is 10,000 shares × £2.50), representing a £5,000 'gain' (i.e. £25,000 − £20,000).

Employee A cannot raise £20,000 to exercise the option, so the company offers a 'cashless' exercise facility whereby the employee, a nominated stockbroker and the company agree that sufficient shares will be sold immediately on exercise to pay the company the exercise price.

Thus, as soon as the option is exercised, the stockbroker sells 8,000 shares at £2.50 to provide the company with the required £20,000 (8,000 × £2.50 = £20,000). Employee A is then free to decide whether to retain the balance of the remaining 'gain' as shares (i.e. 10,000 shares − 8,000 shares = 2,000 shares) or to sell the shares immediately and receive tax-free cash £5,000 (2,000 shares × £2.50 = £5,000).

---

### TEST YOUR KNOWLEDGE 15.4

**a** What is the maximum value of shares a participant may receive under an HM Revenue & Customs-approved CSOP?

**b** How long must the participant wait until options granted under a CSOP vest?

**c** Must options be granted to all employees of a company under a CSOP?

**d** What does 'cashless' exercise mean? How does it work?

# 7  Enterprise management incentives

## 7.1  Key features

Enterprise management incentives (EMIs)

- are suited to smaller companies wishing to operate a tax-efficient scheme;
- allow employees to receive up to £250,000 worth of options;
- feature options which can be exercised between three and ten years after grant;
- require fewer formalities than a CSOP.

These points are discussed next.

## 7.2  Operation

EMIs are intended to help smaller, high-risk companies with potential for growth to recruit and retain high-calibre employees and to reward employees for taking a risk by investing their time and skills in helping small companies achieve their potential. The company must employ no more than 250 employees. Eligible employees (which include directors) must generally work at least 25 hours a week for the company. EMIs are operated as HM Revenue & Customs-approved schemes, but there is no approval or clearance mechanism as with other approved plans. All an employer is required to do is to notify the HM Revenue & Customs (in this instance the Small Company Support Centre) within 92 days of grant of an EMI option of the following:

- notification of grant using the prescribed HM Revenue & Customs form;
- declaration from the employee in respect of the 25 hour per week requirement;
- declaration from a secretary or director confirming the company meets the requirements to be eligible to participate in the EMI;
- copy of the option agreement issued to evidence the grant of options (all EMI options must be evidenced in writing, setting out the key terms of the grant).

EMI options can be offered by independent trading companies with gross assets not exceeding £30 million. The company's trading activity must be carried on wholly or mainly in the UK. If employers are in doubt as to whether their company qualifies, they can submit details of the company to HM Revenue & Customs and seek pre-approval before the EMI options are granted. Options over shares worth up to £250,000 at the time of grant can be granted to employees and a company may have up to £3 million shares in value under EMI option at any one time.
Other key features of the EMI provide that:

- An individual may receive options up to a market value of £250,000 (including any amount granted under an approved CSOP) which may qualify as EMI options.
- The shares subject to the option must be fully paid up and not redeemable.
- Options must be exercisable for no more than ten years. Options may also be subject to performance conditions, at the discretion of the employer.
- No employee or director with more than a 30% interest in the share capital of the company may participate.
- Any number of qualifying employees may participate (subject to the £3 million limit). EMIs may therefore also be operated on an all-employee (rather than discretionary) basis.

## 7.3  Tax implications

If the exercise price is the market price of the shares at the date the option is granted, under normal circumstances there is normally no income tax or NIC charge when the options are exercised. If options are granted at less than the market value then there is an income tax charge at the time of exercise based on the value of the discount. Any shares sold following exercise of options are subject to capital gains tax.

> **STOP AND THINK 15.1**
>
> EMIs provide a combination of tax efficiency with reduced administrative burden. Both of these factors would be important to a qualifying company when considering the appropriate design of an employee share scheme (see section 3).

# 8 Long-term incentive plans

The use of **long-term incentive plans (LTIPs)** as a form of share incentive has increased over recent years. LTIPs are usually operated on a discretionary basis, but there is no reason why an employer could not choose to operate an LTIP on an all-employee basis. LTIPs are also usually provided by listed companies, but there is nothing to prevent an unlisted company from providing such an incentive.

There is no HM Revenue & Customs-approved structure for the operation of an LTIP and therefore it is necessary for the employer to structure the LTIP in a way that takes into account, *inter alia*, the need to provide a meaningful incentive whilst minimising tax liabilities for the employer, employee and trust (see below). The nature of such tax planning structures is beyond the scope of this study text.

The structure and operation of the plan will vary from employer to employer. However, a typical LTIP arrangement provides for:

- Shares which are to be allocated into a trust, which may be located offshore in order to minimise tax liabilities. The main purpose of the trust is to 'warehouse' the shares and release the appropriate number of shares to the participant against the valid satisfaction of the performance period, performance conditions and any waiting period (see below).
- An award of shares to the participant which is conditional or deferred over a performance period. The performance period is usually two or three years and the number of shares which can be awarded at the end of the period is subject to satisfactory achievement of one or more performance conditions.
- A potential further waiting period of two or three years prior to release. The participant would have successfully completed the performance period and would be beneficially entitled to the shares; however, the plan would provide that the shares must remain in a trust for the waiting period.
- Concessionary features which will allow the participant to receive at least a pro-rated award of shares if he has involuntarily left the company prior to the end of the performance or waiting period.

## 8.1 LTIPs and option plans: a comparison

A company may need to consider whether to operate an LTIP or an option plan. An LTIP differs from an option plan as follows:

- The usual arrangement under an LTIP is to make a conditional or deferred award of shares. An option scheme does not award shares, as the options are merely a contractual right to acquire shares.
- The allocation of shares into a trust usually means that the employer must fund the cash at the time of the award to purchase the shares because the employer is working on the assumption that the shares will increase in value over time and it would be cheaper to acquire the shares at the time of award rather than at the end of the performance period (a 'hedging' strategy) .The company's cash flow position therefore needs to be taken into account in considering the appropriate design of a scheme.
- The value to the participant of an option is if the difference over which the market price of the share exceeds the option price and if the option is underwater it is unlikely to have any meaningful value. However, under an LTIP the participant is usually entitled to the whole share and will receive some benefit, no matter what the market price of the share.

# 9 Introducing and administering an employee share scheme

Despite the advantages of giving employees an interest in the company, employee share schemes are medium- to long-term benefits, and employers should consider all the issues carefully before introducing a scheme. The overall aim is to provide a meaningful incentive to employees which the company is able to afford and its shareholders are able to endorse.

## 9.1 Design of the employee share scheme

Key design features and issues the company will need to consider and of which the secretary should be aware include the following:

- How will any new employee scheme compliment other existing share schemes or benefits?
- How will any proposed scheme fit with other incentives and ensure that the combination of incentive arrangements target the desired employee audiences?
- All-employee or discretionary?

The employer will need to decide whether to operate a scheme for all employees or operate a discretionary plan for the purposes of motivating a select group of employees. Many companies operate both kinds.

### Whether to operate an HM Revenue & Customs-approved scheme
The company will need to weigh the benefits of the tax reliefs available under an HM Revenue & Customs approved scheme against the potential additional flexibility of a scheme which is tailored to the needs of its workforce but may not necessarily gain HM Revenue & Customs approval.

### How the scheme will affect the finances of the company
The company will need to consider the financial impact of operating an employee share scheme. For example, some schemes may require that the shares are purchased in the market at the outset and therefore require an immediate cash input from the company. Shares purchased for the purposes of an employee share scheme are exempted from the general rule that a company cannot assist in the purchase of its own shares (CA 2006, s. 682).

### Whether shareholders would be prepared to tolerate the dilution impact on the issued share capital
New shares issued under employee share schemes are exempted from the general provision that shares must be offered to all existing shareholders on a pre-emptive rights basis (see Chapter 12). As shareholders will be affected by the employee share scheme's dilutive impact, the introduction of a new scheme requires shareholder approval (ordinary resolution). Approval is likely only if the shareholders consider the dilution impact is outweighed by the positive motivational effect the share scheme will have on the workforce to improve the company's performance.

## General cost and administrative burden to the company

If the scheme is particularly complex or if there is a large number of participants, there will be increased costs and administration for the company. Many companies contract out the administration of their share schemes to third parties and it is often the duty of the secretary to manage the relationship with the external contractor.

## Potential for discrimination

Any discretionary scheme will involve the selection of participants by the board or board committee. It is important that participants are selected fairly and that non-participating employees cannot claim they have been unfairly discriminated against (for example, on the ground of gender).

## 9.2 Scheme rules

There are some principal features common to many employee share schemes. These are usually contained in the scheme rules, which are often drafted by the company's legal advisers or, for HM Revenue & Customs-approved schemes, they may follow a model provided by the HM Revenue & Customs.

Typical features in scheme rules include:

- *Name* – Each employee share scheme should have a unique name.
- *Duration* – The date the employee share scheme was approved by shareholders and HM Revenue & Customs approval (if applicable), as well as the date the scheme expires.
- *Authority to make grants* – A provision that the board (or a committee of the board) has authority to make grants to participants.
- *Number of options or shares available* – Either a maximum number of shares or options available under the employee share scheme.
- *Definition of who is eligible to participate* – This usually takes the form of a description of an eligible employee or director of the company, or subsidiary company.
- *Form of documentation* – A general provision empowering the directors to decide or modify the specific form of documentation to be issued in respect of grants, exercises or other key events. This permits flexibility so that the scheme rules do not have to be amended each time the documentation changes.
- *Description of option price, shares, incentive or other benefit* – Either an exhaustive description of how the option price, shares, incentive or other benefit shall be determined and calculated; or a more generic description of the calculation with authority for the directors to determine certain specific issues at the time of grant.
- *Concessionary features for involuntary leavers* – Features which permit employees who have left involuntarily to exercise options or receive shares or other incentives early in situations where they would not normally be entitled had they remained in employment. This recognises that the company may have denied the employee the possibility of remaining in employment until the time when the benefit would have vested.
- *Potential loss of benefits for voluntary leavers* – Certain restrictions on the ability to exercise an option or receive a share or other incentive where the employee has left voluntarily.
- *Exercise period and procedure* – The general period and manner in which participants may exercise their option or receive their other share incentive.
- *Power to modify the scheme rules* – A provision allowing directors to make minor modifications to the scheme rules, for example, to benefit the administration of the employee share scheme. Any major modifications usually require shareholder approval.
- *Variations of share capital* – Power for the directors to adjust the value and/or number of options, shares or other incentives granted in the event of a capital transaction such as a rights issue, subdivision or consolidation of the share capital (see chapter 12). For example, if an employee had been granted 10,000 shares at £2 per share under a LTIP and the company underwent a two shares for one subdivision of share capital, the directors would be authorised to adjust the grant retrospectively to 20,000 shares at £1 each, thus preserving the original value of the award.

- *Takeover or change of control of the company* – If the company is taken over by another organisation, it may no longer be appropriate to continue to operate the employee scheme using the shares of the acquired company. Scheme rules usually contain provisions which allow some or all of the option, share or other incentive to be received early. Alternatively, the scheme rules may contain authority to exchange the benefit into options or shares of the acquiring company.
- *Treatment of incentive in case of winding up, insolvency, scheme of arrangement, etc.* – How the incentive will be affected by such corporate events affecting the company. If the company is being wound up, there may be a risk of forfeiture of the incentive if action is not taken within a set time.

If the employee share scheme is HM Revenue & Customs-approved, the scheme rules are also drafted to reflect the requirements of the HM Revenue & Customs.

## 9.3 Role of HM Revenue & Customs

HM Revenue & Customs sets the qualifying conditions for the operation of approved share schemes. As these conditions are subject to change from time to time, secretaries involved in administering share schemes should ensure they keep up to date with any changes. Extensive information is available on the HM Revenue & Customs website (see Directory).

Annual tax returns must be submitted to the HM Revenue & Customs for each employee share scheme. The tax returns include information on options exercised or shares granted or transferred and enable the HM Revenue & Customs to determine whether HM Revenue & Customs-approved schemes have been managed in accordance with their requirements. The tax returns also provide information for HM Revenue & Customs to determine any tax liabilities or reliefs.

All modifications to HM Revenue & Customs-approved schemes should be submitted to the HM Revenue & Customs for approval before they can be effected. Failure to do so could jeopardise the approved status of the scheme, which could have serious tax consequences. The secretary should maintain a file which clearly shows any such modifications, together with a copy of the board minute (and general meeting minute if applicable) resolving the modification and letters received from the HM Revenue & Customs approving the modifications.

It is important to consider how arrangements under employee share schemes will be taxed. Allowances and exemptions may be available which will reduce the employees' tax liability. This gives approved schemes an advantage over unapproved arrangements and encourages employees to retain the shares to minimise their liability. The HM Revenue & Customs website has extensive information on employee share schemes. Their Employee Share Schemes team will comment on proposed employee share schemes.

## 9.4 Establishing an employee share scheme

Establishing an employee share scheme requires much work to be done and the secretary is an important part of ensuring the process is a success. The following is an outline of the key points of a typical process in establishing an employee share scheme:

### Prior to obtaining approval

1 *Consider the most appropriate type of employee share scheme:* The company will need to consider which type of scheme is best suited for both the company and its employees.
2 *Draft required documentation:* Each employee scheme will require rules, option or other grant certificates, explanatory booklets, an employee presentation, maturity documentation and other support materials.
3 *Check Articles of Association:* To ensure there is nothing to prevent the directors from operating an employee share scheme. Any amendment to the Articles will require a special resolution.
4 *If applicable, consult HM Revenue & Customs:* If a scheme is to meet applicable HM Revenue & Customs requirements for approved schemes, it may be prudent at this stage to discuss the scheme with them on an informal basis.

5 *If applicable, consult with major institutional shareholders:* Listed companies may need to consult with their major institutional shareholders prior to obtaining board approval to ascertain if they would be willing to support the proposal.

## Obtaining approval and making an initial grant

1 *Obtain board approval:* The scheme rules, other key documentation and a description of the scheme should be presented to the board for their consideration and approval.

2 *Obtain shareholder approval:* This is required in most cases and an ordinary resolution should suffice. If the employee share scheme involves the issue of shares from its unissued share capital, it is not necessary to obtain separate authorisation to allot shares. Pre-emption rights do not apply to shares allotted under an employee share scheme. When obtaining shareholder approval in a listed company, the company must also disclose the full text of the scheme (this is usually contained in the scheme rules) or the details of its most important terms in a shareholder circular. If the scheme rules are not circulated to shareholders, details should be given in the shareholder circular of where the scheme rules are available for inspection.

3 *Obtain formal HM Revenue & Customs approval, if applicable:* A copy of the scheme rules and any other required documents must be submitted to HM Revenue & Customs for approval.

4 *Board or duly authorised committee of the board to approve first grant:* The rules might stipulate a timescale or procedure which must be followed in making grants to participants and such requirements must be observed.

5 *Prepare and issue documentation and begin employee briefings:* Option or other grant certificates must be issued to employees together with explanatory booklets. If employees are unfamiliar with the scheme, then appropriate briefings should be carried out.

## 9.5 Role of the company secretary

The secretary is often central to the responsibilities and duties involved in establishing and administering an employee share scheme. In larger organisations, some of these responsibilities are contracted out to third party service providers. No matter who performs the duties, the work required is the same:

1 *Establish and maintain a register of participants* – It is necessary to establish a robust system, with supporting administrative procedures, to ensure an accurate register of participants is kept. Necessary precautions and procedures must be taken regarding data security, integrity and protection. If directors of a listed company participate in the employee share scheme, any such participation must be notified to the market via a RIS.

2 *Establish and maintain a central file of documentation* – A central file with all pertinent documentation relating to the employee share scheme (e.g. the scheme rules, HM Revenue & Customs letters of approval if applicable, pro-forma option or grant certificates) should be maintained and updated as appropriate.

3 *Issue grant documentation* – The secretary is often responsible for issuing grant documentation and for monitoring the level of interest shown by employees following the issue of such documentation.

4 *Monitor achievement of performance conditions, vesting and lapses* – Some employee incentives (e.g. LTIPs) require performance conditions to be satisfied prior to any shares being transferred. The secretary is responsible for monitoring performance conditions and often this will require calculation and verification by the company's accountant or auditor. Even if the employee share scheme has no such conditions, the secretary is responsible for keeping track of when prior grants are going to mature or vest and when they are due to lapse.

5 *Deal with queries* – It is essential that the secretary is familiar with the scheme rules and other formal documentation to ensure he is able to deal with any queries raised by participants or the board. This will involve the secretary keeping up to date with HM Revenue & Customs regulations regarding employee share schemes. The secretary may also be responsible for administrative matters, such as a participant's change of address, or dealing with share scheme documentation for a participant who has left the company. The secretary will also need to deal with third parties, such as the HM Revenue & Customs or those enquiring on behalf

of participants. For example, most scheme rules provide that the personal representatives of a deceased participant may exercise the participant's options up to twelve months following the death of the participant. The secretary would, therefore, need to deal with the personal representatives and need to ensure that they are authorised to represent the deceased (e.g. the secretary would require sight of the grant of probate).

6 *Complete annual tax returns* – HM Revenue & Customs has pro-forma tax returns which need to be completed and returned each year. As most of the information required by the HM Revenue & Customs can be found from the register of participants or the central files of documentation, the secretary is often best placed to provide most of the information.

7 *Manage ad hoc events:* For example:

a) Scalebacks may need to be implemented for all employee schemes where the employees are invited to apply for options or shares. The scheme rules for all employee schemes usually contain a provision as to the maximum amount of options or shares which are available. In the event that participants have applied for more options or shares than are available, a scaleback will be initiated to reduce the number of options or shares to no more than the maximum permitted.

b) Any variations in share capital (e.g. a rights or a bonus issue) may need to be reflected in the employee share scheme. Calculations will need to be made to adjust the number and/or value of options or shares granted and explanatory documentation will need to be issued to participants. In the case of a rights issue where shares are held in a trust and the employee is beneficially entitled to those shares, the employee may need to be offered the opportunity to take up his rights (by paying the cash subscription price) or to sell his rights.

8 *Prepare and issue maturity packs* – Employees should be made aware when options, shares or other incentives have vested and should be briefed on the choices available to them and the timescales in which they must take action prior to any lapse. It is good practice to issue a maturity pack to the participant prior to vesting to inform them in good time before they need to take any action.

9 *Issue ad hoc documentation* – Some employee schemes provide that participants will receive information on a regular basis or ad hoc basis (for example, the annual report). It is usually the duty of the secretary to ensure the register of participants is accurate and up to date and to ensure participants receive the required documentation.

---

**STOP AND THINK 15.2**

It is always useful to review employee share scheme documentation first hand. If you have a friend or relative that participates in an employee share scheme, ask them if you may review the paperwork. Alternatively, if you work for an organisation, consider what would be an appropriate type of employee share scheme.

Browse the HM Revenue & Customs website. This contains model forms, guidance booklets and checklists for both participants and employers.

---

**TEST YOUR KNOWLEDGE 15.6**

a What are the key factors to be considered in the design of an employee share scheme?
b What do scheme rules usually state in respect of (i) the authority to make grants; (ii) concessionary features for involuntary leavers?
c What is the purpose of a tax return in respect of an employee share scheme?
d What considerations should a company secretary take into account when establishing and maintaining a register of participants?
e When managing an employee share scheme, what queries should a company secretary expect?

## 10 Using treasury shares in employee share schemes

The Companies (Acquisition of Own Shares) Regulations 2003 permit companies to acquire their own shares and hold them in a treasury share account. In certain circumstances, treasury shares may be used in satisfaction of employee shares schemes (see Chapter 12).

## 11 Additional issues for listed companies

The UK Corporate Governance Code (see the Corporate Governance syllabus for more details) and the Listing Rules recommend that shareholders should approve the introduction of any new employee share scheme.

### 11.1 Guidelines issued by institutional shareholders

As part of the drive for good corporate governance, the ABI, with the support of the NAPF, has published guidelines on share incentive schemes in listed companies. These guidelines can be viewed via the Institutional Voting Information Service website (see Directory). The key recommendations are:

- The ABI emphasises the principle of linking remuneration to performance, but recommends limits on the proportion of shares available for employee acquisition (no more than 10% of the issued share capital should be available in any ten-year period), limits in participation and clear evaluation and disclosure of cost.
- Grants of options should be phased, with awards being made on a sliding scale in relation to the achievement of demanding and stretching performance criteria.
- While participation in share incentive schemes and other forms of share-based payment are seen as significant and integral components of remuneration packages for senior executives, it is recommended that the costs of running the scheme be made as transparent as possible.
- Participation in share incentive schemes should be restricted to bona fide employees and executive directors, and be subject to appropriate limits for individual participation, which should be disclosed. NEDs should not participate in any form of share incentive scheme although they may have their fees paid in the form of shares purchased at the full market price.
- Listed companies should provide for the grant of options in a 'window' following the announcement of half-year or annual published results. The guidelines state that share options should be granted within 42 days following the date of any announcement of results of the company and no grant should be made later than ten years after the establishment of the scheme.

### 11.2 Other considerations for listed companies

Directors and certain other employees of listed companies are subject to the Model Code (see Chapter 6), which restricts their ability to deal in the shares of the company during certain periods. 'Dealing' is defined in the Model Code to include the grant or exercise of options under option schemes (with an exception for all-employee schemes) and the transfer or disposal of shares or other rights under other employee share schemes. Under the DTRs, announcements of changes to directors' interests in the shares and options of the company have to be advised to the Stock Market via a Regulatory Information Service.

The secretary needs to consider the documentation which must be submitted to UKLA for any new shares issued under an employee share scheme. Certain exemptions are permitted under the block listing regime so that a prospectus does not have to be produced in connection with new shares issued. (Further information in respect of block listings are provided in Chapter 12.)

Listed companies are subject to the Directors' Remuneration Report Regulations 2002. These require extensive disclosure of directors' remuneration, including participation in employee share schemes, to be made in the company's annual report and accounts.

## CHAPTER SUMMARY

■ Employee share schemes provide employees and directors with an incentive to improve personal performance and encourage loyalty by offering a financial stake in the company.

■ The company secretary is usually responsible for helping to establish a scheme and for maintaining the scheme's records.

■ Schemes which are HM Revenue & Customs-approved provide tax reliefs for the employer and/or employee. However, such schemes must be run in accordance with HM Revenue & Customs requirement at all times. Help and guidance are available from HM Revenue & Customs.

■ Some schemes are provided on an all-employee basis; others are operated on a discretionary basis. This will be one of the factors in determining an appropriate design of a scheme for the company.

■ There are specific requirements on listed companies regarding the introduction and approval of employee share schemes and in the disclosure of participation of directors. Listed companies are encouraged to abide by the recommendations published by the ABI and the NAPF.

## PART 4 PRACTICE CASE QUESTIONS

These questions are based on the case scenario outlined at the beginning of Part Four. You will also need to refer to content throughout this study text part to provide the answers.

### 💼 PART CASE QUESTION 4.1

Assume for the purposes of question 1 and question 2 only that you are now the Assistant Secretary of Multiple plc. In order to ensure that Accurate Registrars provide the best service to the shareholders of Multiple plc, you have agreed to go on a six-month secondment to Accurate Registrars to help improve their procedures and processes. The following enquiries are received during your first week at Accurate Registrars:

a) Mr Powers is a shareholder of Multiple plc and has one share certificate for 20,000 shares. Mr Powers wishes to transfer 5,000 of his shares to Mrs Penny for £10,000. Mr Powers is unfamiliar with the share transfer process and has asked if he could be provided with a guidance note of all the steps and procedures he, Mrs Penny or the registrar will take.

b) A covering letter and a Power of Attorney have been received from Mr Wealthy, who holds 500,000 shares in Multiple plc. In his letter, Mr Wealthy states that he is going abroad on a three-month luxury cruise and would like his solicitor, Mr Legal, to sell 50,000 shares in Multiple plc on his behalf whilst he is away. You intend to produce a checklist of steps Accurate Registrars should take after they receive the letter and the Power of Attorney.

Provide the advice as requested in a) and b) above.

### 💼 PART CASE QUESTION 4.2

The following week, you receive a number of letters from shareholders of Multiple plc. You agree to prepare responses to each of the letters so that future responses from Accurate Registrars can be based on your work. The letters you receive are as follows:

a) Mr Bust has run up large debts and expects to be made bankrupt. He has written to you and explained that he does not understand the bankruptcy process. He wants to know what steps are likely to occur in respect of the 2,000 shares he holds in his sole name.

b) Mrs Smith writes to you explaining that she married last month and that as a result her name has changed from Miss Jones. She also provides you with a new address to which she and her husband have moved. Mrs Smith asks you what documentation, if any, needs to be sent to the registrar regarding her change of name and address. Mrs Smith also mentions that her friend suggested that she asks for her dividends to be mandated in the future. However, she does not know what this means and is not sure whether there would be any benefit in this for her.

c) Mr Cash writes to you stating that he has noticed Multiple plc plans to introduce a scrip dividend. He has been keen for some time to increase his interest in Multiple plc and asks you what a scrip dividend is, how it operates and if there might be any benefits in it for him. He also asks you to explain all the documents he would expect to receive in a scrip dividend and what he would need to do with them.

Write suitable letters in respect of each of a)–c) above.

## PART CASE QUESTION 4.3

As part of Multiple plc's expansion plans, you are in the confidential planning stages of acquiring Major Concern plc. Multiple plc will need to raise additional financing if the proposed acquisition is to be a success. As the proposed acquisition is in the planning stage, it is not known yet to the public and the queries below are raised with you:

a) The chief executive asks you to provide advice on the different methods by which the company may make an issue of shares.

b) A non-executive director has seen a reference to 'underwriting' in the draft acquisition timetable. The NED is not familiar with the underwriting process, or the reasons for needing it, and would like the matter briefly explained.

c) Assuming that the acquisition is financed via the issue of new shares, the finance director points out that the company would like to allot shares in large blocks to certain major institutional investors only. Would this be possible to approve this at the forthcoming general meeting which will consider the acquisition?

d) The chairman knows that when the proposed acquisition is announced to the public next month, Big Prospects' share price is likely to rise substantially. He plans to buy 100,000 shares in Big Prospects plc shortly and has asked if he could buy them now rather than after the announcement has been made. He also asks whom, if any, he needs to advise before making the purchase of shares.

Write a memorandum to the board which deals with the matters raised in a)–d) above.

## PART CASE QUESTION 4.4

The board wishes to encourage every employee to acquire shares in Multiple plc. They have decided to introduce a savings-related share option scheme. As the Company Secretariat department is responsible for operating share schemes, this will be your responsibility. Prepare a working programme indicating all the matters which will need to be considered and prepared.

## PART CASE QUESTION 4.5

As company secretary of Multiple plc, it is vital that the work of the department is planned properly throughout the forthcoming year. Assume the date today for the purposes of this question is 1 January 2012. You are drawing up your work programme and timetable for the period 1 January 2012 – 31 January 2013. The following matters are all relevant in preparing your work programme:

- the financial year-end is 31 December and the half year-end is on 30 June. The company does not issue quarterly results;
- the last AGM was held on 28 May 2011;
- the last annual return was made up to 1 July 2011;
- Mr Old is due to retire as a director on 1 November 2012, when he shall sell his shares to Mr New, who will be appointed to the board on the same date;
- the board, which has the requisite authority, is due to approve an allotment of shares to shareholders on a pre-emptive basis on 1 August 2012;
- the company intends to issue awards under its Company Share Option Plan on 5 April 2012.

Executive directors are among the expected recipients of the awards;

- a special resolution will be proposed at a general meeting of the company on 1 September 2012 in respect of the alteration of the company's articles of association;
- Board meetings are expected to be held on the first business day of each month during 2012;
- final dividends are typically paid each year in June. Interim dividends are typically paid each year in December.

Produce a work programme and timetable for the department taking into account:

- the deadlines in respect of the above transactions or events;
- what documents, if any, must be filed with the Registrar of Companies or UKLA and what notifications should be sent through a Regulatory Information Service;
- the last date on which such documents may be filed plus a brief explanation of the applicable statutory timescales.

# APPENDIX 1

# Model articles for private companies limited by shares

## INDEX TO THE ARTICLES

# PART 1 INTERPRETATION AND LIMITATION OF LIABILITY

## Defined terms

1. In the articles, unless the context requires otherwise –

'articles' means the company's articles of association;

'bankruptcy' includes individual insolvency proceedings in a jurisdiction other than England and Wales or Northern Ireland which have an effect similar to that of bankruptcy;

'chairman' has the meaning given in article 12;

'chairman of the meeting' has the meaning given in article 39;

'Companies Acts' means the Companies Acts (as defined in section 2 of the Companies Act 2006), in so far as they apply to the company;

'director' means a director of the company, and includes any person occupying the position of director, by whatever name called;

'distribution recipient' has the meaning given in article 31;

'document' includes, unless otherwise specified, any document sent or supplied in electronic form;

'electronic form' has the meaning given in section 1168 of the Companies Act 2006;

'fully paid' in relation to a share, means that the nominal value and any premium to be paid to the company in respect of that share have been paid to the company;

'hard copy form' has the meaning given in section 1168 of the Companies Act 2006;

'holder' in relation to shares means the person whose name is entered in the register of members as the holder of the shares;

'instrument' means a document in hard copy form;

'ordinary resolution' has the meaning given in section 282 of the Companies Act 2006;

'paid' means paid or credited as paid;

'participate', in relation to a directors' meeting, has the meaning given in article 10;

'proxy notice' has the meaning given in article 45;

'shareholder' means a person who is the holder of a share;

'shares' means shares in the company;

'special resolution' has the meaning given in section 283 of the Companies Act 2006;

'subsidiary' has the meaning given in section 1159 of the Companies Act 2006;

'transmittee' means a person entitled to a share by reason of the death or bankruptcy of a shareholder or otherwise by operation of law; and

'writing' means the representation or reproduction of words, symbols or other information in a visible form by any method or combination of methods, whether sent or supplied in electronic form or otherwise.

Unless the context otherwise requires, other words or expressions contained in these articles bear the same meaning as in the Companies Act 2006 as in force on the date when these articles become binding on the company.

## Liability of members

2. The liability of the members is limited to the amount, if any, unpaid on the shares held by them.

# PART 2 DIRECTORS

## DIRECTORS' POWERS AND RESPONSIBILITIES

### Directors' general authority

3. Subject to the articles, the directors are responsible for the management of the company's business, for which purpose they may exercise all the powers of the company.

## Shareholders' reserve power

4. (1) The shareholders may, by special resolution, direct the directors to take, or refrain from taking, specified action.

   (2) No such special resolution invalidates anything which the directors have done before the passing of the resolution.

## Directors may delegate

5. (1) Subject to the articles, the directors may delegate any of the powers which are conferred on them under the articles –
   
   (a) to such person or committee;
   
   (b) by such means (including by power of attorney);
   
   (c) to such an extent;
   
   (d) in relation to such matters or territories; and
   
   (e) on such terms and conditions;
   
   as they think fit.

   (2) If the directors so specify, any such delegation may authorise further delegation of the directors' powers by any person to whom they are delegated.

   (3) The directors may revoke any delegation in whole or part, or alter its terms and conditions.

## Committees

6. (1) Committees to which the directors delegate any of their powers must follow procedures which are based as far as they are applicable on those provisions of the articles which govern the taking of decisions by directors.

   (2) The directors may make rules of procedure for all or any committees, which prevail over rules derived from the articles if they are not consistent with them.

# DECISION-MAKING BY DIRECTORS

## Directors to take decisions collectively

7. (1) The general rule about decision-making by directors is that any decision of the directors must be either a majority decision at a meeting or a decision taken in accordance with article 8.

   (2) If –
   
   (a) the company only has one director, and
   
   (b) no provision of the articles requires it to have more than one director, the general rule does not apply, and the director may take decisions without regard to any of the provisions of the articles relating to directors' decision-making.

## Unanimous decisions

8. (1) A decision of the directors is taken in accordance with this article when all eligible directors indicate to each other by any means that they share a common view on a matter.

   (2) Such a decision may take the form of a resolution in writing, copies of which have been signed by each eligible director or to which each eligible director has otherwise indicated agreement in writing.

   (3) References in this article to eligible directors are to directors who would have been entitled to vote on the matter had it been proposed as a resolution at a directors' meeting.

   (4) A decision may not be taken in accordance with this article if the eligible directors would not have formed a quorum at such a meeting.

## Calling a directors' meeting

9. (1) Any director may call a directors' meeting by giving notice of the meeting to the directors or by authorising the company secretary (if any) to give such notice.

   (2) Notice of any directors' meeting must indicate –
   
   (a) its proposed date and time;
   
   (b) where it is to take place; and

(c) if it is anticipated that directors participating in the meeting will not be in the same place, how it is proposed that they should communicate with each other during the meeting.

(3) Notice of a directors' meeting must be given to each director, but need not be in writing.

(4) Notice of a directors' meeting need not be given to directors who waive their entitlement to notice of that meeting, by giving notice to that effect to the company not more than 7 days after the date on which the meeting is held. Where such notice is given after the meeting has been held, that does not affect the validity of the meeting, or of any business conducted at it.

## Participation in directors' meetings

10. (1) Subject to the articles, directors participate in a directors' meeting, or part of a directors' meeting, when –
    (a) the meeting has been called and takes place in accordance with the articles, and
    (b) they can each communicate to the others any information or opinions they have on any particular item of the business of the meeting.

(2) In determining whether directors are participating in a directors' meeting, it is irrelevant where any director is or how they communicate with each other.

(3) If all the directors participating in a meeting are not in the same place, they may decide that the meeting is to be treated as taking place wherever any of them is.

## Quorum for directors' meetings

11. (1) At a directors' meeting, unless a quorum is participating, no proposal is to be voted on, except a proposal to call another meeting.

(2) The quorum for directors' meetings may be fixed from time to time by a decision of the directors, but it must never be less than two, and unless otherwise fixed it is two.

(3) If the total number of directors for the time being is less than the quorum required, the directors must not take any decision other than a decision –
    (a) to appoint further directors, or
    (b) to call a general meeting so as to enable the shareholders to appoint further directors.

## Chairing of directors' meetings

12. (1) The directors may appoint a director to chair their meetings.

(2) The person so appointed for the time being is known as the chairman.

(3) The directors may terminate the chairman's appointment at any time.

(4) If the chairman is not participating in a directors' meeting within ten minutes of the time at which it was to start, the participating directors must appoint one of themselves to chair it.

## Casting vote

13. (1) If the numbers of votes for and against a proposal are equal, the chairman or other director chairing the meeting has a casting vote.

(2) But this does not apply if, in accordance with the articles, the chairman or other director is not to be counted as participating in the decision-making process for quorum or voting purposes.

## Conflicts of interest

14. (1) If a proposed decision of the directors is concerned with an actual or proposed transaction or arrangement with the company in which a director is interested, that director is not to be counted as participating in the decision-making process for quorum or voting purposes.

(2) But if paragraph (3) applies, a director who is interested in an actual or proposed transaction or arrangement with the company is to be counted as participating in the decision-making process for quorum and voting purposes.

(3) This paragraph applies when –
   (a) the company by ordinary resolution disapplies the provision of the articles which would otherwise prevent a director from being counted as participating in the decision-making process;
   (b) the director's interest cannot reasonably be regarded as likely to give rise to a conflict of interest; or
   (c) the director's conflict of interest arises from a permitted cause.

(4) For the purposes of this article, the following are permitted causes –
   (a) a guarantee given, or to be given, by or to a director in respect of an obligation incurred by or on behalf of the company or any of its subsidiaries;
   (b) subscription, or an agreement to subscribe, for shares or other securities of the company or any of its subsidiaries, or to underwrite, sub-underwrite, or guarantee subscription for any such shares or securities; and
   (c) arrangements pursuant to which benefits are made available to employees and directors or former employees and directors of the company or any of its subsidiaries which do not provide special benefits for directors or former directors.

(5) For the purposes of this article, references to proposed decisions and decision-making processes include any directors' meeting or part of a directors' meeting.

(6) Subject to paragraph (7), if a question arises at a meeting of directors or of a committee of directors as to the right of a director to participate in the meeting (or part of the meeting) for voting or quorum purposes, the question may, before the conclusion of the meeting, be referred to the chairman whose ruling in relation to any director other than the chairman is to be final and conclusive.

(7) If any question as to the right to participate in the meeting (or part of the meeting) should arise in respect of the chairman, the question is to be decided by a decision of the directors at that meeting, for which purpose the chairman is not to be counted as participating in the meeting (or that part of the meeting) for voting or quorum purposes.

## Records of decisions to be kept

**15.** The directors must ensure that the company keeps a record, in writing, for at least 10 years from the date of the decision recorded, of every unanimous or majority decision taken by the directors.

## Directors' discretion to make further rules

**16.** Subject to the articles, the directors may make any rule which they think fit about how they take decisions, and about how such rules are to be recorded or communicated to directors.

# APPOINTMENT OF DIRECTORS

## Methods of appointing directors

**17.** (1) Any person who is willing to act as a director, and is permitted by law to do so, may be appointed to be a director –
   (a) by ordinary resolution, or
   (b) by a decision of the directors.

(2) In any case where, as a result of death, the company has no shareholders and no directors, the personal representatives of the last shareholder to have died have the right, by notice in writing, to appoint a person to be a director.

(3) For the purposes of paragraph (2), where two or more shareholders die in circumstances rendering it uncertain who was the last to die, a younger shareholder is deemed to have survived an older shareholder.

## Termination of director's appointment

**18.** A person ceases to be a director as soon as –
   (a) that person ceases to be a director by virtue of any provision of the Companies Act 2006 or is prohibited from being a director by law;

(b) a bankruptcy order is made against that person;

(c) a composition is made with that person's creditors generally in satisfaction of that person's debts;

(d) a registered medical practitioner who is treating that person gives a written opinion to the company stating that that person has become physically or mentally incapable of acting as a director and may remain so for more than three months;

(e) by reason of that person's mental health, a court makes an order which wholly or partly prevents that person from personally exercising any powers or rights which that person would otherwise have;

(f) notification is received by the company from the director that the director is resigning from office, and such resignation has taken effect in accordance with its terms.

## Directors' remuneration

19. (1) Directors may undertake any services for the company that the directors decide.

(2) Directors are entitled to such remuneration as the directors determine –

(a) for their services to the company as directors, and

(b) for any other service which they undertake for the company.

(3) Subject to the articles, a director's remuneration may –

(a) take any form, and

(b) include any arrangements in connection with the payment of a pension, allowance or gratuity, or any death, sickness or disability benefits, to or in respect of that director.

(4) Unless the directors decide otherwise, directors' remuneration accrues from day to day.

(5) Unless the directors decide otherwise, directors are not accountable to the company for any remuneration which they receive as directors or other officers or employees of the company's subsidiaries or of any other body corporate in which the company is interested.

## Directors' expenses

20. The company may pay any reasonable expenses which the directors properly incur in connection with their attendance at –

(a) meetings of directors or committees of directors,

(b) general meetings, or

(c) separate meetings of the holders of any class of shares or of debentures of the company, or otherwise in connection with the exercise of their powers and the discharge of their responsibilities in relation to the company.

# PART 3 SHARES AND DISTRIBUTIONS

## SHARES

### All shares to be fully paid up

21. (1) No share is to be issued for less than the aggregate of its nominal value and any premium to be paid to the company in consideration for its issue.

(2) This does not apply to shares taken on the formation of the company by the subscribers to the company's memorandum.

### Powers to issue different classes of share

22. (1) Subject to the articles, but without prejudice to the rights attached to any existing share, the company may issue shares with such rights or restrictions as may be determined by ordinary resolution.

(2) The company may issue shares which are to be redeemed, or are liable to be redeemed at the option of the company or the holder, and the directors may determine the terms, conditions and manner of redemption of any such shares.

## Company not bound by less than absolute interests

**23.** Except as required by law, no person is to be recognised by the company as holding any share upon any trust, and except as otherwise required by law or the articles, the company is not in any way to be bound by or recognise any interest in a share other than the holder's absolute ownership of it and all the rights attaching to it.

## Share certificates

**24.** (1) The company must issue each shareholder, free of charge, with one or more certificates in respect of the shares which that shareholder holds.

(2) Every certificate must specify –

(a) in respect of how many shares, of what class, it is issued;

(b) the nominal value of those shares;

(c) that the shares are fully paid; and

(d) any distinguishing numbers assigned to them.

(3) No certificate may be issued in respect of shares of more than one class.

(4) If more than one person holds a share, only one certificate may be issued in respect of it.

(5) Certificates must –

(a) have affixed to them the company's common seal, or

(b) be otherwise executed in accordance with the Companies Acts.

## Replacement share certificates

**25.** (1) If a certificate issued in respect of a shareholder's shares is –

(a) damaged or defaced, or

(b) said to be lost, stolen or destroyed,

that shareholder is entitled to be issued with a replacement certificate in respect of the same shares.

(2) A shareholder exercising the right to be issued with such a replacement certificate –

(a) may at the same time exercise the right to be issued with a single certificate or separate certificates;

(b) must return the certificate which is to be replaced to the company if it is damaged or defaced; and

(c) must comply with such conditions as to evidence, indemnity and the payment of a reasonable fee as the directors decide.

## Share transfers

**26.** (1) Shares may be transferred by means of an instrument of transfer in any usual form or any other form approved by the directors, which is executed by or on behalf of the transferor.

(2) No fee may be charged for registering any instrument of transfer or other document relating to or affecting the title to any share.

(3) The company may retain any instrument of transfer which is registered.

(4) The transferor remains the holder of a share until the transferee's name is entered in the register of members as holder of it.

(5) The directors may refuse to register the transfer of a share, and if they do so, the instrument of transfer must be returned to the transferee with the notice of refusal unless they suspect that the proposed transfer may be fraudulent.

## Transmission of shares

**27.** (1) If title to a share passes to a transmittee, the company may only recognise the transmittee as having any title to that share.

(2) A transmittee who produces such evidence of entitlement to shares as the directors may properly require –

(a) may, subject to the articles, choose either to become the holder of those shares or to have them transferred to another person, and

(b) subject to the articles, and pending any transfer of the shares to another person, has the same rights as the holder had.

(3) But transmittees do not have the right to attend or vote at a general meeting, or agree to a proposed written resolution, in respect of shares to which they are entitled, by reason of the holder's death or bankruptcy or otherwise, unless they become the holders of those shares.

## Exercise of transmittees' rights

**28.** (1) Transmittees who wish to become the holders of shares to which they have become entitled must notify the company in writing of that wish.

(2) If the transmittee wishes to have a share transferred to another person, the transmittee must execute an instrument of transfer in respect of it.

(3) Any transfer made or executed under this article is to be treated as if it were made or executed by the person from whom the transmittee has derived rights in respect of the share, and as if the event which gave rise to the transmission had not occurred.

## Transmittees bound by prior notices

**29.** If a notice is given to a shareholder in respect of shares and a transmittee is entitled to those shares, the transmittee is bound by the notice if it was given to the shareholder before the transmittee's name has been entered in the register of members.

# DIVIDENDS AND OTHER DISTRIBUTIONS

## Procedure for declaring dividends

**30.** (1) The company may by ordinary resolution declare dividends, and the directors may decide to pay interim dividends.

(2) A dividend must not be declared unless the directors have made a recommendation as to its amount. Such a dividend must not exceed the amount recommended by the directors.

(3) No dividend may be declared or paid unless it is in accordance with shareholders' respective rights.

(4) Unless the shareholders' resolution to declare or directors' decision to pay a dividend, or the terms on which shares are issued, specify otherwise, it must be paid by reference to each shareholder's holding of shares on the date of the resolution or decision to declare or pay it.

(5) If the company's share capital is divided into different classes, no interim dividend may be paid on shares carrying deferred or non-preferred rights if, at the time of payment, any preferential dividend is in arrear.

(6) The directors may pay at intervals any dividend payable at a fixed rate if it appears to them that the profits available for distribution justify the payment.

(7) If the directors act in good faith, they do not incur any liability to the holders of shares conferring preferred rights for any loss they may suffer by the lawful payment of an interim dividend on shares with deferred or non-preferred rights.

## Payment of dividends and other distributions

**31.** (1) Where a dividend or other sum which is a distribution is payable in respect of a share, it must be paid by one or more of the following means –

(a) transfer to a bank or building society account specified by the distribution recipient either in writing or as the directors may otherwise decide;

(b) sending a cheque made payable to the distribution recipient by post to the distribution recipient at the distribution recipient's registered address (if the distribution recipient is a holder of the share), or (in any other case) to an address specified by the distribution recipient either in writing or as the directors may otherwise decide;

(c) sending a cheque made payable to such person by post to such person at such address as the distribution recipient has specified either in writing or as the directors may otherwise decide; or

(d) any other means of payment as the directors agree with the distribution recipient either in writing or by such other means as the directors decide.

(2) In the articles, 'the distribution recipient' means, in respect of a share in respect of which a dividend or other sum is payable –
(a) the holder of the share; or
(b) if the share has two or more joint holders, whichever of them is named first in the register of members; or
(c) if the holder is no longer entitled to the share by reason of death or bankruptcy, or otherwise by operation of law, the transmittee.

## No interest on distributions

**32.** The company may not pay interest on any dividend or other sum payable in respect of a share unless otherwise provided by –
(a) the terms on which the share was issued, or
(b) the provisions of another agreement between the holder of that share and the company.

## Unclaimed distributions

**33.** (1) All dividends or other sums which are –
(a) payable in respect of shares, and
(b) unclaimed after having been declared or become payable, may be invested or otherwise made use of by the directors for the benefit of the company until claimed.
(2) The payment of any such dividend or other sum into a separate account does not make the company a trustee in respect of it.
(3) If –
(a) twelve years have passed from the date on which a dividend or other sum became due for payment, and
(b) the distribution recipient has not claimed it, the distribution recipient is no longer entitled to that dividend or other sum and it ceases to remain owing by the company.

## Non-cash distributions

**34.** (1) Subject to the terms of issue of the share in question, the company may, by ordinary resolution on the recommendation of the directors, decide to pay all or part of a dividend or other distribution payable in respect of a share by transferring non-cash assets of equivalent value (including, without limitation, shares or other securities in any company).
(2) For the purposes of paying a non-cash distribution, the directors may make whatever arrangements they think fit, including, where any difficulty arises regarding the distribution –
(a) fixing the value of any assets;
(b) paying cash to any distribution recipient on the basis of that value in order to adjust the rights of recipients; and
(c) vesting any assets in trustees.

## Waiver of distributions

**35.** Distribution recipients may waive their entitlement to a dividend or other distribution payable in respect of a share by giving the company notice in writing to that effect, but if –
(a) the share has more than one holder, or
(b) more than one person is entitled to the share, whether by reason of the death or bankruptcy of one or more joint holders, or otherwise, the notice is not effective unless it is expressed to be given, and signed, by all the holders or persons otherwise entitled to the share.

# CAPITALISATION OF PROFITS

## Authority to capitalise and appropriation of capitalised sums

**36.** (1) Subject to the articles, the directors may, if they are so authorised by an ordinary resolution –
(a) decide to capitalise any profits of the company (whether or not they are available for distribution) which are not required for paying a preferential dividend, or any

sum standing to the credit of the company's share premium account or capital redemption reserve; and

(b) appropriate any sum which they so decide to capitalise (a 'capitalised sum') to the persons who would have been entitled to it if it were distributed by way of dividend (the 'persons entitled') and in the same proportions.

(2) Capitalised sums must be applied –

(a) on behalf of the persons entitled, and

(b) in the same proportions as a dividend would have been distributed to them.

(3) Any capitalised sum may be applied in paying up new shares of a nominal amount equal to the capitalised sum which are then allotted credited as fully paid to the persons entitled or as they may direct.

(4) A capitalised sum which was appropriated from profits available for distribution may be applied in paying up new debentures of the company which are then allotted credited as fully paid to the persons entitled or as they may direct.

(5) Subject to the articles the directors may –

(a) apply capitalised sums in accordance with paragraphs (3) and (4) partly in one way and partly in another;

(b) make such arrangements as they think fit to deal with shares or debentures becoming distributable in fractions under this article (including the issuing of fractional certificates or the making of cash payments); and

(c) authorise any person to enter into an agreement with the company on behalf of all the persons entitled which is binding on them in respect of the allotment of shares and debentures to them under this article.

# PART 4 DECISION-MAKING BY SHAREHOLDERS

## ORGANISATION OF GENERAL MEETINGS

### Attendance and speaking at general meetings

37. (1) A person is able to exercise the right to speak at a general meeting when that person is in a position to communicate to all those attending the meeting, during the meeting, any information or opinions which that person has on the business of the meeting.

(2) A person is able to exercise the right to vote at a general meeting when –

(a) that person is able to vote, during the meeting, on resolutions put to the vote at the meeting, and

(b) that person's vote can be taken into account in determining whether or not such resolutions are passed at the same time as the votes of all the other persons attending the meeting.

(3) The directors may make whatever arrangements they consider appropriate to enable those attending a general meeting to exercise their rights to speak or vote at it.

(4) In determining attendance at a general meeting, it is immaterial whether any two or more members attending it are in the same place as each other.

(5) Two or more persons who are not in the same place as each other attend a general meeting if their circumstances are such that if they have (or were to have) rights to speak and vote at that meeting, they are (or would be) able to exercise them.

### Quorum for general meetings

38. No business other than the appointment of the chairman of the meeting is to be transacted at a general meeting if the persons attending it do not constitute a quorum.

### Chairing general meetings

39. (1) If the directors have appointed a chairman, the chairman shall chair general meetings if present and willing to do so.

(2) If the directors have not appointed a chairman, or if the chairman is unwilling to chair the meeting or is not present within ten minutes of the time at which a meeting was due to start –

      (a)    the directors present, or

      (b)    (if no directors are present), the meeting, must appoint a director or shareholder to chair the meeting, and the appointment of the chairman of the meeting must be the first business of the meeting.

  (3)   The person chairing a meeting in accordance with this article is referred to as 'the chairman of the meeting'.

## Attendance and speaking by directors and non-shareholders

**40.** (1)   Directors may attend and speak at general meetings, whether or not they are shareholders.

  (2)   The chairman of the meeting may permit other persons who are not –

      (a)    shareholders of the company, or

      (b)    otherwise entitled to exercise the rights of shareholders in relation to general meetings, to attend and speak at a general meeting.

## Adjournment

**41.** (1)   If the persons attending a general meeting within half an hour of the time at which the meeting was due to start do not constitute a quorum, or if during a meeting a quorum ceases to be present, the chairman of the meeting must adjourn it.

  (2)   The chairman of the meeting may adjourn a general meeting at which a quorum is present if –

      (a)    the meeting consents to an adjournment, or

      (b)    it appears to the chairman of the meeting that an adjournment is necessary to protect the safety of any person attending the meeting or ensure that the business of the meeting is conducted in an orderly manner.

  (3)   The chairman of the meeting must adjourn a general meeting if directed to do so by the meeting.

  (4)   When adjourning a general meeting, the chairman of the meeting must –

      (a)    either specify the time and place to which it is adjourned or state that it is to continue at a time and place to be fixed by the directors, and

      (b)    have regard to any directions as to the time and place of any adjournment which have been given by the meeting.

  (5)   If the continuation of an adjourned meeting is to take place more than 14 days after it was adjourned, the company must give at least seven clear days' notice of it (that is, excluding the day of the adjourned meeting and the day on which the notice is given) –

      (a)    to the same persons to whom notice of the company's general meetings is required to be given, and

      (b)    containing the same information which such notice is required to contain.

  (6)   No business may be transacted at an adjourned general meeting which could not properly have been transacted at the meeting if the adjournment had not taken place.

## VOTING AT GENERAL MEETINGS

### Voting: general

**42.** A resolution put to the vote of a general meeting must be decided on a show of hands unless a poll is duly demanded in accordance with the articles.

### Errors and disputes

**43.** (1)   No objection may be raised to the qualification of any person voting at a general meeting except at the meeting or adjourned meeting at which the vote objected to is tendered, and every vote not disallowed at the meeting is valid.

  (2)   Any such objection must be referred to the chairman of the meeting, whose decision is final.

## Poll votes

**44.** (1) A poll on a resolution may be demanded –

    (a)   in advance of the general meeting where it is to be put to the vote, or

    (b)   at a general meeting, either before a show of hands on that resolution or immediately after the result of a show of hands on that resolution is declared.

  (2) A poll may be demanded by –

    (a)   the chairman of the meeting;

    (b)   the directors;

    (c)   two or more persons having the right to vote on the resolution; or

    (d)   a person or persons representing not less than one tenth of the total voting rights of all the shareholders having the right to vote on the resolution.

  (3) A demand for a poll may be withdrawn if –

    (a)   the poll has not yet been taken, and

    (b)   the chairman of the meeting consents to the withdrawal.

  (4) Polls must be taken immediately and in such manner as the chairman of the meeting directs.

## Content of proxy notices

**45.** (1) Proxies may only validly be appointed by a notice in writing (a 'proxy notice') which –

    (a)   states the name and address of the shareholder appointing the proxy;

    (b)   identifies the person appointed to be that shareholder's proxy and the general meeting in relation to which that person is appointed;

    (c)   is signed by or on behalf of the shareholder appointing the proxy, or is authenticated in such manner as the directors may determine; and

    (d)   is delivered to the company in accordance with the articles and any instructions contained in the notice of the general meeting to which they relate.

  (2) The company may require proxy notices to be delivered in a particular form, and may specify different forms for different purposes.

  (3) Proxy notices may specify how the proxy appointed under them is to vote (or that the proxy is to abstain from voting) on one or more resolutions.

  (4) Unless a proxy notice indicates otherwise, it must be treated as –

    (a)   allowing the person appointed under it as a proxy discretion as to how to vote on any ancillary or procedural resolutions put to the meeting, and

    (b)   appointing that person as a proxy in relation to any adjournment of the general meeting to which it relates as well as the meeting itself.

## Delivery of proxy notices

**46.** (1) A person who is entitled to attend, speak or vote (either on a show of hands or on a poll) at a general meeting remains so entitled in respect of that meeting or any adjournment of it, even though a valid proxy notice has been delivered to the company by or on behalf of that person.

  (2) An appointment under a proxy notice may be revoked by delivering to the company a notice in writing given by or on behalf of the person by whom or on whose behalf the proxy notice was given.

  (3) A notice revoking a proxy appointment only takes effect if it is delivered before the start of the meeting or adjourned meeting to which it relates.

  (4) If a proxy notice is not executed by the person appointing the proxy, it must be accompanied by written evidence of the authority of the person who executed it to execute it on the appointor's behalf.

## Amendments to resolutions

**47.** (1) An ordinary resolution to be proposed at a general meeting may be amended by ordinary resolution if –

    (a)   notice of the proposed amendment is given to the company in writing by a person entitled to vote at the general meeting at which it is to be proposed not less than 48 hours before the meeting is to take place (or such later time as the chairman of the meeting may determine), and

(b) the proposed amendment does not, in the reasonable opinion of the chairman of the meeting, materially alter the scope of the resolution.

(2) A special resolution to be proposed at a general meeting may be amended by ordinary resolution, if –

(a) the chairman of the meeting proposes the amendment at the general meeting at which the resolution is to be proposed, and

(b) the amendment does not go beyond what is necessary to correct a grammatical or other non-substantive error in the resolution.

(3) If the chairman of the meeting, acting in good faith, wrongly decides that an amendment to a resolution is out of order, the chairman's error does not invalidate the vote on that resolution.

# PART 5 ADMINISTRATIVE ARRANGEMENTS

## Means of communication to be used

**48.** (1) Subject to the articles, anything sent or supplied by or to the company under the articles may be sent or supplied in any way in which the Companies Act 2006 provides for documents or information which are authorised or required by any provision of that Act to be sent or supplied by or to the company.

(2) Subject to the articles, any notice or document to be sent or supplied to a director in connection with the taking of decisions by directors may also be sent or supplied by the means by which that director has asked to be sent or supplied with such notices or documents for the time being.

(3) A director may agree with the company that notices or documents sent to that director in a particular way are to be deemed to have been received within a specified time of their being sent, and for the specified time to be less than 48 hours.

## Company seals

**49.** (1) Any common seal may only be used by the authority of the directors.

(2) The directors may decide by what means and in what form any common seal is to be used.

(3) Unless otherwise decided by the directors, if the company has a common seal and it is affixed to a document, the document must also be signed by at least one authorised person in the presence of a witness who attests the signature.

(4) For the purposes of this article, an authorised person is –

(a) any director of the company;

(b) the company secretary (if any); or

(c) any person authorised by the directors for the purpose of signing documents to which the common seal is applied.

## No right to inspect accounts and other records

**50.** Except as provided by law or authorised by the directors or an ordinary resolution of the company, no person is entitled to inspect any of the company's accounting or other records or documents merely by virtue of being a shareholder.

## Provision for employees on cessation of business

**51.** The directors may decide to make provision for the benefit of persons employed or formerly employed by the company or any of its subsidiaries (other than a director or former director or shadow director) in connection with the cessation or transfer to any person of the whole or part of the undertaking of the company or that subsidiary.

## DIRECTORS' INDEMNITY AND INSURANCE

### Indemnity

**52.** (1) Subject to paragraph (2), a relevant director of the company or an associated company may be indemnified out of the company's assets against –

    (a) any liability incurred by that director in connection with any negligence, default, breach of duty or breach of trust in relation to the company or an associated company,

    (b) any liability incurred by that director in connection with the activities of the company or an associated company in its capacity as a trustee of an occupational pension scheme (as defined in section 235(6) of the Companies Act 2006),

    (c) any other liability incurred by that director as an officer of the company or an associated company.

  (2) This article does not authorise any indemnity which would be prohibited or rendered void by any provision of the Companies Acts or by any other provision of law.

  (3) In this article –

    (a) companies are associated if one is a subsidiary of the other or both are subsidiaries of the same body corporate, and

    (b) a 'relevant director' means any director or former director of the company or an associated company.

### Insurance

**53.** (1) The directors may decide to purchase and maintain insurance, at the expense of the company, for the benefit of any relevant director in respect of any relevant loss.

  (2) In this article –

    (a) a 'relevant director' means any director or former director of the company or an associated company,

    (b) a 'relevant loss' means any loss or liability which has been or may be incurred by a relevant director in connection with that director's duties or powers in relation to the company, any associated company or any pension fund or employees' share scheme of the company or associated company, and

    (c) companies are associated if one is a subsidiary of the other or both are subsidiaries of the same body corporate.

# APPENDIX 2

# Model articles for public companies limited by shares

## INDEX TO THE ARTICLES

# PART 1 INTERPRETATION AND LIMITATION OF LIABILITY

## Defined terms

1.  In the articles, unless the context requires otherwise –

    'alternate' or 'alternate director' has the meaning given in article 25;

    'appointor' has the meaning given in article 25;

    'articles' means the company's articles of association;

    'bankruptcy' includes individual insolvency proceedings in a jurisdiction other than England and Wales or Northern Ireland which have an effect similar to that of bankruptcy;

    'call' has the meaning given in article 54;

    'call notice' has the meaning given in article 54;

    'certificate' means a paper certificate (other than a share warrant) evidencing a person's title to specified shares or other securities;

    'certificated' in relation to a share, means that it is not an uncertificated share or a share in respect of which a share warrant has been issued and is current;

    'chairman' has the meaning given in article 12;

    'chairman of the meeting' has the meaning given in article 31;

    'Companies Acts' means the Companies Acts (as defined in section 2 of the Companies Act 2006), in so far as they apply to the company;

    'company's lien' has the meaning given in article 52;

    'director' means a director of the company, and includes any person occupying the position of director, by whatever name called;

    'distribution recipient' has the meaning given in article 72;

    'document' includes, unless otherwise specified, any document sent or supplied in electronic form;

    'electronic form' has the meaning given in section 1168 of the Companies Act 2006;

    'fully paid' in relation to a share, means that the nominal value and any premium to be paid to the company in respect of that share have been paid to the company;

    'hard copy form' has the meaning given in section 1168 of the Companies Act 2006;

    'holder' in relation to shares means the person whose name is entered in the register of members as the holder of the shares, or, in the case of a share in respect of which a share warrant has been issued (and not cancelled), the person in possession of that warrant;

    'instrument' means a document in hard copy form;

    'lien enforcement notice' has the meaning given in article 53;

    'member' has the meaning given in section 112 of the Companies Act 2006;

    'ordinary resolution' has the meaning given in section 282 of the Companies Act 2006;

    'paid' means paid or credited as paid;

    'participate', in relation to a directors' meeting, has the meaning given in article 9;

    'partly paid' in relation to a share means that part of that share's nominal value or any premium at which it was issued has not been paid to the company;

    'proxy notice' has the meaning given in article 38;

    'securities seal' has the meaning given in article 47;

    'shares' means shares in the company;

    'special resolution' has the meaning given in section 283 of the Companies Act 2006;

    'subsidiary' has the meaning given in section 1159 of the Companies Act 2006;

    'transmittee' means a person entitled to a share by reason of the death or bankruptcy of a shareholder or otherwise by operation of law;

    'uncertificated' in relation to a share means that, by virtue of legislation (other than section 778 of the Companies Act 2006) permitting title to shares to be evidenced and transferred without a certificate, title to that share is evidenced and may be transferred without a certificate; and

    'writing' means the representation or reproduction of words, symbols or other information in a visible form by any method or combination of methods, whether sent or supplied in electronic form or otherwise.

Unless the context otherwise requires, other words or expressions contained in these articles bear the same meaning as in the Companies Act 2006 as in force on the date when these articles become binding on the company.

## Liability of members

2.  The liability of the members is limited to the amount, if any, unpaid on the shares held by them.

# PART 2 DIRECTORS

## DIRECTORS' POWERS AND RESPONSIBILITIES

### Directors' general authority

3.  Subject to the articles, the directors are responsible for the management of the company's business, for which purpose they may exercise all the powers of the company.

### Members' reserve power

4.  (1) The members may, by special resolution, direct the directors to take, or refrain from taking, specified action.
    (2) No such special resolution invalidates anything which the directors have done before the passing of the resolution.

### Directors may delegate

5.  (1) Subject to the articles, the directors may delegate any of the powers which are conferred on them under the articles –
    (a)  to such person or committee;
    (b)  by such means (including by power of attorney);
    (c)  to such an extent;
    (d)  in relation to such matters or territories; and
    (e)  on such terms and conditions;
    as they think fit.
    (2) If the directors so specify, any such delegation may authorise further delegation of the directors' powers by any person to whom they are delegated.
    (3) The directors may revoke any delegation in whole or part, or alter its terms and conditions.

### Committees

6.  (1) Committees to which the directors delegate any of their powers must follow procedures which are based as far as they are applicable on those provisions of the articles which govern the taking of decisions by directors.
    (2) The directors may make rules of procedure for all or any committees, which prevail over rules derived from the articles if they are not consistent with them.

## DECISION-MAKING BY DIRECTORS

### Directors to take decisions collectively

7.  Decisions of the directors may be taken –
    (a)  at a directors' meeting, or
    (b)  in the form of a directors' written resolution.

### Calling a directors' meeting

8.  (1) Any director may call a directors' meeting.
    (2) The company secretary must call a directors' meeting if a director so requests.
    (3) A directors' meeting is called by giving notice of the meeting to the directors.
    (4) Notice of any directors' meeting must indicate –
    (a)  its proposed date and time;
    (b)  where it is to take place; and

(c)  if it is anticipated that directors participating in the meeting will not be in the same place, how it is proposed that they should communicate with each other during the meeting.

(5)  Notice of a directors' meeting must be given to each director, but need not be in writing.

(6)  Notice of a directors' meeting need not be given to directors who waive their entitlement to notice of that meeting, by giving notice to that effect to the company not more than 7 days after the date on which the meeting is held. Where such notice is given after the meeting has been held, that does not affect the validity of the meeting, or of any business conducted at it.

## Participation in directors' meetings

**9.**  (1)  Subject to the articles, directors participate in a directors' meeting, or part of a directors' meeting, when –
   (a)  the meeting has been called and takes place in accordance with the articles, and
   (b)  they can each communicate to the others any information or opinions they have on any particular item of the business of the meeting.

   (2)  In determining whether directors are participating in a directors' meeting, it is irrelevant where any director is or how they communicate with each other.

   (3)  If all the directors participating in a meeting are not in the same place, they may decide that the meeting is to be treated as taking place wherever any of them is.

## Quorum for directors' meetings

**10.**  (1)  At a directors' meeting, unless a quorum is participating, no proposal is to be voted on, except a proposal to call another meeting.

   (2)  The quorum for directors' meetings may be fixed from time to time by a decision of the directors, but it must never be less than two, and unless otherwise fixed it is two.

## Meetings where total number of directors less than quorum

**11.**  (1)  This article applies where the total number of directors for the time being is less than the quorum for directors' meetings.

   (2)  If there is only one director, that director may appoint sufficient directors to make up a quorum or call a general meeting to do so.

   (3)  If there is more than one director –
   (a)  a directors' meeting may take place, if it is called in accordance with the articles and at least two directors participate in it, with a view to appointing sufficient directors to make up a quorum or calling a general meeting to do so, and
   (b)  if a directors' meeting is called but only one director attends at the appointed date and time to participate in it, that director may appoint sufficient directors to make up a quorum or call a general meeting to do so.

## Chairing directors' meetings

**12.**  (1)  The directors may appoint a director to chair their meetings.

   (2)  The person so appointed for the time being is known as the chairman.

   (3)  The directors may appoint other directors as deputy or assistant chairmen to chair directors' meetings in the chairman's absence.

   (4)  The directors may terminate the appointment of the chairman, deputy or assistant chairman at any time.

   (5)  If neither the chairman nor any director appointed generally to chair directors' meetings in the chairman's absence is participating in a meeting within ten minutes of the time at which it was to start, the participating directors must appoint one of themselves to chair it.

## Voting at directors' meetings: general rules

**13.**  (1)  Subject to the articles, a decision is taken at a directors' meeting by a majority of the votes of the participating directors.

   (2)  Subject to the articles, each director participating in a directors' meeting has one vote.

(3) Subject to the articles, if a director has an interest in an actual or proposed transaction or arrangement with the company –
   (a) that director and that director's alternate may not vote on any proposal relating to it, but
   (b) this does not preclude the alternate from voting in relation to that transaction or arrangement on behalf of another appointor who does not have such an interest.

## Chairman's casting vote at directors' meetings

**14.** (1) If the numbers of votes for and against a proposal are equal, the chairman or other director chairing the meeting has a casting vote.
   (2) But this does not apply if, in accordance with the articles, the chairman or other director is not to be counted as participating in the decision-making process for quorum or voting purposes.

## Alternates voting at directors' meetings

**15.** A director who is also an alternate director has an additional vote on behalf of each appointor who is –
   (a) not participating in a directors' meeting, and
   (b) would have been entitled to vote if they were participating in it.

## Conflicts of interest

**16.** (1) If a directors' meeting, or part of a directors' meeting, is concerned with an actual or proposed transaction or arrangement with the company in which a director is interested, that director is not to be counted as participating in that meeting, or part of a meeting, for quorum or voting purposes.
   (2) But if paragraph (3) applies, a director who is interested in an actual or proposed transaction or arrangement with the company is to be counted as participating in a decision at a directors' meeting, or part of a directors' meeting, relating to it for quorum and voting purposes.
   (3) This paragraph applies when –
      (a) the company by ordinary resolution disapplies the provision of the articles which would otherwise prevent a director from being counted as participating in, or voting at, a directors' meeting;
      (b) the director's interest cannot reasonably be regarded as likely to give rise to a conflict of interest; or
      (c) the director's conflict of interest arises from a permitted cause.
   (4) For the purposes of this article, the following are permitted causes –
      (a) a guarantee given, or to be given, by or to a director in respect of an obligation incurred by or on behalf of the company or any of its subsidiaries;
      (b) subscription, or an agreement to subscribe, for shares or other securities of the company or any of its subsidiaries, or to underwrite, sub-underwrite, or guarantee subscription for any such shares or securities; and
      (c) arrangements pursuant to which benefits are made available to employees and directors or former employees and directors of the company or any of its subsidiaries which do not provide special benefits for directors or former directors.
   (5) Subject to paragraph (6), if a question arises at a meeting of directors or of a committee of directors as to the right of a director to participate in the meeting (or part of the meeting) for voting or quorum purposes, the question may, before the conclusion of the meeting, be referred to the chairman whose ruling in relation to any director other than the chairman is to be final and conclusive.
   (6) If any question as to the right to participate in the meeting (or part of the meeting) should arise in respect of the chairman, the question is to be decided by a decision of the directors at that meeting, for which purpose the chairman is not to be counted as participating in the meeting (or that part of the meeting) for voting or quorum purposes.

## Proposing directors' written resolutions

**17.** (1) Any director may propose a directors' written resolution.

(2) The company secretary must propose a directors' written resolution if a director so requests.

(3) A directors' written resolution is proposed by giving notice of the proposed resolution to the directors.

(4) Notice of a proposed directors' written resolution must indicate –

(a) the proposed resolution, and

(b) the time by which it is proposed that the directors should adopt it.

(5) Notice of a proposed directors' written resolution must be given in writing to each director.

(6) Any decision which a person giving notice of a proposed directors' written resolution takes regarding the process of adopting that resolution must be taken reasonably in good faith.

## Adoption of directors' written resolutions

**18.** (1) A proposed directors' written resolution is adopted when all the directors who would have been entitled to vote on the resolution at a directors' meeting have signed one or more copies of it, provided that those directors would have formed a quorum at such a meeting.

(2) It is immaterial whether any director signs the resolution before or after the time by which the notice proposed that it should be adopted.

(3) Once a directors' written resolution has been adopted, it must be treated as if it had been a decision taken at a directors' meeting in accordance with the articles.

(4) The company secretary must ensure that the company keeps a record, in writing, of all directors' written resolutions for at least ten years from the date of their adoption.

## Directors' discretion to make further rules

**19.** Subject to the articles, the directors may make any rule which they think fit about how they take decisions, and about how such rules are to be recorded or communicated to directors.

# APPOINTMENT OF DIRECTORS

## Methods of appointing directors

**20.** Any person who is willing to act as a director, and is permitted by law to do so, may be appointed to be a director –

(a) by ordinary resolution, or

(b) by a decision of the directors.

## Retirement of directors by rotation

**21.** (1) At the first annual general meeting all the directors must retire from office.

(2) At every subsequent annual general meeting any directors –

(a) who have been appointed by the directors since the last annual general meeting, or

(b) who were not appointed or reappointed at one of the preceding two annual general meetings, must retire from office and may offer themselves for reappointment by the members.

## Termination of director's appointment

**22.** A person ceases to be a director as soon as –

(a) that person ceases to be a director by virtue of any provision of the Companies Act 2006 or is prohibited from being a director by law;

(b) a bankruptcy order is made against that person;

(c) a composition is made with that person's creditors generally in satisfaction of that person's debts;

(d) a registered medical practitioner who is treating that person gives a written opinion to the company stating that that person has become physically or mentally incapable of acting as a director and may remain so for more than three months;

(e) by reason of that person's mental health, a court makes an order which wholly or partly prevents that person from personally exercising any powers or rights which that person would otherwise have;

(f) notification is received by the company from the director that the director is resigning from office as director, and such resignation has taken effect in accordance with its terms.

## Directors' remuneration

**23.** (1) Directors may undertake any services for the company that the directors decide.

(2) Directors are entitled to such remuneration as the directors determine –
- (a) for their services to the company as directors, and
- (b) or any other service which they undertake for the company.

(3) Subject to the articles, a director's remuneration may –
- (a) take any form, and
- (b) include any arrangements in connection with the payment of a pension, allowance or gratuity, or any death, sickness or disability benefits, to or in respect of that director.

(4) Unless the directors decide otherwise, directors' remuneration accrues from day to day.

(5) Unless the directors decide otherwise, directors are not accountable to the company for any remuneration which they receive as directors or other officers or employees of the company's subsidiaries or of any other body corporate in which the company is interested.

## Directors' expenses

**24.** The company may pay any reasonable expenses which the directors properly incur in connection with their attendance at –
- (a) meetings of directors or committees of directors,
- (b) general meetings, or
- (c) separate meetings of the holders of any class of shares or of debentures of the company, or otherwise in connection with the exercise of their powers and the discharge of their responsibilities in relation to the company.

# ALTERNATE DIRECTORS

## Appointment and removal of alternates

**25.** (1) Any director (the 'appointor') may appoint as an alternate any other director, or any other person approved by resolution of the directors, to –
- (a) exercise that director's powers, and
- (b) carry out that director's responsibilities, in relation to the taking of decisions by the directors in the absence of the alternate's appointor.

(2) Any appointment or removal of an alternate must be effected by notice in writing to the company signed by the appointor, or in any other manner approved by the directors.

(3) The notice must –
- (a) identify the proposed alternate, and
- (b) in the case of a notice of appointment, contain a statement signed by the proposed alternate that the proposed alternate is willing to act as the alternate of the director giving the notice.

## Rights and responsibilities of alternate directors

**26.** (1) An alternate director has the same rights, in relation to any directors' meeting or directors' written resolution, as the alternate's appointor.

(2) Except as the articles specify otherwise, alternate directors –
- (a) are deemed for all purposes to be directors;

    (b)   are liable for their own acts and omissions;

    (c)   are subject to the same restrictions as their appointors; and

    (d)   are not deemed to be agents of or for their appointors.

(3)  A person who is an alternate director but not a director –

    (a)   may be counted as participating for the purposes of determining whether a quorum is participating (but only if that person's appointor is not participating), and

    (b)   may sign a written resolution (but only if it is not signed or to be signed by that person's appointor).

No alternate may be counted as more than one director for such purposes.

(4)  An alternate director is not entitled to receive any remuneration from the company for serving as an alternate director except such part of the alternate's appointor's remuneration as the appointor may direct by notice in writing made to the company.

## Termination of alternate directorship

**27.** An alternate director's appointment as an alternate terminates –

    (a)   when the alternate's appointor revokes the appointment by notice to the company in writing specifying when it is to terminate;

    (b)   on the occurrence in relation to the alternate of any event which, if it occurred in relation to the alternate's appointor, would result in the termination of the appointor's appointment as a director;

    (c)   on the death of the alternate's appointor; or

    (d)   when the alternate's appointor's appointment as a director terminates, except that an alternate's appointment as an alternate does not terminate when the appointor retires by rotation at a general meeting and is then re-appointed as a director at the same general meeting.

# PART 3 DECISION-MAKING BY MEMBERS

## ORGANISATION OF GENERAL MEETINGS

### Members can call general meeting if not enough directors

**28.** If –

    (a)   the company has fewer than two directors, and

    (b)   the director (if any) is unable or unwilling to appoint sufficient directors to make up a quorum or to call a general meeting to do so, then two or more members may call a general meeting (or instruct the company secretary to do so) for the purpose of appointing one or more directors.

### Attendance and speaking at general meetings

**29.** (1)  A person is able to exercise the right to speak at a general meeting when that person is in a position to communicate to all those attending the meeting, during the meeting, any information or opinions which that person has on the business of the meeting.

(2)  A person is able to exercise the right to vote at a general meeting when –

    (a)   that person is able to vote, during the meeting, on resolutions put to the vote at the meeting, and

    (b)   that person's vote can be taken into account in determining whether or not such resolutions are passed at the same time as the votes of all the other persons attending the meeting.

(3)  The directors may make whatever arrangements they consider appropriate to enable those attending a general meeting to exercise their rights to speak or vote at it.

(4)  In determining attendance at a general meeting, it is immaterial whether any two or more members attending it are in the same place as each other.

(5)  Two or more persons who are not in the same place as each other attend a general meeting if their circumstances are such that if they have (or were to have) rights to speak and vote at that meeting, they are (or would be) able to exercise them.

## Quorum for general meetings

**30.** No business other than the appointment of the chairman of the meeting is to be transacted at a general meeting if the persons attending it do not constitute a quorum.

## Chairing general meetings

**31.** (1) If the directors have appointed a chairman, the chairman shall chair general meetings if present and willing to do so.

(2) If the directors have not appointed a chairman, or if the chairman is unwilling to chair the meeting or is not present within ten minutes of the time at which a meeting was due to start –

(a) the directors present, or

(b) (if no directors are present), the meeting, must appoint a director or member to chair the meeting, and the appointment of the chairman of the meeting must be the first business of the meeting.

(3) The person chairing a meeting in accordance with this article is referred to as 'the chairman of the meeting'.

## Attendance and speaking by directors and non-members

**32.** (1) Directors may attend and speak at general meetings, whether or not they are members.

(2) The chairman of the meeting may permit other persons who are not –

(a) members of the company, or

(b) otherwise entitled to exercise the rights of members in relation to general meetings, to attend and speak at a general meeting.

## Adjournment

**33.** (1) If the persons attending a general meeting within half an hour of the time at which the meeting was due to start do not constitute a quorum, or if during a meeting a quorum ceases to be present, the chairman of the meeting must adjourn it.

(2) The chairman of the meeting may adjourn a general meeting at which a quorum is present if –

(a) the meeting consents to an adjournment, or

(b) it appears to the chairman of the meeting that an adjournment is necessary to protect the safety of any person attending the meeting or ensure that the business of the meeting is conducted in an orderly manner.

(3) The chairman of the meeting must adjourn a general meeting if directed to do so by the meeting.

(4) When adjourning a general meeting, the chairman of the meeting must –

(a) either specify the time and place to which it is adjourned or state that it is to continue at a time and place to be fixed by the directors, and

(b) have regard to any directions as to the time and place of any adjournment which have been given by the meeting.

(5) If the continuation of an adjourned meeting is to take place more than 14 days after it was adjourned, the company must give at least 7 clear days' notice of it (that is, excluding the day of the adjourned meeting and the day on which the notice is given) –

(a) to the same persons to whom notice of the company's general meetings is required to be given, and

(b) containing the same information which such notice is required to contain.

(6) No business may be transacted at an adjourned general meeting which could not properly have been transacted at the meeting if the adjournment had not taken place.

## VOTING AT GENERAL MEETINGS

## Voting: general

**34.** A resolution put to the vote of a general meeting must be decided on a show of hands unless a poll is duly demanded in accordance with the articles.

## Errors and disputes

**35.** (1) No objection may be raised to the qualification of any person voting at a general meeting except at the meeting or adjourned meeting at which the vote objected to is tendered, and every vote not disallowed at the meeting is valid.

(2) Any such objection must be referred to the chairman of the meeting whose decision is final.

## Demanding a poll

**36.** (1) A poll on a resolution may be demanded –

(a) in advance of the general meeting where it is to be put to the vote, or

(b) at a general meeting, either before a show of hands on that resolution or immediately after the result of a show of hands on that resolution is declared.

(2) A poll may be demanded by –

(a) the chairman of the meeting;

(b) the directors;

(c) two or more persons having the right to vote on the resolution; or

(d) a person or persons representing not less than one tenth of the total voting rights of all the members having the right to vote on the resolution.

(3) A demand for a poll may be withdrawn if –

(a) the poll has not yet been taken, and

(b) the chairman of the meeting consents to the withdrawal.

## Procedure on a poll

**37.** (1) Subject to the articles, polls at general meetings must be taken when, where and in such manner as the chairman of the meeting directs.

(2) The chairman of the meeting may appoint scrutineers (who need not be members) and decide how and when the result of the poll is to be declared.

(3) The result of a poll shall be the decision of the meeting in respect of the resolution on which the poll was demanded.

(4) A poll on –

(a) the election of the chairman of the meeting, or

(b) a question of adjournment, must be taken immediately.

(5) Other polls must be taken within 30 days of their being demanded.

(6) A demand for a poll does not prevent a general meeting from continuing, except as regards the question on which the poll was demanded.

(7) No notice need be given of a poll not taken immediately if the time and place at which it is to be taken are announced at the meeting at which it is demanded.

(8) In any other case, at least 7 days' notice must be given specifying the time and place at which the poll is to be taken.

## Content of proxy notices

**38.** (1) Proxies may only validly be appointed by a notice in writing (a 'proxy notice') which –

(a) states the name and address of the member appointing the proxy;

(b) identifies the person appointed to be that member's proxy and the general meeting in relation to which that person is appointed;

(c) is signed by or on behalf of the member appointing the proxy, or is authenticated in such manner as the directors may determine; and

(d) is delivered to the company in accordance with the articles and any instructions contained in the notice of the general meeting to which they relate.

(2) The company may require proxy notices to be delivered in a particular form, and may specify different forms for different purposes.

(3) Proxy notices may specify how the proxy appointed under them is to vote (or that the proxy is to abstain from voting) on one or more resolutions.

(4) Unless a proxy notice indicates otherwise, it must be treated as –

(a) allowing the person appointed under it as a proxy discretion as to how to vote on any ancillary or procedural resolutions put to the meeting, and

(b) appointing that person as a proxy in relation to any adjournment of the general meeting to which it relates as well as the meeting itself.

## Delivery of proxy notices

39. (1) Any notice of a general meeting must specify the address or addresses ('proxy notification address') at which the company or its agents will receive proxy notices relating to that meeting, or any adjournment of it, delivered in hard copy or electronic form.

    (2) A person who is entitled to attend, speak or vote (either on a show of hands or on a poll) at a general meeting remains so entitled in respect of that meeting or any adjournment of it, even though a valid proxy notice has been delivered to the company by or on behalf of that person.

    (3) Subject to paragraphs (4) and (5), a proxy notice must be delivered to a proxy notification address not less than 48 hours before the general meeting or adjourned meeting to which it relates.

    (4) In the case of a poll taken more than 48 hours after it is demanded, the notice must be delivered to a proxy notification address not less than 24 hours before the time appointed for the taking of the poll.

    (5) In the case of a poll not taken during the meeting but taken not more than 48 hours after it was demanded, the proxy notice must be delivered –

    (a) in accordance with paragraph (3), or

    (b) at the meeting at which the poll was demanded to the chairman, secretary or any director.

    (6) An appointment under a proxy notice may be revoked by delivering a notice in writing given by or on behalf of the person by whom or on whose behalf the proxy notice was given to a proxy notification address.

    (7) A notice revoking a proxy appointment only takes effect if it is delivered before –

    (a) the start of the meeting or adjourned meeting to which it relates, or

    (b) (in the case of a poll not taken on the same day as the meeting or adjourned meeting) the time appointed for taking the poll to which it relates.

    (8) If a proxy notice is not signed by the person appointing the proxy, it must be accompanied by written evidence of the authority of the person who executed it to execute it on the appointor's behalf.

## Amendments to resolutions

40. (1) An ordinary resolution to be proposed at a general meeting may be amended by ordinary resolution if –

    (a) notice of the proposed amendment is given to the company secretary in writing by a person entitled to vote at the general meeting at which it is to be proposed not less than 48 hours before the meeting is to take place (or such later time as the chairman of the meeting may determine), and

    (b) the proposed amendment does not, in the reasonable opinion of the chairman of the meeting, materially alter the scope of the resolution.

    (2) A special resolution to be proposed at a general meeting may be amended by ordinary resolution, if –

    (a) the chairman of the meeting proposes the amendment at the general meeting at which the resolution is to be proposed, and

    (b) the amendment does not go beyond what is necessary to correct a grammatical or other non-substantive error in the resolution.

    (3) If the chairman of the meeting, acting in good faith, wrongly decides that an amendment to a resolution is out of order, the chairman's error does not invalidate the vote on that resolution.

# RESTRICTIONS ON MEMBERS' RIGHTS

## No voting of shares on which money owed to company

41. No voting rights attached to a share may be exercised at any general meeting, at any adjournment of it, or on any poll called at or in relation to it, unless all amounts payable to the company in respect of that share have been paid.

## APPLICATION OF RULES TO CLASS MEETINGS

### Class meetings

**42.** The provisions of the articles relating to general meetings apply, with any necessary modifications, to meetings of the holders of any class of shares.

# PART 4 SHARES AND DISTRIBUTIONS

## ISSUE OF SHARES

### Powers to issue different classes of share

**43.** (1) Subject to the articles, but without prejudice to the rights attached to any existing share, the company may issue shares with such rights or restrictions as may be determined by ordinary resolution.

(2) The company may issue shares which are to be redeemed, or are liable to be redeemed at the option of the company or the holder, and the directors may determine the terms, conditions and manner of redemption of any such shares.

### Payment of commissions on subscription for shares

**44.** (1) The company may pay any person a commission in consideration for that person –

(a) subscribing, or agreeing to subscribe, for shares, or

(b) procuring, or agreeing to procure, subscriptions for shares.

(2) Any such commission may be paid –

(a) in cash, or in fully paid or partly paid shares or other securities, or partly in one way and partly in the other, and

(b) in respect of a conditional or an absolute subscription.

## INTERESTS IN SHARES

### Company not bound by less than absolute interests

**45.** Except as required by law, no person is to be recognised by the company as holding any share upon any trust, and except as otherwise required by law or the articles, the company is not in any way to be bound by or recognise any interest in a share other than the holder's absolute ownership of it and all the rights attaching to it.

## SHARE CERTIFICATES

### Certificates to be issued except in certain cases

**46.** (1) The company must issue each member with one or more certificates in respect of the shares which that member holds.

(2) This article does not apply to –

(a) uncertificated shares;

(b) shares in respect of which a share warrant has been issued; or

(c) shares in respect of which the Companies Acts permit the company not to issue a certificate.

(3) Except as otherwise specified in the articles, all certificates must be issued free of charge.

(4) No certificate may be issued in respect of shares of more than one class.

(5) If more than one person holds a share, only one certificate may be issued in respect of it.

### Contents and execution of share certificates

**47.** (1) Every certificate must specify –
    (a)   in respect of how many shares, of what class, it is issued;
    (b)   the nominal value of those shares;
    (c)   the amount paid up on them; and
    (d)   any distinguishing numbers assigned to them.
  (2) Certificates must –
    (a)   have affixed to them the company's common seal or an official seal which is a facsimile of the company's common seal with the addition on its face of the word 'Securities' (a 'securities seal'), or
    (b)   be otherwise executed in accordance with the Companies Acts.

### Consolidated share certificates

**48.** (1) When a member's holding of shares of a particular class increases, the company may issue that member with –
    (a)   a single, consolidated certificate in respect of all the shares of a particular class which that member holds, or
    (b)   a separate certificate in respect of only those shares by which that member's holding has increased.
  (2) When a member's holding of shares of a particular class is reduced, the company must ensure that the member is issued with one or more certificates in respect of the number of shares held by the member after that reduction. But the company need not (in the absence of a request from the member) issue any new certificate if –
    (a)   all the shares which the member no longer holds as a result of the reduction, and
    (b)   none of the shares which the member retains following the reduction, were, immediately before the reduction, represented by the same certificate.
  (3) A member may request the company, in writing, to replace –
    (a)   the member's separate certificates with a consolidated certificate, or
    (b)   the member's consolidated certificate with two or more separate certificates representing such proportion of the shares as the member may specify.
  (4) When the company complies with such a request it may charge such reasonable fee as the directors may decide for doing so.
  (5) A consolidated certificate must not be issued unless any certificates which it is to replace have first been returned to the company for cancellation.

### Replacement share certificates

**49.** (1) If a certificate issued in respect of a member's shares is –
    (a)   damaged or defaced, or
    (b)   said to be lost, stolen or destroyed, that member is entitled to be issued with a replacement certificate in respect of the same shares.
  (2) A member exercising the right to be issued with such a replacement certificate –
    (a)   may at the same time exercise the right to be issued with a single certificate or separate certificates;
    (b)   must return the certificate which is to be replaced to the company if it is damaged or defaced; and
    (c)   must comply with such conditions as to evidence, indemnity and the payment of a reasonable fee as the directors decide.

## SHARES NOT HELD IN CERTIFICATED FORM

### Uncertificated shares

**50.** (1) In this article, 'the relevant rules' means –
    (a)   any applicable provision of the Companies Acts about the holding, evidencing of title to, or transfer of shares other than in certificated form, and
    (b)   any applicable legislation, rules or other arrangements made under or by virtue of such provision.

(2) The provisions of this article have effect subject to the relevant rules.

(3) Any provision of the articles which is inconsistent with the relevant rules must be disregarded, to the extent that it is inconsistent, whenever the relevant rules apply.

(4) Any share or class of shares of the company may be issued or held on such terms, or in such a way, that –

    (a) title to it or them is not, or must not be, evidenced by a certificate, or

    (b) it or they may or must be transferred wholly or partly without a certificate.

(5) The directors have power to take such steps as they think fit in relation to –

    (a) the evidencing of and transfer of title to uncertificated shares (including in connection with the issue of such shares);

    (b) any records relating to the holding of uncertificated shares;

    (c) the conversion of certificated shares into uncertificated shares; or

    (d) the conversion of uncertificated shares into certificated shares.

(6) The company may by notice to the holder of a share require that share –

    (a) if it is uncertificated, to be converted into certificated form, and

    (b) if it is certificated, to be converted into uncertificated form, to enable it to be dealt with in accordance with the articles.

(7) If –

    (a) the articles give the directors power to take action, or require other persons to take action, in order to sell, transfer or otherwise dispose of shares, and

    (b) uncertificated shares are subject to that power, but the power is expressed in terms which assume the use of a certificate or other written instrument, the directors may take such action as is necessary or expedient to achieve the same results when exercising that power in relation to uncertificated shares.

(8) In particular, the directors may take such action as they consider appropriate to achieve the sale, transfer, disposal, forfeiture, re-allotment or surrender of an uncertificated share or otherwise to enforce a lien in respect of it.

(9) Unless the directors otherwise determine, shares which a member holds in uncertificated form must be treated as separate holdings from any shares which that member holds in certificated form.

(10)A class of shares must not be treated as two classes simply because some shares of that class are held in certificated form and others are held in uncertificated form.

## Share warrants

**51.** (1) The directors may issue a share warrant in respect of any fully paid share.

    (2) Share warrants must be –

        (a) issued in such form, and

        (b) executed in such manner, as the directors decide.

    (3) A share represented by a share warrant may be transferred by delivery of the warrant representing it.

    (4) The directors may make provision for the payment of dividends in respect of any share represented by a share warrant.

    (5) Subject to the articles, the directors may decide the conditions on which any share warrant is issued. In particular, they may –

        (a) decide the conditions on which new warrants are to be issued in place of warrants which are damaged or defaced, or said to have been lost, stolen or destroyed;

        (b) decide the conditions on which bearers of warrants are entitled to attend and vote at general meetings;

        (c) decide the conditions subject to which bearers of warrants may surrender their warrant so as to hold their shares in certificated or uncertificated form instead; and

        (d) vary the conditions of issue of any warrant from time to time, and the bearer of a warrant is subject to the conditions and procedures in force in relation to it, whether or not they were decided or specified before the warrant was issued.

    (6) Subject to the conditions on which the warrants are issued from time to time, bearers of share warrants have the same rights and privileges as they would if their names had been included in the register as holders of the shares represented by their warrants.

(7) The company must not in any way be bound by or recognise any interest in a share represented by a share warrant other than the absolute right of the bearer of that warrant to that warrant.

# PARTLY PAID SHARES

## Company's lien over partly paid shares

**52.** (1) The company has a lien ('the company's lien') over every share which is partly paid for any part of –

  (a) that share's nominal value, and

  (b) any premium at which it was issued, which has not been paid to the company, and which is payable immediately or at some time in the future, whether or not a call notice has been sent in respect of it.

(2) The company's lien over a share –

  (a) takes priority over any third party's interest in that share, and

  (b) extends to any dividend or other money payable by the company in respect of that share and (if the lien is enforced and the share is sold by the company) the proceeds of sale of that share.

(3) The directors may at any time decide that a share which is or would otherwise be subject to the company's lien shall not be subject to it, either wholly or in part.

## Enforcement of the company's lien

**53.** (1) Subject to the provisions of this article, if –

  (a) a lien enforcement notice has been given in respect of a share, and

  (b) the person to whom the notice was given has failed to comply with it, the company may sell that share in such manner as the directors decide.

(2) A lien enforcement notice –

  (a) may only be given in respect of a share which is subject to the company's lien, in respect of which a sum is payable and the due date for payment of that sum has passed;

  (b) must specify the share concerned;

  (c) must require payment of the sum payable within 14 days of the notice;

  (d) must be addressed either to the holder of the share or to a person entitled to it by reason of the holder's death, bankruptcy or otherwise; and

  (e) must state the company's intention to sell the share if the notice is not complied with.

(3) Where shares are sold under this article –

  (a) the directors may authorise any person to execute an instrument of transfer of the shares to the purchaser or a person nominated by the purchaser, and

  (b) the transferee is not bound to see to the application of the consideration, and the transferee's title is not affected by any irregularity in or invalidity of the process leading to the sale.

(4) The net proceeds of any such sale (after payment of the costs of sale and any other costs of enforcing the lien) must be applied –

  (a) first, in payment of so much of the sum for which the lien exists as was payable at the date of the lien enforcement notice,

  (b) second, to the person entitled to the shares at the date of the sale, but only after the certificate for the shares sold has been surrendered to the company for cancellation or a suitable indemnity has been given for any lost certificates, and subject to a lien equivalent to the company's lien over the shares before the sale for any money payable in respect of the shares after the date of the lien enforcement notice.

(5) A statutory declaration by a director or the company secretary that the declarant is a director or the company secretary and that a share has been sold to satisfy the company's lien on a specified date –

(a)   is conclusive evidence of the facts stated in it as against all persons claiming to be entitled to the share, and

(b)   subject to compliance with any other formalities of transfer required by the articles or by law, constitutes a good title to the share.

## Call notices

**54.** (1)   Subject to the articles and the terms on which shares are allotted, the directors may send a notice (a 'call notice') to a member requiring the member to pay the company a specified sum of money (a 'call') which is payable in respect of shares which that member holds at the date when the directors decide to send the call notice.

(2)   A call notice –

(a)   may not require a member to pay a call which exceeds the total sum unpaid on that member's shares (whether as to the share's nominal value or any amount payable to the company by way of premium);

(b)   must state when and how any call to which it relates it is to be paid; and

(c)   may permit or require the call to be paid by instalments.

(3)   A member must comply with the requirements of a call notice, but no member is obliged to pay any call before 14 days have passed since the notice was sent.

(4)   Before the company has received any call due under a call notice the directors may –

(a)   revoke it wholly or in part, or

(b)   specify a later time for payment than is specified in the notice, by a further notice in writing to the member in respect of whose shares the call is made.

## Liability to pay calls

**55.** (1)   Liability to pay a call is not extinguished or transferred by transferring the shares in respect of which it is required to be paid.

(2)   Joint holders of a share are jointly and severally liable to pay all calls in respect of that share.

(3)   Subject to the terms on which shares are allotted, the directors may, when issuing shares, provide that call notices sent to the holders of those shares may require them –

(a)   to pay calls which are not the same, or

(b)   to pay calls at different times.

## When call notice need not be issued

**56.** (1)   A call notice need not be issued in respect of sums which are specified, in the terms on which a share is issued, as being payable to the company in respect of that share (whether in respect of nominal value or premium) –

(a)   on allotment;

(b)   on the occurrence of a particular event; or

(c)   on a date fixed by or in accordance with the terms of issue.

(2)   But if the due date for payment of such a sum has passed and it has not been paid, the holder of the share concerned is treated in all respects as having failed to comply with a call notice in respect of that sum, and is liable to the same consequences as regards the payment of interest and forfeiture.

## Failure to comply with call notice: automatic consequences

**57.** (1)   If a person is liable to pay a call and fails to do so by the call payment date –

(a)   the directors may issue a notice of intended forfeiture to that person, and

(b)   until the call is paid, that person must pay the company interest on the call from the call payment date at the relevant rate.

(2)   For the purposes of this article –

(a)   the 'call payment date' is the time when the call notice states that a call is payable, unless the directors give a notice specifying a later date, in which case the 'call payment date' is that later date;

(b)   the 'relevant rate' is –

(i)   the rate fixed by the terms on which the share in respect of which the call is due was allotted;

(ii) such other rate as was fixed in the call notice which required payment of the call, or has otherwise been determined by the directors; or

(iii) if no rate is fixed in either of these ways, 5% per annum.

(3) The relevant rate must not exceed by more than 5 percentage points the base lending rate most recently set by the Monetary Policy Committee of the Bank of England in connection with its responsibilities under Part 2 of the Bank of England Act 1998(2).

(4) The directors may waive any obligation to pay interest on a call wholly or in part.

## Notice of intended forfeiture

**58.** A notice of intended forfeiture –

(a) may be sent in respect of any share in respect of which a call has not been paid as required by a call notice;

(b) must be sent to the holder of that share or to a person entitled to it by reason of the holder's death, bankruptcy or otherwise;

(c) must require payment of the call and any accrued interest by a date which is not less than 14 days after the date of the notice;

(d) must state how the payment is to be made; and

(e) must state that if the notice is not complied with, the shares in respect of which the call is payable will be liable to be forfeited.

## Directors' power to forfeit shares

**59.** If a notice of intended forfeiture is not complied with before the date by which payment of the call is required in the notice of intended forfeiture, the directors may decide that any share in respect of which it was given is forfeited, and the forfeiture is to include all dividends or other moneys payable in respect of the forfeited shares and not paid before the forfeiture.

## Effect of forfeiture

**60.** (1) Subject to the articles, the forfeiture of a share extinguishes –

(a) all interests in that share, and all claims and demands against the company in respect of it, and

(b) all other rights and liabilities incidental to the share as between the person whose share it was prior to the forfeiture and the company.

(2) Any share which is forfeited in accordance with the articles –

(a) is deemed to have been forfeited when the directors decide that it is forfeited;

(b) is deemed to be the property of the company; and

(c) may be sold, re-allotted or otherwise disposed of as the directors think fit.

(3) If a person's shares have been forfeited –

(a) the company must send that person notice that forfeiture has occurred and record it in the register of members;

(b) that person ceases to be a member in respect of those shares;

(c) that person must surrender the certificate for the shares forfeited to the company for cancellation;

(d) that person remains liable to the company for all sums payable by that person under the articles at the date of forfeiture in respect of those shares, including any interest (whether accrued before or after the date of forfeiture); and

(e) the directors may waive payment of such sums wholly or in part or enforce payment without any allowance for the value of the shares at the time of forfeiture or for any consideration received on their disposal.

(4) At any time before the company disposes of a forfeited share, the directors may decide to cancel the forfeiture on payment of all calls and interest due in respect of it and on such other terms as they think fit.

## Procedure following forfeiture

**61.** (1) If a forfeited share is to be disposed of by being transferred, the company may receive the consideration for the transfer and the directors may authorise any person to execute the instrument of transfer.

(2) A statutory declaration by a director or the company secretary that the declarant is a director or the company secretary and that a share has been forfeited on a specified date –
  (a) is conclusive evidence of the facts stated in it as against all persons claiming to be entitled to the share, and
  (b) subject to compliance with any other formalities of transfer required by the articles or by law, constitutes a good title to the share.
(3) A person to whom a forfeited share is transferred is not bound to see to the application of the consideration (if any) nor is that person's title to the share affected by any irregularity in or invalidity of the process leading to the forfeiture or transfer of the share.
(4) If the company sells a forfeited share, the person who held it prior to its forfeiture is entitled to receive from the company the proceeds of such sale, net of any commission, and excluding any amount which –
  (a) was, or would have become, payable, and
  (b) had not, when that share was forfeited, been paid by that person in respect of that share, but no interest is payable to such a person in respect of such proceeds and the company is not required to account for any money earned on them.

## Surrender of shares

**62.** (1) A member may surrender any share –
  (a) in respect of which the directors may issue a notice of intended forfeiture;
  (b) which the directors may forfeit; or
  (c) which has been forfeited.
(2) The directors may accept the surrender of any such share.
(3) The effect of surrender on a share is the same as the effect of forfeiture on that share.
(4) A share which has been surrendered may be dealt with in the same way as a share which has been forfeited.

# TRANSFER AND TRANSMISSION OF SHARES

## Transfers of certificated shares

**63.** (1) Certificated shares may be transferred by means of an instrument of transfer in any usual form or any other form approved by the directors, which is executed by or on behalf of –
  (a) the transferor, and
  (b) (if any of the shares is partly paid) the transferee.
(2) No fee may be charged for registering any instrument of transfer or other document relating to or affecting the title to any share.
(3) The company may retain any instrument of transfer which is registered.
(4) The transferor remains the holder of a certificated share until the transferee's name is entered in the register of members as holder of it.
(5) The directors may refuse to register the transfer of a certificated share if –
  (a) the share is not fully paid;
  (b) the transfer is not lodged at the company's registered office or such other place as the directors have appointed;
  (c) the transfer is not accompanied by the certificate for the shares to which it relates, or such other evidence as the directors may reasonably require to show the transferor's right to make the transfer, or evidence of the right of someone other than the transferor to make the transfer on the transferor's behalf;
  (d) the transfer is in respect of more than one class of share; or
  (e) the transfer is in favour of more than four transferees.
(6) If the directors refuse to register the transfer of a share, the instrument of transfer must be returned to the transferee with the notice of refusal unless they suspect that the proposed transfer may be fraudulent.

## Transfer of uncertificated shares

**64.** A transfer of an uncertificated share must not be registered if it is in favour of more than four transferees.

## Transmission of shares

**65.** (1) If title to a share passes to a transmittee, the company may only recognise the transmittee as having any title to that share.

(2) Nothing in these articles releases the estate of a deceased member from any liability in respect of a share solely or jointly held by that member.

## Transmittees' rights

**66.** (1) A transmittee who produces such evidence of entitlement to shares as the directors may properly require –

(a) may, subject to the articles, choose either to become the holder of those shares or to have them transferred to another person, and

(b) subject to the articles, and pending any transfer of the shares to another person, has the same rights as the holder had.

(2) But transmittees do not have the right to attend or vote at a general meeting in respect of shares to which they are entitled, by reason of the holder's death or bankruptcy or otherwise, unless they become the holders of those shares

## Exercise of transmittees' rights

**67.** (1) Transmittees who wish to become the holders of shares to which they have become entitled must notify the company in writing of that wish.

(2) If the share is a certificated share and a transmittee wishes to have it transferred to another person, the transmittee must execute an instrument of transfer in respect of it.

(3) If the share is an uncertificated share and the transmittee wishes to have it transferred to another person, the transmittee must –

(a) procure that all appropriate instructions are given to effect the transfer, or

(b) procure that the uncertificated share is changed into certificated form and then execute an instrument of transfer in respect of it.

(4) Any transfer made or executed under this article is to be treated as if it were made or executed by the person from whom the transmittee has derived rights in respect of the share, and as if the event which gave rise to the transmission had not occurred.

## Transmittees bound by prior notices

**68.** If a notice is given to a member in respect of shares and a transmittee is entitled to those shares, the transmittee is bound by the notice if it was given to the member before the transmittee's name has been entered in the register of members.

# CONSOLIDATION OF SHARES

## Procedure for disposing of fractions of shares

**69.** (1) This article applies where –

(a) there has been a consolidation or division of shares, and

(b) as a result, members are entitled to fractions of shares.

(2) The directors may –

(a) sell the shares representing the fractions to any person including the company for the best price reasonably obtainable;

(b) in the case of a certificated share, authorise any person to execute an instrument of transfer of the shares to the purchaser or a person nominated by the purchaser; and

(c) distribute the net proceeds of sale in due proportion among the holders of the shares.

(3) Where any holder's entitlement to a portion of the proceeds of sale amounts to less than a minimum figure determined by the directors, that member's portion may be

distributed to an organisation which is a charity for the purposes of the law of England and Wales, Scotland or Northern Ireland.

(4) The person to whom the shares are transferred is not obliged to ensure that any purchase money is received by the person entitled to the relevant fractions.

(5) The transferee's title to the shares is not affected by any irregularity in or invalidity of the process leading to their sale.

# DISTRIBUTIONS

## Procedure for declaring dividends

**70.** (1) The company may by ordinary resolution declare dividends, and the directors may decide to pay interim dividends.

(2) A dividend must not be declared unless the directors have made a recommendation as to its amount. Such a dividend must not exceed the amount recommended by the directors.

(3) No dividend may be declared or paid unless it is in accordance with members' respective rights.

(4) Unless the members' resolution to declare or directors' decision to pay a dividend, or the terms on which shares are issued, specify otherwise, it must be paid by reference to each member's holding of shares on the date of the resolution or decision to declare or pay it.

(5) If the company's share capital is divided into different classes, no interim dividend may be paid on shares carrying deferred or non-preferred rights if, at the time of payment, any preferential dividend is in arrear.

(6) The directors may pay at intervals any dividend payable at a fixed rate if it appears to them that the profits available for distribution justify the payment.

(7) If the directors act in good faith, they do not incur any liability to the holders of shares conferring preferred rights for any loss they may suffer by the lawful payment of an interim dividend on shares with deferred or non-preferred rights.

## Calculation of dividends

**71.** (1) Except as otherwise provided by the articles or the rights attached to shares, all dividends must be –

(a) declared and paid according to the amounts paid up on the shares on which the dividend is paid, and

(b) apportioned and paid proportionately to the amounts paid up on the shares during any portion or portions of the period in respect of which the dividend is paid.

(2) If any share is issued on terms providing that it ranks for dividend as from a particular date, that share ranks for dividend accordingly.

(3) For the purposes of calculating dividends, no account is to be taken of any amount which has been paid up on a share in advance of the due date for payment of that amount.

## Payment of dividends and other distributions

**72.** (1) Where a dividend or other sum which is a distribution is payable in respect of a share, it must be paid by one or more of the following means–

(a) transfer to a bank or building society account specified by the distribution recipient either in writing or as the directors may otherwise decide;

(b) sending a cheque made payable to the distribution recipient by post to the distribution recipient at the distribution recipient's registered address (if the distribution recipient is a holder of the share), or (in any other case) to an address specified by the distribution recipient either in writing or as the directors may otherwise decide;

(c) sending a cheque made payable to such person by post to such person at such address as the distribution recipient has specified either in writing or as the directors may otherwise decide; or

(d)    any other means of payment as the directors agree with the distribution recipient either in writing or by such other means as the directors decide.

(2)  In the articles, 'the distribution recipient' means, in respect of a share in respect of which a dividend or other sum is payable –

(a)    the holder of the share; or

(b)    if the share has two or more joint holders, whichever of them is named first in the register of members; or

(c)    if the holder is no longer entitled to the share by reason of death or bankruptcy, or otherwise by operation of law, the transmittee.

## Deductions from distributions in respect of sums owed to the company

**73.** (1)  If –

(a)    a share is subject to the company's lien, and

(b)    the directors are entitled to issue a lien enforcement notice in respect of it, they may, instead of issuing a lien enforcement notice, deduct from any dividend or other sum payable in respect of the share any sum of money which is payable to the company in respect of that share to the extent that they are entitled to require payment under a lien enforcement notice.

(2)  Money so deducted must be used to pay any of the sums payable in respect of that share.

(3)  The company must notify the distribution recipient in writing of –

(a)    the fact and amount of any such deduction;

(b)    any non-payment of a dividend or other sum payable in respect of a share resulting from any such deduction; and

(c)    how the money deducted has been applied.

## No interest on distributions

**74.** The company may not pay interest on any dividend or other sum payable in respect of a share unless otherwise provided by –

(a)    the terms on which the share was issued, or

(b)    the provisions of another agreement between the holder of that share and the company.

## Unclaimed distributions

**75.** (1)  All dividends or other sums which are –

(a)    payable in respect of shares, and

(b)    unclaimed after having been declared or become payable, may be invested or otherwise made use of by the directors for the benefit of the company until claimed.

(2)  The payment of any such dividend or other sum into a separate account does not make the company a trustee in respect of it.

(3)  If –

(a)    twelve years have passed from the date on which a dividend or other sum became due for payment, and

(b)    the distribution recipient has not claimed it, the distribution recipient is no longer entitled to that dividend or other sum and it ceases to remain owing by the company.

## Non-cash distributions

**76.** (1)  Subject to the terms of issue of the share in question, the company may, by ordinary resolution on the recommendation of the directors, decide to pay all or part of a dividend or other distribution payable in respect of a share by transferring non-cash assets of equivalent value (including, without limitation, shares or other securities in any company).

(2)  If the shares in respect of which such a non-cash distribution is paid are uncertificated, any shares in the company which are issued as a non-cash distribution in respect of them must be uncertificated.

(3) For the purposes of paying a non-cash distribution, the directors may make whatever arrangements they think fit, including, where any difficulty arises regarding the distribution –

    (a) fixing the value of any assets;

    (b) paying cash to any distribution recipient on the basis of that value in order to adjust the rights of recipients; and

    (c) vesting any assets in trustees.

## Waiver of distributions

77. Distribution recipients may waive their entitlement to a dividend or other distribution payable in respect of a share by giving the company notice in writing to that effect, but if –

    (a) the share has more than one holder, or

    (b) more than one person is entitled to the share, whether by reason of the death or bankruptcy of one or more joint holders, or otherwise, the notice is not effective unless it is expressed to be given, and signed, by all the holders or persons otherwise entitled to the share.

# CAPITALISATION OF PROFITS

## Authority to capitalise and appropriation of capitalised sums

78. (1) Subject to the articles, the directors may, if they are so authorised by an ordinary resolution –

    (a) decide to capitalise any profits of the company (whether or not they are available for distribution) which are not required for paying a preferential dividend, or any sum standing to the credit of the company's share premium account or capital redemption reserve; and

    (b) appropriate any sum which they so decide to capitalise (a 'capitalised sum') to the persons who would have been entitled to it if it were distributed by way of dividend (the 'persons entitled') and in the same proportions.

(2) Capitalised sums must be applied –

    (a) on behalf of the persons entitled, and

    (b) in the same proportions as a dividend would have been distributed to them.

(3) Any capitalised sum may be applied in paying up new shares of a nominal amount equal to the capitalised sum which are then allotted credited as fully paid to the persons entitled or as they may direct.

(4) A capitalised sum which was appropriated from profits available for distribution may be applied –

    (a) in or towards paying up any amounts unpaid on existing shares held by the persons entitled, or

    (b) in paying up new debentures of the company which are then allotted credited as fully paid to the persons entitled or as they may direct.

(5) Subject to the articles the directors may –

    (a) apply capitalised sums in accordance with paragraphs (3) and (4) partly in one way and partly in another;

    (b) make such arrangements as they think fit to deal with shares or debentures becoming distributable in fractions under this article (including the issuing of fractional certificates or the making of cash payments); and

    (c) authorise any person to enter into an agreement with the company on behalf of all the persons entitled which is binding on them in respect of the allotment of shares and debentures to them under this article.

# PART 5 MISCELLANEOUS PROVISIONS

## COMMUNICATIONS

### Means of communication to be used

**79.** (1) Subject to the articles, anything sent or supplied by or to the company under the articles may be sent or supplied in any way in which the Companies Act 2006 provides for documents or information which are authorised or required by any provision of that Act to be sent or supplied by or to the company.

(2) Subject to the articles, any notice or document to be sent or supplied to a director in connection with the taking of decisions by directors may also be sent or supplied by the means by which that director has asked to be sent or supplied with such notices or documents for the time being.

(3) A director may agree with the company that notices or documents sent to that director in a particular way are to be deemed to have been received within a specified time of their being sent, and for the specified time to be less than 48 hours.

### Failure to notify contact details

**80.** (1) If –

(a) the company sends two consecutive documents to a member over a period of at least 12 months, and

(b) each of those documents is returned undelivered, or the company receives notification that it has not been delivered, that member ceases to be entitled to receive notices from the company.

(2) A member who has ceased to be entitled to receive notices from the company becomes entitled to receive such notices again by sending the company –

(a) a new address to be recorded in the register of members, or

(b) if the member has agreed that the company should use a means of communication other than sending things to such an address, the information that the company needs to use that means of communication effectively.

## ADMINISTRATIVE ARRANGEMENTS

### Company seals

**81.** (1) Any common seal may only be used by the authority of the directors.

(2) The directors may decide by what means and in what form any common seal or securities seal is to be used.

(3) Unless otherwise decided by the directors, if the company has a common seal and it is affixed to a document, the document must also be signed by at least one authorised person in the presence of a witness who attests the signature.

(4) For the purposes of this article, an authorised person is –

(a) any director of the company;

(b) the company secretary; or

(c) any person authorised by the directors for the purpose of signing documents to which the common seal is applied.

(5) If the company has an official seal for use abroad, it may only be affixed to a document if its use on that document, or documents of a class to which it belongs, has been authorised by a decision of the directors.

(6) If the company has a securities seal, it may only be affixed to securities by the company secretary or a person authorised to apply it to securities by the company secretary.

(7) For the purposes of the articles, references to the securities seal being affixed to any document include the reproduction of the image of that seal on or in a document by any mechanical or electronic means which has been approved by the directors in relation to that document or documents of a class to which it belongs.

## Destruction of documents

**82.** (1) The company is entitled to destroy –

    (a)   all instruments of transfer of shares which have been registered, and all other documents on the basis of which any entries are made in the register of members, from six years after the date of registration;

    (b)   all dividend mandates, variations or cancellations of dividend mandates, and notifications of change of address, from two years after they have been recorded;

    (c)   all share certificates which have been cancelled from one year after the date of the cancellation;

    (d)   all paid dividend warrants and cheques from one year after the date of actual payment; and

    (e)   all proxy notices from one year after the end of the meeting to which the proxy notice relates.

   (2)  If the company destroys a document in good faith, in accordance with the articles, and without notice of any claim to which that document may be relevant, it is conclusively presumed in favour of the company that –

    (a)   entries in the register purporting to have been made on the basis of an instrument of transfer or other document so destroyed were duly and properly made;

    (b)   any instrument of transfer so destroyed was a valid and effective instrument duly and properly registered;

    (c)   any share certificate so destroyed was a valid and effective certificate duly and properly cancelled; and

    (d)   any other document so destroyed was a valid and effective document in accordance with its recorded particulars in the books or records of the company.

   (3)  This article does not impose on the company any liability which it would not otherwise have if it destroys any document before the time at which this article permits it to do so.

   (4)  In this article, references to the destruction of any document include a reference to its being disposed of in any manner.

## No right to inspect accounts and other records

**83.** Except as provided by law or authorised by the directors or an ordinary resolution of the company, no person is entitled to inspect any of the company's accounting or other records or documents merely by virtue of being a member.

## Provision for employees on cessation of business

**84.** The directors may decide to make provision for the benefit of persons employed or formerly employed by the company or any of its subsidiaries (other than a director or former director or shadow director) in connection with the cessation or transfer to any person of the whole or part of the undertaking of the company or that subsidiary.

## DIRECTORS' INDEMNITY AND INSURANCE

### Indemnity

**85.** (1) Subject to paragraph (2), a relevant director of the company or an associated company may be indemnified out of the company's assets against –

    (a)   any liability incurred by that director in connection with any negligence, default, breach of duty or breach of trust in relation to the company or an associated company,

    (b)   any liability incurred by that director in connection with the activities of the company or an associated company in its capacity as a trustee of an occupational pension scheme (as defined in section 235(6) of the Companies Act 2006),

    (c)   any other liability incurred by that director as an officer of the company or an associated company.

(2) This article does not authorise any indemnity which would be prohibited or rendered void by any provision of the Companies Acts or by any other provision of law.

(3) In this article –

    (a) companies are associated if one is a subsidiary of the other or both are subsidiaries of the same body corporate, and

    (b) a 'relevant director' means any director or former director of the company or an associated company.

## Insurance

86. (1) The directors may decide to purchase and maintain insurance, at the expense of the company, for the benefit of any relevant director in respect of any relevant loss.

    (2) In this article –

        (a) a 'relevant director' means any director or former director of the company or an associated company,

        (b) a 'relevant loss' means any loss or liability which has been or may be incurred by a relevant director in connection with that director's duties or powers in relation to the company, any associated company or any pension fund or employees' share scheme of the company or associated company, and

        (c) companies are associated if one is a subsidiary of the other or both are subsidiaries of the same body corporate.

# Glossary

**abbreviated accounts** A company which qualifies as small or medium-sized may file simplified accounts consisting of an abbreviated balance sheet, a statement from the directors that they are taking advantage of the exemptions available, and a report from the auditor stating that the requirements for exemption have been met.

**accounting reference date** The date on which the accounting reference period (the company's financial year) ends. In the case of a newly incorporated company the accounting reference date is the last day of the month in which the anniversary of incorporation falls.

**administration order** A court order which gives power to manage the business to the administrator.

**administrative restoration** A procedure available under CA 2006 whereby the Registrar may restore a company to the register without the need for a court order, provided certain criteria are met.

**administrator** An insolvency practitioner appointed by the court under an administration order.

**alternate director** A person appointed by a director to represent him as a director, particularly at board meetings that the appointer is unable to attend.

**annual general meeting (AGM)** A general meeting of the members which, following the year of the company's incorporation, must for public limited companies be held in each calendar year within six months of the financial year-end. Private limited companies are not required to hold an AGM.

**annual information update** A document, pursuant to the Prospectus Rules, requiring a listed company each year to publish through a regulatory information service all the information that the company has released to a regulatory information service or otherwise made public pursuant to the Companies Act over the previous twelve months.

**Articles of Association** The regulations governing a company's internal management – the rights of shareholders, the conduct of meetings and the appointment, removal and powers of directors. Separate Model Articles for public and private limited companies are in force for companies incorporated from 1 October 2009. This forms part of the company's constitution.

**BACS** The Bankers' Automated Clearing System, an electronic payment system, used by many companies to make payments directly to banks and building societies.

**blank transfer** Used when a shareholder completes a stock transfer form leaving the name of the transferee blank, usually when using shares as a form of security (e.g. for a loan). In the event of default by a shareholder a transferee will be inserted on the stock transfer form and shares sold.

***bona vacantia*** A grant of administration appointing the Treasury Solicitor to act on behalf of a person or organisation in the absence of any formal arrangements, e.g. to administer the estate of a deceased person who died domiciled in England and Wales leaving no relative and no valid will.

**bonus issue** Fully paid shares of the same class issued free of charge to existing shareholders in proportion to their existing holding. Also referred to as capitalisation issue.

**business review** A review which forms part of a company's annual report and accounts which describes, inter alia, the company's performance, future trends affecting the company's development and the company's principal risks and uncertainties.

**charge** A mortgage or a loan secured against some or all of the assets of the company.

**charging order** A court order charging assets (for example a shareholder's shares) for the benefit of his creditors (e.g. the shares are sold to pay the debts).

**City Code on Takeovers and Mergers** Regulations governing takeovers and mergers for companies whose shares are traded on the London Stock Exchange, AIM or PLUS Market.

**class meetings** A meeting of the holders of a class of a company's shares. Class meetings are held whenever the rights of the holder are to be varied by an action proposed by the company.

**close period** Generally the 30-day or 60-day period leading up to the announcement of results for a listed company. Persons discharging managerial responsibility of a listed company are generally prohibited from dealing in the shares of that company during such a period.

**Community Interest Company (CIC)** A corporate entity to encourage the provision of products and services to benefit community, social and environmental needs. Companies wishing to qualify for CIC status are required to satisfy the community interest test.

**companies limited by guarantee** In a company limited by guarantee the Memorandum contains an undertaking by members to contribute a specified amount towards the payment of its debts and the expenses of winding up while they are members or within one year after ceasing to be members.

**company share option plan (CSOP)** An HM Revenue & Customs-approved employee share scheme which may be operated on a discretionary basis. Employees may be awarded up to £30,000 worth of share options which they may exercise, usually between three and ten years following the award. Sometimes referred to as an executive share option plan (ESOP).

**connected person** The director's spouse, civil partner, minor children, stepchildren (which includes equivalent relationships arising through civil partnerships), business partner(s) and companies in which the director has an interest of 20% or more. It also includes the director's parents, children or step-children over 18 years and other persons to whom the director has an enduring family relationship (CA 2006, ss. 252–256).

**consolidation of shares** Where shares are consolidated to increase the nominal value of each share.

**continuing obligations** Part of the Listing Rules and Disclosure and Transparency Rules. The regulations and obligations which listed companies have to comply with once they have been admitted to the Official List.

**contributory** The holder of a partly paid share who is required to pay the unpaid element on his shares on a winding up.

**corporate governance** 'The system by which companies are directed and controlled' (Cadbury). Corporate governance is concerned with how the company is structured and controlled internally to ensure that the business is run lawfully and ethically, with due regard for its employees and shareholders.

**cumulative dividend** If any dividend due is not paid, it accrues to the shareholder and is payable with the next dividend due at the next payment date. Usually associated with preference shares.

**dawn raid** Where a company planning a takeover bid acquires a substantial shareholding in the target company before the price rises.

***de facto* director** A person who has not been properly appointed but who is 'occupying the position of a director'.

**debenture** A written acknowledgement of a debt evidencing a loan to the company by investors who usually receive interest at a fixed rate. Debentures are loans secured on the assets of the company and rank ahead of the payment of preference shares and ordinary shares and in repayment of capital in a liquidation. They are not a class of shares as such and debenture holders are not members of the company.

**deferred shares** Commonly carry very few rights – their rights are deferred to the ordinary shares, therefore they usually carry no right to vote or receive a dividend. They have the right of repayment of their capital value in a winding up.

**dematerialisation** A paperless system of holding shares, represented by electronic accounts.

**derivative claim** A claim brought by a member under CA 2006, ss. 260–269 against a director for an actual or proposed act or omission involving negligence, breach of duty or breach of trust by a director of a company. The claim is brought by the member for and on behalf of the company itself.

**dilution** When shares are allotted, for example in an employee share scheme, the number of new shares issued expressed as percentage of the issued capital is known as dilution.

**disqualification (voluntary) undertaking** An out of court procedure under IA 2000 whereby a director accepts a binding undertaking not to act as a director for a defined disqualification period without the consent of the court.

**distributable profits** Profits within the company which may be used to pay dividends.

**dividend** A payment made to members out of a company's distributable profits, in proportion to their shareholding.

**dividend tax voucher** The statement and explanation for the shareholder showing the number of shares on which payment has been made, the tax credit and the net amount payable.

**dividend waiver** Shares on which dividends should not be paid, for example, certain types of employee trusts or shares held in treasury.

**dividend warrant** A document, rather like a cheque, issued to the shareholder which authorises the company's bank to pay the dividend when it is presented by the shareholder.

**dormant company** A company which has no significant accounting transactions during a financial year.

**DRIP dividends** Dividend reinvestment plans occur when the company offers a facility to a shareholder to purchase additional shares on the stock market with the net proceeds of a dividend payment. The difference between scrip and DRIP is that with DRIP the shares received are already in issue, whereas with scrip new shares are issued.

**enterprise management incentive (EMI)** An HM Revenue & Customs-approved employee share scheme for smaller companies. EMIs are usually operated as discretionary schemes.

**extraordinary general meeting (EGM)** Before CA 2006, a term used to describe any general meeting held by a company which was not an AGM. While it is not used in the legislation an EGM may still be referred to in company's Articles which have not been updated to reflect CA 2006 changes.

**final dividend** Dividend paid in respect of the financial year-end.

**floating charge** A loan secured on present and future assets, such as raw materials or finished products, which change during the course of the company's business. A floating charge crystallises over the assets in the event of a default on the loan.

**founder shares** Shares issued to the founders or promoter of a company which may carry enhanced rights over other classes of share.

**grant of probate** A document issued following a person's death where the deceased has a valid will. The probate of a will is a document sealed by the Court of Probate after the will has been proved and is evidence of the executor's authority to act as personal representative.

**grant of representation** The collective description of probate and letters of administration.

**'in the money' option** When the market value of a share is greater than the exercise price.

**incorporation** The process by which a legal entity is formed separate from its owners and registered at Companies House. After incorporation, the company may start trading.

**inside information** Information of a precise nature in relation to a listed company which is not generally available. If such information were generally available, it would be likely to have a significant effect on the share price of the company.

**insider dealing** Dealing in shares of a company by an individual who has knowledge of undisclosed 'inside information' that comes from an inside source.

**insider lists** A requirement of the Listing Rules and Disclosure and Transparency Rules obliging listed companies and their advisers to maintain a register of persons who have access to inside information of a listed company.

**institutional shareholders** Pension funds and insurance companies; the group of investors holding the most shares in companies quoted on the London Stock Exchange.

**interim dividend** Dividend paid during the year.

**issued share capital** The number of shares which has been issued and taken up by members.

**issuing house** A merchant bank which is a general corporate financial adviser as well as acting as a sponsor of capital issues and sales of securities to the public.

**letter of allotment** Written confirmation that shares have been allotted to an individual and that share certificates will be issued by a certain date.

**letter of administration** A document issued following a person's death where the deceased did not have a valid will. The court appoints an administrator to act as personal representative in respect of the deceased.

**lien** A statement that share certificates have been deposited as security for a loan or other advance. A company receiving such notice should note it, but not acknowledge receipt.

**limited liability partnership (LLP)** A limited liability partnership has the organisational flexibility of a partnership and is taxed as a partnership, but the liability of the partners is limited. In most other respects it is very similar to a limited company.

**liquidator** An insolvency practitioner authorised to undertake the winding up of a company. This involves realising the company's assets and distributing them to the creditors according to statutory requirements. Any assets which remain following distribution are divided among the members of the company.

**listed company** A company which has been admitted to UKLA's Official List.

**Listing Regime** A set of rules made by UKLA comprising the Listing Rules, Disclosure and Transparency Rules and Prospectus Rules to regulate the admission to listing and continuing obligations on listed companies.

**long-term incentive plan (LTIP)** An employee share scheme, usually discretionary. Shares awarded to the employee are held in a trust and released on completion of a deferred time or qualifying condition(s).

**market abuse** Behaviour in relation to securities or investments traded on a UK market which amounts to misuse of information, misleading/false impression or market distortion.

**matching shares** Free shares given by the company to employees participating in a share incentive plan in a ratio not to exceed 2:1 to partnership shares.

**members** A shareholder in a company limited by shares, or guarantor in a company limited by guarantee. A shareholder becomes a member when his name is entered in the register of members.

**Memorandum of Association** A short document containing historical details of the company's initial subscribers for shares and their agreement to form a company. This forms part of the company's constitution.

**Model Code** A code, published in the Listing Rules, which governs dealing in securities by directors and other 'persons discharging managerial responsibility' to avoid the possibility of insider dealing. Each listed company must either adopt the Model Code or establish its own procedures, which must be at least as stringent as the Model Code.

**negotiable instrument** Property which may be transferred by simple delivery or by delivery with endorsement (usually by way of a signature).

**nomad** A nominated adviser drawn from a register of approved firms kept by the London Stock Exchange appointed by a company wishing to join AIM.

**nominal value** The value attached to a share when it is issued. The nominal value of a share need not bear any correlation to the market value of that share.

**nominee shareholder** A person, group of people or company whose name appears on a company register of members instead of the beneficial owner.

**non-executive director (NED)** A director who is not an employee of the company and who has no executive responsibilities.

**non-statutory accounts** Any balance sheet or profit and loss accounts of a company dealing with a complete financial year, other than as part of its statutory accounts. This includes data in newspaper advertisements and prospectuses, employee accounts, preliminary announcements and, to the extent that they include comparative information relating to a complete financial year, interim accounts.

**'off the shelf' company** Companies which have already been registered with a Memorandum, Articles and name, usually by third parties (known as formation agents). The new owners purchase the company from the formation agent and then adapt the company details for their own needs.

**offer for sale** An offer of new or existing securities which are first acquired by an issuing house and then offered to the public.

**offer for subscription** An offer of new securities issued directly to applicants by the company concerned.

**offeree** A company subject to a takeover bid.

**offeror** The bidding company in a takeover.

**Official List** UKLA's list of securities listed on the London Stock Exchange.

**official receiver** An insolvency practitioner appointed through the insolvency service of the BIS to administer company liquidations and individuals who have been declared bankrupt. Official receivers are officers of the court.

**omnibus transfer** A document showing the aggregated details of the transfers necessary to put the shares into the name of the successful bidding company following a takeover.

**open offers** The same as a rights issue except that the benefit of the right is not permitted to be traded.

**ordinary business** In the case of an AGM, the routine business of receiving the accounts, approving dividends and the appointment and reappointment of directors and auditors.

**ordinary resolution** A resolution passed by a simple majority (CA 2006, s. 282).

**ordinary shares** Shares entitling the owner to receive a dividend (if one is paid) only after the payment of a set dividend to the holders of preference shares.

**ostensible authority** Apparent or seeming authority; the authority that one can assume a person purporting to be an agent has.

**oversea company** A company incorporated outside the UK which has opened an establishment within the UK.

**paid up capital** The amount of issued capital which has actually been paid.

(Shares are not always paid in full at the time they are taken up.)

**partnership shares** Shares which a member of a share incentive plan can purchase out of pre-tax earnings in addition to any free allocation which he receives by participating in the scheme.

**person discharging managerial responsibility (PDMR)** A director or a senior executive of a listed company who has regular access to inside information relating to the company. PDMRs have power to make managerial decisions affecting the future development and business prospects of the company.

**phoenix company** A new company formed with a name the same as or similar to that of a company that has gone into insolvent liquidation and having the same director(s) as the failed company.

**placing** Where securities are purchased by an issuing house are placed directly with investment clients with only a small proportion being sold through the market.

**preference shares** Shares giving the holder preferential rights in respect of dividends and sometimes in respect of a return of capital on a winding up.

**presenter** A person authorised to file company documents with Companies House on behalf of a company.

*prima facie* On the face of it; at first sight.

**primary market** The Stock Exchange market for new issues of securities

**prohibited period** A period during which persons discharging managerial responsibility of a listed company may not deal in the securities of their company. This period consists of any close dealing period; and any time where inside information exists.

**PROOF (PROtected Online Filing)** A service offered by Companies House to help deter fraudulent returns being sent to the Registrar. Companies must register with Companies House and file documents electronically.

**prospectus** A document containing information about the company and its shares which enables prospective investors to decide whether to invest.

**proxy** A person appointed by a member entitled to vote at a general meeting to attend the meeting in his place. The proxy can speak at the meeting and vote on a show of hands and on a poll. The proxy need not be a member of the company.

**proxy card** A form issued to a member to appoint a proxy and to vote on a poll.

**public offer** A takeover offer made to all the shareholders of a company to acquire all or a proportion of their holdings.

**qualifying floating charge holder** A floating charge entered into after 15 September 2003 under EA 2002 which comprises a charge over the whole or substantially whole of the company's property. The charge holder has the right to appoint an administrator out of court.

**qualifying person** An individual who is a member of the company, a representative of a corporation, appointed under CA 2006, s. 323 for the purposes of that meeting or a proxy of a member appointed for that meeting.

**quasi-loan** A loan where the company reimburses the director's creditor.

**quorum** The minimum number of people necessary for the transaction of business at general meeting or board meeting. A company's Articles usually specify the quorum for general meetings, but if there is no such provision, the Companies Act will apply.

**receiver** A person appointed under a debenture or other instrument secured over the assets of a company. In the event that the company defaults under the terms of the debenture or other instrument, the receiver is appointed to manage and realise the secured assets for the benefit of the charge holder.

**recognised investment exchange (RIE)** An authorised investment exchange.

**record date** The date used to determine the members eligible to receive a dividend if one is paid, or who are able to participate in any other corporate transaction. All members on the register of members at the specified date will be eligible.

**redeemable shares** Shares that will be redeemed by the company at their nominal or par value at some stated date in the future.

**redemption** The process of redeeming (buying back) redeemable shares.

**register of members** A statutory register of information, it is the definitive list of members of a company.

**regulatory information service** An information provider approved by the FSA to disseminate information to the market. Under the continuing obligations of the Listing Rules, listed companies must notify a regulatory information service of any major developments in their business of any change in their financial condition.

**resolution** The formal way in which a decision is proposed and passed.

**rights issue** The issue of shares to existing shareholders in proportion to their existing holdings.

**rolling settlement** The period between a share trade being executed and settlement (i.e. payment) of that share transaction. For example, 'T + 3' means that settlement will occur three business days following the trade.

**SAYE (Save As You Earn) schemes** HM Revenue & Customs-approved, all-employee savings schemes whereby employees save for a fixed period towards the purchase of shares by exercising their share option.

**scheme of arrangement** Under CA 2006, s. 899, an agreement, for example, to restructure between a company and its members (or in the case of a liquidation, a company its creditors) approved by the court.

**scrip dividends** New shares issued fully paid to a shareholder instead of a cash dividend. They are different from bonus issues as the shareholder is usually given the choice of electing to take shares or cash.

**secondary market** The market for securities once they are launched.

**securities** A general name for stocks and shares of all types.

**shadow director** Any person in accordance with whose directions or instructions the directors are accustomed to act, except where that person gives advice in a professional capacity (e.g. a solicitor or accountant).

**share** A fixed and indivisible section of the capital of a company.

**share incentive plan (SIP)** A flexible, all-employee share scheme with three key award components: free shares, partnership shares and matching shares. SIPs are HM Revenue & Customs-approved.

**share premium** The difference between the issue price of a share and its nominal value.

**share warrant to bearer** A document issued by the company entitling the bearer (holder) to the number of shares in a company stated in the warrant. Share warrants can be issued by any limited company if the Articles allow.

**single alternative inspection location (SAIL)** A location, other than the registered office, where a company may keep statutory registers.

**societas europaea** A public company corporate vehicle which operates across the European Union by reference to laws applicable in each EU member state. Companies which have operations across several EU states will be able to benefit by simplifying their corporate structures and harmonising applicable legislation.

**special business** Accounts, dividends, directors and auditors when considered at a general meeting other than an AGM, or non-ordinary business transacted at an AGM.

**special notice** Special notice is required for certain ordinary resolutions if removing a director or removing, appointing or reappointing an auditor (CA 2006, s. 312).

**special resolution** Used for significant decisions (e.g. changes of name). Requires a 75% majority to pass, and must be described as a special resolution in any notice, which should set out the exact text of the resolution.

**sponsor** A merchant bank, lawyer, accountant or broker who sponsors capital issues and the sale of securities to the public generally. They advise on the form that the issue should take, timing, any capital reorganisation that may be required and the issue price. They also share the responsibility for the accuracy of the information provided in the prospectus.

**stake-building** Purchase of individual blocks of shares by a member or concert party, often as a prelude to a takeover bid.

**statement of affairs** A document sworn under oath which summarises the company's financial position (i.e. its assets, liabilities and creditors) during liquidation or insolvency proceedings.

**statutory accounts** The individual or group accounts which are required to be filed with the Registrar of Companies. These may be full accounts or abbreviated accounts which qualifying small and medium-sized companies may deliver.

**statutory declaration of solvency** A statement made by the board which confirms that the company is solvent and will be able to meet all liabilities which arise within twelve months from the commencement of the voluntary liquidation.

**Stewardship Code** A code developed by the FRC setting out the best practice for institutional investors in respect of their stewardship of UK listed companies.

**summary financial statement** A shortened form of the annual report and accounts of the company which may be circulated to shareholders instead of the full report. All companies have the choice of issuing summary financial statements.

**techMark** The market for innovative technology markets, a 'market within a market' of the London Stock Exchange.

**The Gazette** The official publication of BIS, published on each business day, in which formal announcements concerning companies are made (e.g. administration orders, compulsory liquidations). *The Gazette* is published in three editions in London, Edinburgh and Belfast. This can be viewed online (see directory)

**third party debt order** A court order charging income or interest (for example a shareholder's dividends) to the benefit of the creditor(s).

**three-way proxy** A proxy form which must be used by a listed company to enable a member to vote in favour of a resolution, vote against or to give another person discretion how to vote. In the absence of any instructions, the proxy may vote as he wishes, or not at all.

**transfer** The process where the ownership of share passes from one person to another as a result of sale or gift.

**transmission** The legal process where the ownership of a share passes from one person to another (e.g. following the death or bankruptcy of a member). This is not the same as transfer.

**UK Corporate Governance Code** The Code on Corporate Governance maintained by the FRC which applies to UK listed companies. It is a voluntary code rather than a legal requirement. The UK Listing Rules require listed companies to disclose in their annual report the extent of their compliance and to explain any non-compliance.

**unconditional** In a takeover, if acceptances reach the level where the bidder will control more than half the voting shares of the target company, he has the right to declare the offer unconditional and he is bound to acquire.

**'underwater' option** When the market value of a share is lower than the exercise price.

**underwriting** An agreement usually made between the company and a merchant bank or broker for the bank or broker to take up shares in an issue if they are not fully taken up by the public. Underwriting removes the risk that the company will not receive its full subscription monies.

**unregistered transfer** Transfers which have not yet been registered, and where the name of the transferee has not yet been listed in the register of members.

**vendor consideration issue or vendor placing** Securities which are issued to a company instead of cash by a purchaser when the company is acquired.

**vesting order** A court order requiring a change of owner of the shares, usually applied when removing a trustee.

**voluntary arrangement** An agreement approved by the court in which the company formally agrees with its creditors the terms for the settlement of its debts.

**warrant** A document entitling the holder to subscribe for equity capital of a company at a future date(s) at a price determined when the warrant is issued. Some warrants can be traded on the London Stock Exchange.

# Directory

## Further reading

### Company law

B. Hannigan, *Butterworths' Corporate Law Service* (Butterworth). Multi-volume, loose-leaf/CD-ROM work, which embraces all aspects of company law. It contains numerous forms, precedents, procedural tables, model accounts and checklists.

The Rt Hon The Lord Millett, Alistair Alcock, Michael Todd QC, AJ Boyle, Andrew Keay and David Bennett *Gore-Browne on Companies* (Jordans). A two-volume, loose-leaf work.

Morse, Geoffrey K., *Palmer's Company Law* (Sweet & Maxwell). A comprehensive book on UK company law.

### Company statutes

*Butterworths' Company Law Handbook* (Butterworth). Annual editions. The relevant texts of the most important statutes, statutory instruments and European legislation, as well as certain FSA regulation.

Walmsley, Keith, *The ICSA Companies Act 2006 Handbook*, 2nd edition (ICSA Publishing). Complete text of the Act with commentary and indexes.

### Company secretarial practice

Birds, J. and Boyle, A. J., *Boyle and Birds' Company Law* (Jordans, 2011).

Armour, Douglas, *The ICSA Company Secretary's Handbook* (ICSA Publishing). Regular editions).

Armour, Douglas, *The ICSA Company Secretary's Checklists* (ICSA Publishing). Regular editions. Procedural checklists, timetables and other quick reference material associated with the statutory functions and responsibilities of company secretaries, presented in A–Z format.

Lai, Jerry, *Tolley's Company Secretary's Handbook* (Tolley). Annual editions.

Leighton, H. G. M., Van Duzer, Peter and Gillard, Cecile, *Jordans' Company Secretarial Precedents*, 6th edition (Jordans, 2011). A comprehensive selection of precedents aimed primarily at private companies.

Smith, Charles G. S., *Company Precedents* (Sweet & Maxwell). A two-volume, loose-leaf work, which contains over 300 precedents, also available on CD ROM.

Venus, David, *Butterworths' Company Secretarial Procedures and Precedents* (Butterworth). A single-volume, loose-leaf work which provides commentary as well as checklists and precedents.

Walmsley, Keith and Hamer, Andrew, *Company Secretarial Practice* (ICSA Publishing). Comprehensive information service available in print, CD and online. Regularly updated. Covers all aspects of company secretarial functions, especially in listed companies.

### Directors

Bruce, Martha, *Rights and Duties of Directors*, 11th edition (Bloomsbury Professional Publishing, 2011).

Brian Coyle, *The Non-Executive Directors Handbook 2nd Edition* (ICSA Publishing 2011)Loose, Peter, Griffiths, Michael and Impey, David, *The Company Director, The Powers, Duties and Liabilities*, 11th edition (Jordans, 2011).

### Meetings

Hamer, Andrew, *The ICSA Meetings and Minutes Handbook*, 2nd edition (ICSA Publishing, 2009). A practical guide to running company meetings, which addresses the law and practice in both public and private companies.

Stephen Davies QC, Nicholas Briggs, Bethan Evans, Tom Ellis, David Impey *The Modern Law of Meetings*, 2nd edition (Jordans, 2009).

Madeleine Cordes; John Pugh-Smith; Geraldine Caulfield; James Burton; Catherine Dobson; Zack Simons, *Shackleton on the Law and Practice of Meetings*, 12th edition (Sweet & Maxwell, 2012).

## Magazines and journals

*Chartered Secretary.* The monthly magazine of the ICSA covering news and features on developments in all areas of interest to company secretaries.

*The Company Secretary.* ICSA's monthly technical newsletter for company secretaries.

*Tolley's Company Secretary's Review* (Butterworths/Tolley).

*PLC* (PLC Publications) A monthly magazine focusing on technical legal issues for in-house lawyers and company secretaries.

*The Register* (Companies House). A free, quarterly magazine on Companies House and other company law developments.

## Other sources of information

### Companies House guidance booklets

For a full list of booklets available and to view or print the pages, see the Companies House website: www.companieshouse.gov.uk. Copies of company forms are also available via the site.

### ICSA guidance

The ICSA Policy Unit produces a range of Best Practice Guides and Guidance Notes to support company secretaries. Download from www.icsa.org.uk.

### HM Revenue & Customs guidance

HM Revenue & Customs provides guidance and updates on taxes (e.g. Stamp Duty). It also provides detailed guidance on employee share schemes. See www.hmrc.gov.uk.

### London Stock Exchange and Financial Services Authority

The Listing Rules, Prospectus Rules and Disclosure and Transparency Rules are available from the Financial Services Authority (www.fsa.gov.uk).

AIM Rules (for Companies and Nomads), Rules of the London Stock Exchange, details of fees and forms, all of which are regularly updated, available to download from www.londonstockexchange.com.

## Web resources

**The CIC Regulator**
www.cicregulator.gov.uk

**Companies House**
(see Registrar of Companies)

**Competition Commission**
www.competition-commission.gov.uk

**The Department for Business, Innovation & Skills**
www.bis.gov.uk

**Euroclear UK & Ireland Ltd**
www.euroclear.co.uk

**Financial Reporting Council (including Financial Reporting Review Panel)**
www.frc.org.uk
www.frrp.org.uk/frrp

**Financial Services Authority**
www.fsa.gov.uk

**FTSE International**
www.ftse.co.uk

**HM Revenue & Customs**
www.hmrc.gov.uk

**ICSA Publishing**
www.icsabookshop.co.uk

**ICSA Software International**
www.icsasoftware.com

**ICSA Training/Conferences**
www.icsatraining.co.uk
www.icsaevents.co.uk

**Information Commissioner**
www.ico.gov.uk

**The Insolvency Service**
www.insolvency.gov.uk

**The Institute of Chartered Accountants in England and Wales**
www.icaew.com

**The Institute of Chartered Accountants of Scotland**
www.icas.org.uk

**The Institute of Chartered Secretaries and Administrators (ICSA)**
www.icsa.org.uk

**The Law Society**
www.lawsociety.org.uk

**The London Gazette**
www.gazettes-online.co.uk
(includes Edinburgh and Belfast Gazettes)

**The London Stock Exchange**
www.londonstockexchange.com

**The Office of Fair Trading**
www.oft.gov.uk

**UK Statutory legislation (includes the Office of Public Sector Information and Her Majesty's Stationery Office)**
www.legislation.gov.uk/

**The Panel on Takeovers and Mergers**
www.thetakeoverpanel.org.uk

**The PLUS Market (formerly OFEX)**
www.plusmarketsgroup.com

**The Registrar of Companies for England & Wales Companies House**
www.companieshouse.gov.uk

**UK Listing Authority**
www.fsa.gov.uk

# Index